THE HITE REPORT ON THE FAMILY

By the same author

Sexual Honesty By Women, For Women (1974)
The Hite Report on Female Sexuality (1976)
The Hite Report on Men and Male Sexuality (1981)
Women and Love: A Cultural Revolution in Progress
(The Hite Report on Love, Passion and
Emotional Violence) (1987)
Fliegen mit Jupiter (1993)
Women as Revolutionary Agents of Change:
Selected Essays in Psychology and Gender 1972–1993 (1993)

The Divine Comedy of Ariadne and Jupiter (1994)

Shere Hite

THE HITE REPORT ON THE FAMILY

Growing Up Under Patriarchy

Grove Press
New York

First published in Great Britain in 1994 by Bloomsbury Publishing Ltd.
First Grove Press edition, May 1995

Printed in the United States of America

Library of Congress Cataloging-in-Publication Data
Hite, Shere.
    The Hite report on the family: growing up under patriarchy /
Shere Hite.
    Includes bibliographical references and index.
    ISBN 0-8021-1570-5
    1. Family—Psychological aspects. 2. Patriarchy. 3. Parent and
child. 4. Children and sex. 5. Sex (Psychology) 6. Family life
surveys. I. Title
HQ518.H57 1995   306.85—dc20   94-42157

Grove Press
841 Broadway
New York, NY 10003

10 9 8 7 6 5 4 3 2 1

Contents

CONTENTS

CONTENTS

CONTENTS

CONTENTS

CONTENTS

CONTENTS

CONTENTS

CONTENTS

A Special Preface to the US Edition

Some things, like the Statue of Liberty, we take for granted. Barbara Seaman, one of the most influential women in the twentieth-century women's movement, is something like that. It was Barbara who made sure that this book—already published in ten other countries—was also published in the US, as it was Barbara who had earlier introduced me to the editor of the first Hite Report. A woman of great personal charm and energy as well as a seminal author, she has written such books as *Free and Female* and *The Doctor's Case Against the Pill*; she is the co-founder of The Women's Health Network, and her work has led to Congressional hearings and procedural changes on the part of the world's physicians and pharmaceutical companies. As Jane O'Reilly remarked on meeting her, "Do you know who that is? That woman has saved thousands of lives!"

For their help in getting this book published in the US, I would also like to express my profound gratitude to Phyllis Chesler, Naomi Weisstein, Jesse Lemisch, Barbara Ehrenreich, Kate Millett, Ruby Rohrlich, Andrea Dworkin, Gloria Steinem, Susan Faludi, and Stephen Jay Gould, as well as to Jennifer Gonnerman, Marcia Gillespie, Janet Wolfe, Jessica Velmans, Allison Draper, Gillian Taylor, Karla Jay, Lin Crouch, Cecile Rice, Victoria McKee, and many others, especially those who have answered my questionnaires and so improved the quality of my life during the last years.

Shere Hite
January 15, 1995

Notes on Research and Methodology*

This research is based on over 3,000 completed essay questionnaires received from men and women, boys and girls, from different countries, over a period of fifteen years.

Half of the completed questionnaires came from the United States, 35 per cent from the UK and Western Europe, and the remaining 15 per cent from the countries listed on page xxiii. All respondents were asked not to sign their names, because I believe that allowing people the privacy of total anonymity makes it easier for them to be open, and creates an atmosphere of freedom and dignity. I am grateful to all those who responded, and thank them for their insight and frankness.

I have always preferred to us: the probing, in-depth format of essay questions, rather than the more usual and simplified multiple-choice, as I wanted to get a picture of childhood unblemished by preconceptions, a fresh picture built on primary data. A multiple-choice questionnaire would have presented people with pre-set categories from which to choose, limiting their responses. Additionally, I have always preferred the arduous task of distributing a questionnaire to anonymous participants because of the rewards: the freedom and beauty of the voices. The reader hears people describe *in their own words* experiences and feelings they might not express elsewhere. Readers can use these records of other people's experiences as a way of discovering new perspectives on their own life, and understanding how their own childhood resembles or differs from others'.

I also offer theoretical conclusions to readers as a possible new vantage point from which to think about their childhood and psycho-sexual identity, and the impact of these on their adult life.

Acknowledgements

The questionnaires were distributed in the countries listed on page xxiii. I would like to thank the following groups, who, among others, helped to distribute these questionnaires: *Emma Magazine*, Germany; *Everywoman*, UK; *Amazon*, Oxford, UK; *Corridor*, Cambridge, UK; National Student Union

* See also p. 377 and the Appendices.

Association, US; YWCA, US; YMCA, US; Women Against Fundamentalism, UK; Bradford University; *Penthouse International*; *Mujeres y Podor*, Spain; *Woman Magazine*, Spain; *La Vanguardia*, Spain; *Viva*, Holland; *Max*, Germany; *Marie Claire*, Italy; *Nouvelles Questions Féministes*, France; Centre Audiovisuel de Simone de Beauvoir, France; *Elle*, Germany; *Zitty Magazine*, Germany. Of course, questionnaires were distributed in a diversity of other ways as well.

For reading portions of this book or enabling me to understand various theoretical perspectives on the family, I would like to thank: Barbara Seaman, Barbara Ehrenreich, Kate Millett, Ti-Grace Atkinson, Ruby Rohrlich, Phyllis Chessler, Ellen Cole, Bonnie Strickland, Fatima Mernissi, Florence Rush, Janet Wolfe, Leah Shaeffer, Dale Spender, Bill Granzig, Bernard Zilbergeld, Albert Ellis, Andrea Dworkin, Lois Banner, Diana Leonard, Christine Delphy, Naomi Weisstein, Jesse Lemisch, Herb Klein, Stephen J. Gould, and Alice Miller. None of these, of course, bears responsibility for this manuscript, as the conclusions of this research are entirely my own.

I would also like to thank my editors at Bloomsbury, and Ayse Amon, Belinda Budge, Iris Brosch, Delphine Seyrig, Cecile Rice, Joanna Briscoe, Silvia de Bejar, Corona Machemer, Leah Fritz, Karen Clark, Uschi Neubauer, Gillian Taylor, Harriet Griffey, Mic Cheetham and Friedrich Horicke.

A New Type of Debate and Discussion

I

Readers of this report will choose those respondents with whom they wish to identify, agree or disagree. The presentation of my research takes the form of a debate between those participating (from whom I quote extensively to give readers direct access) and myself, as together we try to sift through the information and experiences presented, and come to various conclusions and understandings. This represents a new, interdisciplinary, feminist methodology, a more interactive type of research than the "under the microscope" approach to "research subjects".*

I am gratified to observe that others have also begun to use this method of presentation of their research, although few use my type of data-gathering, as it is enormously time-intensive and financially costly. This is because of the essay nature of the questionnaires. Research based on in-depth interviews, such as those therapists sometimes conduct with clients, is extremely valuable but often limited to smaller data bases. In my research, I am trying to combine the best of both worlds.

---

* A more elaborate and extensive discussion of the methodology used in this work, as well as a theoretical perspective on methodologies used in the social sciences, can be found on page 387.

What Is the Best Way to Study Children's Psycho-sexual Identity? A Slight Departure, a New Direction

Basing my research on information drawn from several countries represents a slight departure and change in focus from my previous reports. The focus here is at least as much psychological and theoretical as statistical. In the past, I have based my research principally on one country, the United States, and endeavoured to make my statistical base, insofar as possible, reflect the make-up of that country's population—not because I was trying to do a standard market-research "survey", but because I hoped in that way to include, in democratic fashion, as many diverse voices as possible: those of different races, ethnic backgrounds and ages, as well as occupations and educations, reflecting the country's diversity.

In this report I am turning the focus less towards documenting social patterns in any specific country, and more towards a theoretical, psychological re-conception of the experience of childhood. By using participants from different countries, I endeavour to include cultural differences in that upbringing, while retaining a basic focus on the crucial similarities in psychology in the countries in which the "holy family" model is seen as the only "right" model. How *are* people faring in this family, that is, how do children learn about themselves—form their psycho-sexual identity—through the lens of this archetype? What are people's underlying feelings? Are their "true" feelings different from the clichés?

Is This Report Psychology or Sociology?

Although the Hite Reports are often referred to as "surveys", they are in fact reports, in-depth studies combining research, hypotheses and theory, as is standard in the field of psychology. With regard to the issue of "science", it is important to point out that one's work can be scientific without being a survey. It is considered methodologically standard* in psychology to present papers based on samples of ten to thirty non-randomly selected people, on the basis of which the psychologist generalizes about human behaviour.

My research methods can best be seen as a combination of sociology, psychology, and cultural history, together with innovations relating to feminist methodology. They have been explained at many professional gatherings, including the founding first meeting of the National Association of Women's Studies, at two annual meetings of the American Association for the Advancement of Science, the Society for Women in Philosophy in the United States, the Organization of American Historians, the American Association of Sex Counselors, Educators and Therapists, and the American Anthropological

* For example, Freud used a sample of only three upper-class Viennese women for his "scientific" theories on female psycho-sexuality.

Association. Internationally I and others have presented lectures on my methodology to the International Sociological Association, the German Psychological Association, and the Cambridge University Forum.

This Hite Report in particular has a research approach similar to other works on children and the family, although their samples tend to be smaller and their findings based on observation and personal interviews.* Those influenced by Margaret Mead and Ruth Bendick, for example, focus on the idea of personality as bringing together all the human sciences: sociology, anthropology and psychology, with the emphasis that personality is a product of culture.

Historical relativism of the family

I am also setting forth here a view of the family as a political institution, placing family in the context of its (partial) history, and interpreting the changes going on now in the family as part of a transformation, a beneficial change, in social structure and human relationships. Contrary to a fundamentalist interpretation of events, I hypothesize that these changes do not represent the "collapse of society", but in fact its rebirth, its renaissance.

As relationships and "love" between adults were covered extensively in the last two Hite Reports, here the spotlight is on children and how they construct their identities in the context of the family. Through children's eyes, we see in a new way some underlying causes of the many problems in the family that appear in the headlines of newspapers day after day.

Concerns about Hite Research Methodology

Various misunderstandings have arisen in the press, and I would like to address them here for the record, though most have been responded to in previous works, as well as in speeches and academic writings.

It has been said that my reports do not fully categorize those speaking, and I have not categorized people's statements by "country of origin" or nationality in this book. This is not to say that there were not cultural differences between people of different countries. However, this is not a study in cultural relativism, it is a study of the patterns inherent in the patriarchal family model, a model which most respondents experience, whether personally or in the culture. I was interested to know how people feel about this model in the light of the changes in the family that have already taken place: the development of a new pluralism, the large-scale exodus from the nuclear family reflected in the divorce rate, and the increase in women working outside the home.

* Others include Alice Miller, Bruno Bettelheim, Florence Rush, R.D. Laing, and Karen Horney.

I am equally interested in the theoretical realm, that is, discovering whether people's feelings match the myths and symbols of the society.* Do people feel what they are "supposed" to be feeling? Human behaviour can form a counterpoint to the institutions of society—and when it does, this tells us something significant, that the institutions are out of step, due for change. In this way, we can get some idea of the future direction of society: it makes prediction possible.†

I have not presented my work in terms of categories of class or race, such as "Afro-American women say this . . .", while "white, middle-class women say that . . .", although I have spent an enormous amount of time making such classifications and comparisons for my own use as a background for actual presentation of data. For example, in my first report, I was interested in how many women need relatively direct clitoral stimulation in order to orgasm. The point was not to break this down into race and class and compare incidences. Similarly, for my last report, I spent much time making sure that an elderly population was included, since I wanted to see how women felt about "love" over a lifetime.

In this book, people of various nationalities express opinions, and it may not always be clear in which country the speaker lives; sometimes the replies are translated. The point is not, I believe, to display how many children, for example, are sexually abused in one country as compared with another but to present the experiences and feelings of those who have been abused, so that we can begin to understand what type of family structure causes sexual abuse. Finding the larger patterns amongst the detail seems to me the way to go forward in understanding the psycho-sexual identity which is the basis of our society.

It is always difficult to know how much to edit or standardize the spelling and grammar of people's replies. I faced this in the past when I received replies with misspellings obviously representing a particular region or lower educational level. I was advised that to present these replies without reasonably standard English would cause readers to look down on these participants, since spelling and punctuation in the more highly educated replies were corrected. I tried in all ways to retain the flavour of the speaker; in no case have words been changed, nor anything added, only deletions made for the sake of brevity. It has been frustrating to me over the years when critics have drawn the erroneous conclusion that my sample was overwhelmingly middle-class, even though my statistical charts showed that it was not.

I dislike the idea of categorizing people. Stereotypes cling to our outmoded ideas of class, economic level and education. A "poor migrant agricultural

* My research has proved itself valid in the area of prediction before: the previous Hite Report was the first to say that women, not men, were initiating divorce. This turned out to be true, when later government statistics in the US and UK also found that the majority of divorces are initiated by women. Previously, it had been assumed that women were being left by their husbands.
† The questionnaire for *The Hite Report on the Family* is reproduced in full detail on page 377.

worker" may be read and "heard" very differently than if the same reply were labelled as being from an "Oxford University professor". I have received incisive comments from people with no education, as well as those with several degrees. With the method of presentation here, the reader can decide independently with whom to agree or disagree.

Because some of the replies are translated into English, there is a danger that they may sound American or British when they are not. Without making the book even longer than it is—and adding divisions to the book which deviate from its central purpose—how could this problem be overcome? It seemed best to stick to a cohesive style of presentation.

One matter that has concerned me at various points in presenting this research is the fact that the reader has no guide to knowing what age the respondent is. Could it be a problem that people are speaking of childhoods so far removed that they are no longer relevant, since families have changed so much? To avoid this, I have concentrated mainly on those who are now under the age of thirty-two, so that most of those taking part would have been children and teenagers during the last twenty-five to thirty years, the years of the rapid change in women's status and the years since men's questioning of the family in the 1960's. In other words, almost all respondents in this study grew up after "sexism" had become a common word in the Western vocabulary, and gender relations in the family had begun to change.

As this is not explicitly a study of differences in children brought up in the 1960's and those brought up in the 1970's and '80's—just as this is not a study in cultural relativism—it was inappropriate to interrupt the text with constant references to age.

Media Criticisms of Hite Report Methodology

It is hard to write about sex in our society without being trivialized or distorted. There is an amazing amount of misinformation in the popular press. Of course, this is not unique to my case. Alfred Kinsey* experienced a similar situation, so that he eventually began to carry with him a large index-card file of reporters' names, noting the errors in their articles about his work, and attempting to reply to each reporter to set the errors right.

The theoretical side of my work has often been lost in the media frenzy over the question "Can her statistics be true?" Whether or not the statistics are "perfect" surely the issues raised deserve to be addressed. For example, is what I term "emotional violence" more or less important if 80 per cent rather than 75 per cent of women suffer from it? What is more important—the statistic or the issue I have defined and raised?

There are also elements of the process that Susan Faludi described in her

---

* Alfred C. Kinsey, *Sexual Behavior in the Human Male*, and *Sexual Behavior in the Human Female* (Philadelphia, W.B. Saunders, 1948, 1953).

bestselling book *Backlash*. She writes of the media distortions of my research methods and personality, pointing out that certain parts of the media and society are intent on stamping out the influence of feminism on society in the hope of returning to "traditional values".

On a personal note, I would like to mention that it becomes more and more difficult for me to work and publish in a climate of media hostility and suspicion. It is increasingly hard to write in an atmosphere of attack, which is especially so in the United States. A defence committee, formed to aid me in 1988, stated at a press conference: "Terribly important issues that concern women's lives and health, in particular the emotional, psychological and physical abuse of women, are being obscured and trivialized by the media's assault on Shere Hite's work . . . The attack on Hite's work is part of the current conservative backlash. These attacks are not so much directed against a single woman as they are directed against the rights of women everywhere."

Statistics:
Population Breakdown

Who Answered: Study Participants

Age	5–10	11–15	16–19	20–30	31–40	41–50	51–65	66–80
Per cent of participants	2%	16%	20%	23%	19%	11%	5%	4%

Education	grade school	high school or technical school	university ed.	other profess. ed.
Per cent	22%	51%	19%	8%

Income	under £3,000 year	£3,100–6,000	£6,100–10,000	£10,100–20,000
Per cent	10%	22%	31%	14%

	£21,000–40,000	over £41,000 per year
Per cent	17%	6%

Religious affiliation	Protestant	Catholic	Jewish	Agnostic	Atheist	Muslim
Per cent	35.6%	29%	15%	17%	3%	0.4%

Marital status of those over 18	Married	Divorced	Separated	Single, never married	Widowed
Per cent	21%	20%	16%	37%	6%

Occupation:
  Professional   13%
  Manual labour   11%
  Factory   9%

Service industry	19%
Unemployed	8%
Disabled	2%
Student	38%

Total number of respondents 3,208: male 1,047 and female 2,161

Race or Ethnicity

Middle Eastern	6%
"White" Western	71%
African or African descent	11%
Asian or Asian descent	5%
Hispanic	7%

Country–Nationality

US	50%
UK	14%
Germany	10%
Holland	6%
Spain	3%
France	2%
India	1%
Pakistan	1%
Turkey	2%
Mexico	1%
Haiti	1%
Canada	3%
Sweden	1%
Russia	2%
Italy	2%
Brazil	1%

Your children are not your children . . .
Your children come through you but not from you,
And though they are with you yet they belong not
to you.

You may give them your love but not your thoughts,
For they have their own thoughts.
You may house their bodies but not their souls,
For their souls dwell in the house of tomorrow, which you
cannot visit, not even in your dreams.
You may strive to be like them, but seek not to make them
like you.
For life goes not backward nor tarries with yesterday.

Kahlil Gibran, *The Prophet*

Introduction

Icons of the heart

Archetypal Definitions of Love and Power in the Family

Love and anger, love and obedience, love and power. Love and hate. These emotions are all present in family relationships. It's easy to say that they are inevitable, that this is "how it has to be", that stresses and strains are unavoidable, given "human nature". To some extent this is true, but these stresses and strains are clearly exaggerated by a tense and difficult family system that is imposed upon our emotions and our lives, structuring them to fit its own specified goals.

Is the family as we know it, have known it for so long, the only way to create safe, loving and caring environments for people? The best way? To understand the family in Western tradition, we must remember that everything we see, say and think about it is based on the archetypes that are so pervasive in our society—the icons of Jesus, Mary and Joseph. (There is no daughter icon.) This is the "holy family" model that we are expected, in one way or another, to live up to. But let's look at this model: is it really the right one for people who believe in equality and justice? Does it teach a good understanding of love and the way to make relationships work when we become adults?

Too often, we see those we love only "through a glass darkly", through the filtered archetypes and symbols of the "family", rather than as themselves, for themselves. If we can only see others through the hazy and distorting filter of the archetypes, we may never really *see* each other at all.

The family was left out of the democratizing of political life beginning in the West over two centuries ago. Only now is this process affecting private life, with very positive results. Some people, of course, are alarmed by these changes. Reactionary fundamentalist groups (claiming to be religious but which are in fact political) have even gone on the offensive to try and stop this democratization process,

1

offering as their battle cry such pronouncements as: "The collapse of the family will mean the collapse of civilization as we know it."

This investigation was begun several years ago, and offers, instead of hysteria, real data on which to base the debate about the family: what it is, what it should be, what it can be. My report offers many verbatim testimonies about growing up in the family: experiences of developing sexuality and identity; and relationships with parents. I offer a new theoretical interpretation of psycho-sexual development, which as well as its individual focus attempts to place "family" against a larger cultural backdrop.

Debate is important: without taking a thorough look at our beliefs about the family and making rational choices about how we want to define its future, our civilization will never make progress. Freedom and self-determination are energizing: repression in a rigid structure is unlikely to create a flourishing society, either economically, or in terms of spiritual values.

As we hear girls and women, boys and men, speak here about the family—how they came to see themselves within it—we can begin to decide what it is about the traditional family and its "love" that is positive. We can decide what we want to salvage from that tradition, and what we want to discard—what kind of new families and relationships we want to build; for, after all, we all have the right to create our own form of family.

There is a positive new diversity springing up in families and relationships today in Western society. This pluralism should be valued and encouraged: far from being a sign of the breakdown of society, it is a sign of a new, more open and tolerant society springing up, a new world being born out of the clutter of the old.

S.H.

PART I

Memories of early childhood

Chapter 1

The Eroticism of the Mother

Dream Sequences of Childhood

Most of us have a sensory memory, a feeling-memory of being wrapped in a bodily embrace. A memory of being surrounded by a body larger than ours providing warmth. We may also have violent memories of our infancy, but almost all of us were also held, nursed and fed, carried and handled. Sometimes this was by fathers; it was most often by mothers.

Often the focus here is on mothers—especially mothers and daughters. Why? This relationship is very disturbed in our society. Perhaps it is possible to get back to what it is all about if we start at the very beginning.

Many people's—both women's and men's—descriptions of their earliest memories of their mother, their early days with her, are quite lyrically beautiful:

"I would never give up the memory of those warm soft summer days, nestling with my head against my mother's breasts as I leaned back against her, lying in her lap as we sat on the grass under a tree, she reading to me from a book she held on my lap. I wonder if I have ever felt so happy and physically satisfied since.

"I remember that the whole back of me was completely surrounded by her warm body, the perfume of her smell (I can still remember it) floating around me. From just above my head, all the way down my back and the backs of my legs—which I twirled and kicked from time to time, probably tearing her stockings, as I think of it now—I could feel her warm presence. When she would breathe and speak, I could feel her chest rise and fall, quivering slightly, or when she would turn a page, the loose skin of her upper arm would brush against my face. All of this was wonderfully satisfying, comforting, a peaceful reverie.

"I could have sat there for hours. Usually on these picnics my father

5

would announce at the end of the story that it was time for 'us guys' to go play ball, and not wanting to offend, I would stand up and trot off after him."

"My mother had her dressing-table in my bedroom. She would often comb or brush her long hair while I was falling asleep. I remember the sounds she made, the sounds the brush made, the bottle of face cream with its pearl label, the soft smell of her hair and the loose garments she wore, the scent of her skin as she kissed me goodnight.

"Later, even when I was in my middle teens, my mother would bring me into her room when I had a severe earache at night and lay me down with my ear on her chest. When I look back at it now, it seems an act of great tenderness and gentleness."

This sharing of a daily activity, an ordinary physical activity, is still somehow tinged with an atmosphere of great tenderness—yet almost casual "naturalness". This type of interaction between a parent and child is very profound. The gentleness and caring shown makes a real relationship possible between the two—rather than the parent being distant and formidable, trying to seem perfect. (Taking an "I'm the parent, you're the child, you must fear me—and obey me" attitude.)

What comes through here is great trust. Especially in the second example, the woman is sharing not just her role as a mother, but she is letting her child see her doing something for herself; she is not serving others, as one thinks of a mother, she is "serving" herself—and this lets her child know her as a human being. It opens up a space for the expression of feelings, questions, ideas—for oneself.

Although this chapter is about the eroticism of the mother, the beauty and sensuality of childhood experiences of being close to her—or how the child first experiences the physical—the following story is one in which a woman describes her father:

"My favourite time was bedtime. After my brother and I were into our pyjamas and ready for bed every night, my father would read us our bedtime story. This took place in one or the other of our bedrooms. The three of us sat in a row at the side of the bed, one of us on either side of Dad. As we settled in, he always enveloped us, reaching one of his big arms all the way around each of us, and then squeezing us up to him in a loud and lusty bear hug.* We, in the meantime, would be in a state

---

* Men's teasing is often a way men have of making fun of their own sentiments (or "gooey emotions"), disassociating themselves by affectionate teasing, or ending a compliment with a joke. See *Women and Love: A Cultural Revolution in Progress.*

of gleeful suspense, anticipating 'the big tickle'. Because the end of one of these hugs was always polished off with him tickling us, and the two of us laughing and trying to wriggle away. It was a unique part that was always missing when a babysitter was the reader of the story."

Why are we focusing mainly on mothers in this chapter? To explore those very early feelings, that connection between mother and child. And because, interestingly, more people wrote descriptions of their mothers than their fathers, when asked to write their memories of their years before the age of five. Why? Perhaps because early memories are quite physical—and most children spend more time physically close to their mothers than their fathers. This could be due partially to the way in which fathers tend to hold children, as shown by many studies, that is, further away from the body, and for less sustained periods of time, than mothers. (Is this because of the fear boys are taught to have of seeming "feminine"—that is, "holding babies" is a frequently portrayed image of the mother archetype? I doubt very much that it is because body contact feels less good to men!)

As children are generally physically closer to their mother after birth, so respondents to my questionnaire presented more memories of their mother. After all, there is a different form of physical attachment to the mother from the beginning: each child knows (consciously or unconsciously) that she or he came out of the mother's body (an amazing fact). Usually it is upon the mother's breast that a child may be placed the moment after birth, into her arms—and in the mother's bed that she or he may lie for the first few days after birth. In many cases the child is fed by the mother's own body, her milk—so that even though we do not remember all of these things consciously, we feel them. Somehow the smell of our mother's skin reminds us of those days and that time.

This intimate physicality in the first few days and weeks of life creates profound body memories, and it is "natural" that a child would later remember or turn to that body for warmth and comfort—that the memory of this body, its shapes and forms, would be deeply imprinted in her or his mind. And as it is usually the mother who continues the most intimate forms of daily interaction—feeding, preparing food, spoon-feeding and bathing the child—this physicality is continued. As men begin to do more of this early intimate "work"—carrying and cuddling, feeding, holding a bottle or spoon, washing and changing, and the handling of the child that goes with this, more children will remember the smells of their father's body, remember their great physical intimacy with him—as some do here.

Memories of the Mother's Breasts
Age Six–Twelve

Later memories—how different they sound! Distant and almost alienated—yet still sexually charged.

Are these children longing to touch, but not/no longer daring to?:

"I remember watching my mother breast-feeding my baby brother when I was about six. I think I remember this because I was so amazed she would take her breasts out of her blouse in front of other people—when I had been taught so strictly that one should never take one's clothes off in front of others. I remember in particular when we were at a friend of hers house, and she casually unbuttoned the front of her blouse and reached inside, lifting out one of her rather large (I thought) breasts, and leaning it over my brother, so he could reach up to suck. There was some milk on the end of her nipple that had slightly wet her bra. I remember this was all very sensuous and heavy-feeling—her smell, the odour of her skin, slightly moist from her body heat. How her hand looked around her breast, the beautiful pinkish-brown nipple next to the pale-beige of her skin.

"Was I jealous of my brother? I don't know, probably I was. I just remember staring and staring—but nobody noticed me, as they were all chatting and drinking tea, and not thinking anything about me.

"I remember the sound the fabric made as she unbuttoned her blouse, the way it flowed around her breast, clinging a little. The feeling was almost like the sensuality I saw in religious paintings when I was much older (or was it in religious comics I saw when I was still in grade school?), paintings of large women in sumptuous fabrics of many colours swirling around them, as they, half-nude, ascended into the sky. Rubens, Titian, Tintoretto . . . except my mother was not blonde nor red-haired, fair, as in those paintings, she was a brunette, with heavy brown locks she wore back off her face in waves, in that style so popular in the '40's with hair going up over the forehead, making the face seem taller than it was.

"As she sat casually talking with her friends, her clothes loosely enveloping her shoulders, she touched my brother with the most casual

8

sensuality. She had a heavy sensuality, musky, almost unconscious. Her build was medium, neither thin nor fat, but rounded. Her bones must have been quite heavy—when she swung her arms when walking or working, they seemed to fall as if attached to some large weight, moving like a pendulum, of their own accord . . .

"She had a brown mole, larger than a pound coin, on the side of her upper thigh. She loved to swim, she wished she didn't have this birth mark—or 'beauty mark' (she was always debating which it was). She also had a small mole on her face which emphasized her features in a heavy, charismatic way. She moved with a strange, sensual, feline languor, deliberateness, a personal style of moving and gesturing that pervaded every part of her persona."

"I came into the bedroom and there was my sister-in-law on the bed, breast-feeding her new baby. She was dressed in a beautiful negligee (new, I guess), and she was lying on the bed (which was perfectly made up) as if she were ready to have a photo taken by *House Beautiful*. The feeling was almost sterile somehow.

"It was a sort of creamy-white nylon gown with lace around the shoulders, a long, semi-transparent gown. She was looking down at the baby, but the nursing didn't seem to be very effective, I couldn't see any milk coming out. The baby looked confused too; it would try but nothing was there, and stop and just lie there. She would get it to try again, encouraging it to keep trying. This went on for several times, almost as if she wanted to be served, it was she who was supposed to have the experience, present the perfect picture of the perfect Mother, Giving to Her Child. There was something revolting and forced, unnatural, about it. I was glad when they let me go and I didn't have to witness any more of it, it was painful to watch.

"The baby's expression wasn't one of adoration or involvement, just unto itself, tired and bored maybe."

"When I was about eight, I remember swimming in a lake with my mother and some friends. She got very sunburned around the shoulders and arms. When we came home, I was in my room and she came in stripped to the waist and asked me to rub her shoulders with suntan lotion. I remember how large her breasts and how beautiful her nipples were. The curiosity was planted in me to see more of her and what the rest of her looked like. That was the extent of it, just wanting secretly to see her undressed and have the sensation of closeness and trust in her, knowing what her body was like."

Others' early memories are not as positive, hinting at a darker side:

"The nipples on her large breasts had enormous brown areolae—the circles around them were rather pronounced, beige, against her skin. The nipples were ivory tinged with pinkish centres. We used to take showers together, and I would be standing, facing her, just at the height to see them.

"Mine were pink and flat to my chest. The most curvaceous thing on my body (in front, where I could see) was my belly-button, which went in in a very nice way. My hips and arms seemed strong and healthy to me and I felt secure looking at them—they were me, and I looked strong!

"I thought I was a good-shaped physical object—as if my limbs proved my existence somehow. My legs were even stronger, from riding a bicycle (it took me for ever to learn). I also liked the hair on my arms, the way it all went symmetrically in one direction, how the water made waves in it, made it seem slightly darker and glossier—although it was shiny anyway.

"I didn't like my mother's breasts, I found them sort of physically repulsive. I didn't like her smell either. When we stood together in the shower, she being taller than me, they were right in my face, almost. They seemed to hang down and be very big, and with those big brown circles around the nipples, be asking you to suck them. I didn't want to suck them. The idea made me want to throw up, sick to my stomach. Why? Did I not want her inside me that much? Was who she was repellent to me? Or was this a sort of weird hidden attraction?"

"The strongest memory I have from around that time is of seeing my mother's breasts during the year she was nursing my little brother. He was about seven years younger than me. Sometimes they were slightly leaking milk. That gave me a nauseous feeling. Why? Did that repulse me because I knew it was for him, that I was forbidden it? Was I angry? Maybe my stomach clenched in a spasm of rage. I don't know, really I think it was just something about her skin and her personality that was abhorrent to me.

"Her skin was beautiful and it was not. It was a lovely colour, but it seemed to have a slight crêpiness to it, a sallowness, a coarse selfishness about it. That's it! I felt she didn't want to give any of this, her body, to me. She wanted it only for herself! And she wanted only to feel pleasure with her body with her lovers, as she made amply clear in various ways . . . Wait, maybe she didn't do or say anything like this, maybe it was my grandmother who was always muttering about my mother being too interested in men, 'You'll wind up just like your mother,' etc., etc., meaning having too many men—too much sex.

"Anyway, the whole situation made me feel sick, utterly out of the

10

picture, that I could never compete with all the others in her life for her attention or her love."

Reactions of two people to one boy's memories

One boy remembers being with his mother:

"Half unconsciously I seem to recall sensually the feeling of nursing at my mother's breasts. She had large and beautiful breasts. I remember that well because, while nursing my brother, when I was about six or seven, she occasionally showed me that she still cared for me by letting me also nurse at her breasts. And, there was one occasion later (I must have been close to puberty) when we were playing in bed and I touched her breasts and she bared them, let me fondle them and suck them as she cradled me in her arms. It was beautiful."

This statement sparked a controversy between two people in the Hite Report office:

"This paragraph bothers me, because it sounds more like a sexual interaction than a simple childhood memory. This was a dangerous thing for the mother to do, because at his age, he could have been damaged. If he had been younger, it would have been clear that they were simply being affectionate; if he had been older, it would have been clear that they were being sexual. But as he was adolescent, at such a vulnerable age, it is totally unclear what they were doing—and could have damaged him."

"How would it have damaged him? It doesn't sound sexual at all to me, it sounds to me like a sincere homage to a memory of the closeness that they once had, a last time in their lives when it would be possible to relive the beauty of childhood and their intimacy together."

"I still can't agree. I think that the language used in this testimonial intimidates people into silence, even though it might make them feel uncomfortable, because it is difficult to contradict someone evoking a 'beautiful' moment with his mother. I can't argue with someone who is talking about a personal moment that made him happy. However, I can't stop feeling the sexual undercurrent of this paragraph, especially when words like 'suck' and 'fondle' are used. I think also because the action seems to have gone on for a while—first they play, then he touches, then she bares, then he fondles etc.—it seems (to me) more erotic than I would want it to be."

"But you are trying to make it either 'sexual' or 'not sexual'. Isn't there room for a category between the two? Would that be so terrible? If the tone of the writing were different, I might agree. However, it does seem to me unusually different in tone—neither prurient (despite the words you point out, which to me seem merely descriptive), nor

11

goody two-shoes unaware. I am not saying his experience should be an everyday thing, but I think it is interesting as a unique way one family tried to indicate to each other that they did remember, that they hadn't forgotten—even though society makes no provision for older children and parents to approach each other affectionately—not sexually, affectionately. Aren't you just feeling uncomfortable with breaking a social taboo, not because it really hurts anybody?"

"I guess we'll have to agree to disagree. We have opposite views on this."

How do you feel about this one?:

"At a very young age my parents explained sex to us. Since we didn't have any brothers, they let us touch my dad's penis. I remember it felt like velvet. It certainly helped me not to have a lot of inhibitions or fears about the penis."

This began another discussion . . .

Standing immobile watching another brother or sister being breast-fed

It is interesting to note that in so many of the memories here, there is a clear picture of the older child standing immobile, in an almost frozen posture, watching with fascination the mother breast-feed another child, unable to move or approach or make her or his own feelings or thoughts known.

This is not to say that the child "should" approach and take the breast herself or himself—or even lean on the shoulder of the mother. But the earlier memories that opened this chapter show a spontaneity of touching, of interaction, a warmth that is no longer there in most of the others.

It is as if the child is in a transitional stage: she or he hasn't yet forgotten (as adults have) what it was like to be so close to the body of the parent, but now "knows" that she or he no longer has the "right" to relate to this body in any way. It is not that the older child wants to "take the breast, suck the milk" so much as that the act of physical intimacy reminds the watcher of a past experience and of the subsequent prohibition on intimacy, which represents the entire closing out or "rejection".

If a child were still able to cuddle closely with the mother or father, if the sight of nudity and breasts had not become an anomaly, then would these children have stood and stared with such frozen fascination? Remarking on every detail? Probably not. But if they were only staring because they were jealous of the younger child, this would still prove the point. It is standard knowledge that jealousy is not caused by the number of people a loved one knows, but by the quality of the relationship one has (or does not have) with the beloved. By the age of five, in most cases, the child's relationship with the mother has been traumatically reduced, cut off; it has not proceeded gradually to another kind of family warmth and affectionate closeness—except in some rather rare families.

The following family seems to be very physically affectionate, as compared to most:

"With my father, we were periodically close and distant. But, we did kiss. He always insisted on kissing me (usually wetly) on my mouth. It was only after I went away to college that I began insisting on a "manly" handshake. Still, I remember the kisses as loving and sensuous. My relationship with my mother was also warm, affectionate and close. We frequently hugged and kissed each other, as did my grandparents."

A girl describes watching her mother from afar, unable to approach:

"I remember one summer—I must have been seven—my mother had poison ivy all over her body, and was very sick. She was lying on the bed, on a large double mattress which she had us bring into the centre of the living room, she said it was cooler than in her room. She was partially covered by a sheet, a rumpled white cotton sheet; she was dazed from the medication they had given her. She had to have salve rubbed on her every hour, she said she was in agony. She lay there writhing around for several days. I never approached the bed too closely, I hung about the edge of the room. I knew I wasn't supposed to rub the ointment on her body. Her own husband (my stepfather) wouldn't like it, and also, it was somehow clear to me that her body was now his, and off-limits to me. We had separated, so to speak. I could only look, not touch."

The Isolation of the Body

"My mother was always affectionate with me up until the day when my father told her she was babying me too much."

When You're "Too old" To Be Touched

"He's too old to cuddle."
Children go for about ten years without body contact.

When you think about it, children are almost completely physically cut off from others between the age of five and fifteen. They are not supposed to touch anyone, or be touched, more than perfunctorily. They cannot kiss more than quickly and shyly, or feel themselves kissed back, lie pressed together chest to chest, feeling the full length of their body pressed next to another's for more than a second, or sleep close together.

At what moment does it begin? When does one become aware (just aware enough to stop) that one shouldn't touch too much, shouldn't explore, shouldn't ask questions? That there is something about the body, especially the naked body, that is not quite proper? Especially that there is something about genitals that is "different"? Is it the first time or two that one is firmly taken out of the parent(s)' bed and marched back to one's own bed? (This is more common in the West, with its one-bed-for-each-child system, than in many other parts of the world.)

Girls and boys learn very quickly not to touch or rub themselves against their parents, and especially their nude parents, and *especially* not any part that might be "genital" or "sexual" (though they usually don't know the words); that it will cause a strange reaction in adults, e.g., their parents—even if they touch their own genitals.

14

The loneliness of the body: feeling pushed away
"It was never explained, but I'm sure I got messages that said not to ask too many questions about my mother's sexuality."

Children are so incredibly sensitive to parental approval that one word, one glance of disapproval, one frozen and cold posture, is enough to teach the child that to get love, to keep on being accepted, she or he must avoid certain topics or gestures.

And yet, people frequently say such things as, "I have a child who is only two years old, and my gosh, this child at two, even at two, knows that boys play sports and girls do dishes. It must be biologically innate!" They do not see the messages they are themselves sending out.

Interestingly, one of the activities women and men described as being most valuable to them during "sex", in both *The Hite Report on Female Sexuality*, and *The Hite Report on Men and Male Sexuality*, is something our society has no name for. What they enjoyed (and many found absolutely essential for their well-being) was the full body-to-body embrace, the lying next to the other person, pressing together, touching from head to toe—chests, arms around each other, legs side by side, and their heads close enough to be able to smell the other person, feel them with their lips. Without this, they said they would not enjoy coitus in anything like the same way, that it would not have the same power and intensity for them, or the same comforting qualities; that this was something they in fact missed during oral sex. Touching head to toe is integral to "sex", and yet, what do we call it? It must deserve a name.

The lesson of bodily distance is learned for all of life
The physical loneliness of the child is clear when we think of most children's reaction when put in their bed, or told to go to bed: they don't want to, they want a drink of water, they want a story, they want to be tucked in. We require them to sleep alone ("Be a big boy"), when we don't require that of ourselves. Adults don't usually like to sleep alone, and yet it is "automatic" to teach our children this first discipline.

The terrors of being alone in the night—or the dreams of an irrational world where one is totally (at times) powerless—and whose rules one has to learn and accept nevertheless—were superbly chronicled by Lewis Carroll in his unforgettable classics.

Sleeping with dolls—or guns

We give our children cuddly animals to sleep with, to hold near them—and often a child develops a fondness for a certain blanket or doll that it cannot sleep without, or even doesn't want to go out without. The child likes to sleep with this object near it, usually near its face, especially its mouth and nose.

In terms of toys, what do we try to give children? Dolls for girls, and frequently, war/combat/aggressive-hero toys for boys. Why? Is it only because of the gender stereotypes involved (though that would be quite enough)?

Strangely, these toys bear an odd resemblance to the actual defences the two genders will be called upon to use later in life: as women we are taught that our best defence or power in life will be our sexuality, our bodies, our appearance. Boys learn that they will have to fight, engage in combat, perhaps use guns (whether really or symbolically), because for boys to "get ahead" in the world, they must "overcome" the others. "Life is hierarchical, and you must climb to the top of the heap."

Am I saying children should sleep with their parents? With each other? With cuddly toys? Dogs and cats? I'm not sure of the solution, or how we can provide more physical intimacy for our children. I only know that we are blinding ourselves to the fact that children have feelings which are the same as ours in circumstances of physical isolation—and that this enforced way of living, enforced by the parents, can have profound consequences.

Body Intimacy in Families

Some families accept an openness about the body between children and parents:

"My parents were not modest about being naked. They didn't parade around, but if we saw them nude, it was totally normal. I still have no serious reservations about my father walking into the bathroom if I'm on the toilet or in the tub."

But most parents do not allow any extended physical intimacy with their children:

"My parents did not show any affection towards each other. I remember coming upon them once when my mother was sitting in my father's lap. As soon as she saw me, she leapt up, very embarrassed. I remember feeling that I had done something wrong and feeling some resentment towards her and anger towards my father for 'making' her do something that she didn't want to do!"

The Family Defines "Sex" for the Child
(Forbidden Adult–Child Dialogues)

Children's views of their parents' sexuality

Children might grow up (if this were a different world) making a softer transition into "sexuality", rather than thinking that "sex" and closeness are discrete categories or institutions. As it is, children learn—from just such a situation as seen above, that there is a different kind of touching that adults do, that mothers do with fathers—which is secret, hidden, too taboo even to talk about, totally different from the child's own experience of its body, and touching.

One message children get obliquely is that their own physical (erotic? sensual?) feelings and longings are not the "real" sensations.

The "real" sensations will come later when a child becomes "old enough" to enter the sacred institution of heterosexuality. Only then will one's "sexuality" be "awakened", only then will one enter, be

17

initiated into, the secret adult world, the Magic Mountain—let back into paradise, the paradise of pleasure and of touch, the senses.

Another family gives the same message—but mixed with some openness:

"In my family (working class, white, I'm one of two daughters), we often ran back and forth between bathroom and bedrooms naked, and so did our mother. However, my father would never let us see him even in his underpants, if he could help it—he was very embarrassed if we happened to come into the bedroom when he was dressing—so seeing a penis was the only experience that seemed utterly strange and new to me. When I first saw my husband's penis, I had only seen a few pictures of statues from Greece and had no idea what a man really looked like!"

Fathers' sensuality with their children

One woman remembers her father when she was a child:

"My mother usually read me a bedtime story, but sometimes if she was busy, my father would tell me one instead. He would always make up a totally nonsensical tale involving bunnies and monkeys that would invariably end with all the bunnies going to bed. I thought these were hysterically funny and loved them. Also when I was little he would nibble on my ears, which made me giggle and scream—I didn't know if I liked it or not.

"My father didn't spend a whole lot of time with me, but I have good memories. Since my mother was the disciplinarian, my father was never the bad guy to me. My father never got very involved in child raising, probably least of all with me, the daughter."

Fathers' time with their children is covered in more depth in Chapters 6 and 11.

Archetypes of the Mother

The Mother as the Erotic Centre of the Home

Is the mother "Mary the Virgin"—or the erotic centre of the family?

Why do both of these descriptions sound wrong?

"My mom has always been an angel in my mind. My favourite memory is of her comforting me when I cried and she held me like a baby as I listened to her soothing heartbeat. Even when I was bad she held me. It was the most beautiful feeling I have ever had."

Are we being overly sentimental in our memories of the mother? She is indeed central to the child's world, but are we responding to an archetype of "the mother", her symbolism, and not her reality? Yes and no.

The mother is the erotic centre of the family, and of the home. She represents the sexuality of the family. *Her* bedroom, hidden deep within the house, represents the hidden centre of the household, that area from where the rest of the family issues—that is, the children come from her centre, and she is centred in the bedroom: a woman's domain, it is said, is the home.

Why do we never speak of the eroticism of the mother? Is it not supposed to exist? Is it a taboo even to recognize its existence? That eroticism is all around us, as children's memories show. This doesn't apply only to mothers who behave in "feminine" ways, or wear "nice" lingerie: whatever a mother's body size, she is still erotic.

In fact, the hatred and anger most teenagers feel towards their mother can be seen as a form of repressed desire for physical intimacy. Physical closeness creates a safe and luxurious space for talking and sharing—emotional and physical satisfaction combine to make a rich experience in adult relationships. Wouldn't children feel this too?

The eroticism of the mother

But what do we mean by "eroticism"? Do we mean that the mother is sexual, the sexual centre? And if so, would we mean, "is a sexy person", "turns people on"—or "has the sexual parts necessary to reproduce"?

Or, if we don't mean (by "erotic") "sexual"—then do we mean she is "feminine"?

The mother's body is very important and very visible to all the members of the household—and to the society, including the other female members. Yes, there has been too much emphasis on women as "sex objects". But if children were not "owned" by men, if women were not seen by society as reproductive organs for men, would society, even a matriarchal society, still not value the woman's body as a miraculous piece of art that could reproduce?

Especially within a household, which has so much to do with affection and nestling, and the physical pleasures of lying in a bed and sleeping, the mother's body is a strong part of the consciousness of all the members. It is somehow the centre, in a way that cannot quite be put into words—the erotic centre.

The problem here is the language. Since our culture defines "sex" as an institution, has only one allowable form of physical sexual contact for everyone in the world—namely, heterosexual reproductive contact—this statement may be difficult to comprehend. The problem is that if a society tries to force all erotic activity into one type of behaviour—and our society has no other institutions for physical intimacy, no institution called "intimacy"—then there is no "acceptable" category for discussion here; our language knows of no such thing as eroticism for its own sake, as its own poetry or beauty.

Our culture is rigid: its words and institutionalized forms of behaviour are so narrow that we cannot imagine intimate closeness without or beyond "sex".

The Taboo Against Women Touching or Being Intimate

"The closest I've been to a woman is when my mother breast-fed me, probably. Recently, I've hugged friends but only on momentous occasions, and I've touched the other women in my self-defence class as we practise getting out of one another's grip."

Mothers are the unacknowledged erotic centre for girls too. While there is some cultural acknowledgement that boys might "someday" see their mother as "erotic" (since "men desire women"), or notice that she was "erotic" to "men her own age"—"heterosexuality is a drive natural to human beings"—there is little understanding that there is also "erotic" (for lack of a better word) attraction between girls and their mothers. (See Chapters 3 and 4.)

THE EROTICISM OF THE MOTHER

Looking at the mother, watching her

Both men and women remember how they loved to watch their mother get dressed (how many have tried on their mother's shoes or dresses?), comb her hair or put on make-up. They were fascinated by these operations and manipulations done on the body, the identity. Mostly, one gets the impression that it was the sensuousness of it they liked . . . much as animals like to groom each other, here was a chance to play together and to share in, learn, "adult" secrets and mysteries at the same time.

Boys may be all the sooner prohibited from these pastimes, being told they are "sissy" and "feminine", usually by their fathers.

By the age of five or six, in the great majority of families, this is now the only way mothers and children (usually girls) can be close, participate in body warmth—watching the other touch herself, or touching only the body extremities of the other. This is a pattern that continues pleasurably in many girls' friendships later, as they go shopping with their girlfriends, or do their hair and make-up, try on clothes together, and talk about their dates (touching others, thus touching each other by empathizing).

Almost all touching is strictly off limits between mother and daughter, and between father and daughter, after five or six, except for hairbrushing, kissing hello and goodbye, etc., and spanking. This, interestingly, is almost the same age at which a large number of girls begin masturbating.

Some mothers and daughters develop special systems of relating after this "cut-off age"—utilizing first-rate verbal and body-language skills as a pleasurable substitute.

Mothers doing their daughter's hair

Most children, after very early childhood, do not have much affectionate physical contact with their parents. As one woman puts it, "No one touched you—except maybe for a spanking."

However, frequently mothers continue "doing girls' hair"—with a mixture of fondness and pained resentment.

While of course most girls' hair is longer than most boys', and thus may need more grooming than many girls can manage, how did this particular custom come to be so common? Is this an allowable substitute for, or channelling of, the physical contact that girls and mothers love but have had to give up?

Do mothers do this because it is an allowable way to touch and almost cuddle, get body contact with their child? The head is an "okay" place to touch, after all—especially the back of it.

Are some mothers trying to prolong the period of sensuality and touch allowed with their children, by doing such things as bathing and grooming the child? It seems that sensuality between mother and daughter assumes many more acceptable forms than between mothers and sons.

This at least continues some form of physical contact, as these women describe:

"I was always a bit of a 'tomboy', although my mom got into tying ribbons into my braids and cutting my bangs just so, even buying me pretty dresses. I heard the word 'ladylike' frequently, but it wasn't a reproach for my boyish behaviour so much as a kind of sensuality she seemed to be trying to express."

"When my mother used to sew clothes for my doll (the one that I slept with, 'Sleepy'), it was like we were both playing house together, we would hold the fabric and drape it around my doll-baby, pick the colours we liked best. I remember feeling very close when we did this. I can even remember the smell of the sewing-machine oil and her hair, as she leaned over me and the doll—see the texture of her skin on her arms."

"My mother was affectionate with me during my childhood. She used to tuck me in every night, until I was, as my father said, 'too old for that'. That was a fairly traumatic thing, for these were times we spent quietly talking about things that had happened, worries, and it was a special 'only mother–daughter' thing. Now that I'm 'grown-up', we've just moved the ritual into the kitchen, where we chat late at night over cups of tea about my latest 'love', school, her concerns about my brothers and my father. It means a lot to me that she confides in me now, too. She often asks what I think about my brothers or other family matters."

One woman paints a particularly vivid picture of going shopping with her mother, one of the new ways of "touching" the mother:

"One time my mother and I went shopping for a blouse. This was the 1950's when nylon see-through blouses were popular. The style was to wear one of these see-through blouses, with a bra and slip underneath, so you couldn't see anything of the body, but you could see the underwear (usually pink or white) underneath—and the shape of the breasts. That was worn with a suit—a tailored suit with a jacket.

"I remember staring at my mother's chest, her torso, through one of these blouses, and thinking it was astonishing, magnificent. It wasn't only me who thought so, she was considered to be a beautiful woman, people would say so, with classic proportions—good shoulders, good-sized breasts, strong neck.

"I wonder if I felt I could never be as sexual or look as powerful as she? That I was much smaller? Of course, I was! And I had no breasts yet. No one told me I one day would have them. Did I think of myself as always the thin one, the smaller one—was my identity set at that time?"

The "natural" expression of closeness would clearly seem to be physical affection. Physical affection does and does not mean "sex". Once again, a problem with our society's institutionalization of human needs, brought up in all three Hite Reports, is that the whole spectrum of physical affection is basically barred from acceptable behaviour unless it is channelled into the area of "sex", meaning that one has to have "sex" in order to get affection and/or physical closeness. This includes prolonged hugging, for example, or even satisfying kissing or hand-holding. All these, though slightly more acceptable for women in the nineteenth century, were put off limits by a "strong family unit" mentality, which seems to have become, in some ways, even more rigid in the late twentieth century.

Do kids need a "twin friend" for affection?
If children go for about ten years without lengthy, affectionate bodily contact (except briefly, perhaps, from each other in play), how can we rectify the situation? Parents, or grandparents, could easily be more affectionate without "risking" anything—as will be discussed later.

There should also be other sources of love and affection, especially physical affection, for children and teenagers. Someone for whom they are "the special one". Perhaps important friendships between children should be given more status. There could be a new term coined for such a best friend—this could be called, not just a friend, but a "twin friend".

Mary the Icon: Clichés About Mothers

Do children really love their mother as much as memories of these early years show, or is this to sentimentalize the relationship? There are many myths about the "mother". She is good and all-giving. She is Mary, never complaining. She is the Virgin, above sexuality and self.

This chapter asks what the family could have been, and can still be, if it were not violently forced to change gears, turn its relationships upside down, at the time of children's puberty (and even earlier). The reason, in large part, for the sexual repression and taboo on information is this: reproduction "has" to be put at the service of men, therefore the whole focus of the family has to be consciously shifted from the mother to the father, i.e., girls and boys have to come to adopt their place in the system, accept "the father" as the legitimate "head" of the household and the world. And as more "sexual".

In the patriarchal mind, the mother is thought of as asexual, mothers being "good", the opposite of "loose women". Mothers are thought of as "older women" whilst their daughters are "Lolitas" and "sexpots". In the early ancient world, the myth of Oedipus places the hero, strangely to our ears, in the position of falling in love with his mother. Age is never mentioned; his only problem, it seems, is breaking the gods' taboo against incest. Nothing is said about it being "unnatural" to find an older woman sexually attractive, or this being in any way a problem for him.

Of course, it is out of style to voice such complete, unabashed, love and adoration for one's mother. These "sentimental" feelings were heard more frequently in Victorian times—in letters, songs of the day, and biographies. More recently, since the 1942 book *A Nation of Vipers* by Philip Wylie (which coined the term "smothering" to refer to women who loved their children "too much"), and with the growing tendency after World War II towards armchair "psychoanalysing" of mothers (negatively so), mothers were generally portrayed as villains—too clinging and sugary for the child's own good. (Wylie's book was a bestseller in the US.)

In the 1970's, women began to be criticized for just the reverse: not

24

loving home and family "enough". With the numbers of mothers who worked outside the home increasing, mothers began to read in popular magazines that they were selfish, and should be giving much more love to their children! (Obviously they can never do anything right.) In reality, the vast majority of mothers are the ones who are doing the primary care for the child—washing, cooking, nursing, dressing AND loving. Mothers in the late 1940's, like today, were "damned if they did, damned if they didn't", i.e., wrong if they didn't give up their World War II jobs and stay at home with the children*, and wrong if they did stay at home with the children and take care of them all day because then they were "loving too much" and "smothering" them.

* Bowlby's influential post-war work on maternal deprivation was based on the exceptional experiences of evacuated children—not children whose mother was simply working outside the home. Many of these children, not surprisingly, suffered the effects of separation in these exceptional circumstances. However, the conclusions of this work did much to make mothers feel guilty if they worked or were separated *at all* from their children. Much of this attitude remains today, and continues to be hotly debated. Bowlby, John, *Attachment and Loss*, Vols 1 & 2 (London, Hogarth Press, 1969).

Do Parents Own the Child's Body?

One woman has a different recollection of her feelings of being cut off from real intimacy and touch after the age of five or so. She remembers feeling owned, having her body controlled, from outside—there was much contact, but no reciprocal contact. It was a proprietary, invasive kind of contact.

Here she remembers being given a bath by her mother—feeling that her body was possessed not by her but by her mother:

"I remember standing in the bathtub (with very little water in the bottom—another economy, we were poor) feeling cold, and being told not to keep fiddling with my hands, that *she* was washing me, not to interfere. She put soap all over my body, rather roughly I thought, then she washed between my legs, she washed the folds of my lips around my vulva, moving her fingers in between them, back and forth, then one quick wipe up towards my ass, and that was it.

"I was left feeling rather possessed, invaded—I felt my body belonged to her to touch as she wanted, to do with as she wanted, that I had no power over her, I could do nothing to stop her occupation of my body. She didn't hurt me, it wasn't sexual, but I had no choice.

"She seemed to control every bodily function of mine. She prepared every meal I ate, she chose the food, she insisted I eat it, she told me to clean my plate, I had to eat everything whether I liked it or not. She told me I should be grateful. In the mornings before I went to school, she used to push a cold metal spoon with foul-smelling cod liver oil deep down my throat, which always made me gag (I guess to be sure I swallowed it she pushed it down so far). I swallowed it, but I couldn't digest it, I kept burping it up all morning and tasting it again.

"The clothes I wore to school were the clothes she made or approved of, I don't remember if I was allowed to select which ones in the beginning, I think maybe it was whichever ones she had time to clean and iron, but later, I could select from among the approved garments. I often went to school thinking I looked rather stupid, but I also thought that made me ungrateful because she had worked so hard

26

to 'put clothes on our backs', as she said—and I did see that ironing was hard work, and she did work hard.

"But for a long time, I didn't feel my body was something I owned, it seemed like something, an object, that was there in space—I was only in my head, my mind. That, no one could touch. I didn't share it."

Another girl, during a private bath, defiantly claims her body as her own:

"I was sitting in the bathtub, supposed to be bathing myself. The door was closed but not locked (that would have been a strange thing to do in our house, so I didn't even think of it). I was sitting in shallow water, I must have been about seven, playing around—it was early evening, and my mother and grandmother were in the kitchen cooking dinner. I could vaguely hear them. I started to explore myself. I don't remember doing it before or after in the bathtub, but that day, I remember trying to put something up my vagina. Maybe I was washing there, and it felt good, so I thought I would try some more.

"I decided to mix some of my mother's face powder with water and put it up there—heaven knows why! I think I had a glass or something to mix it in. I tried to mix it up, the powder didn't really dissolve in the water but I got it as dissolved as I could, then leaned back, and just as I was starting to pour it in, the door opened and my mother stood there, surprised, gasping, 'Christine! What are you doing???'

"My initial reaction was to know I should feel embarrassed, but for some reason—I don't know where it came from, I wasn't similarly self-possessed at other times—I felt this was a silly question, since it was impossible not to see what I was doing. So, after a minute, I turned my head in her direction (the tub was so my back was to the door) and looked archly at her: 'Well???' as in, 'Want to make something of it?' This look of disdain in her direction seemed to make her shrink back, she shrugged her shoulders, closed the door and left! She never mentioned it to my grandmother—I mean, I could just tell, there was no tension in the air, no eyes looking away, no nothing! And my grandmother could be really punitive when she wanted to.

"I don't know where that look I gave my mother came from, or how I had the courage to face her down like that. It was an almost involuntary reaction, I didn't even think about it before doing it. Maybe I was just disgusted to be interrupted in the middle of an important discovery I hoped to make! Or maybe I was frustrated because I wasn't getting the feeling I had hoped for when starting to pour. I definitely had an urge inside me to feel something—I didn't know what. The water wasn't doing it, whether it was because most of it just ran down the sides of

me, not into me—or whether it didn't go into me enough, or something
. . . but it wasn't satisfying. Maybe that was the look of impatience I
gave my mother.

"Neither of us ever mentioned it again. At that time, we had
never talked about sex or menstruation or pregnancy or anything.
I wonder how I would have felt if she had stayed in the bathroom,
and sat down (on the nearby toilet seat) to have a chat with me about
'those things'. I probably would have half liked it, and half resented
her staying there then. She might have giggled at me, or been sort
of superior in knowing what I'd done, what I'd tried—her knowing
everything, and my knowing nothing. This way, it was *mine*—no one
was telling me what I should or shouldn't do. (Well, I knew I shouldn't
be doing it! Even though no one told me. How? Maybe because I never
saw anybody else touch themselves there?) Maybe she should have talked
to me sometime, some other time, shared some of her knowledge about
her own sexuality, with me. But she never did. I resent that."

Mothers Talk About Their "Sexual" Feelings for Their Children

A small minority of parents are aware of, or willing to discuss, erotic
feelings they may have for their children:

"I'm surprised at the sexual pleasure I feel playing with my three-year-
old daughter, and she sometimes seems to be mocking intercourse when
she mounts my husband. It's okay as long as she's young, but I can feel
our self-consciousness increasing with her age."

"With my kids, yes, I'm turned on to them. I try to stay accepting of
their feelings, while encouraging them to explore with friends their own
age. We've talked about people, bodies, having babies, contraception and
abortions and know we'll keep on talking. I have a harder time accepting
my own feelings of being turned on to them. I have two boys, ages five
and seven."

"I have felt sexual feelings when I breast-fed both my daughter and
son. I was startled at first. But nursing is such an intimate thing that it
isn't really that surprising, I suppose. It feels good. (Also nursing and
sex both release oxytocin, I found out.) My son, who is four months
old, always giggles when I clean his penis. I try not to overdo it."

"My older daughter (she's eight years old) likes to touch my breasts.
Unfortunately I can't handle it, and recoil."

"I've had sexual feelings for all members of the family. I love them,
it's hard to separate love from sexual feelings."

"I have sexual feelings towards my daughter—mixed with intense love. I think it's okay if I don't act on it."

Fathers also express these feelings (see also Part III):
"I find myself aroused by close physical playing and loving with my two-year-old sons. I am curious about incest and the origin of the taboos, and if it might be all right to make love with my sons someday."

Sisters' and brothers' erotic awareness of each other
Sisters and brothers too sometimes have sexual thoughts about each other; are these curiosity, or more ominous?

"I have had sexual feelings for my sister who is a few years younger. I do not think too much about it—obviously I am not going to act on any feelings I might have. The feelings are much more a desire for increased closeness than a desire for any sexual relationship."

"There were some feelings of attraction for my older brother (three years older) during our adolescence. We were very afraid of each other and hardly communicated—probably for this reason. He and my younger brother both went through a phase (age fourteen–sixteen) of peeping in at me while I dressed. Now I wish we could have been more comfortable about our curiosity."

"I have a younger sister who is very beautiful, and I have had fantasies of having sex with her. I've never told her this, because I think she'd be upset. She is very beautiful and her body is wonderful to look at."

"I'm crazy for my older brother! If he weren't my brother, I would like to have sex with him—my fantasies go wild over my brother."

Sensuality, Eroticism and Sexuality in the Family

Why is childhood sexuality repressed? Is it necessary for the incest taboo? For decency? To uphold our values?

These two fathers describe how they observe their young children, or interact with them in a sensual way:

"I have two daughters. The younger one was having orgasms when she was three or four years old from holding her Teddy bear between her legs. My wife and I left the room. Childhood's sexuality is irrepressible, but most parents don't know anything about it (and only a little bit about their children in general)."

"I have a daughter, seven, and a son, nine. When *I* was that age, I only got a book from my mother—*Being Born*—which she read to my sister and brother and me. It was stupid! Now my wife and I are trying to raise our kids differently, to understand that responsible sexual behaviour is part of being human. And also to give them enough affection. We snuggle together while reading or watching TV. We often shower together. They know what human bodies look like. We frequently bathe together—all of us!"

One young woman remembers with pleasure how her mother continued body contact with her even beyond her very earliest years:

"My mother was very affectionate with me. She used to scratch or caress my back while we lay in front of the fireplace, or tickle my feet. She gave me baths and washed and combed my long hair. She was always gentle and made sure I never got soap in my eyes. She used to let me hold a towel over my face. And when I was sick, she pampered me and waited on me."

Can parents and children touch? How much?

Is it "natural" for parents to stop touching their children after the age of five? Is this part of the "normal and necessary" "separation process" that is theorized by some schools of psychology?

A patriarchal social structure, with the family system constructed as ours is, has made it necessary for physicality to be off-bounds between most of its members, in any sustained way. How else could rigid authoritarian and hierarchical relationships be maintained? But now many people are questioning the glorification of "discipline" and "not showing feelings", the not being "too affectionate" motto of the "traditional family".

By looking at family relationships early on, we can ask: Isn't the cut-off of touching artificial, i.e., demanded by the culture and not by actual necessity?

If we didn't live in the social structure that we do, would we stop touching our children so early in life? Wouldn't we behave differently? Would we hear, "She/he's too old for that now, don't babyfy her/him, turn him into a sissy, spoil her." If children were free to come and go, if they weren't locked into the family system by having no alternatives (no group-male or female houses, as in the Polynesian Islands), then would love be stronger, because it would not be forced?

This is not to say that in some ideal world we would all live happily ever after, in love with/in bed with our parents. Our family system informs parents that they should stop touching children, and thus cuts off a vital form of communication and love (and makes "sex" more alluring?), while deliberately separating parents from children.

New structures of affection could grow "naturally" out of family love and contact, if touching weren't artificially prohibited by the "family" system after children are considered old enough to sleep alone. We need to create these channels for affection and shared physicality.

Chapter 2

Violent Physical Intimacy

The Construction of Sexuality and Eroticism Through Spanking and Physical Punishment

For many children, especially after about the age of five or six, the only intimate physical contact they have with anyone is with their parents when they are punished. When the parent actually lays hands on and takes physical power over the child's body, touching it and moving it about in some way. At the same time, the parent is usually showing a (gratifying?) degree of emotional agitation, passion and involvement.

When asked, "Did your parents touch and cuddle you?" many people answer, "No—only through spanking."

Spanking and beating give a strong unspoken message connecting power, violence and sexuality. Spanking especially is an invasive "sexual" experience which defines the child's body and connects the buttocks and genitals with violence—and sometimes pleasure.

The majority have been hit only once or twice, as this girl describes:

"Apparently I was just about a model child. I was only hit once in my life. I was about four and ran out in a parking lot and narrowly escaped getting wiped out by a car. My mother spanked me for that."

Infrequent and relatively non-brutal spankings such as this are less traumatic than repeated violent abusive eruptions, often premeditated, as other people describe in this chapter. But almost all spankings are still very much remembered.

Girls and boys are equally frequently struck, according to this study, but in different ways. Girls tend to be punished by the mother, usually in a more spontaneous, "slapping" or hitting way. If a father punishes a daughter, this is more likely to be non-spontaneous ("Go to your room and wait for your punishment there"), and to involve spanking or lashing

32

with a belt. A father's punishment is usually more severe and feared—he seems bigger, more overwhelming and frightening. It is much more frequently fathers who strike boys (fathers also strike sons more often than daughters)—although the fear is always there for girls too, in such warnings as "Wait until your father hears about this!"

Spanking and physical abuse: girls' stories*
Here several girls describe the context in which they experienced abuse:
"When I think back to my childhood, it seemed my mother was always angry about one thing or another. Growing up under her hand meant lashings with the belts my father left behind when he was thrown out. You might say those were the only things he contributed to our welfare besides alimony cheques. I cannot remember my father, as my mother kicked him out when I was very little. He has come back for important family events, like graduations, but stays too briefly for me to gain any lasting impressions. My memory is mainly of a tall, slow-speaking man with a deep voice.

"My mother said she loved me but her manner was always too critical, too snide, too restrictive and domineering for me to believe her. Speaking sweetly and singing to us were never her style. She had to perform all the household chores, including keeping us clean and well fed—after all, there was no one else."

"My mother would hit me with a hairbrush and scream and scream at me. I hated first grade because that's when it started to get really bad. I went from being an extrovert and an artistic child to being quiet, reclusive and shy, lacking self-confidence.

"I despised and felt overwhelmed by my mother's dark, enormous sexuality. I look so little like her and was made to feel inadequate. I hated her lusty, crude appraisal of men, the way she talked about going around with men.

"I was very close to my father, to the jealousy of my mom, till I was about five. But my father stopped being close to me or my sisters the older—and more female—we got."

"My father and I never got along. I hated him. He was never affectionate, he used to hit me. He was a disciplinarian and would never give me a reason other than that he was my father. He was narrow-minded, old-fashioned and unintelligent. They argued daily. My mother always spoke badly of him, she said he was stupid and 'a nothing'. I believe my dad wanted a son. He always complained about being surrounded by girls, my mom and the three of us daughters."

* See Part III for boys' stories.

"My mother once beat me with a brush until it broke, and then with a flyswatter until it broke, then used the wires until they broke, and then her hand until she got tired. Why? Only because my shoes were such a mess in the closet that I couldn't find a complete pair. That was when I was about nine or ten. I could never respect her. I kept a diary and for many years I would not capitalize her name or the word 'mother' because I felt she didn't deserve this respect. She had a quick temper, very little understanding, she often beat me.

"Today, when I understand my mother better, I can get some understanding of the way she was. But somehow it doesn't make it any better. I was never close to my father, and he was not very affectionate with me either. He was dominated by my mother, but I liked him from a distance, and I did always know that if he hit me or spanked me, I deserved it."

"My father was and still is cruel, mean and brutal. Living at home, during high school, I became depressed, developed an ulcer and was under a doctor's care for my nerves as well. I told a girlfriend (she saw the bruises on my back) about how he would beat me, and she threatened to call the Children's Aid. I was petrified, begged her not to, became hysterical. I knew that if she did that, he'd beat me till I died. She let the matter drop and after that I took extra care never to let on to anyone what the situation was."

And another, describing her mother with sympathy, says, "Maybe she couldn't help hitting me":

"I was close to both parents, probably equally. Mom died when I was nine, so I didn't know her too well. She would slap me a lot, but I guess she couldn't help it, she spent a lot of time in hospitals for depression. She had a lot of problems, obviously. Her death was a suicide. So maybe she couldn't help hitting me. I'm very short-tempered too and I'm so scared, if I am ever blessed enough to have babies, that I might lose my cool and hit them. I wouldn't want to, though. Ever. When I see a mother even yell at her little children, such as in a store, and especially if she slaps them, I get so angry with her.

"My parents must have made a good impression on me when I was small, because all I want in my life is a husband and children. I don't want a career at all. I think a woman should be home and raise her own babies. I see working mothers, they almost have their kids 'raised' by babysitters, and these kids are wild. My parents loved me. Daddy does what's right for me. If he tries to tell me something, I know it's for my own good.

"I am fairly close to my dad. We never kiss anymore, but I hug him once in a while. I can talk to him pretty well. It's getting so now that I'm older I can 'almost' talk of anything with him. Sex is still a biggy! I love him. I only fear him if I've done something bad, something wrong, and there's no way out of it, I gotta tell him, and I know he's gonna be mad. We argue about money. He saves it a lot. I spend it. Also, he doesn't understand my moods. He thinks I have to be cheerful all the time, and I just can't.

"I remember when I was little, Dad and Mom would fight just like Dad and I do now. When Mom would cry or be upset, he wouldn't understand. Even now, I can be hurting like hell (my feelings) and if I cry, he gets mad and tells me I'd better get a hold of myself—I'm being 'too hard' on him!"

Love-Hate for Parents

One girl gives a vivid picture of the confusing overtones of the violence in her home:

"I felt very close to my family yet very alienated. They were extremely loving but harsh disciplinarians at the same time. My mother was very loving, but punished me often—usually verbally, but also by hitting me. I had a love-fear relationship with her. It was rather confusing. I would often ponder and pray, not understanding what was going on.

"She would control me by yelling, hitting and using the Bible against me, which she knew I believed in. She would harp on the verses of submission of children to parents, and of women to everyone, and would often tell me to shame myself and feel guilty for my sins. These 'sins' were usually a difference of opinion between us (length of skirts, relationships to people). It took years of being away from her to be able to see things in a clearer perspective. I did like the areas she trained me well in—self-discipline, consideration for others, responsible living, honesty.

"My mother was affectionate in her good moods and would praise me occasionally. When she did speak sweetly to me it was generally manipulative to get me to do what she wanted. (Always the tense point.) She sang lullabies to us when we were babies, and as a young child she bathed me and put up my hair. But later we were constantly clashing. She was angry if there wasn't immediate compliance to her wishes, particularly in public.*

"Today I see her for what she is, a complicated mess. I still love her

---

* Was her mother feeling a lack of respect from the society as well, so that this was the last straw? This is a common feeling and experience. See *Women and Love*.

but have no desire to be with her, as she cannot feel or think beyond her own narrow little world. I have tried to expand it, to suggest other ways of looking at things, but have found her to be incapable of comprehension, although she is highly intelligent.

"My childish memories of my father, who died when I was six, include jumping all over him when he came home from work and riding on his shoulders. My father was always kind to me. I remember an incident where a dog was hurt by a car in front of our house and we looked at each other and equally felt the pain without uttering words. He took me fishing, which did not interest me—but being with him did. I loved and respected him, I don't remember personal fear of him, but knew he could get very angry with my brothers."

Another woman describes a very distressing childhood:

"My mother was obese, somewhere in the neighbourhood of two hundred pounds. I didn't like her much. In her moments of lucidity, I was always surprised at the measure of sensitivity she showed.

"Arguments were punishable. Rebellion unheard of. (Or, at least punishable.) Punishment meant pain or withdrawal, and then an insistence on cowering. Much humiliation.

"In their defence, I will say that my parents were deeply involved in their own struggles. My mother never forgave herself for the fact that my sister was born with Erb's palsy. My dad was busy being a nice guy to the whole world and never had time for us. I was given food, shelter and clothing and a dosage of verbal and physical abuse. The verbal abuse took the form of being called a 'son-of-a-bitch-bastard' (one word) every day of my life. I'm not sure my mother knew my name.

"The physical abuse came from being beaten with a wooden hanger and having my face scratched with the metal end. My parents were unable to give love in a meaningful way. My mother (I have since been told) was probably psychotic to some degree.

"Somehow, only recently, have I come sufficiently through the pain and anger to find some measure of forgiveness for her. This is something she cannot do for herself. She did not love me in what was an acceptable manner. Yet somehow, I felt secure in the dependability of the insanity.

"My parents always argued, and today they continue to fight in their mutual hysteria. I feel sorry for the guilt that destroys their lives. There are no friends and little left of what was family. I have been angry that they did not make a better life for themselves, that my mother didn't do better for herself, that she denied me the privilege of knowing how to make a better life (though I have found much of that myself), that she never helped my sister to deal with her life appropriately, or herself—that she never knew enough forgiveness.

"My mother in all her insanity saw sex as dirty, saw body parts as dirty, they had numbers not words, or were called 'down below', 'potato', etc. To this day, a bathing suit is deemed inappropriate and sex is the most horrendous kind of thing one could possibly know (yet she loved Marilyn Monroe and took great pleasure in beautiful women. One of the few positive attitudes she had).

"I was always supposed to be a good girl. That would mean coming home early, staying at home and never doing anything that involved any human being or could not be visibly noted as anything but pristine pure. I never quite figured out what was 'good' since everything seemed 'bad'. I really was most unsuccessful in avoiding that which was 'not nice' or 'bad'.

"I don't remember masturbating as a child. I was well into adulthood when I started. My education about masturbating came when my mother threw a book, *Calling All Girls*, at me as a teenager and said, 'Read this.' I remember thinking, I know all this stuff already.

"Today, my mother sits blinded by diabetes, unable to walk, in a wheelchair, overweight, in constant pain, unable to control her bodily functions. She gets up only to go to the table to eat. The only thing alive is her mind and it dwells on cruel commentary and unkindness about the entire world. My father has become her nurse. They are locked into a relationship of hate and dependency. He remains a gentle man at times. There are remembrances of that gentility in him. It may have been my saving grace."

Punishment, Discipline and the Definition of Love

One young woman discusses what happened to her as a child, how she was spanked in her very "normal family" ("not often")—and what it was like for her. She wonders about the emotions of "love" and "respect" she felt for her parents, and what they meant:

"Were you spanked by your parents?"
(Averted eyes, shifting in seat) "Yes, I remember they used to take out after us, me and my brother, with a shoe horn—a long one. My father's shoe horn. My brother and I used to hide it. (Under the stairs, I think.) This really got my father angry. My mother used to say always, 'Wait until your father comes home!' She used to leave it to him to punish us. This wasn't fair of her, leaving the dirty work to him. So as a result, I think I kind of grew up fearing him . . .

"Well, I guess he came home, he wasn't particularly angry, because he wasn't there to get angry when it all happened, so it must have been strange, to come home and find oneself in the role of having to be 'angry' and punish someone. But why do you think she left it to him? Why didn't she do it herself? It was a dirty job, and maybe she didn't want to have to do it. I don't know."

"Why did she become so angry?"
"Well, of course, we were so used to her, we didn't take any notice of what she told us, we just kept jammering away all the time, we didn't really take her threats seriously."

"So she got angry when you would talk back and not respect her, things like that?"
"Yes, smart answers, the two of us against her, she was home all the time . . ."

"Maybe she felt she couldn't make you stop, no matter what, or that only your father could discipline you—since you respected him more, he had more power?"
"Yes, he had the power, the whole family was built around helping him get off to work, keeping quiet so he could rest, waiting for him to come home at night so we could have supper—things like that. He

38

made all the money. And he was the one we respected most, we feared the most."

"Well, where did they/he hit you with the shoe horn? On the buttocks?"

"On the upper thighs, near the hips."

"Not on the posterior, the behind? Did you have to bend over or get in a certain position to be 'spanked'?"

(Averted eyes) "No, on the thighs . . . that's all I remember. But I wonder . . . maybe there are things I don't remember."

"What kind of influence or effect did being hit have on you?"

(Thoughtful, distant expression) "I wonder . . . I'm not sure . . . it must have had a lot of effect, effects I'm not even aware of."

"I wonder how it is for a baby in a crib who gets smacked by an angry adult. It must be terrifying, this huge adult hitting it, while it is in terror, and has absolutely no defence against what's happening—and if it cries more or keeps on crying out, it gets hit more. So the baby tries to contain itself.

(Still looking far away) "Yes, there must be a great fear . . . Maybe that is why I feared my father, because he did hit me, or had hit me . . ."

"But do you blame your mother for 'making' him hit you? After all, he didn't have to do what she said. They must have agreed that the policy of spankings was okay, otherwise if she were the only one, he would have had a talk with her and said, 'Look here, I can't carry out these punishments for you, let's think of another way to resolve what's going on.' But I notice you don't feel he was as much to blame as your mother."

"Well, it was her idea. Admittedly, we were provoking her, acting bratty to her, not to him. He wasn't there, we were constantly with her. If we had been with him as much, we might have respected him less and been just as bratty with him . . . I don't know. It's strange, isn't it?"

"What were your feelings for your father?"

"The main feeling I remember is respect, I remember I respected my father a lot. My brother and I both did."

"Why?"

(Puzzled look and pause) "He used to bring us candy home sometimes . . . but then my mother made us special cakes and pies. Maybe it was just the way she seemed to look up to him . . . in a way, but not in other ways. She let him take the lead, she prepared everything for him at home, she centred herself around his comfort, he seemed very very important. Without him the family wouldn't survive. But of course without my mother it wouldn't have survived, either, so I don't know why the most prominent emotion I felt for him, the emotion that comes to mind when I think of my childhood, is respect. Love, yes, but love I felt for my mother too . . . the love was different, for him it was a kind of respect-love. Maybe it's true what they say, punishing people makes them love you, I hate to say it, but maybe it's because he punished us and didn't just yell at us like my mom did, that we respected him."

"*So it was better to be hit? Then you took him seriously?*"

"Well, I guess then we had no choice. But then I should have resented him too. But I resent my mother more. Why? Or is 'respect' a cold form of love, that is, love mixed with resentment? Is the coldness and distance I feel mixed with the love, hate—and disbelief that he could hurt us like that? That he could be so cold as to actually assault us, who were so much physically smaller and weaker?"

"*Why didn't you experience it as anger? Possibly one can't afford anger in those situations. After the punishment the child is supposed to be sorry—after all, it was the child who supposedly did the wrong thing. The child is not allowed to be angry with the parent, the child is not allowed to judge morally the parents, the child must simply love and obey.*"

"Yes, I felt rage and anger . . . and I couldn't bear to believe he wouldn't love us, that he would hit us. It was easier to believe that my mother made him do it, I knew why she was mad, I had seen her anger and could even see her side of it. I knew what those fights were all about.

"I guess I always showed my anger to my mother, so I still felt very warm and close to her, not distant and 'respectful' as I did with him . . . the relationship with him was emotionally distant, for both me and my brother. I know my brother used to wonder if other boys talked more to their fathers. Well, if you have to choose between being close and not respecting a parent, or being distant and respectful, I don't know. As a future parent, I don't know which one I'd choose."

"*Maybe there's a happy medium!*"

It can be helpful if friends talk to each other about these experiences, get them out in the open and clear the air—since often, without noticing it, people carry around guilty shadow-feelings, memories of this early "shame", as part of their adult personae.

But the preceding conversation shows just how difficult and delicate it can be for one person, even an adult today, to describe being spanked during childhood to another person.

Spanking and Sado-masochism

The Influence of Spanking and Beating on Fantasies

"I was very young, maybe six, when I first masturbated to orgasm. It was on my own, with a lot of guilt. Until I was twelve, I fantasized about being spanked while masturbating, rubbing against a pillow. Then I stopped feeling guilty and used my fingers. At the same time, I stopped fantasizing about being spanked."

"We used to play house. I was the mommy and my brother was the daddy. I would fix dinner, and then we would do dishes. Mommy would complain that Daddy wasn't putting the dishes away. He would say, 'If Mommy isn't nice, I'm going to have to spank Mommy.' Then he would put me over his knee and spank me. I wouldn't cry during the spanking (it didn't hurt), then we would say okay, now it's time for bed, and lie down together (on the floor or ground) as if we were in Mommy and Daddy's bed, to go to sleep. I wonder if we wondered what they did there."

The aim of physical punishment, according to many childcare books, is to break the child's will: the child must learn to obey unquestioningly. This is more important than actual physical pain. Thus, to be most effective, the event must be set up in advance, say fifteen minutes or so, during which the child is told to "wait" in his or her room for the spanking. After the event, the child "should ask to be forgiven", thus colluding with the "rightness" of the parent, and the "deservedness" of the punishment.

These are also basic elements of sado-masochistic activity. The teaching of these connections between power and genitals often creates a strong love-hate, fear-intimacy bond with the abusive parent or person. Philip Greven suggests, in *Spare the Child* (Knopf, 1991), that sado-masochistic sex may be a way for some people to re-enact these scenes (emotionally and psychologically re-experience them), but make them come out with a different end result.

Other interpretations of sado-masochistic sexuality stress that such

41

activity is not "harmless" or (even less) "therapeutic" in any way; it merely demonstrates how deeply people have been imprinted with horribly deformed definitions of "love" as hate, fear and submission—or aggression and control—and so, can only "love" in this way. In particular, it is notable that in heterosexual sado-masochistic pornography, it is almost always the woman who is made to experience pain and domination of her body. Sado-masochism is a statement about the power relationship between men and women, and sometimes an incitement to men to abuse women. Yet its erotic appeal in our culture cannot be denied.

The Hierarchical Psyche: Spanking and Sexuality

Punishments for the psyche and the body

How exactly are the connections made in the child's mind between the parents' power, the private violent invasion of the body, the "rule" that the child cannot resist or fight back—and possible simultaneous sexual stimulation?

When a child is hit on the buttocks, blood rushes to the area, causing a tingling in the genitals. Girls, according to this research, seem slightly more likely to be hit on the buttocks, while boys are hit on the back, or backs of the legs. More of girls' sexual anatomy is exposed in the bent-over position than boys'; although the scrotum is vulnerable in such a position, the penis remains in the front of the body, while the vaginal opening, more towards the back of the vulva, is nearer the buttocks, and nearer the blood-flow brought on by the blows.

This kind of violent touch can be sexualized in the child's mind not only because of a real flow of blood into the genitalia, but also because of a longing for intimacy with the parent: if painful physical touch is the only fulfilment of that longing, then this can "feel good".

According to some studies, the vast majority of the US population has been physically disciplined.* Has the "vast majority" of the British? German? French? Indian? population also been physically assaulted, "disciplined"?

In the UK in 1990, 90 per cent of those responding to a *Woman's Own*

---

* Murray Straus, Richard Gelles, and Suzanne Steinmetz, *Behind Closed Doors: Violence in the American Family* (NY, Simon and Schuster, 1980); this book contains documentation and asserts the fact that domestic violence is normal throughout the USA. Physical punishments of children, these authors argue, are violent acts that underpin subsequent violence within families and between spouses.

survey admitted to smacking their children, although more than half regretted doing so. Five European countries—Sweden (1979), Finland (1983), Denmark (1985), Norway (1987), and Austria (1989)—have outlawed physical punishment of children. In the UK, EPOCH (End Physical Punishment of Children) is campaigning for the same legislation.

Children are generally forbidden to act/react appropriately and effectively in these situations to defend themselves from assault and invasion. Indeed, if they try to defend themselves or fight back, the punishment may be more severe, they are told. The "best thing" for them is to submit. Thus the associations of love, fear and pain begin early and remain embedded in the unconscious mind for life, unless removed.

According to Greven, following also Alice Miller, "Spanking, whippings, and beatings are the painful origins of much adult sado-masochism. The astonishing absence of studies of sado-masochism in our history and culture is evidence of the denial that most people experience concerning the long-term consequences of physical punishments both for the psyche and sexuality. It is the early fusion of pain and love and the eroticization of coercion through the assaults upon the body and the anus that often shape the creation of sado-masochistic feelings, fantasies and behaviours in adults."*

If spanking and physical punishment are widespread in a society, it is logical that sado-masochism will also be. It may not be an aberration, it can be inherent in a culture, any culture in which children suffer from painful physical punishments and humiliation, and are subject to more powerful authorities.

And yet, adherents of corporal punishment and "discipline" for children (often members of fundamentalist religious groups, as their child-rearing manuals can attest) refuse to admit to the sexual aspects of what they are doing, or even to the fact that such "pointing out" of the genitals of the child in this "humiliation" setting (yet one full of attention and passion) could have profound effects on the sexual feelings and emotional poles of the child. The absence of "sexuality" in these situations has always been stressed by advocates of corporal punishments for children. Yet this is clearly self-deceptive.

Astutely, Greven also points out, "The unconscious association of love with anal punishments is surely among the psychic sources of much of the fear and hatred of homosexuality and of sodomy rampant in the Christian right today. Homophobia is as central to the ideology and

* *Spare the Child*, Philip Greven (NY, Knopf, 1991), p. 175.

43

psychology of the Christian right today as anti-Semitism was to Nazis in the 1930's and 1940's."*

Further important sources in this area include:

Alice Miller, *For Your Own Good: Hidden Cruelty in Child-Rearing and the Roots of Violence* (NY, Farrar, Straus and Giroux, 1983).
Erin Pizzey and Jeff Shapiro, *Prone to Violence* (London, Hamlyn Paperbacks, 1982).
Linda Godon, *Heroes of Their Own Lives: The Politics and History of Family Violence* (NY, Viking, 1988).

* Greven, op. cit., p. 184.

What Does This Physical Assault Mean?

The assault on a part of the child's body this close to her/his genitals (usually our society believes genitals "should" be covered; it is "shameful" to show them) must have confusing meanings for the child. What can it mean? That the parent desires to be intimate with the child—but the child must be punished because this desire is the child's fault? That this part of the child is so shameful (genitals are shameful) that the parent wants to beat them? That the parent now wants to destroy the genitals or "that part", the "not nice part", of the child's body?

Certainly, in the case of spanking (as opposed to beating), the child must feel she or he is being punished not only by being struck, but also by the humiliation of having to "bend over" and "show" this shameful part of her/himself. All of these ideas and many more pass through the child's mind in a flash of reality, before the blur of "society's reality" covers over this insight and "tells" him or her the "right interpretation" of what has happened, i.e., "it was necessary, and the parent had to do it, you deserved it, and it will make you a better person—straighten you out."

Yet lingering somewhere in the unconscious, the child must also have many of these questions stored up, and even know she or he has a power over the adult, to provoke in the adult such a show of desire/aggression/intimacy.

Another part of the problem affects not the sexual identity of the child, but the psyche: the child is helpless against the assault. Whether or not "justice" is involved is not the point; whether or not she or he has done anything really wrong or particularly terrible is irrevelant. It is the power dynamic that is being imprinted on the brain: the child experiences the fact of being terrified and overwhelmed by a physical assault coming from someone she or he also loves/gets love from (in some form, even if just food and a place to sleep) at other times.

In fact, the child is often told to ask the parents' forgiveness and apologize after the assault—forcing a further submission of self. In these cases, where does the rage go? Without expression, there is nowhere it can go, except to become internalized and to turn into self-hate. The punishment becomes a deeply traumatizing experience, far beyond the pain involved. Why? *Because there is no way the child can react against it, children are generally forbidden to defend themselves or take revenge, and so they are left with an impotent, powerless rage*—which sometimes even blots out memory, leaving a haze of alienated emotion over the rest of life. The primary image is gone, but the atmosphere remains. And love's definition becomes more confused, especially as there is no memory of this process happening.

Parents' denial that they hit their children

Some people block out, don't remember their childhoods at all. For example: "I don't remember much about my parents from my childhood. My childhood memories do not include memories about my parents, or my siblings, for that matter. My memories are vague to nonexistent."

The great majority of both girls and boys who were hit frequently say that, later in life, when they mention being spanked or hit, and try to talk about this as adults with their parents, their parents say they absolutely cannot remember having done it. Even repeated attempts at communication (in many cases) still lead to blank looks and attitudes of disbelief on the part of the parents. As one young woman recounts:

"Luckily my sister was there (we slept in the same room at the time) and she still remembers very well what happened. But both of my parents, neither one of them 'remembers' a thing!"

Most children, however, when they grow up, never bring up these incidents with their parents. As with the subject of sexuality, this too cannot be mentioned. Perhaps it is too private and personal—and embarrassingly intimate—or even too passionate.

Also, it is interesting to note the language: spanking or hitting is usually described by parents and children as "discipline", i.e., "They disciplined me," not, "He hit me," or, "We spanked her." The sentence is softened, the word "discipline" with a broader meaning is usually used at first, until the questions asked become more precise.

With this language, the children in a way deny to themselves the aggression, what really happened, and blame themselves. Girls (as opposed to boys) think, I was an unruly child, it was necessary. Boys more often speak of their punishment with anger and pride (and some shame) while girls speak mostly with shame and self-blame.

Does most of the "disciplining" start after the age of five, and take place between the ages of five and ten? Or does it take place earlier, when the child/infant is even more defenceless?

VIOLENT PHYSICAL INTIMACY

Physical abuse generally stops when the child's body is almost as large as the parents' bodies (late puberty). Sometimes in the case of particularly brutal relationships between fathers and daughters, it is replaced with sexual abuse.

Toilet training

Do children learn from toilet training, just as much as from spanking, that their genitals are "dirty"?

What parent or sibling hasn't, when changing a diaper, inevitably turned his or her nose up, saying, "Yuck! Ick! Dirty!" and pulled the diaper away from the body, holding it as far away from the nose as possible, ready to drop it into the disposal bin or washer?! It's a natural reaction, but the child cannot help but feel embarrassed or even ashamed, knowing she or he is the cause of this reaction.

Maybe our society is doomed to think of sex as "dirty", because toilet training is inevitable, and so intertwined in our minds are genitals, urination, defecation, and sexual secretions that there is no way to avoid this. Will the connection between sex and "dirt" always be part of the appeal of sex? Should we just understand and accept this?

The fact is, no matter how "dirty" a baby learns her or his defecation and urination are, and thus too are "those parts", if the family were more open and accepting of sexuality, this "dirtiness" would not be taken to the extreme.

Enemas

One man describes how anal penetration became an integral part of his sex life after his early experiences with enemas as a child—demonstrating the close connection between very early physical experiences with genitals and erotic identification:

"In my childhood I discovered that enemas and suppositories gave me a charge. I had an aunt that took warm enemas almost every day—I would see her go to the kitchen and make a large pitcher of soapy water, the suds flowing over the top of the pitcher—then she would go to the bathroom with a fountain syringe in the other hand and stay for quite a time. I was told she did that to make her bowels 'move'.

"When I was much younger they would hold me over their knees and take a small bulb syringe and squirt a little water up my rectum to make me 'go out'—other times they would take a soap stick (made of octagon soap) and with a knife slim it down to about the size of the middle finger. They would dip one end in warm water and insert it up my rectum and hold it for a few moments. It felt good—but I never let anyone know it!

MEMORIES OF EARLY CHILDHOOD

"As I got older enemas attracted me and I still take them. I use them with sex on many occasions. I even have a very private soap stick and a red rubber fountain syringe with a large black nozzle packed away in my travel bag."

Sexual Abuse of Girls

Of course, the earliest sexual experiences of many children, but especially girls, are of sexual abuse. As documented by this study and many others (see Diana Russell and Florence Rush, for example), fathers, and especially stepfathers, brothers and male relatives or friends are almost always the abusers, and girls are almost always the objects of the abuse. Boys, according to almost all studies, are rarely sexually abused. Almost no boys wrote about having been sexually abused in this study.

One girl explains what happened between her and her brother:

"When I was nine, I walked in on my older brother who was masturbating. He was fourteen. He was lying in bed with his pants open and holding his penis. I remember I immediately saw his big penis, bigger than his hand, the top sticking up over his hand. Big and red.

"I don't remember when I had seen a penis before, never one that big. It was hard and seemed to be wet or shiny. His face was flushed and he seemed very excited.

"I started to leave, and he said, 'Come over here. Don't be afraid. Don't you want to see?'

"I went over by the bed and looked at his hand on his penis, his whole fist around it, clutching it kind of spasmodically. 'Watch while I come,' and he proceeded to move his hand until some white jerky stuff came out, all over the bed and his jeans. He started to breathe more normally after that.

"'Don't you want to touch it? Here, put your hand around it, like mine.' I did. I was so fascinated and almost hypnotized, I knew I shouldn't be doing it, but it was so amazing and something in me felt very excited. Then he put his hand over mine, very roughly, and then he shot wads of white liquid all over the bed and my clothes. It was kind of a mess. Then his penis got smaller.

"He looked at me, 'Don't you play with yourself down there?' I looked down, he must have known from my embarrassment that I did, but I said, 'No.' He told me he could show me how his girlfriend did it—'And then you can do it to yourself whenever you want.'

49

"'Come on, take your pants down, it won't hurt. Hurry up before mom and dad come home.' He started loosening my pants. I let him take them down. I was so used to him dressing me and undressing me when I was smaller, helping me tie my shoes, all kinds of things, this seemed so normal. Once my pants were down, his penis began to get big again, and his breathing was fast again. But he was trying to control himself, I think. He lay between my legs, his head looking up at me, and began to rub my genitals I guess until I got very wet, liquid came out and I was starting to jerk.

"Then we heard the car in the drive, and jumped up, both of us pulled our pants up quick in panic, and I ran from the room. We never discussed it again until I was twenty-one and on my twenty-first birthday, we joked about it (in a private whisper).

"Was I molested? Should I feel mad? Am I somehow disfigured because my first 'sexual encounter' was with my brother? I don't know. He was very good-looking, I thought, and his penis was amazing to my eyes then. I feel more affectionate towards him today because of that moment we shared, like we know each other better, somehow. We feel no shame with each other. We both have a sexual life and there's nothing wrong with it."

A woman, whose daughter was sexually abused by her husband, now, at sixty-five, explains her life and why she didn't leave her husband:

"I was not in love when I married, but I grew increasingly fond of my husband over the years. Before my marriage, I used to think I was in love, but I seemed always to pick someone who drank too much or who wasn't in love with me. So then I deliberately picked someone to marry who I thought would be acceptable to my parents, who had a bright future—and who I thought would be a good father. I was wrong on the last premise.

"My husband abused me and the children verbally, and he sexually abused my oldest daughter, his stepdaughter, from the time she was eight until she was eighteen—which I only recently discovered when she was hospitalized for a serious depression.

"I wanted to leave him, but we have been together for thirty-two years and I feel guilty about leaving him now, as he is ill. Also, we really don't have enough money to live on separately.

"He has done some really bad things in our married life. He forced me to have four children when only two were planned. He insisted I had to have a hysterectomy when it really wasn't necessary. (He insisted he wouldn't have sex with me until I did it.)

"I was faithful to him until I met a widower who lives in our building and I thought we loved one another. It wasn't a good relationship, as he had other women and wasn't interested in marrying again. I wanted a lot more intimacy than I got. My husband was very jealous and upset, although he had encouraged me to have this affair.

"I think he has many problems in his life, he has very low self-esteem and needs to be more in touch with his own feelings, wants and needs. He won't talk on any subject where he might be emotionally involved. He hides behind endless sporting events and doesn't want to talk about feelings at all, ever. I feel cheated because I have to retreat into myself and cannot discuss anything serious with anyone.

"Over the years I've become very repressed emotionally (a great deal like my father), and this has brought on physical pain which my doctor diagnoses as osteo-arthritis. It has shown up since finding out about my husband's excesses, so this is probably psychosomatic, as is his bronchial asthma (first showed up recently).

"I'm in this marriage and I can't get any therapy as I don't want to be single and I am more comfortable in this relationship for the little it gives us. After all, I am sixty-five years old. I'm white, female, Jewish, with two years of college. I devoted all my time after marriage to home and family, I didn't have any work experience, so what would I do if I were single?

"Now that we are retired and living in a condo in Florida, I enjoy golf and social life with a little travelling. I'm happy most of the time but have no really close relationship with anyone. My husband and I have a good companionship now but no sexual life, as he turned off that about three years ago. He is seventy and seems happy to forgo sex. I wasn't happy about that but have adjusted to it. I've always simulated orgasm unless we were having oral sex or I masturbated.

"I've had many upsetting things happen with my children. One daughter died at thirty-four (multiple sclerosis), one son spent a year in jail on a drug arrest, and another daughter is divorced and raising four children alone. Also, two nieces who lived with us for eight years are both divorced now and have recently moved in here with their three children each.

"As a child I was very close to my mother and loved my father, but he was an introverted man, unable to give much love. Very quiet! He never showed my mother any affection, neither did she to him, nor did they argue. (My father later came to live with us, my husband and me, for twenty-three years.) My mother was affectionate to me and my sister, but extremely overprotective. I did everything to become popular, as I knew that's what would please her. I had many friends and went out many nights during high school, and during college, I dated five nights a week."

Are children who are abused political prisoners?

The violence in family situations such as these is often not even "seen" by those involved, who have come to live with "the situation", "accepting" the interpersonal dynamics as "the way it is", and eventually, perhaps even justifying them as "right" and "just"—or "what had to happen". But it is just these dynamics, learned in the authoritarian family system, that are re-enacted in political systems of oppression.

During this century, we have seen fascist political systems which convinced whole groups of people not to "see" the torture and murder of others. In just the same way, we often still do not want to "see" the physical or even sexual assaults on children as the forms of human rights abuses they are.

The obedience learned in families has political consequences. This psychological relationship to power becomes fixed in the psyches of many individuals, and influences their decisions later as adults. Thus many dictatorial regimes right now are being supported by people used to a stern-father ideal—who are, therefore, afraid to challenge the power of the dictator. Dishearteningly, many people will support a strong-father figure in whatever he does, since they have learned in the traditional family that male power must always be feared, respected and obeyed.

The subject of incest is discussed in Chapter 6.

Afterword

The purpose of these two chapters has been to open up a topic which very much needs to be looked at, so that together we can find creative solutions.

It is impossible to know exactly what physical relationships "should be" between parents and children; after all, we are seeing now the result of two thousand years or more of accreted behaviour patterns; to re-think this behaviour will take time, and needs many people to talk and write about it. The data and ideas presented here are meant as part of that re-thinking, to reflect and aid the process of democratizing the family that is currently going on.

Offered here is not only personal testimony, but also a new way to see the situation: the "traditional family" hierarchy (whether or not the iconography was replicated perfectly in our own houses) is a way of life that we, who were children once, have internalized and integrated into our own personality structures—and forgotten, come to consider "normal" and inevitable, "the way things are".

If we can remember back to the early questions we had when we were small children, as we hear the memories and voices of people in this book, we can begin to unravel the problems of formation of the person from what we now so easily insist are "the characteristics of human nature"—including exaggerated and misdirected violence and aggression.

We create much of this violence by our social order, especially through the traditional authoritarian family order. We impress values of power and dominance on children, even infants, when they are so helpless and small, that it is no wonder that the lessons remain learned for all of life, in most cases. We do violence to our children, and yet we do not explain that violence, even to ourselves. We give children rules, and yet we don't explain why those rules exist—perhaps because we do not even know. And so our children grow up in turn to rule their own families in the same way—with rules that are not clear to anyone but simply continued because they are "the way it is done", "tradition".

The worst thing we teach, without realizing it, is that power and might are the most "real" and important things in the world. Through the family system, we say over and over again that one must "respect" the hierarchy of man-on-top, that those in power (the parents) deserve power, that we must "respect" them—only because this is the way *we* had to live and see our parents when *we* were children.

We have reached a stage in society in which we must think more clearly about the source of the desire to dominate others. If we can do this, we can find a way out of our increasingly violent and aggressive (winner-take-all and don't-care-about-the-others) world. Our global problems—child poverty in the streets of cities such as Rio, Calcutta and Lagos, our assault on the natural environment, the terrible religious and political wars in ex-Yugoslavia and Afghanistan—show that we must begin to re-construct our world, from our largest, most public political institutions to our most personal, private relationships, and so end this sort of needless violence.

The roots of this violence are laid within an outmoded family structure—an authoritarian structure which needs to be democratized. This structure is creating a mind-set, a psychological landscape which focuses on power, and respect for, fear of, desire for power. Yet this structure has also changed enormously in the last twenty-five years. We need to acknowledge and reinforce the good in these changes, and find a gentler way of living together.

PART II

Growing up female:
why no daughter icon?

Girls Fight the System: Alice Asks Questions of Wonderland*

The secret thoughts of girls between the ages of ten and twelve, their fresh, clear-eyed take on things—this is territory that has offered many children's writers rich material. L. F. Baum's *The Wonderful Wizard of Oz*, Louisa May Alcott's *Little Women*, and Lewis Carroll's *Alice's Adventures in Wonderland* all present lively heroines of this age, full of curiosity.

Girls everywhere, as documented in this research, soon discover that they have to deal with a rather upside-down world, that is, a world that doesn't make sense to them, that is run by a kind of complicated and quirky hierarchy which gets you into trouble (especially as a girl) if you don't follow its rules. Alice observes that no one can explain the "rules" directly to her, the inhabitants are all "too far gone", so enmeshed in the system that they no longer "see" it like she does; she has to learn about this topsy-turvy, quirky and absurd world by observing it all on her own. By memorizing the rules, not trying to understand their meaning and logic—since there is none!

Alice in Wonderland and Dorothy in Oz both are very close to the hearts and spirits of girls here, as they start the teen years as "tomboys" and free spirits. The young heroines in this section, just like Alice and Dorothy, are busy "seeing" the world in their own new ways, trying to make sense of it, and today, questioning it out loud.

Dorothy has her own opinions!
Yet a second problem girls face here, which they also share with Alice and Dorothy, is that of not having their views of the world taken seriously by those around them. When Dorothy comes home from Oz and tries to tell Aunt Em and the rest of the family what happened, they won't listen, they can't hear her. Nobody "at home" thinks she has anything important to say. Aunt Em tells Dorothy, "Now, go find a place out of the way where you won't bother anybody or cause us any trouble!"

* As there is no daughter amongst the icons of the "holy family"—only a son—Alice has a lot of questions indeed!

How Real Is Reality?

This attitude leaves girls wondering whether the experience of the world they have is "real"—is what they see and feel real, or is "reality" the world "out there"? They learn to live on two levels, in two cultures at the same time—their own, the "female subculture" documented in *Women and Love*, and the dominant, mainstream culture, inside which they also function. In *their* culture, they are not second class; in the world's culture, they are. Their very important friendships with other girls keep this subculture and inner identity alive.

The early teenage world of girls is one of action. Does it have to end? No, and increasingly it doesn't. It is often the "tomboys" like Dorothy who have created the revolution in family life we are seeing now, the democratization of the family. And, maybe, these "tomboys" will create a new political system.

Who are Alice and Dorothy today?

What *are* girls thinking about today in their heart of hearts? The world has changed for the better for girls in the last thirty years, as the family and women's position is changing. Are girls still having to compromise and live in their dreams? Or can they express themselves fully—their "tomboy" selves, their "femininity", their intellects, their sexual energy, and their creativity? A progress report.

Chapter 3

Girls' Secret Sexuality and Identity
Age Five–Twelve

Being a Tomboy*

Glorious Descriptions of Freedom, Using Their Bodies, Feeling Able To Do All Things

"She (my best friend and I) were cowboys, with guns and holsters. We rode horses, like the guys! (In our minds—we lived in the city.) I didn't know which sex I was—I was neither. I wasn't like my father, I wasn't like my mother. I was smaller. I was a cowboy."

Many girls enjoy a brilliant period of independence and freedom just before adolescence, a period which stands out with clarity in their statements, so different is it from the period of imposed sexual identity that comes down (or tries to come down) heavily just after, and which continues in one form or another (reproductive choices, worry about menopausal "looks", feminist and post-feminist "do's" and "don't's") for the rest of their lives.

This period is like an Indian summer of the self, the undisturbed self, before the child is "heavily trained" in "sexual identity" by the society.

"Were you ever a tomboy?"
69 per cent of women answered yes to this question, and proceeded to describe with relish a period in their lives of independence and freedom,

---

* Why is there no equivalent word for boys who behave in "feminine" ways, or play girls' games? Of course there is one: "sissy". Why is this term much more derisive than "tomboy"?

fun, physical daring and action. The reason for their surprisingly long answers is clearly their pleasure in writing them down and thinking about them.

The clarity with which they remember those days is like a snapshot taken with a perfectly focused camera:

"I was a tomboy in grade school. Until second grade (when we moved into a regular neighbourhood with lots of kids), I played mostly by myself, exploring fields, streams, and woods, making up stories and plays. After second grade I played with both girls and boys in the neighbourhood, but mostly girls. We played 'Muffy' dolls a lot (does anyone remember them?), rode bikes, married our cats (?!), played 'Red-Rover, Red-Rover', played on the school playground equipment a half-block away, played in the woods, went bob-sledding in the winter (a great big sled—the neighbourhood kids all piled on and were pulled behind a car), played with the whole neighbourhood (there must have been ten or twelve 'regulars') on an amazing truck inner-tube, bouncing on and off, went sledding down a giant hill. I was never warned against acting too rough or being a tomboy. My dad played catch with me (baseball and mitts), I picked up snakes and loved to dangle them in front of my thoroughly disgusted mother (that may be the only example I can think of where she showed a 'feminine' trait)."

"Was I a tomboy! Man, there wasn't a tree within a fifty-mile radius that I didn't at least take a try at climbing. I loved the power of sitting up there, being able to see far, far. On the other hand, I spent a good bit of my childhood in casts, and, of course, incurred the wrath of both my parents for these exploits. Mother devoted her life to trying to make a proper lady of me. I think her greatest woe is her miserable failure in this. I had all the usual prohibitions—modulate the voice, sit with my knees together, don't eat too much, don't expect too much of life, don't chase boys, don't smoke, don't do too well in school (I was a very bright little girl), don't look for a career. My mother and I cleaned the house, did the laundry, all that kind of thing. I was expected to be cleaner than boys.* My brother was not expected to help with the domestic chores. Also, I was taught to cook, whereas my brother wasn't. My mother still brags that I baked my first 'from scratch' cake at seven. Quite an achievement, I suppose."

"I remember most of my early childhood being considered a tomboy—it was said to be because there were lots of male children and only one other female child in the neighbourhood. I don't (in the early years) recall being hassled for my tomboy behaviour. Later, of

---

* This is still the attitude of beauty-industry magazines!

course, I was chided for not sitting correctly and for wanting to have male friends (we were ten or eleven) sleep over.

"Being a tomboy—it was just being a kid and doing kid stuff—I climbed trees a lot. I can remember the feelings, the freedom and the openness of standing in one specific tree down the road from our house. I could see the sky opening up above and around me from the perch and I felt strong and (I realize now) clean and in control. Ah . . . I guess if this is tomboy-like behaviour (the term 'tomboy' stinks!) then it is vital and powerful.

"My mother showed me how to be feminine in the way she dressed me and did my hair, and in more subtle ways— behaviours and privileges (my father did this too): 'If you don't (be a certain way in looks, dress, manners), no one will want you.' There was a real 'job' description for females. My mother and I did 'typically' female things like housework, shopping, and cooking that my brother was not invited to participate in. In fact, there would have been concern had he wanted to do these kind of things.

"Told to be a 'good girl'? You bet! My father cornered me in our kitchen the day I began menstruating and said, 'Now you have to be a good girl.' As opposed to what! The way I'd been prior to twelve? Jerk! (Yes, I am angry). My mother drummed those words into me every time I left the house, from both of them. It had to do with sex. Good girls don't do anything sexual and if by chance they do, they needn't bother to bring their problems home to their parents!"

"I lived with my grandparents on a farm during World War I (from the age of nine until ten) and I was a tomboy. When there were complaints about my 'rough' behaviour, I rebelled by refusing for months to answer to any name but 'Jack'."

"A tomboy?! I must've been the original. There wasn't anything I didn't dare do. I climbed higher in the trees than anyone else. I ran faster than the boys. I trained myself to be a trapeze artist on a rope in my backyard. I enjoyed playing softball. I rode my bicycle at top speed down hills with my feet on the handlebars, and no hands! I'd really be upset if my daughter did those things.

"I had one bad experience as a tomboy. When I was visiting my mother's sister and family, I got carried away trying to show off the muscles in my arms and I socked some boy on his arm. My aunt was so horrified at my doing this, she made me go and sit in the car for the rest of the day. I'll never forget the awful feeling I had about myself that day. She made me feel I was evil. My aunt came and sat in the car with me for a while, but she was so serious and stern, I could only cry tears of shame."

"Yes, I was a tomboy. I loved to climb trees, shoot my bow and arrow, dream of some day running away to Darkest Africa and living a life like Tarzan's. I'm sure my mother was disappointed in me, that I wasn't more feminine. I remember once I got a doll for Christmas (perhaps I was about eight or nine), one she so wanted me to have and like. I just pretended to play with it to avoid hurting her feelings."

"I loved to run, pretend I was a horse, swim, jump on the trampoline and roller skate. But in the orphanage the girls and boys were separated and our lives were so ordered and structured that there wasn't much leeway for sports.

"I very much wanted a chemistry set (which my father and aunt ignored, as if they hadn't heard) and to work on the orphanage farm as a chore. They wouldn't let girls, only boys. It was just solid immutable fact like the sunrise that certain things were for boys, certain things for girls.

"When I moved back with my dad, I would sit and watch my stepmother dress and put on make-up and do her hair. I loved to do that too, and go shopping with her. My tomboyhood was over."

"I was definitely a tomboy. I could take on any boy in the neighbourhood and win. I was a fat kid, so all I had to do was sit on somebody I disagreed with (sounds like my father). I was told to be a lady but it never came off. I realized my father was the strongest personality in the family, and I followed his way. Consequently I was just as tough as my older brother. I had a knife like my brother and I went fishing like my brother. But after a while my father wouldn't let me do what my brother was doing 'because he was a boy and I was a girl'."

"I climbed trees, swam in rivers and had fist fights most days until I was ten. The neighbours grew almost apoplectic at my wearing only navy knickers and a brown, bare skin all summer. Mama was in a hospital at the time. I think other kids were warned against playing with me. Toffee-nosed neighbours said I was gypsyish."

"I was a tomboy. One of the proudest moments of my life was when I beat up a boy in my seventh grade. I don't think I ever told my mother about that."

Athleticism and "ladylike" activities can go together—they are combined in quite a few girls' lives:

"I think I was a feminine tomboy with the right mixture of rough-house, Barbie-doll games, school, and kickball."

"I never thought of myself as a tomboy, but I had a horse from the age of fourteen, drove the tractor, worked in the fields and garden, cut trees, helped my dad with all the chores, sailed, swam, and water-ski'd. I also took ballet and piano and violin. My mother is a violinist and we spent many marvellous hours playing duets with my sister at the piano."

"Until I was eleven we lived in New Mexico, we had some land and some horses and chickens, and we played cowboys and Indians as well as Barbie dolls. I learned how to shoot and paint alongside cooking, cleaning and sewing."

"Girls at home helped with kitchen chores, laundry, sewing and house cleaning. The males in our house were waited on hand and foot. (My brother is beginning to pay for this in his inability to care for himself and in his relationships with women.) Also my brother got to join a Little League team and I didn't. (There was no girls' Little League at the time.) However . . .

"Was I ever a 'tomboy'? I still am. I like to do things that are generally considered 'macho': motor-cycle riding, karate, scuba diving, wind surfing, skiing (snow), mountain climbing, hiking, camping, canoeing, chemistry. However, I am a woman and I like being a woman. My parents seem to enjoy the fact that I was and still am enjoying these 'boyish' activities. I behave like a lady when necessary so I don't upset them."

Through anti-tomboy rules imposed on many girls by their early teens, girls are systematically kept from developing physical strength (and in similar ways, are inhibited from developing their economic-educational strength)—possibly making them more submissive and less assertive as adults:

"My parents fostered the idea that I was weak. Our family doctor diagnosed me as anaemic, and they had me excused from gym. What bunk!"

Only a minority of those responding say they were never tomboys:

"I don't think I was ever a tomboy, I played with boys at games like cowboys and Indians and cops and robbers, but was nearly always a cowgirl or a lady 'baddie'."

"I was not a tomboy but my sister sure was. I did not like a lot of the rough-and-tumble games she enjoyed. I was much more hesitant and a bit of a mommy's girl. I liked playing with her and my brother, yet I also enjoyed my time alone just sitting and watching the trees and birds. I enjoyed reading a great deal."

"I was never a tomboy—in fact, I was a pretty vain little kid who liked to wear party dresses all the time. I was never warned against playing 'boy games', I don't think I had any interest in them."

What's in a word?

There are some other interpretations of being a tomboy:

"I did like boys' subjects at school—maths, physics, computers. Being at a girls' school I always came out on top in these subjects because I wasn't in competition with boys. Now at university I find the competitive attitude of the men very traumatic."

"I was something of a tomboy because I would rather play in the mud than with dolls, but I was never good at any kind of physical activity, so I don't quite fit the stereotype of baseball, trees, etc. The boys weren't too keen on me playing with them and I wasn't too keen on playing with the girls, so I was something of a loner."

"We grew up like clumsy tomboys, not because we wanted to, but because we couldn't live up to my mother's 'feminine' standards. Our father accepted us as 'comrades' and helpers around the house and garden, which was a comfort to our pride—and a blessed thing for the future: to be able to mend broken furniture, to paint walls and put up wallpaper."

"I was the middle child, a tomboy, a rebel, an agitator, incorrigible. I don't think either parent loved me, I think they put up with me, I was their 'cross to bear'."

For most girls, being a tomboy doesn't necessarily mean playing with boys—it just means taking part in activities usually reserved for boys:

"I grew up with eight brothers. My sisters were a bit shy and shallow, so I avoided them. But there was nonetheless an invisible line that I was not to cross, being a girl. When playing with my brothers, I was never completely one of their 'gang'. I was never told to be ladylike, other than being warned not to show hostility openly (i.e., punching, kicking)."

For a small minority, being associated with boys, not girls, is the basic point:

"I was definitely a tomboy. I liked to climb trees, fish, play with turtles and frogs, and liked hanging around the boys in the neighbourhood. One of my favourite pastimes was picking up pieces of dog crap and throwing it at the other little girls in the neighbourhood. It was really funny to see the look on their faces. In fact, I was considered 'one of the guys' for a long time."

Many girls object to the heavy conditioning implied by use of the word "tomboy" to label their interests/them (who says that these are boys' activities in the first place?):

"In California, climbing trees was no big deal. Many of us preferred baseball and such things to sewing and cooking, but no one ever made anything out of it."

"I did all the boy things, but I wasn't called a name like 'tomboy'. I just enjoyed it—I was not discouraged or encouraged."

It's a big mistake to label girls "boys", just because they're *active*!

But one girl poignantly describes the pressure (lots of nagging):
"They said no one would want to marry me if I stayed a tomboy."

Grown-up tomboys: conformism and rebellion

Of course women can be "tomboys" at any age:

"I have always been and always will be rebellious, feisty, and a wild thing. I value this greatly in myself, and have the attitude that I can do anything."

"At the age of forty-four, I recently climbed a couple of trees to steal some apples from neighbours who were gone for the winter. There was a period when I was very rebellious, and still am to some extent, when expected to conform to someone else's stereotyped expectations."

Girls' Ownership of Their Own Bodies

Perhaps women's extreme pleasure in remembering the time when they were tomboys shows how tortured we feel, without even realizing it . . . so used are we to carrying around the burden of how the world sees our bodies. Tomboy-hood was for most women a time when they could enjoy their bodies with little self-consciousness and few worries about "beauty culture".

We should be able, as women, to enjoy our bodies! To use them for our pleasure and needs—rather than as outward symbols of pleasure for others. This is our reality, our stamina, our physical action, being stolen from us. Don't let it be! If we reclaim it, this strength will inform and create our true identities.

Girls' First Images of Their Sexuality: Menstruation and Masturbation

Girls' Early Masturbation Experiences
Age Five–Twelve

Most girls begin masturbating quite early. 45 per cent of girls, according to these findings, begin masturbating by the age of seven, and over 60 per cent by the age of eleven or twelve.

The age at which girls have their first experiences can vary widely—from four to forty—but most girls begin as children, and most of the rest during their very early teens.

They almost always discover masturbation alone, by themselves, and secretly. Sometimes girls try masturbation because they have heard it is possible, but far more commonly, they simply discover it by listening to their own bodies or finding one day that something they do feels very good.

It is such a positive sign that girls, without any encouragement and without anyone to teach them, manage to develop quite naturally through exploring their bodies, and learn about the pleasures of orgasm. (Perhaps it might be "natural" too, if society were structured differently, for girls to learn about their sexuality by playing games with other girls, as boys do with boys—but is there not a little beauty in girls' private discovery of their bodies?) Also, from this (as noted in *The Hite Report on Female Sexuality*) we have a very valuable biological record, a record with no cultural input or socialization, as to what stimulation for orgasm feels best to women.

The downside is that so many girls learn to associate shame and guilt with touching themselves and with sex in general. Feeling guilty for feeling pleasure . . . all too often, the messages become inextricably intertwined. Later, the guilt and "danger" can become part of the fun. Fantasies of exhibitionism are often demonstrations of a desire not to hide sexually, to show that part of the self, the sexual existence, even that one is sexually beautiful and "good"—and not partially invisible as a person. Wanting people to look at one's genitals, at least in fantasy—but

66

in reality, being terrified that a lover will look too closely, carefully keeping the light turned out during sex, propping the sheets strategically around one, worrying about what he or she is thinking and sees during cunnilingus . . . yet fantasizing like mad during sex that hundreds are watching one's crotch. Ironically, this is a common juxtaposition in many women's psycho-sexual identities.

The stories girls and women tell about first masturbation, how their sexuality developed as a secret life right under the eyes, almost, of their parents, without being detected—these are stories of a private identity being developed. And underneath the pleasure, always the connection to the double standard, i.e., "'Bad girls do this,' am I 'too sexual', am I a 'slut' underneath it all? Will I be punished? Shouldn't I try to control my sexuality, control myself, not let myself do this?" And "adult" sex and sensuality become the land of forbidden pleasures, only accessible in the future, when one will be "grown-up".

Secret Pleasures

93 per cent of parents questioned are usually unaware, or pretend to be, of girls' private life of masturbation during junior school and secondary school. (These same parents are probably living in terror that someone will find out about their own!)

"Did you masturbate as a child? How old were you when you started? Did your parents know?"
"When I was very young, about eight or nine, there was something that made me feel very good. My sister and I would play a game that we called 'lead guy'. This meant we would masturbate in our own beds at the same time. But we never did any more than that, we never had any sexual contact together as children, or experienced it with my brother. My mother once caught me masturbating in her room—I was late for dinner. She jokingly, but with a surprised and angry feeling, announced my activity at the dinner table. I was so embarrassed. Looking back in retrospect I am surprised at my mother's open-mindedness—I guess that my age and activity knocked her for a loop!"

"Masturbation felt good. I didn't realize what it was, but I knew, when I was about nine years old, that while sitting in school if I moved around in the hard seat a certain way it gave me a nice warm feeling. As time went by I could give myself that nice feeling with my hands. I always felt relaxed after it. And I knew it was not something I should share information about with my parents!"

"I first started masturbating when I was about four or five. Looking at myself in mirrors. I was curious. Even before I knew or understood what it was all about. I think I orgasmed then, very young. I used to put myself to sleep that way. All clitoral. My mother caught me once, and said it would ruin everything when I got married, and sort of explained things. So I figured I'd been doing it so many years, my chances were already shot, but I tried to put things in my vagina, even then, so I would feel good about it. I was about eight."

"I began at eleven—no, maybe ten. No one ever knew. I had already been told that touching was a mortal sin and I was Catholic, but I couldn't help it. I never entered myself with my fingers for, being a virgin, my imaginings never could go that far."

"I did it for as long as I can remember, but didn't know what it was till about fifteen or sixteen. (My parents will never know. Only you and me.)"

"I liked to fall asleep on my right side, sucking my thumb, with my right hand between my thighs, sometimes pressing it against my labia. Eventually I discovered that if I rubbed myself in a certain way it felt good.

"I was ten when I had my first orgasm that way. I had no idea what it was. My parents caught me in sex play with a girlfriend once, and with a boy once, but they were surprisingly calm about it both times, just told me not to do it again. I don't know if they knew I masturbated. I knew it was one of the many things I'd better keep secret. My mother has told me that even as an infant I liked to touch and stroke whatever was near me. I was very sensually aware of things—the fabrics of my clothes, the humidity in the air, the feeling of sun, air, soft shirts on my arms and legs—and I loved having my hair brushed, and the feeling of cool sheets. I would slowly move my legs to feel the sheets against my skin."

"At about five or six, I used to rub myself on the sheets and fantasize about a Western hero. In a few minutes, I would feel a warm pleasure! My parents never knew (I suppose)—or they never considered it to be their business."

"My mother caught me once—she looked into my bedroom window! We never mentioned it, and pretended that neither of us knew what the other knew. It was a very embarrassing, awkward few days."

"Maybe I was five or six—and my parents knew. Mama talked to the doctor about what to do, and he said to keep me off eating hot porridge oats. I was shamed a little, but it pleasured and comforted me. Like Portnoy, it was the only thing I had of my own. However, I object to the word 'masturbation'—and to slang terms even more."

"I masturbated for years in the bathroom, but had no idea what I was doing. I played with my breasts a lot, never my genitals. I'm sure my parents knew something was up, as I locked myself in the bathroom for hours after my bath."

"When I was about twelve, I can remember my father telling me at the breakfast table not to 'do that' (I was rubbing myself). After that, I was more careful."

"My sister and I used to pretend that two beautiful princes came to our beds and caressed us, in that very shameful place where it felt so nice. But we were very quiet and whispered to our princes, and our parents never knew. We were in our early teens."

"I did masturbate—although I didn't know that was what it was till much later. I remember a tingling sensation of just feeling good inside that was unconnected with my image of sex. It was just something I could do to my body to feel warm. When I learned what I had been doing years later (I masturbated in grade school), I was not shocked or ashamed. I have pleasant memories."

"I didn't know what exactly I was doing, but it felt good. I couldn't do it very often because I shared a double bed with a younger sister."

"I used to feel terribly guilty about masturbating. Up to the age of fifteen or so, I periodically confessed to my parents that I had been doing it, and promised not to do it again. But I always found myself unable to keep that promise. I know that the modern point of view is that the guilt and fears that I suffered were unnecessary, deplorable, and unhealthy—but I place great value on the whole experience, guilt and all. I view the fact that I did continually masturbate, in spite of my guilt and my fears, as a very positive act of courage and self-assertion, as a dawning recognition of, and respect for, a power that I did not understand, a power greater than my parents and other authority figures. I think masturbation is very important during adolescence. It establishes contact and intimacy with one's body, and strengthens one's sense of a private, unique and inviolable self."

"I rub my body against the mattress, but don't touch myself with my hands. I started two years ago, I do it very seldom, my parents do not know."

"I remember discovering masturbation around the age of fourteen. I felt that it was wrong, but also that my labia and vagina were really unexplored territory and I wanted to simulate the experience of having a man's penis inside me, so I stuck my fingers up myself while imagining that. My parents certainly did not know!"

"It was one of the nightmares of my childhood because when I was five or six, it brought all kinds of punishment at school and at home.

Then I went through a period when I didn't do it at all. Now I only do it in bed at night once or twice, and not every night."

A minority of girls do not masturbate:
"I don't remember doing it ever. I remember my mother telling me never to stick things in my vagina. I understood that to mean hairgrips or dirty things from which I might catch germs, but subconsciously I interpreted that as never to feel or touch myself. It never occurred to me to masturbate, I'm sure my mother never masturbated, and so that prudishness rubbed itself off on me."

One girl was sexually molested in early childhood and wonders whether this caused her to masturbate "early":
"I started masturbating at about five or six. I had been regularly molested by my stepgrandfather (without my parents' knowledge) from the age of two until I was about five, and this awakened my sexual desires very early, according to the doctor. I can remember being very horny at the age of five. I know that my mother knew of one instance when I masturbated when I was about eight, but I don't think she knew more than that."

As we have seen, her masturbation is not "early", according to data for this study. It is quite common for girls to masturbate to orgasm this early. Most understanding of when masturbation begins has been based on the model of boys, who don't generally begin to masturbate to orgasm until puberty. (See Part III.)
In rare cases, women and girls report that their fathers or brothers taught them to masturbate (see also Sexual Abuse of Girls, page 49):
"I was thirteen when I first masturbated. My stepfather took it upon himself to show me how—against my wishes. I tried hard not to do it—because I knew he wanted me to—for he'd be thinking I was. But I eventually did."

Parents' attitudes to masturbation of girls (age five–twelve)
There are perhaps surprisingly few stories of being "caught" or observed masturbating told by girls or boys, and surprisingly few acknowledgements by family members (men or women) of having seen other family members doing "anything". Perhaps this is because children hide so well. Or perhaps it is because adults don't want to have to disclose or think to themselves that they do this too.
Parents say many things, by not "saying" anything:
"About masturbating, I did it, but I never got any warnings from

my parents, sex was just never discussed. I mean, they never told me a thing about sex, absolutely nothing. It's incredible when you think how stupid that is. Obviously I got the message somehow never to discuss it with them, or never to let on that I did it. To hide all the time."

"We used to have a lot of friends to visit us during the summer. My mother instructed us that beds must be changed if men slept in them for one night, but they could be used again if women slept in them. She explained about there being some marks that men sometimes made on the sheets. I realized later that she was referring to wet dreams."

What Do Mothers Today Tell Their Daughters About Masturbation?

One girl tells a story of her mother's acknowledgement and recognition:

"I masturbated as a child. I started when I was about seven or eight years old. My mother knew, she would tell me to be private about it and go to my room, not do it in front of my brothers or her."

When mothers are asked what they are telling their own daughters *now* about masturbation, many say they do try to talk and have a positive attitude:

"I know my two daughters masturbate; at least, I know they play with themselves. When my second daughter was about five, and I came to put her to bed one evening, she held up her fingers to me, saying, 'Mommy, smell this: that's the best smell in the world!' I agreed—she'd been playing with herself. My older daughter, overhearing, came in and said, 'Do you do that, too? I thought I was the only one.' I told them that most people enjoy their bodies in this way, but I didn't tell them about myself, in detail.

"My two sisters, both of whom are younger than me, have talked with me about many of our intimate experiences. I have been open to them since they were in their late teens, when they seemed ready. Both of them saw me as worldly and sophisticated, but were afraid to confide in me in their early teens."

Do Girls Masturbate Together?

According to my research for this book, while almost 60 per cent of boys in my sample have masturbated together, only approximately 9 per cent of girls have. Boys' masturbation is much less hidden. The

71

contrast between women's descriptions of their first masturbation and men's is remarkable (see Chapter 10).

A few girls describe brief experiences with other girls:

"My mother did catch my girlfriend and me, at eight, tickling each other on the crotch on the front lawn as we were wrestling. She spanked us both and sent my friend home."

"I never saw anyone masturbate—*wait*! Yes, I did, when I was in 4th grade, or around then, we had a vibrator and my friend used it under the covers in bed. She didn't move much and said she came. It was my first time with a vibrator and I didn't come. (That was also the only time I didn't with it!)"

"My first orgasm was accidentally discovered when I was seven. We had a swingset in the backyard and I was shimmying up to the top one day when something wonderful and unexpected happened. I taught my best friend and we climbed up the pole often. We felt guilty and tried to stop but weren't too successful. No one ever said anything—but I cannot imagine we were that good at concealing it. Before we learned its proper name, we called it 'tickle, tickle'. This is a story I've never told anyone but Rick."

"My parents didn't know a thing about my masturbation. How did I learn? Once at a sleepover some girl showed us how to do 'it' with a pillow!"

"My earliest memory of masturbation is at five years old. At first, I masturbated by myself and felt very guilty and dirty. Then I started to play 'doctor' with my girlfriend, who was the same age. We were having fun until a little bit of cloth we were playing with got stuck in my anus. At this point we had to tell our mothers what we had been doing. I thought this was a sure sign from God that we were sinners and would be punished.

"My mother made sure I was punished. She publicly humiliated me in front of my father and my brother by telling them what I had done. We all stood by the phone while my mother called the doctor to tell him this 'dirty deed'. He was to tell me what the punishment would be. Of course, he said not to worry and the cloth would come out naturally. My mother watched me constantly after that. I stopped masturbating for a while."

Teenage Girls' Acceptance of Masturbation Today

Despite all this hiding, according to these findings there is a major change in how girls feel about masturbation today, as compared to the 1970's: most have a positive attitude towards masturbation: 61 per cent now, as opposed to 29 per cent in the 1970's, feel no shame but even a kind of pride in their skill and knowledge about their own bodies, especially by their teenage years—as does this sixteen-year-old:

"Masturbation is important—it's healthy, it gets you very tuned into your body. Sure, I can imagine any woman masturbating. I use my hand or a vibrator—I rub the clitoris, the mound above it and the area around it fast. Sometimes I insert several fingers inside myself or I use my other hand to touch my breasts, my face and body. I don't move much, I fantasize, and keep my legs far apart.

"My best fantasy? I get backstage at a Rolling Stones concert or the Band concert, and the huskiest, most gorgeous lead guitarist looks at me and says, throatily, 'I need you.' I start to explain to him that I'm not a groupie, but he kisses me wildly and deeply, pushes me gently down on the bed that just happens to be there, does cunnilingus to me while I thrash in ecstasy and then he makes love to me, dominantly, and I am fulfilled!

"Since my father is an analyst, I used to read all his books on sex for the dirty parts. The scientific studies told me nothing I didn't know except that I wasn't masturbating vaginally, that I wasn't coming vaginally, what was wrong with me? At least that's how I felt. I can't see where pornography can serve that much of a purpose. A woman with doubts about her sexuality, for instance, will feel a hell of a lot better after reading the Hite Reports!"

Finally, as pointed out earlier, most children and teenagers (and adults!) have learned not to wonder if their mother or father masturbates. They have learned this so well that they have even forgotten to wonder or ask themselves the question—not to mention asking their parents, or bringing up the subject.

Girls' First Menstruation and Family Denial

"Did your parents discuss menstruation with you? Your mother? Your father? Were you prepared for it when it started?"

78 per cent of girls and women say their mother did mention menstruation, but 72 per cent also say they still felt they were not adequately prepared, as the discussion was so minimal. Only 12 per cent of fathers discussed menstruation with their daughters. 81 per cent of women got most of their information at school, either from a class, their friends, or a school nurse. Not even 10 per cent had been given a celebration.

The "Invisibility" of Girls' Maturing Bodies

It would seem as if girls are not supposed to feel any pride in their maturing adulthood, their bodies.

The beginning of menstruation could be a magical and fascinating moment in a girl's life. It is amazing to see just how little attention is paid to it, in most cases.

Instead there is a kind of hush-hush atmosphere (or rude remarks and innuendoes). It would seem as if girls are not supposed to feel any pride in their maturing adulthood, their bodies. In some more "liberated" families, there is a reaction such as, "Well, it's normal, so what? Don't let's get carried away and make a big deal out of it." This "no-nonsense" attitude seems to be connected to the old cliché that hormones make women "drama queens", and that the "new, modern woman" would not "give in to emotion", i.e., she must "prove" herself especially "stable"—even almost make her period disappear, be as much like "a man" as possible (supposedly calm all the time), and not seem to have a monthly cycle or bleeding.

While menstruation does not interrupt most girls' or women's lives most of the time, it is bizarre for a family not to remark on the changing of their daughter's body into one which now has the amazing capacity to reproduce and create new life.

74

In the 1950's, there was a famous US advertisement which announced that if a woman used that company's tampon, "He'll never know your secret." Hiding was crucially important. *No one* was to know that "smelly bleeding" was occurring—especially "him". After all, he might be turned off.

One of the disgraces of the medical profession *vis-à-vis* women is the dearth of research into the causes of menstrual pain. Ironically, women are often still told by doctors that either: It is all in their mind and they should visit a psychiatrist to find out why they can't "accept periods as a normal, natural part of life" and/or: "It is part of being a woman; women just have to live with pain and suffering, it's part of the price they pay to bear children." Here we hear echoes of the Biblical pronouncement that women are cursed, "doomed to bear children in pain and suffering", because of our "sin" in the Garden of Eden!

Relatively little is known about hormones even now. For example, the connection between low blood sugar and female hormones, between adrenalin and hormones (female or male), or why osteoporosis should occur in some women (and not others) when their body changes to post-reproductive ("menopausal") status. The statistics on "PMS" have been blown up out of all proportion by the media and medical profession, in a kind of parodying of the old clichés "She's got the curse," "Hormones make women irrational bitches." There should be less of this stereotyping of women, and more solid factual research.

Reproduction Becomes Possible!*

(Why is menstruation "your secret"?)
The family should clearly recognize the daughter's body as good. There should be an event or celebration marking this stage in the girl's life, welcoming her.

The *falla* in Valencia, Spain, is a custom whereby girls at puberty participate in many public events held only for and by them and their parents: they dance, recite verses and wear special dresses and hair ornaments. Younger girls look forward to the day when they will be able to participate in the *falla* and be admired by everyone. This is similar in spirit to the Jewish bar mitzvah.

The lack of interest in this new stage of a girl's life also reinforces

---

* In *The Hite Report on Men and Male Sexuality*, one young man, quite in love, recounts having removed his lover's tampon, when they were in bed together having sex, and stuck it in his mouth! This was also later portrayed in Erica Jong's erotic novel, *Parachutes and Kisses*.

the unfortunate "information" coming at her from many parts of the culture as to how unimportant she is—as well as teaching her (yet again) that both she and her sexuality should be secret, hidden, and unexpressed. That her body and its orifices, functions, are all somewhat shameful, certainly not a matter for pride. She is expected to "take care" of menstruation, so that she "doesn't cause a bother". She learns, usually, that she must change pads frequently "to stay clean", and, as one girl put it, "Well, definitely it's nothing to be particularly proud of."

In only 10 per cent of families* according to my research here is the father told when the daughter starts menstruating. In only 24 per cent of families are the brothers informed. However, when boys were asked when they first learned or heard about menstruation, 39 per cent of those from families with sisters said they had heard about it through their sisters. (See Part III.)

What Do Mothers Tell Daughters?

"I remember my mother telling me it was like 'cleaning the house' once a month. A 'good cleaning' or something silly like that. But she explained everything."

"My mother told me about menstruation one day while she was washing my hair. Her manner was very casual, and I was so involved in the hair-washing, that I paid only cursory attention and didn't really understand what she was trying to tell me. When it happened several months later, I was frightened and thought I was ill. After a couple of days, I told her I was bleeding and she reminded me of our earlier discussion and explained it again. I believe she did better with my younger sisters, because they seemed to be more prepared for it than I had been."

"I remember when I started menstruating, I was scared and embarrassed. I did not know what was happening. My mother took me into the bathroom and put a Tampax in herself to show me how to do it. She told my father that evening at the dinner table! I was so embarrassed, I cried."

"My mother discussed the practical aspects with me. She told me I would see blood on my underwear and to tell her right away when it happened. When I did, she went and told everybody—including my father and my girl scout leader! (We were going camping and she wanted to make sure I was okay.) I was so embarrassed!"

---

* Families in which a father is present, or a frequent visitor/strong presence.

"I always had the sense I shouldn't ask my mother these personal things. I knew there was something going on with women, my sister had a big box that was always there with her, Kotex, but it was like the subject of sex or menstruation was taboo and I just knew I wasn't supposed to ask questions. Maybe this was because no one ever spoke about it in a normal conversation among the family."

"I was not really prepared. My mother always told me magazines for teenagers were dirty, but that was the only way I could've found some kind of sex education, since I did not dare ask her. My dad apparently never wanted to have anything to do with that. When I got it and I could not handle having a huge spot of blood on my sheets, she acted as if it were something perfectly natural. She got me some of those plastic panties you are supposed to wear with maxi pads. I had no idea how to use them, how often to change. She never told me anything about the possibility of using tampons. I was twelve and pretty confused, I guess. I don't think it's right to leave a child alone with so many questions."

"My mother found out about six months after I started menstruation. She was hurt that I didn't come to her, but I guess I wished she had said something sooner."

"My mother asked me if I knew about menstruation. I said, 'Yes,' she said, 'Good,' and that was the beginning and end of my sex education. I was knowledgeable but not mentally prepared."

"I remember my mother telling my sister and me about menstruation and sex when she was pregnant with my youngest sister. I was about nine years old. She also showed us what sanitary napkins and tampons were, and how to use them. One sister and I watched with fascination as our mother inserted a tampon into her own vagina. The oldest sister wouldn't watch and said she thought it was disgusting. She still doesn't use tampons."

"When my mother told me (I was eleven), I cried the entire time she was talking to me (super-sensitive kid). When it came on later that year, during class on a warm spring day in the 6th grade, I had to walk home with a sweater knotted at the waist. For the first two years, it used to just start any time—it was a big strain to be constantly on the look out for spotting."

"My mother took me to the Girl Scout movie *and* a town movie that gave me the physical facts, as well as some of the scares about venereal disease, Aids and unwed motherhood. Also, we girls at school had a health course that discussed this and other areas of sexuality, a very good course. Any questions were okay. They could be given or sent to the teacher anonymously. Unusual, I think. She was a good teacher."

"When I finally did get 'it', my mother made me show her my underwear as proof that I had started to menstruate. I was embarrassed but my mother was excited. She told my aunt without even asking me. Even though I was close to my aunt, I didn't want anyone to know; I needed time to absorb the fact myself. When I went over to my aunt's house later, she said, 'Well, you're a woman now!' right in front of my uncle. My uncle replied, 'Not yet,' which, as I look back on that incident, was a disgusting and ignorant thing to say to a young woman. However, his comment certainly keeps alive the patriarchal myth that females aren't women until they have been penetrated by a man."

"Neither my mother or father ever discussed menstruation with me. When it started, I thought something was terribly wrong with me or that I was hurt. Shortly after, my father left a book for children about sex on my bed which explained everything. Nothing was ever mentioned about it again."

"My mom talked to me about it, she down-played my excitement, speaking with disdain even. I started late, I remember being curious and envious and feeling left behind when I heard other girls discuss 'the curse'."

"I was ten and my parents were on a trip. The elderly babysitter gave me a Bandaid to wear for three days!"

"My mother attended a film with me in school about menstruation, but besides that we never had a 'mother-to-daughter' talk. I was not prepared for it, it was a scary experience. I think I had two or three periods before I even told my mother."

"My mother told me about menstruation, and about God and his seed. She may have told me about the blood but I just couldn't believe this would happen to me. When it did, I cried and was mad that I had to wear one of those ugly things for protection. I was eleven at school when it happened and the teacher sent me home. After that, the nurse talked to my mom on the phone. When I went back to school in the afternoon, a boy sang 'I Know Why You Went Home'. I was embarrassed."

"My mother told me about menstruation, I remember it so well, and she told me not to discuss it with any of my friends. (I somehow sensed that this especially included the boys). In the 5th grade, a boy from school kept asking me what a period was. I knew I possessed this secret knowledge, and was quite smug and kept answering with, 'A period is a dot at the end of a sentence.'"

"They tried to discuss it a few times but were awful. One time I got a small amount of blood on the toilet seat and they actually called

78

me in from outside to wash it off! All one of them had to do was use a Kleenex. It was only a tiny amount."

Fathers and Menstruation

"One summer morning at the age of twelve, I began to menstruate. I was terrified; here was the horrible disease I had been dreading—I vowed I would never masturbate again. I kept washing myself and changing my underwear, went swimming, but the bleeding didn't stop. In the evening I told my parents I was bleeding down there! My mother gave me some sanitary napkins and said I ought not to have gone swimming; my father explained things to me.

"I can't remember what he told me; all I know is that he told me very little, and yet he managed to convey the impression that now I 'knew everything'. That's quite a feat, I wish I could remember how he did it! Many years later, I borrowed a box of Kotex from a pregnant neighbour, promising to replace them within a few days. She said, 'Don't worry, I won't be needing them for quite a while.' This was news to me."

"All I have to say about my father and this subject is, once, before I was fifteen, he went to the store to buy my Kotex because I was in bed with cramps. There was never any discussion of it beyond that. He just went to the store, came back, handed my mother the Kotex and she handed them to me."

Most women remember being embarrassed by the thought of their father knowing:

"I was embarrassed when I found out that my mother had told my father it had started because I didn't think men knew anything about it. I thought only women knew about menstruation."

"After my mother left, my father called me in one night and told me that I would start to bleed some day. I was twelve. I knew that he often exaggerated, and so I imagined a haemorrhage. He was very upset about having to tell me. I think he told me I must never mention this subject to anybody. I was terrified every day. When I did start, my stepmother was there and fixed me up with a Kotex. She said I must not tell my father. I didn't understand why not. One day I left a clean Kotex in my room and my father saw it. When I came home from school, the door to my room was shut. My stepmother told me accusingly, 'Your father knows!' I had done something awful, but what?"

"My father took me when I was eight years old to Stanford University where a film was shown on female and male reproductive organs, menstruation, sperm and egg process, detailed growth of babies inside the womb, and menopause. The total. That, though complete, left much unsaid—like feelings—those were 'no-no' questions! He raised the roof whenever I asked about any sort of feeling, or what was going 'too far' on a date, or how does sex feel, or anything. Oh boy, what hell it raised. And if I dared ask, he'd demand to know, who was I seeing and what was I doing?"

Changing Attitudes: A New Mother–Daughter Discussion

There is a great contrast between old and new attitudes towards menstruation, but new attitudes of pride and openness are still unusual:

"I want to say I've handled this very differently with my child. She didn't want to know about menstruation, which I understood, but I told her she had to know. I keep all the pads and tampons in a basket in our bathroom, and I showed them to her. I put a tampon in a glass of water so she could see what happens. We poured water in a pad, too. I made it sound like a fascinating experiment. I showed her the disposable douches we can get nowadays, too.

"One day when she was thirteen, she came to me while I was in the bathroom. She said, 'I started.'

"I said, 'Started what?'

"She said, 'My periods.' She was crying.

"I said, 'Oh I thought it was something serious.'

"She said, 'You don't think this is serious?'

"I said, 'No. From the way you looked, I thought something had happened to the cat.' She laughed.

"I talked to the principal who happens to be a girlfriend of mine. She told me funny stories about how the girls will try to get out of PE and Latin and maths and anything else they don't want to do. I passed on these funny stories-without-names to my daughter. Then she saw she wasn't the first girl in the history of the world to go through this experience. I haven't told her what happened to me. I'm bitter about it, and yet I wouldn't know how to handle my own child if it hadn't been done so badly with me. I'm glad I did it the right way."

"My fourteen-year-old brother told me about menstruation when I was eleven. My mom said she was proud of it, that it was healthy and natural and she always felt good when she had it. I felt the same way and never had a cramp."

"My mother told me, but there was no celebration, which is odd, come to think of it. Sort of a don't-bother-me attitude. When my girls start, I always hug them and tell them congratulations, as well as get a little teary in the eyes. It's a special time for us. I guess my mom was afraid I'd get pregnant, as she seemed mostly irritated when I told her I had started. All the girls discussed it and we just couldn't wait for it."

"I was prepared well enough. I had a new feeling when I got my first period. I liked the feeling, but I didn't know what it was. It was a feeling of belonging to the Earth, a sign of membership here."

"Both my parents discussed menstruation with me. My mother talked with me when I was younger, and after she died, my father was open about it."

"My mother was frank when she was menstruating. Because of her polio, she always did her 'toilet' on the bed, and this was frequently visiting time for us. Short of shutting us out of her room during this hour of toiletry, she could not have avoided our seeing the blood. But even if it hadn't been that kind of physical situation, I am sure she would have talked to us about it. My sister and I used to be quite amused by the advertisements about booklets for 'what girls should know'."

"When my period first started I was on vacation. We were at a beach house. My grandmother gave me a Kotex and I remember feeling quite excited and proud to be finally a 'woman'. I kept looking in my underwear every half hour to see the pad and if it needed changing. My father teased me with, 'Susan can't go in the water.' I was mortified that he knew."

"Menstruation was marvellous for me! My mother, who was a nurse, handled this terrifically. She told my sister and me about it when I was eight and my sister was ten. It sounded exciting and very grown up—I was extremely eager to have this happen. When I finally started at twelve years and nine months, my mother announced to my father at dinner that I was now a 'young lady'. I was so proud.

"My older sister was mad and told mother she never made a similar announcement when she started. I might add that though mother explained all this and giving birth, she never told me where men came in. I had no idea what their role was until I heard other girls talk in high school."

The brusqueness and desire to avoid embarrassment of some discussions, hiding under a matter-of-fact façade, is quite amazing:

"My parents never discussed menstruation. When I was twelve I began. I told my mother I was bleeding. She got a belt and a Kotex from an older sister and merely said it would happen every month."

"My mother slapped my face (lightly) when I got my period—a barbaric Jewish custom that probably traumatizes an awful lot of young girls. (My mother never hit me before or since that I can remember.)"

Some women remember thinking that they were in danger of bleeding to death; they imagined they had a rare disease:

"I started right after my sled crashed into a tree. I thought I was bleeding to death. I was scared for months until I had a class in school that explained what was happening in my body. What a relief! I should not have had to go through that by myself."

The famous "booklet approach": many parents can't seem to handle talking, and give their daughters medical booklets, leave the room and never talk to them at all about it:

"My mother wordlessly handed me a booklet by Modess Corp. I instinctively knew I was supposed to read it and not ask questions. The only problem with the book was that the 'star' was too pretty and superclass for me to identify with. I felt ashamed for not being pretty and rich."

"My mom gave me a booklet on menstruation when I was about ten and told me to read it. I couldn't pronounce half the words. It prepared me for the 'blood coming from my body once a month'."

Now There Are New Rules of Comportment: "Be a Lady"

"Be a Good Girl" (Restrain Yourself!)

Suddenly, after the period of freedom, which society calls being a tomboy, girls are expected to change their behaviour dramatically. The onset of puberty and menstruation is greeted with the cry, "Be a good girl," according to 97 per cent of those in this study.

One young woman compares her mother's meaning to her father's meaning:
"My mother's meaning:
a. Don't draw attention to yourself excessively by 'succeeding' (and making mother envious) or by 'failing' (and making mother ashamed).
b. Don't succeed better than your brother.
c. Obey mother—do not question mother—agree with mother—take mother's side in fights—like mother's relatives better than father's relatives—love who mother loves—hate who mother hates—tell lies for mother.
d. Look up to mother—don't judge mother objectively.
e. Don't let any man fuck you and dump you.

"My father's meaning:
a. Agree with me.
b. Glorify me.
c. Overachieve—have a flawless school record.
d. Be like me instead of like your mother.
e. Be in the best social group but don't cost me a fortune doing it.
f. Don't let yourself be taken advantage of by others."

"Good girl" often has quasi-religious overtones; after all, the icon of motherhood, Mary, ostensibly did not menstruate or have sex:
"By 'good', my parents meant all the Christian values that they were trying to inculcate in me; i.e., that my place in the world was as a good wife (meek, accepting, God-fearing, dutiful), a good mother and a good Christian person.
"They often openly praised the fact that I was such a good girl,

and I responded by being 'gooder', helping my mother a lot, being good with the babies. My security was in being praised by my parents, even though this caused some jealousy from my elder sister, who was threatened."

"I had to Serve Others. It was the Christian duty of a good girl. I was considered a 'good girl' because I did things before being told and I always waited on family members like a mother hen. Grades in school were just passing, that was all that was expected from the good girl."

"A 'good girl' never did anything that would upset or embarrass her parents. My mother constantly overstressed the importance of 'What will other people think or say?' "

"'Be a good girl' was like a religious chant in my house. It meant be whatever they wanted me to be at the time. It meant be a little Christian, be virginal, be obedient, be passive, be a little mother to my dolls, be a cook, be a homemaker."

"Try to Be More Feminine . . ."

When asked, most women say their mother did not exactly tell them how to be feminine, they just got the picture from how she behaved. 73 per cent say that all they learned about "femininity" was that they should keep the house clean!

"My mother always told me not to bite my nails, it wasn't 'feminine'. The majority of the time we got stuck doing the dishes and the housework, even though both my brother and I theoretically had 'house chores'."

"The only explanation of 'being feminine' was in terms of the things I couldn't do. Girls don't hitch-hike. Girls don't need a bike, girls don't need a radio. Girls need clothes, girls need permanents. Girls are good—good, good, good. Also girls can't stay in the house alone. Girls can't go out at night alone—girls have to telephone when they are going to walk two houses away at night, and girls have to be pretty. Girls can't call boys on the phone. As for a real definition of femininity, I am stumped."

"My mother is beautiful and vain. She told me by example that the way to be feminine was to be pretty, defer to men, and be weak. Other than that, there were definite female chores, cooking, laundry, bed making—boys did lawns, etc."

"Feminine meant having beautiful clothes and conning men."

"My mom showed me how to be feminine by the usual—lots of

84

dolls (she made them pretty clothes to wear), and letting me dress up in her clothes and 'play high-heels'."

"My mom was obsessed with being ladylike and taking the 'Blessed Mother of Christ' as her model."★

"To be 'feminine', according to my mother, was to be like her—neat, nice, well-dressed in 'classy' materials, to have a nightgown with lace, and a room of her own which she kept locked up when she was at work."

"To be feminine was to cook, iron, sew, dust, do household chores. I don't think my mother actually took the time to show me feminine ways."

"My mother would dress me in order to show that I was a lady. She would yell at me when I said a curse, and tell me what a lady is supposed to do. My mother never, never had to deal with fixing things around the house, the car, and the boys didn't cook. I define femininity as being dressed very neatly in a dress, looking very pretty."

"My mother taught me how to be feminine by her interest in fashion, teaching me how to be polite and cordial, as well as a specific role in the family: I helped her in the kitchen; the males were served. Although my parents tried to make the roles less stereotyped, the boys rarely helped to clean up. I was definitely encouraged to do things for my father and brothers as a way of expressing my affection for them: serving food, baking for them, etc."

"Mom used to say, 'It takes pain to be beautiful.' She still feels strongly about male and female roles. We had dresses and pink rooms, we were told things like, 'You don't want to do that, that's for boys.' She'd tell me how to act like a lady, on dates, at dinner, etc. My mother and I did things that my brother wasn't expected to do, especially dishes and dancing."

"She would tell me, 'You look like a man in that.'"

"Smile!" (Don't Look Unhappy)

Another keynote of "femininity training" is the constant injunction to girls to "smile", not to look "unhappy":

"I remember she always used to say to me always have a smile on, no matter what is happening; no one should know."

★ According to the "Christian" model, as traditionally interpreted, all women should be mothers, and all mothers must adore children, just as Mary adored and obeyed Christ, her son. Women can't rebel against being "saints" without becoming "devils".

"I was always told not to yell and to be softspoken."

"I was taught not to display hostility, i.e., towards my brothers. I was told, 'It's not ladylike to be angry, fight or frown.'"

"My mother told me constantly to smile, saying I looked sullen with a straight face. Now I'm told I have a beautiful smile, but it annoys me that women are expected to smile all of the time. She used to try to get me to sit with my knees together, but I've never felt comfortable sitting that way, and she gave up on that after I was about twelve. I wear trousers, so I don't have to sit in a prissy position, and I can sit cross-legged."

Anger and Independence are Forbidden (A Rebellious Girl is a "Demon-Child")

Anger and any sign of rebelliousness are definitely not a part of "femininity", although they are often praised and received with interest and respect in boys.

How mothers and fathers deal with daughters' anger and resentment is very troubling. I doubt most parents truly realize what damage they are doing by not allowing girls to be angry about anything, no matter how wrong.

As one woman describes this repression and blighting of her self-awareness, her spirit:

"My family's—and especially my mother's—depiction of me was always as someone who explodes. I was 'the one' in the family they all said had a 'wild temper', was 'likely to explode', and they used to rag me about this. I don't think it was true. I only became upset when there was something really to be upset about. Usually something they did that they didn't want to admit.

"Today I think thank goodness they couldn't turn me into a docile woman. It's just stereotyping girls or women to refuse them the right to get angry. Men have this right all the time, and so did my brother. But my grandmother too, she used to call being angry (in girls) 'being ugly'. 'Don't look ugly,' she would say when I was wailing or expressing displeasure about something.

"It's just this that has got women (like my best friend) turning anorexic: awful things are done to us and we can never express our outrage. So women take it out on themselves, they try to kill themselves, make themselves take up as little space in the universe as possible. Since nothing they can do is right (except 'being pretty'), they try to stop doing anything, and be as thin and 'pretty' as possible. This is wicked, really, it is. We have to be allowed our anger, not have our personality and minds lopped off."

Another woman, born in France, remembers how she got this message:

"Mother often used to tell me to stop '*le petit cinéma que tu faites*', implying that I was only 'unhappy' and making scenes to get attention. She made me feel I had no right to say what I was saying, or feel what I was feeling. That my words, the content, were not legitimate, the situation didn't exist, wasn't how I thought it was. And that I was a horrible, ridiculous child for expressing any of this.'

Mothers are the traditional family's Control Police for girls. Unfortunately.★ (See also Chapter 5.)

One woman says she got the feeling, "Don't think for yourself or be different, or we'll send you to a shrink":

"When I began to have my own ideas and thoughts and they differed from my mother's, that was when she began to act like she hated me. As long as I was a model child, and I maintained straight 'A'-type grades all through college (even during a nervous breakdown I had that rendered me a zombie, unable to carry on my life functions unassisted, I still made the honour roll), as long as I wore clothes she liked, hung around with boys and girls she approved of and said things she felt were okay to say, it was fine. But if I went counter to popular opinion in *any* way, I was unnatural, I was bad, wrong. She threatened to send me to a shrink, her worst threat ever; I begged her please to do so, and she called me 'smart'. I finally went myself, years later."

"Keep Your Legs Together!"

Another part of the new identity expected of girls is taught through the frequent admonition, "Keep your legs together!":

"Keeping my legs together (I'm laughing as I write this) was a big issue in 'acting like a lady'. I remember thinking that I had to act most like a lady when wearing a dress (which I hated for quite a long time), when in church and when serving punch at my parents' parties."

"Knees together, hands folded in lap, don't talk to strangers, especially men. No similar restrictions for my brother."

★ Women used to be afraid to be called "aggressive" or "loud"; and now they're afraid to be called "feminist"—there's no difference! How far have we come?

"Femininity: properly crossing my legs and sitting like a lady. Clean language, and caring about my appearance."

"Sit properly and listen more than talk. Be modest and ladylike in dress, speech and mannerisms."

"Girls always wore dresses, and so my mother would remind me to keep my skirt down and not show my underpants."

"I was told that a lady didn't sit with her legs apart, so I tried not to, but she never told me *why*!"

Other sexual references began to be made to girls about that time:

"I was told by an older cousin, while having a picture taken by my father with my mother present, that I could be sexy now, I was old enough (I was about thirteen). I didn't know what she meant."

"I often played outside with my brother and his friends. His friends thought I was a bit funny for a girl. At the age of twelve I remember one of the lads calling me names for sitting, quite innocently, on the ground with my legs sprawled out. It must have had some effect on me, as the incident has stuck in my mind."

Boys Have More Rights

Most girls in this research think (with reason!) that it is terribly unfair that they have to do more cleaning and washing-up than their brothers; 79 per cent of those now in their teens and twenties say that this was or is still the case in their families:

"I remember being on holiday with my aunt and uncle and having to stay behind with my aunt to do the washing-up, whilst my brother went into town with my uncle. I thought it was unfair, and ran off to hide for several hours. I know I was expected to help around the house more."

"I knew that if my brother didn't do the washing-up when it was his turn, my mum would have to do it, so I did it instead. My brother didn't seem to think about my mum having to do the housework, not as much as I thought about it."

"My mother and I did the housework, which my brothers were not expected to concern themselves with (they being potential breadwinners, and me a potential wife). I was heartily encouraged to take pleasure in housework."

Most girls and women say that boys are still given more money, encouragement and opportunities for educational and business advancement than they are. This gender-different treatment in the family intensifies as children reach the end of their teens:

"When it came time to graduate from high school, my only escape was to get married. Yes, I was in love, but I also desperately wished to escape from home and I was never given any career guidance, it was never suggested I go on to college. Two years later my parents went so far as to borrow money and support my brother as best they could into college. He worked his ass off, too, at some miserable jobs, and spent many sleepless nights, but I always resented the fact that they guided him into college and not me." (See also Chapters 4 and 5.)

Positive Pictures of "Femininity"

On the other hand, 28 per cent of women say they received a positive picture of femininity:

"She never really tried to put me into a feminine role and was genuinely pleased when I joined the Marines. I can't say as much for my father."

"To be feminine—growing up on a farm gives a woman a mix of what she should be. On the one hand, I was to be a 'lady': keep your skirts down, panties concealed, ankles crossed, and don't be rude or look sexy. Only tramps look sexy, they have no respect for themselves. Don't let any male touch you in 'those' places. Keep the bathroom door closed.

"On the other hand, I was driving a tractor by the time I was in 5th grade, and I'd done field work much earlier. I milked cows, I rode horses, and except when it came to muscle strength, women could function on the farm the same as men. I saw a lot of strong women, physically strong women, around me. And the men considered them feminine and desirable too. We didn't fit in at all with the thin women in the fashion magazines I saw later.

"I still like the looks of those great, sturdy women of my family best."

"We just lived plain lives, no great emphasis on 'femininity'. Basically I think I always believed that I was a member of the human race. My parents both wanted me to make them proud of me, so I became an achiever in school. Only later in life did I think male or female made any difference—that was perhaps something one got concerned about later."

The number of girls given a positive picture of femininity or womanhood increases to 54 per cent if only replies from girls and women who have grown up with "single" mothers are included. There are also higher percentages for girls who have mothers with jobs outside the home.

"Femininity": An Attack on Women, or a New Definition?

Is femininity, then, nothing but cleaning the house, fixing your hair, and reproducing—quietly, and with a smile on your face? Or, "helping your mother, no matter what she's doing"?

I do not want to imply here in a simplistic way that "femininity" is "bad", that it hurts women, or that if we could just throw it overboard, everything would be fine. In fact, what are known as "women's values", or what I have called "women's self-culture", has strong and positive qualities which are politically important today. I spent several years researching the third Hite Report, *Women and Love*, and presenting my findings regarding changing definitions of love and female identity. I cannot reproduce this entire complex debate here, but hope that interested readers will consult that volume.

The restrictions put on women in the name of "femininity" do hurt women, and these should be removed immediately. Women should not accept them. Still, "femininity", in the sense of standing for "softness", empathy and understanding, co-operation, not competition, obviously has an increasing relevance for the world now; boys, too, should be taught to have more of these "feminine" qualities. Governments should relate to each other and the environment via this "women's value system" (which is not a system "all women" and "no men" adhere to, of course).

Without the training to do so, would girls choose to be "feminine" in the sense of cultivating the behaviour that is pushed on them, i.e., being "graceful", interested in clothes, keeping their legs together, etc.? Would boys avoid such behaviour? Some would and some wouldn't. These are individual human likes and dislikes; in a society less obsessed with imprinting gender patterns, it is likely that values which we associate with the terms "femininity" or "masculinity" would be picked up by some individuals of both genders, if left to their own devices and development.

If our gender–culture behaviour is not innate, has society made a wise move in instilling it? Does male aggression ensure survival of the species? Does female empathy ensure reproduction so that mothers take care of children? This is a specious, self-serving argument. We do not need these hierarchical separations for creation of happy families, happy living spaces for people. They are designed not for preservation of the species but for preservation of male dominance in the family and society.

Pornographic and Beauty-Industry Images of Female Sexuality

At the same time that girls are expected to hide their sexuality (masturbation, menstruation, or questions about their parents' physical relationship), they are confronted with a barrage of overtly sexual, pre-defined images of "themselves", in television and magazine ads, as well as in films and videos. Do girls even get a chance to form an individual style of sexuality, make their own definition of eroticism?

Girls see pornography and media images of "their" sexuality
"Sexual" images of women are everywhere in films, on television, and in magazines. From a very early age, girls see pornographic magazines on news-stands. In many countries, even in a pram, or being pushed by her mum or dad in a pushchair, a girl can find herself at eye-level with a nude model on a magazine cover.

However, even by the time their children are twelve or even sixteen, few parents have discussed this with their daughters (or sons), or listened to them while they try to think through how they feel about these images of sexuality and what they mean.

It is amazing that parents are still behaving as though their daughters don't see pornography.

What "should" parents say? What can they say? Well, for example, they can start by asking their daughter's opinions, and then sharing their own.

What Do Girls Think When They First See Pornography?

"How did you feel when you first saw pornography? How old were you? What does pornography tell you about what it means to be a woman?"
How does seeing these images, and especially the nude images, influence girls' discovery and definition of their sexuality?

"When I first saw it, I was so excited! I felt so *adult*, so sexy!"

"I was at my boyfriend's house waiting for him to come home from work. There was nobody else there, and I found it under the couch. Probably his dad's. I only looked at it for a minute; I was afraid Doug would come in and find me with it. I put it back."

"I used to love it, I would look at it with my best friend, and we would wonder where the models bought all the underwear."

"The nude bodies of the women turned me on. I was in the grocery store looking at it. I was surprised to see that there were hardly any men, just women. Why? Was the magazine meant only for men, or was I supposed to be turned on by women? Was *I* supposed to look like that? Would I look like that when I was having sex? When I was older? I used to worry about it, I didn't like their expressions, or something about the atmosphere of it all. I hoped my experiences wouldn't be anything like the pictures seemed—although the idea of doing all those things was incredibly exciting."

"At first I was shocked, but now I find it more instructional. Maybe it's because my friend wanted to shock me. Some boys left it in our locker at school, with our names written on the girls' nude bodies, and other things scrawled on it too."

"When I first saw it I was embarrassed but now I'm not (though sometimes disgusted). I had grown up being told that you are never supposed to go around nude, no one in our house went around nude, even after a shower you put a towel or a robe on. You took off your clothes in private. It was at a party I went to, when the parents were out of the room, some kids pulled it out and started showing it around. I didn't want to run out of there but I felt like it, I felt so embarrassed. But I stayed. The part I found really hard to even look at was when they had their legs apart and you could see the raw-looking flesh."

"The first time I saw porn it was in the form of a *Playboy* belonging to my stepfather. I felt awed (wonder, at those women) and I felt sort of hopeless. I would never look like that! No one will want me. I felt sort of deformed. I don't know if other women have experienced this reaction, but I would be curious to know. Pornography tells women they have to look like the air-brushed woman with the perfect body and be extremely passive, in a vulnerable position, or posturing, to be what every man desires. The expressions on their faces say, 'Every man desires me.' I sure never looked air-brushed, not even on my best days. And I certainly don't walk around thinking every man desires me. And I don't put myself in that kind of vulnerable position at the hands of a million strange men. It's funny, but I never formulated those thoughts quite that way. That's how I feel about pornography. Basically, it stinks . . . it seems demeaning to me—and, honestly, to men."

Girls' descriptions of their first views of pornography are surprising, full of mixed emotions—often excited, worried, relieved, confused. Sometimes young girls want to be "with it" and "go with the flow", they want to seem more "grown-up" than they are by not being shocked or negative; sometimes they are curious, and sometimes they hate it:

"I think pornography has made it difficult for me to look at sex as a natural drive of mankind. Instead it makes me feel that sex is something deemed 'bad' by society. I think sex is too exploited and the media has turned it into a money-making business. It makes me wonder what my role can be since it always shows women in a negative way. The word 'pornography' has an evil meaning for me."

"Initially pornography intrigued me. The first time I saw it was while I was babysitting. I was about fifteen. I could never talk to my mother about it, even though I am close to her. Most of the people who I babysat for had many pornographic magazines in their homes. The articles were about sexual practices unknown to me and I found it difficult to believe that people would actually buy this smut. Most magazines were really demeaning to women. But it helped me feel normal about my sexuality to know others did these things, at the same time that it made me realize how much sexuality can be abused in society."

"I was interested in porn from the age of eight or so. I wasn't upset by it, but I thought that it did put down the women who actually posed for it—for all the world to see. I felt really confused, but why should I mind it as long as it is done discreetly? But it gave me a creepy feeling, like I might be an animal just like those girls."

"My mother was very reasonable about sex when I was twelve and I bought her a *Playgirl* magazine for her thirty-seventh birthday. She laughed and we looked at it together."

"I was in a barber shop waiting while my dad got his hair cut. There were stacks of *Playboy* and *Penthouse* to read. I must have been about eight. I was thrilled because I was doing something that I knew was wrong! The idea of anybody's nudity, male or female, was titillating and horrifying at the same time. (My paternal grandmother, a fairly devout Baptist, was a major influence over my way of thinking at this time.) I was both embarrassed and amused. Pornography tells me that women have a long way to go before they really are accepted on equal terms with men in society, and also that a lot of people are sadly lacking in imagination if they need images like that to turn them on."

"When I first saw it, I felt that I shouldn't be watching, but I was glued to the TV. I was fascinated. Hooked. It happened about five years ago when my parents put in cable."

"My first encounter with pornography was with my father's magazines. I looked at them with curiosity. Also, in high school I knew this guy who covered his walls with *Playboy* pin-ups. I thought he was sick and never liked to go in his room. I've never used pornography to get off, although in my late teens I became involved with Women Against Violence in Pornography and Media, so I did look at pornography. I mostly felt disgusted about how degrading it is to women."

"I was about twelve and I went crazy with excitement! I ran to my room and I think I masturbated and came about ten times, right in a row. I couldn't believe there were things like that. Then, after I calmed down, I went back to the living room (there was no one home) and looked more carefully. I was curious."

"I laughed. It was ridiculous. I was unconcerned."

Parents talk about whether or not their children have seen pornography in an off-hand, matter-of-fact way—if they talk of it at all:

"Some of my older kids have, I'm sure, seen some porn. They can handle it—it's up to them."

"I feel sorry for my son, who at this age can look but not touch. When he is older I hope he can transfer these feelings that have to be restrained for so many years. As for my daughter and the rest of the women, I wish them lots of luck."

"I'm a mother, and I'm sure my son and my daughter have seen plenty of pornography—but what can I do? It's out there, they're going to see it sometime. They're young yet, I'll talk to them when they're a little older. It didn't affect the way I felt about myself when I first saw it, maybe it won't affect them. But I worry about it and I don't like it when the woman is the sex object and the man is not. I like them to be equals."

Who Is "Beautiful"? Who Is "Sexy"?

Beauty pornography and media-created images of women
Television, cosmetic and beauty-industry advertisements, media images—the effects of these on girls, younger and younger girls, are massive and de-individualizing. Yet some girls feel these images are also empowering:

"When I was a child, my mother worried because I ran around imagining myself to be one of the heroines in *Charlie's Angels* (a TV series with three gorgeous girls who also were smart detectives and knew karate). Even at age nine, I wanted to bleach my hair and wear make-up and look like them, I was very into fashion magazines.

"But to me it wasn't a brainwashed thing, it was me being free, daring and adventurous. Now, however, I think it would have been nice if I had grown up with some models of physically active women (like Navratilova) who weren't so into make-up and all that."

"I love Madonna, but my mother gets mad when I say this. She says I shouldn't copy her. But I feel *good* when I see her!"

Sexuality is packaged and pre-defined for girls at an early age
With so many images coming at them of the "beautiful" and the "sexy", there is very little or no chance for girls to discover sexuality and create it for themselves. In any case, in the past, the reproductive ideology enforced the definition of "sex", which everyone learned anyway. So girls hardly had a chance to define themselves then either, although at least they didn't have to deal with the violent images of today all around them. The idea learned then did not include women being tied up, beaten or raped—as is frequently portrayed in magazine layouts now.

Pornography as we know it, in the negative context for women that our society has created (with its double standard of "good girls" and "bad girls", its definition of "sex" as intercourse and so on), more or less slaps girls in the face with the message, "Female sexuality is raunchy and women who are sexual are dominated. If you want to have sex, if you like sex, you'll be like this: cheap. You'll degrade yourself. A female who really likes sex is promiscuous, once she starts she can't stop, she becomes a whore, she'll 'do it' for any man who wants it," plus thousands of other absurdly distorted notions.

The contemporary world—in which almost any girl can walk to any neighbourhood corner shop and see pictures of women with leashes around their necks, wearing very little except make-up, feigning "sexy" poses, or else "fashion pictures", in which the women look cold, remote, and extremely skinny, but supposedly represent objects of desire and sensuality—this is almost enough to make one long for the "good old days", when a girl, despite repressive messages from her parents, school, etc., could find her own sexual style. Today she seems to be "told" by the media that it's dominatrix, masochist, or nothing.

Is this a simplistic view? After all, couldn't the argument be that, by seeing so many photos, at least the message comes across to girls that somehow sex is okay, that there *is* a world of sex out there?

Might a girl not look at these pictures and dislike them, make up her own mind, create her own style in reaction? The figures *are* sometimes strong and powerful (this doesn't mean there is an equation between being a dominatrix and power). And some of the women in fashion magazines sometimes look strong—though they always all seem to be the same age.

While there may be some truth to these arguments, the problem is that the whole concept of "sex" in our society is so shot through with plain, old-fashioned sexism that the picture layouts, the directing of the models' poses and expressions, the sets—everything reeks of it.

This subject features strongly in the Hite Reports already in print and will be covered in detail in a future Hite Report.

Sexual Lies in the Family

The Beginnings of the Double Standard: "Good Girls and Bad Girls"

The family tries to construct girls' psycho-sexual identity

Girls' sexual identity is formed in the following context:

The unspoken, unacknowledged fixation of the family on the mother as its erotic centre.
Girls' secret sexual life of masturbation.
Denial of menstruation (it doesn't happen, it is a secret, don't make a fuss or a big deal out of it); certainly it is not a matter of pride.
Spanking or punishment being genitally located.
The expectation that the girl does not need to hold or sleep next to someone after the age of five, even though adults do.

The messages that are received/given in the family all seek to take away a girl's power; menstruation is not your power, masturbation is not your power, pride in your body being female is not your power. Also, girls can have no information, so they cannot have that power, either.

Yet, there is a feeling that all this *is* part of whatever power the mother has. The child senses that her sexuality is terribly important, and looks with fascination at whatever tangible accoutrements are necessary to accentuate this mysterious "thing", or which help to define her body presence.

One woman describes a time when she walked in on her older sister who was nude, and muses on why her sister ran to cover herself:

"I remember my sister, after swimming, running away to the bedroom to hide when she took off her swimming suit. She must have been about eighteen, and I was nine. Why did she close the bedroom door with such fright? Once I opened it by mistake, and she grabbed her wet suit and clutched it in front of her, hoping I wouldn't see her body. Why? Why that scurrying away? She couldn't look me in the eyes, or smile. Didn't she think she was beautiful?

97

"Our grandmother was so different, almost the opposite. She used to get ready for bed in the summer when we two girls would visit her, and she was not ashamed at all. She would stand there in all her marbled fat, totally sure of her right to be nude. Or she would be getting dressed for church, there in the bathroom. She would take a bath, then sit there putting on her hose and garter belt, then her underwear, put on her lipstick and comb her hair.

"She was extremely plump and wrinkled and in her sixties, but she seemed sure of her right to her own body. She lived alone (widowed). Was that part of the difference? She could therefore take up space in the world without a man to challenge her? I know that my body stance is better when I'm not with a man in the house; otherwise I tend to lean towards him, try to please. Or maybe her independence had to do with coming from the generation she did. I mean, women from years ago seemed to be less afraid to look like 'older women'—they are not afraid to be 'fat', to have white hair, and everything. Like George Bush's wife.

"I admire that, but I'm not sure I'm like that. But I hope I'm not like my sister! Such terror.

"But if she had this attitude, what must sex be like for her? She got married the next year, when she was nineteen. What did she do with her husband—were they intimate? What did they *do*? Was nudity something *they* were ashamed of too? There is some kind of invisible wall so that even today I can't ask her, I am afraid to see that kind of blind terror in her eyes again. I love her and don't want to pain her."

Thousands of little flowers should be blooming, but instead girls are told, even today, to hide menstruation, to be sexual yet ashamed of their (socially constructed) sexuality, to express their sexuality to men only and to be ashamed of that expression when other women are around.

This inner conflict often forms a wound that does not heal. It creates a constant downward pull on many adult women's feelings of well-being and joy, dilutes their strength in making choices about whom to love, how to love, and how they want to spend their lives.

Sexual lies exist in the family: the mother is sensual but has no sexuality, the children have no sexuality. The father probably does, since everybody knows that "men" are sexual by definition; yet there is something that would seem wrong about this, too, being mentioned in the family. Thus the father's sexuality takes on a somewhat shady or illegitimate aura, an outlaw quality.

If mothers can't be sexual, except in secret, is it "bad" to be sexual if you are a woman? If not, why must the mother pretend her sexuality doesn't exist, that she has no sexual life? Or, why has she decided not to have a sexual life? Because Mary, the icon, didn't? Does this imply to daughters that they should have no sexual lives either? Does this create a sexual tension between mother and daughter?

Do mothers have repressed sensual/sexual feelings for their daughters? Even the thought is forbidden.

Why is there no celebration of a girl's first menstruation? Why is it treated as a non-event, or an event to be hidden, kept "your secret", or worse, bemoan? And what do daughters understand of their father's "sexual" identity? (See Chapter 6.)

The remedy to all this is not a "totally open" sexual household, but an open recognition of these issues, and a new determination to make something different of the "family" and our lives in it.

Sexual Identity and the Secretive Family System

What are girls thinking? The family silence about sexuality often begins to breed a separation, an alienation and resentment between the parents and the girl—a sense of shame and lack of pride—and also a separation within the girl herself.

Growing up in this secretive family system, girls construct two identities: one which is "themselves" and another for "sex". In their "sexual" definition, they may take the patriarchal definition—"Yes, I'm a slut during sex, and I love it"—or worry that they have the "wrong fantasies" and try not to have "dirty" associations with sex. Many women also try not to have sex at all, or for extended periods, so as not to have to live in the midst of this double consciousness or double identity, either of which seems to betray the other, creating a feeling of hypocrisy, and so muddying women's inner confidence, their feeling of respect for themselves.

Avoiding what society calls "sex" means not to have to feel off-balance from living with two separate identities, one of which is "shameful". Not to have to hide one's "illegitimate behaviour" and feel guilty (for being politically incorrect, so to speak). Girls want to feel proud and whole. Having a sex life so often makes women feel split and unsure, even during their daily, "public" identity.

What women are doing, especially in their debate over sexuality during the last twenty years, is trying to integrate these two selves, reconstruct another identity which is their own creation.

Chapter 4

The Split Self: Girls' New Sexual Identity Outside the Family
Age Ten–Nineteen

Dating and Crushes: Female Sexuality as Forbidden Power and Pleasure

"When I got into kissing and hugging, I thought *wow*! This is *it*! It made you feel very grown-up, but it was scary too because once in a while you couldn't stop and wanted to go all the way. That was scary. I discussed those feelings with Angela, but not my reason for them. No one knowing made it seem more adult. But I'm closest to my best friend Angela. There's nothing we don't share, good or bad, or even wicked, for that matter."

"The first time I held hands with someone, I was ten years old at primary school. I fell in love with the boy who sat next to me. I used to hold his hand during lessons. It was as thrilling then as sexual intercourse (on occasion) later came to be. He was the first boy I kissed.

"I organized games of 'kiss-chase' specifically to get to kiss him (behind the classroom door of all places)! This passion of mine lasted until I was fourteen years old, after I'd begun dating steadily with another boy. Although I was bolder than my first boyfriend was, I hadn't the guts to push it further. Anyway, like most males, he was at that age less mature and physically developed than I, and also went to a different secondary school. Nevertheless, we exchanged passionate Valentine cards for several years, and declared our love in writing—but never face to face."

"I remember my brother, my cousin and I 'showing ourselves' to each other when I was about eight. Then later, I was desperately excited sucking the breasts of my schoolfriend, to her slight reluctance, at about ten. I had no idea of the fundamentals of reproduction until I was twelve,

100

and then only vaguely and with reference to animals. I remember my cousin and I 'trying it out' (Did we know what?) when we were about eleven—lying on top of each other in the sacks in the barn."

"Although the girls who were boarders at school had secrets about candles, my schoolfriends and I (we went home at night, we lived nearby) were very proper. I remember having bodily responses, excitement at thoughts, but I believed these were all things to be 'put behind me' and sinful. No boys tried more than kissing until I was about eighteen—and then I rather severely discouraged it. I had got the idea that my body was some sort of unfamiliar and dangerous time-bomb, charged with sinful dynamite, which would go off in someone else's hands. Anything 'sexy' was very much reserved for grown-ups, real married people."

"When I was a child I definitely had a lot of sexual curiosity, and maybe feelings, for my four brothers, but it was never expressed. Even today I do, but they are very conservative, and I am shy too. I find their bodies and manners attractive, not just as 'my brothers' but as men. And their teasing, lively criticism of my appearance is an indication of more than just observation."

"In the town I lived in during junior high, there wasn't much real 'dating', you would just meet someone somewhere and perhaps end up necking at the local spot. I was about thirteen when I started to do this. I was very self-conscious and scared, but I liked the idea that someone might want to kiss me. I didn't know what 'going all the way' really meant. Anyway, I was too scared to. I liked it a lot when I found a boy who seemed to like being with me for myself and not just for someone to 'score' with. I was very flattered."

Virginity, Hymens and First Intercourse (Coitus*)

"When I first had sex, it felt very natural and beautiful. I had previously thought I'd feel dirty, but I was surprised to find that I felt like the Virgin Mary after making love! It was so perfect. I didn't tell anybody. I felt it was private, between two people and very special."

"I felt very guilty because I had to lie to my parents when I started dating. To see him I had to sleep at his flat because he lived about an hour's journey away. So I told them I was staying at a girlfriend's. It all got very complicated and out of control."

"My first sexual experience was when I was a freshman in college. It was in the back seat of a car, the inevitable result of too much beer, necking, petting and clitoral stimulation. He was nineteen. My first orgasm was about a year later while under the influence of mescaline and, by God, I came then during intercourse, as well as my first oral sex. Of course under the influence of mescaline almost anything could seem like an orgasm, but I think the drug helped to initiate me into oral sex, making it easier than otherwise since I had been rather squeamish about it."

"I was fifteen the first time I fucked. I was disappointed that it was such an unremarkable event. My hymen ruptured so effortlessly that he even doubted my virginity. I had only a tiny spot of blood to offer as evidence."

"Losing my virginity? Oh dear, oh dear. I had built it up to such a pitch that I was more nerves than anything else. I knew I was going to 'give it away' rather than 'lose' it. Question was, who to? I used it rather as a trump card, waiting until I really wanted to secure a man I was in love with, so when I was worried about his affection turning off—I then produced this prize. After I did it I was so totally consumed, so shattered because it wasn't the experience I thought, that we fought and parted. What a pity."

* Are people still interested in statistics on how old girls are when they first have intercourse, as if this were some kind of indicator of the morality of a society . . . or the degree of freedom in society? Why are they not so fascinated by the age at which boys first have intercourse?

"There was much less pain or bleeding involved than I expected—only a tiny bit. Emotional pain, plenty. But no tears. I was hitch-hiking, far from home, out on a limb, just holding myself together, and twenty years old."

"My first intercourse was a happy occasion—my boyfriend brought me a bottle of champagne and I cut off a lock of his hair as a token. I was thirteen."

"By the time I reached nineteen, I was so hung up about being a virgin that I had a very unpleasant experience with a very insensitive man. He literally dragged me into his bedroom and, after some coaxing, I slept with him. But I had a Tampax inside me, so he didn't get very far! (I didn't remove it because I thought I couldn't get pregnant with it in me—I was very drunk—and so the whole thing was only a technical loss of virginity.)

"If it wasn't for my private delight in masturbation, I would have been really messed up. I liked to make out with boys in high school, I thrived on it. But I felt that if I gave in I'd be ruined for life. Word gets around fast in a small town."

Of course, most girls, even today, go into their first experience of "intercourse" (coitus), thinking that they should have "more pleasure than they've ever had"; that the pleasure should be much greater than during "just petting" or masturbation. But they are often used to having orgasms during these activities (masturbation, or manual stimulation by a boyfriend or girlfriend for example), and are shocked when they do not have orgasms easily during coitus—and find the feelings so different from the clear-cut orgasms they are used to.

The Hite Report on Female Sexuality first demonstrated (in 1976) that it is not the "norm" for women to orgasm from simple coitus ("thrusting in the vagina"), but rather from exterior or "clitoral" stimulation—and that this should become a standard part of "sex" between people. Before that, many women were faking orgasms during intercourse, feeling terribly guilty and "abnormal" if they did not have them, never daring to tell their partner, but instead going into the bathroom to masturbate privately for orgasm, after "sex".

With the continued depiction of women in videos and movies as "coming" from "intercourse", in the same way and at the same time as men do, the reality of most women's need for clitoral stimulation to orgasm has begun to be obscured, and now girls (who have little information from their mothers and rely mostly on magazines, films, and their sexual partners) are again having to go through sometimes several years of experimentation and worry before feeling confident and comfortable with their bodies.

There is a similar problem with the lack of depiction of how people put on condoms in films, sex videos and magazines. Since "no one" there does it, people in general also believe it is not "normal", and they shouldn't have to bother with it either.

How Many Girls Have Hymens?

Are "hymens" as common as they are, in myth, supposed to be? Is it "normal" to have a "hymen"? How many girls really experience any physical pain or bleeding on first intercourse? Strangely, there has been little reliable data on this subject.

Research for this study demonstrates quite surprisingly that most girls do not experience pain or bleeding on first coitus; the percentage of those who do is quite low. In fact, even more surprisingly, it may not be anatomically "normal" for girls to have a painful-to-break "hymen". Those who are "supposed" to know—gynaecologists or paediatricians—in fact have no particular expertise in this, since (1) gynaecologists usually do not see very young girls, and (2) paediatricians usually don't do in-depth or detailed vaginal examinations. Therefore, is the assumption that "normal girls" have hymens, simply based on hearsay, or "learned" in medical textbooks? On what body of knowledge and investigation, if any, are these texts based?

According to my research, only 18 per cent of women felt any painful tearing or saw any blood on first intercourse, or at any time earlier in their lives. This would imply that a belief in the prevalence of a full "hymen" in girls is a myth, and a dangerous one at that, especially for women in cultures that punish women if they are not "virgins" on marriage.

We may be doing a great disservice to girls and their families, causing them needless worry over this question, by letting this assumption continue unchallenged. In the worst scenario, it can cause parents to take their daughters to doctors to be "checked" and "sewn up" before marriage, especially in cultures where hymens are a fetish.

Many men (husbands and boyfriends, or gynaecologists) simply assume that if the woman or girl has no "hymen", she "must have done it", or has "fallen off her bicycle" or something. Or, they say, "Well, of course, there are variations in human anatomy."

Doctors should inform parents and girls themselves that, while some girls may experience bleeding, this is not by far the "average" case; most girls do not.

Erotic Emotional Pleasure

For many girls, petting and erotic affection is more pleasurable and exciting than coitus. Special emotions and feelings go with that eroticism:

"I loved dating. I loved showing off my boyfriends. I only dated hunks. My first kiss was sweet and tender, I remember it vividly. I was fourteen. The first time I made out with a boy, I was fifteen. He was very aggressive and horny. I remember feeling so horny myself! I loved all of that time, the touching, the kissing, the air of suspense and possibility: what will we do? My body was just ready for it all, I was so turned on.

"The first time I had sex was later on, with a boy I loved and waited two years for until he asked me out. And even then, we were fixed up. The time was right for me and him (he was also a virgin). We tried a few times, but couldn't get his penis in. The first time he actually penetrated me (I was eighteen) it was painful and I bled.

"I was scared and told him I couldn't do it again. He agreed. But then a few days later we tried again and it worked. We had intercourse about once a week for the remainder of our relationship.

"My parents knew none of this, of course. I told my best friend and she was appalled. She said I'd get pregnant. But we were using condoms, and I didn't."

"I started dating at exactly sixteen and a half. Funny summer. I saw one guy, nineteen years old, twice; nothing fancy, not a kiss once, but when he moved, he wrote for months after, asking me to marry him.

"That same summer, I met Keith, who was also nineteen, and we dated pretty seriously for over three months (a long time then). My first real kiss was with Keith, and it was great. I decided that kissing was the greatest pastime, and 'made out' with Keith again, loving the feelings I was having. They were not only in my body, they were also in my brain, the emotional rush I got when I thought of him and of kissing him, mixed with the warmth of the affection, being held like that for hours on end. Incomparable! Nothing could beat it! He got a little more adventurous every time we met, and it went beyond kissing, we did all kinds of things. But the best for me was always just that long, leisurely erotic body contact in his car, in the dark."

Confusing Decisions Girls Can't Discuss With "the Family"

Some girls are confused when they start dating, not sure it is "really them", but they go ahead anyway because they feel they should be seeing boys:

"I felt confused when I first started dating. I guess I basically started because I didn't want to be 'left out', as most of my friends were dating. The bloke I dated was crazy for me, but I suppose I didn't feel the same way. I had sex with him at sixteen, quite often, and truthfully I loved it, but not *him*, although I thought (at the time) I did, as I couldn't comprehend why I would do that (have sex) if I didn't love him. I never talked to my parents about it, although my mother knew, but it was like, 'I know it's happening, but I don't want to know.' I talked with my friends about it, in great detail."

"I can remember feeling in 8th grade that I 'should' be asked out by boys and that I 'should' be interested in them. It was the last thing I wanted to do, really, and was wrapped up with all kinds of anxieties. I felt something was wrong with me because I wasn't more affectionate."

When to have "first intercourse" is always a question:

"I was a bit shocked when he pulled a rubber out of the glove compartment and asked if I wanted to. But I stayed a virgin till a week before my twenty-fourth birthday. Funny, I had only known the guy then three weeks. But we were very comfortable with each other and 'it' was fun. Not painful or awful. I was ready for it. My parents worried. They stayed up until I got home, worried some more and still worry. (No one is good enough for their daughter!)"

Peer pressure to be "bad" (not to imply that girls must always be "good"!) is always around:

"The thing I hated the most about high school were the so-called tough girls. The ones who wore black all the time and smoked in the girls' johns. They were on the way to making a mess out of their lives

106

and there they were putting the rest of us down, making us feel like dirt. They made my early high-school years miserable.

"What I did like was the safety and certainty of high school. It was always there, day after day, always the same. I was good at the academic part, and got better in the social part as I grew older. I liked most of my teachers, had some good friends. I loved acting and singing in plays. That helped me get over a lot of shyness and self-consciousness."

There is also pressure to take drugs:

"School was very difficult for me, especially junior and senior high school. I didn't do drugs or drink. At times, it seemed like everybody in the world did one or the other. I have always been very sure of my beliefs and no matter how much easier it would have made my life, I wouldn't go back on my principles. Many boys said they liked me and thought I was pretty, but too heavy."

"In high school I wasn't promiscuous or into drugs, and I liked learning. I made up for this in college though! I got quite a 'drug education'! I never suffered any consequences, I was one of the lucky ones."

Interracial dating, especially black and white, is still not common, and remains problematic:

"The worst thing that happened to me was when my father disowned me for going out with a black guy. It took two years for him to speak to me again, and today I still feel his anger."

The Right to "Sex": How Old Are Girls When They Start Having Sex?

How early do girls have a "right" to sex? And what would that sexuality be? Would it be so coitus-focused as pornography and rock-video depictions imply? Or would it be more diverse, more sensual and erotic, and perhaps even more spiritual?

There is an assumption in psychological literature that girls with little closeness at home with their parents or family tend to start sex sooner—often winding up pregnant. Is this belief supported by this research? Not necessarily. For *some* girls, loneliness and an understandable need for affection make them exchange sex for being held. But many other girls start sex "early", just out of curiosity and simple adventurousness, or even love.

To say that girls only start sex early out of "neediness" is a negative, double-standard way of looking at girls' actions, a "woman as victim" interpretation. In fact, if girls are more curious, or want to touch and be held, this may show that they are less frightened, more ready to engage with the world. These are qualities for which boys are usually praised.

On the other hand, teenage girls—especially those with no good communication ties with their parents or other "substitute" family—are indeed often vulnerable to being harassed into sex, pressured into it. They feel "sex" is the price they pay for being held and spoken to affectionately:

"I started dating at thirteen. I was flattered, I wasn't used to being liked. I always dated a lot of boys. I loved catching them, it was so exciting."

"I wanted boys early, I needed desperately to be held, due to my family situation. All went off without a hitch: I was busy being a good girl and following the rules with people who I knew or my parents could find out about. But older male strangers alleviated the need I had for sex in my darker, hidden life."

"I began to behave like a 'mature' young lady when I started the 7th grade. Older boys noticed me and it made my life worth living, really. It was as though I had never realized my own attractiveness and positive characteristics until a boy said he liked my being quiet or he liked my legs etc., etc."

It can be painful for a girl later if it turns out she was only a notch on someone's belt:

"I was the loneliest when I was a teenager, being used and abused by guys I made it with just to be accepted—huh. What a stupid ass I was. Never again."

"I contemplated suicide when the man I lost my virginity to suddenly turned on me and started treating me like a locker-room joke."

"When I was seventeen I felt rejected and depressed. I was suspicious of everyone I went out with after the bad experiences I had had. I couldn't believe anyone was going out with me because they wanted to get to know me."

But more and more, girls are refusing to believe that it matters if someone else thinks they are a "notch". Girls are judging boys now, and deciding what their own sexual actions do and do not mean. This is part of reclaiming our right to our own bodies.

Do Parents Take Girls' Minds Seriously?

Most parents, remarkably, are still not taking girls' talents and interests seriously. Parents are more likely to pressure girls to "fit in" and "be normal", or to focus on their sexuality, urging them "not to cause trouble" (and not get pregnant!) than they are to spend time and attention encouraging them in their school and future work interests. It is as if they do not take their daughters seriously.*

Most women in this study, even those with little education, enjoyed the academic side of school but got little encouragement from their parents to take it seriously. Even today, it is not a measure of popularity for girls to be "too smart". Yet this is one of the few times in life that many women get to take themselves seriously, and explore their talents and interests:

"High school was good as far as making close friendships with girls went, and individual achievement. I was recognized for music (band and choir), drama, academics, and the newspaper. I was well known and proud of my achievements. If it weren't for high school, I wouldn't have found these capabilities of mine.

"My parents never really seemed interested in the things that were important to me like my music, my acting, my achievements. I believe that they love me, although my mother definitely favoured my brother, and my father always wanted my brother to be 'his son' with Little League baseball, football, train sets, and other male-oriented activities. I was always jealous. I wanted to play too!"

"I was very smart in school. My brother's and my grades were praised equally. However, I was never encouraged to be anything important. I remember wanting to be a dancer one month and then a doctor the next, when I was about six or seven. When someone asked me to decide which I wanted to be because I couldn't be both, I told them I would be a dancing-doctor. Everyone laughed, but I was serious. Shortly after that, my uncle tried to discourage me from becoming a

* But *can* they, in a society in which the model of the "holy family" does not even have a daughter?

109

doctor by telling me that it was a gutsy, gory job—I decided to give up the idea."

"I often received compliments from my parents on how pretty I looked, when what I wanted to hear was how smart or strong or perceptive I was. I remember when I won an academic award, the night of the public awards announcements my father told me how pretty I looked. Never once did I hear how great it was that I was such a scholar. I was treated to a hot fudge sundae afterwards in celebration, but the words are always in my memory, about how I looked."

Rape and Date Rape

When do girls first hear about the existence of something called "rape"? At what age? How does this inform their psycho-sexual identity? Clearly, the prevalence of the issues of "rape" and "date rape" in the press is affecting girls' sexual development.

If parents can't discuss these problems with their daughters, how are the daughters—no matter how "well brought up"—to deal with such a confusing array of choices and pressures?

The following "rape" experiences might have happened to any young and trusting girls:

"One time I did go to a hotel room with someone I hardly knew, someone I met during a rock concert. He pressured me to the point where he was basically holding me down and I was just saying no, and the experience was so frightening, I can't even remember, but I think I was crying the whole time, and he was on drugs, cocaine or something. He finally let me go and I just kept saying I've got to go, I don't want to do this. I think eventually he said okay, fine, anything you want, and for some reason I got out of it, but I do remember him walking me out to my car. He wanted my pantihose—it was like anything, here, just get out of my sight, I don't ever want to see you again. Then I realized he probably wanted to go back and show his friends that he had slept with me and this was the proof of it! If that wasn't it, it was just superkinky. I can remember being very, very frightened, and also realizing how stupid I had been."

"When I was eighteen, I was attacked while I was hitch-hiking. He drove me up into the mountains and started to rape me, but some hunters drove past and I screamed and was rescued. Up until that time I felt that I was invincible. I had gone through a period of feeling very strong and very safe during adolescence so, when he first came close to me, I thought that he wanted to kiss me and I wondered how I could refuse without hurting his feelings, because I didn't want to kiss him.

"He choked me and threatened to kill me. I looked around and we were surrounded—we were in the Sierras in California—we were

111

surrounded by lovely green forests, and under a star-filled sky and I thought, This is such an incongruity. I was terrified. He said he might kill me and leave me in the woods and I believed that—I had a very strong sense that I was going to be dead, lying back in the woods on this mountain, and I could see the newsreels, another nude female corpse is found in the woods, the pictures on the evening news of men carrying away a stretcher with a body on it, and it was awful. Up until that point, I thought that I could go anywhere in the world and do anything I felt like doing."

"The worst was I had an orgasm when I was raped by an ex-convict. I really suppressed it and I think I had a lot of problems because of this but it didn't occur to me for a long time. I told one friend this—he reacted suspiciously, as though something was wrong with me."

"I think the most traumatic thing was being raped as a nineteen-year-old virgin. It took years and years to get through that one. After the initial details were dealt with, I became 'promiscuous'—I figured the excuse of virginity wouldn't hold up any longer, so I had no way now to say no to all the creeps who wanted to sleep with me. Maybe that was the worst outcome of being raped. The other was disillusionment with men. He was a familiar person on campus—in his forties I think—but someone who I knew had fatherly feelings for me that couldn't possibly be sexual because he was so much older, you know?

"Once that all happened, I had a well-founded paranoia about men, but continued to get myself into situations where the only way out was to say okay and then resolve never to see that person again. I think there are remnants of all the forced and unloving sex in my current abstention from sex with my life partner of so many years, as if to say, 'If I can say no, will you still stick around?'"

Parents don't seem to realize the pressures their daughters are under—or at least don't want to talk about them:

"When I was younger I felt that I was pressured a lot, like 'boys only wanted one thing'. When I was a freshman at the university, I had a friend that lived in a dorm across the street, he was an older man of twenty-one. I'd go over to his room and play cards. One time I drank massive quantities of wine. At eighteen it didn't take much for me to have to run to the bathroom down the hall and throw up. When I came back to his room, he was wearing his robe. I said I'd go home because he was obviously going to bed (we had never had anything but a platonic friendship).

"He blocked the door. I really thought he was kidding around. He said I could sleep in the other bed. I was kind of scared by then, or I knew

112

something a little strange was going on, but I felt if I said anything I'd look like a freaked-out kid, so I said okay. He got in his bed and I got in the other with my clothes on. I had a skirt on. He turned out the lights. God, I was so whirly from the wine.

"I can't remember what happened exactly, but he was on top of me. He was naked. I'd only tried to make love to my boyfriend back home a few times. I felt so strange. I was yelling, 'No, no I'm a virgin!' After he finished (I don't remember feeling anything) he said, 'There, that wasn't so bad, was it?' I sort of kept quiet then—I was so disgusted at my helplessness and foolishness at being there. At my trusting him. I thought I'd asked for it by being there.

"It was much much later that I defined it as a rape. I never spoke to him again. Later in college, when I made friends with another guy, we sort of became soulmates. I told him the story. (I thought about it a lot.) It turned out that he was this guy's neighbour and had heard me yelling that night. He and two other guys sat by the wall and listened to the whole thing. It's my rape story, I guess."

"The rape was the biggie. It happened fourteen months ago and I'm still waiting to go to trial. It was all the police department crap that was the worst. Even the actual rape wasn't as bad as feeling really strongly for a guy, and finding out that all you are is a cunt to him. And that's the truth."

"In college, I was raped by a professor. I was sort of in shock at the time. It was so unexpected. I couldn't believe it was actually happening. I did try to fight him off, but I was so much in shock, I was helpless. After, I was pretty upset, and I couldn't concentrate or study. But I never did press charges. No one would have believed me anyway, it was my word against his. I didn't want the exposure of going to court (little chance of conviction) and I couldn't afford the time. I was already doing part-time jobs (a forty-hour week) to put myself through school, while carrying nineteen credit hours, including six graduate courses. I got very little sleep!

"I was determined to go on with my life and did. I felt that if I let it interfere with my life, it was like giving the man even more control over me. Funny, when I graduated, my dad kept telling me it was time to get married. I didn't feel like it."

What Do Parents Say to Girls about Dating? Nothing

Just when girls are starting to enjoy, or at least to explore and have questions about, their sexuality with others (they have, for the most part, already enjoyed their bodies/orgasms for years by themselves), the strain and distance developed in the family over issues of sexuality becomes pronounced.

The negative attitudes and tension reported here surrounding the beginning of dating are remarkable. Girls learn very early (as do boys) that sexuality must not be discussed in the "family"—neither the parents' sexuality, nor their own feelings during masturbation, nor what other kids say at school, nor their own emergent erotic feelings and emotions. Almost nothing to do with "sex" can be discussed.

So, the more important this part of their life becomes—and the more pressing their need to find some way of making sense of all their new feelings and experiences—the more distance is created from the "family", and the more a double identity becomes entrenched as a way of life.

At this point in their lives, many girls (and boys) begin to feel they are living with split identities, or in two completely different worlds:

"My mom gave my brother a pamphlet about Aids, but my brother and I don't think anybody we know has it. The guys I go out with say putting on rubbers wastes time. That is why I have to worry about getting pregnant and Aids. About the pill, my friend told me that it wrecks your face, and that's all that I need know."

"I always feel very uncomfortable telling my parents I am going out on a date, since we have never yet discussed the subject."

Living in Two Worlds:
Dating and Sex—Parents' Attitudes

"What was your mother's attitude when you started dating? Your father's? Did you discuss with your parents what happened when you went out on dates?"

Incredibly, 79 per cent of parents seem to more or less pretend that dating and sexual feelings just aren't happening:

"They don't discuss my dates. They never really ask about anything."

"My parents and I don't discuss this, I think they feel dating is my private life."

"I'll be fourteen in eight days. My sister is getting married in a few months, she is a virgin. Our family is together and happy. My mom teaches us no sex before marriage, but I see nothing wrong with sex. My brother doesn't either, he fucks girls. I also screw with his friends. We do drugs sometimes, but I don't tell my mother, she wouldn't like it."

"I tell my mother where I'm going, but that's all. I tell my best friend *everything!*"

"It's funny, the first time my mother talked to me about anything related to sex was when I was getting married at twenty-seven. She said, 'I think it's time we talk,' and we both laughed."

Parents' loud silence about dating and sexual feelings
The vast majority of girls have no real communication with their parents, or even their sisters or brothers, about their sexuality:

"I feel very uncomfortable talking to my parents. They don't know anything about my sexual development, and if they asked I wouldn't tell them. After not telling me anything when I was younger, I feel they have no right to start discussing my sex life now."

"My parents never knew what was going on with me. Why should they? It was my body."

"My parents would be shocked to hear anything about my love life. Whenever I tried to talk to them, they never understood, they made me feel worse than I originally felt."

One young woman describes how this state of affairs affected her life:

"My parents never mentioned dating. They didn't comment. I don't know what they assumed or thought I was doing. Sometimes when I went out, supposedly to meet just my girlfriends, my mother would order me to be in at a certain time, acting bossy and cross. My father would make it into a joke.

"My mother would express lots of anger and shame. When a young couple 'had to get married' because the girl became pregnant. She would be 'disgusted' by such things and say that she felt pity for the parents. I hated her for saying such stupid, blind things. I wished she could be understanding and listen to me talk."

Not talking can lead to irrational attacks and assumptions:
"My relationship with my mother was always shaky. She definitely didn't understand me. When I was about sixteen, she told me she thought I was on drugs, it was the only way she could explain my behaviour. I wasn't, I had never touched so much as a drink or a joint."

Many teenagers who do try to talk to their parents report dismaying experiences:
"I told my mother the first time I truly wanted to make love, even though I had stopped short of doing it. That met with such shock and disapproval, and consequent restrictions, that I kept quiet from then on, sorry that I couldn't share this new part of me—my sexuality."

"If you have had a sexual relationship, do your parents know? If so, how did they react?"
The majority of parents ignore or do not discuss how a girl feels about dating, and do not learn the problems she might be encountering—almost as if they are turning their backs, expecting the girl to "find her own way", and everything automatically to "turn out right", in the labyrinth of today's rapidly changing and confusing sex-relationship games:
"Sex was never discussed. My brother and I used to compare notes, however, and he would warn me of the dangers of knowing 'certain types of boys'."

"The attitude of both my parents appeared to be one of pride (and relief?) that their daughter was attractive to boys. My mother would even help me prepare for my dates. (She explained that the boy would pay for everything. I could never understand why; I still can't.) My father teased me. Neither parent, however, ever questioned me closely about my boyfriends or really discussed anything. Almost like it was taboo or embarrassing to mention."

"My mother and father were terrified of my dating. I was told by my father that my mother's older sister had been pregnant before marriage, and it seemed that this was the worst thing he could think of. We never discussed my life or dates, really, on any other than a hysterical level (his)."

"My mother and father didn't like the fact that I was so serious with my boyfriend. Because of my mother's disapproval of our relationship, I never told her when we started to have sex. Besides, it was much too important a moment in my life to share with anyone other than my love."

Most girls don't tell their parents anything:

"I am a fifteen-year-old student, from a strict middle-class family from the French West Indies. I'm white with a little black mixed in. Although I live with my parents, across the street lives my best male friend whom I first had sex with. Now we don't have sex but we are friends and tell each other about our sexual experiences with others. Also I can talk to him about my life, of hassling with my family. Sex for me is very separate from my mother's arguments. I keep sex to myself and my friend."

"I never openly told my parents anything, but by the time I was twenty-two and living with a man, they must have known I was having sex! My mother responded by wanting me to get married. I told her that I didn't want to marry the man. I think she was surprised by the statement. My father and stepmother behaved as if we *were* married and treated us as part of the family. They accepted us as we were, and for this I was grateful."

"I wasn't allowed to date until I was sixteen. I felt very restricted, as if they felt any boy I went out with was going to jump on my bones the minute I got in the car. This put a fear in me that all men were after only one thing. I discussed nothing about my dates with them, because the littlest thing they heard would be twisted and misconstrued to be something nasty and terrible."

"They always told them what time I had to be home (eleven o'clock). It was my mother who spoke, never my father. (In fact I have no idea how my father felt, because he never said anything about it.) I never told them what really happened on my dates—I told them the places we went but not the parking we did!"

If most parents can't talk about sex with their heterosexual daughters, imagine their difficulty discussing lesbian love and sex:

"Mother's premise has always been that women friends are significant and true. I know she loves her woman friends, hugs and kisses them, takes walks with them even arm in arm. However, when I told her (in my teens) I had taken a woman lover, she fell apart. 'Why do you have to have . . . *sex* . . . with a friend?' she sobbed. That was a confidence I wish I'd spared her. She was not, and probably never will be, ready for woman–woman love."

"The greatest emotional trauma I've met to date was when my parents confronted me about my sexuality and my relationship with my girlfriend. They went wild. They 'battered' me psychologically with all they could. They threatened to commit me to an insane asylum and to kill me.

"I cried a lot because of these problems. I was especially distraught when my girlfriend told me that she would obey my parents' wishes for us not to see each other. She wanted to wait until we were both out of our parents' homes. I couldn't understand why she wouldn't come away with me. I wanted us both to move out that night. She wanted time to think."

Masturbation and Fantasies: When You Begin to Think You're Gay

Girls' secret lesbian thoughts and feelings

All around children are signposts informing them, "Heterosexuality is *the* way to go."

But what if you are feeling, or beginning to feel, something different? As one girl describes:

"I've been gay for as long as I can remember. I can never recall being attracted to a man, I never fantasized about them sexually. When I was in 3rd grade I used to fantasize about my women teachers. What it would feel like to kiss one of them."

Lesbian feelings between girls

While it is important for mothers and daughters, or parents and daughters, to talk about lesbianism, my research here shows that mothers rarely mention it.

One girl received a vague warning:

"When I was about thirteen, my mother used to say to me when my girlfriend and I would lie on the bed together watching television, 'Don't lie on the bed like that!' She had something in her mind, something bad in her mind. I don't know why she said that, but we stopped doing it so much after that. I have romantic love for my girlfriends, sometimes, but I do not need to have sex with them, I don't want sex with them."

★   ★   ★

The ways in which girls express, very early on, their questions in the area of attraction and feeling for other girls is often rather oblique:

"I was always with guys. Guys were always more interesting to me than girls. I don't know whether that is because they pay more attention to me or flatter me, since I'm not sure I really believe they are more exciting."

"I've been very horny ever since I started self-love as a child. I worry about it and wonder if I am abnormal—frigid? A lesbian? I wish I could relax and not try to be what I 'should'. It is very confusing. I always know when I'm turned on by a woman, but I couldn't accept my feelings for years."

"For several years until very recently I had dreams about my mother and a lot of guilt. I was hostile towards her and felt worse because she is an intelligent person. When she touched herself non-sexually or rubbed her legs while she sat and talked, I wanted to hit her or run away. Now we walk with arms around each other, and it's cool."

"I used to fantasize a lot during masturbation—it just came naturally and definitely helped me climax. When I was pretty young I fantasized about being punished, I guess to relieve my guilt. Then later it was about women usually."

But sometimes girls' references are not oblique at all:

"Especially since my first relationship with another woman, my sexual awareness has about tripled, and being aware of my sexuality makes me hot. I started having sex at fifteen.

"My parents are very educated, open, honest about sex. But one thing I doubt my parents could accept is that I am physically so woman-oriented."

The New Sexual Meaning of "Be a Good Girl"

When "Be a good girl" means "Don't have sex"
Earlier, "Be a good girl" meant don't misbehave, but later the comment is explicitly sexual, i.e., "Just because you're on the pill doesn't mean you now have the right to do things," as girls explain:

"I heard 'Be a good girl' a million times from my father. He meant avoid sex and don't get pregnant, which is exactly the opposite of what I did."

"When I was sixteen my father told me, 'A man can do anything and get away with it, but if a woman does anything, she's considered a tramp. So if a man ever tries anything, give him a good kick where it hurts.' He explained nothing further and I had no idea where I was supposed to kick a man. But I understood he saw the boys I knew as predators."

"I vaguely remember my father telling me to be a 'good girl' because 'boys are only after one thing'. On the other hand, my mother, even though a good Catholic, welcomed the more open society of the '70's. Her advice was to go on the pill and live with somebody before you marry them. That was quite radical for a Catholic who was older than most mothers, but she was talking with the voice of experience."

"When I left for Europe at twenty, my mother told me to be a 'good girl'. It meant don't have sex, but I did. I was very careful about contraception and had a diaphragm. When I told her when I got back, she took it as 'permission' either to start having sex with her lover (later husband) or to be honest and tell me about it. It really changed our relationship. Now we were both 'bad girls', but it was okay, somehow."

"Up to the age of fifteen, my parents (particularly my father) were keen for me to be in by a certain time at night, and didn't like me going out with boys, especially the 'wrong' kind. When they told me to be a 'good girl', it meant not having sex."

"My parents always told me I was a 'good girl'. I respected the way they brought me up. When I'd go out with boys I'd go only so far, then I'd think of my parents and how they'd disapprove, then I'd go home. If I ever got 'into trouble', I'd die of the humiliation and disappointment of my parents, more than my own shame."

Many parents' way of telling a daughter "not to have sex" (rather than discussing with her the interesting new feelings she might be having, as well as things to "watch out for") is to become vaguely distrustful and make "remarks":

"My father and mother were suspicious of every boy whose name I ever mentioned. My mother accused me of sleeping with every boy I dated, even though I remained a virgin until right before I married. In my school, if your father allowed you to date in junior high, you were looked up to and envied. The fact that you could date made you more grown-up than anyone else."

One family's idea of "talking" and "listening" to their daughter consisted of showing her newspaper articles:

"I was shown each and all rape articles and made to read every line. Any boy picking me up for a date was grilled and instructed, as if he were like the guys in the articles. If I admitted to a goodnight kiss, the attitude was, you probably went further."

Fathers' horror at the idea of sexually active daughters

46 per cent of girls say their father exhibited hostile attitudes to their dating, although the following two examples are unusually dramatic:

"The couple of dates I had, my father went hunting for me, looking in all the parked cars. Needless to say, I was not popular."

"Once when I was going out on a date, my father told me he thought I was dressed like a slut. I told him never to say that again if he wanted to stay my father. My mother never said anything like that."

21 per cent of girls have had to hide their dating from their father (for some, it was a secret shared with their mother):

"I started dating when I was eleven. I felt good about dating boys because it gave me new feelings about myself. My mother thought I was too young to date, but went along with it anyway. My father didn't want me to date until I was sixteen, so I had to hide it from him. I didn't like lying to my father, but I enjoyed dating."

"My mother's attitude when I started dating (around twelve) was a mixture of amusement, nostalgia, trepidation and regret at the passing of my childhood. My father thought I was too young and regretted more deeply this step. He was slightly jealous, I think, of any affection I might be directing towards my boyfriends. I certainly didn't discuss with my parents what happened when I was on a date, except perhaps to tell them about a film or something else I'd seen. Of course I did discuss it all with my close friends, particularly the 'petting' aspect!"

"My mother was anxious when I started dating, but she helped prepare me by teaching me to be comfortable dancing. My father tried suddenly to get protective and say things like, 'Who's that nigga?' (We're black.) But it was mostly posturing. My mother always knew who I was with and where we were going."

The double standard re. sons' and daughters' dating

This attitude is alive and well, as girl after girl testifies:

"My opinion of my father isn't very high. He is a 'smart-ass white boy', as African-Americans would say. He acts superior and thinks everything should be done for him. If he ever gets off his skinny ass and actually does something, he expects an award.

"When we were growing up and my younger brother stayed out all night with a girl, my father couldn't wipe the smile off of his face for a month. When I came in late—and hadn't done *anything*—he yelled at me, and I quote, 'Do you spread your legs for everyone?' Unquote.

"Earlier, when we were really young I heard my mother arguing for the $100 it would have taken for me to take ballet and my father saying no, we couldn't afford it. He had this dream of owning a business. Of course when my brother needed football equipment, there was no discussion. He got it!"

"She said things like, 'Nice girls don't go places like that,' or that I couldn't go out for a drink but it was okay if my brother did. After all, he was a *man*. It also seemed okay for my brother (younger) to have friends back fairly late, but I never did. I remember bringing the church youth club (about twenty of us) back home one Sunday. My father stormed in about 10 p.m. and threw them all out. That was the last time friends of mine ever came to the house."

Girls learn to hate themselves for sexual activity (the double standard lives)

One girl more or less overdosed on her first days of freedom—and then hated herself later:

"When I was sixteen and out of town, I slept with about nine guys (I lost my virginity to a guy I knew only about one hour) and kissed at least fifteen others. I didn't think about what I had done, if I had I would have gone nuts. To this day I believe I did all that because I was psychologically unstable. The whole time I was there I felt it wasn't me but rather someone else. After all, would I have sex without birth control about fifteen times with various strange men? Hardly. I must have been someone else.

"I finally came to grips with the whole thing years later, and I can go through whole days, even weeks, without looking in the mirror and seeing a terrible person, a slut. I can finally accept what I did and can once again have a relationship with a guy and even be sexual without thinking I'm a terrible person."

Teenage girls (and boys) integrate the double standard split into their value structure, assumptions and psychological make-up very early:

"The big friend of my early days was Gina. She was overweight, musical, poetic, dreamy, soft, kissed me and taught me lots about myself. We were friends until high-school days, but when she fell in love with a boy and actually made love with him as an expression of love (I'd never heard of such a thing . . . I *knew* sex was dirty), she seemed dirty to me."

Sometimes the identities of girls, despite all these exterior pressures, remain strong because the girl is hiding/safeguarding a serious part of herself deep inside where no one can see it. As we have seen, many young girls as "tomboys" (a needlessly trivializing phrase, as if it were

122

just a "stage" for "identifying with boys", rather than an important way that girls explore the world and themselves) form a relationship with nature. They feel closer to the trees than to the people around them, or for some girls, it is their horse or dog. Often girls who read novels have an active personal life of the imagination which is completely private, which is their "home" for the moment. Who is to say the girl's inner reality—whether with nature or in books—is not as real as the life of her "family" or school around her?

One teenager developed a very severe identity split, trying out all the roles in their extreme:

"Good girl" was me all through high school—grades, clubs, friends, blah, blah, blah. Another masquerade. I was always an officer, a leader. I followed the "good girl" rules and survived with the best permanent file in my class. Mom was pleased. Meanwhile, I hated the charade, and sneaked out at night to perform oral sex on men I'd never seen before in my life, sometimes for money. It was almost schizophrenia.

"I loved my mother in a love/hate chaos, always tried to please, fetched coffee, cowered, was controlled with an invisible tension. It was confused love on all sides, with constant role-playing. It's still a mess since my parents are now going through their second divorce. I try to keep a wall there, for my own sanity, with newsy light letters and rare visits.

"I tried for years to love my mother. She's exactly like me, and my opposite. Physically, she's gorgeous, trained for professional ballet, works as a stripper, yet we communicate and we will never let the other settle for less. We write or call weekly. I want to look like her, be attractive like her, yet I worry that she's self-destructive, and she is an unrelenting bitch sometimes. She's been an invaluable help, too.

"As a child I could be more honest with my father about some things because I knew he was such a redneck—I could call him when I was drunk, bitch about birth control pills, etc. But my father didn't know about my other life, that I got paid for sex.

"I had a string of married men. I loved none of them. They were sex for the flip side of the daytime 'good girl'. They were playful and enjoyed their little transgressions. They enjoyed my demand for discretion.

"All the same, I hated the double life I led in high school. I had suffered for years over an earlier high-school breakup. I still wonder if that is why I became so promiscuous. He wouldn't have sex with me because of his 'wait till marriage' morals. It became a slow drifting apart that I couldn't seem to control. Perhaps he was frightened that I was ready for sex."

Female sexuality in hiding (Can you still be a "lady" by day, if you're a "slut" at night?)

Many girls feel very lonely with their private life and sexual identity not accepted by the "family", *until* they develop close friends. In fact, at this point, sometimes they feel so alienated from their parents that they even hate them. Every little thing the parent does reminds them of that parent's rejection of their identity.

This forcing of the self underground does not strengthen the emotional or psychological development of the person. It puts the individual in turmoil as they try to make sense of the whole picture, as well as their feelings.

Sometimes children who completely reject the "family" at that point are psychologically in better shape than those who do not. Most frequently (out of financial and legal necessity, as well as affection), the individual tries to compromise, and winds up living on several levels at once. This makes her or him feel guilty and cowardly, because she or he feels hypocritical, whoever she or he is with.

Rare acknowledgements of sexuality in the family

Some families acknowledge—to an extent—some of the things that are happening:

"The thing that I like most about my parents is that they trust me. When I am going out, I am not afraid to tell them where I am going or what I am going to do. If I am going to a party where alcohol is being served, I tell them, and they usually respond by telling me to drink in moderation, or spend the night if I do not feel capable of coming home safely. I've told them about kissing and cuddling in the car, but not the details."

"My mother told me about sex when I was six. I asked for a refresher course when I was about eleven and immediately told all my friends—thinking I could hardly wait for it to happen to me. Throughout my teenage years we had long discussions about sex, and I can still talk about it to her (except for premarital sex).

"What she never did mention is my clitoris (Mother, I'll never forgive you), *or* masturbation, oral sex or the different kinds of sexual partners out there (the last probably through lack of experience). She instilled in me a strong will-power over never having sex without birth control or protection from Aids, and thus far I have escaped pregnancy.

"She repeatedly told me sex was a beautiful and wonderful experience, but only in marriage. This hung me up for quite a while and I made many vows to remain a virgin. Then, once I started sex, I vowed to cut it out. Now, I feel I have finally freed myself of this negative attitude about premarital sex. She often tells me about her sex life with my dad, that she reached orgasm on her wedding night and has ever since. I find that hard to believe since she was a virgin, didn't masturbate, I'm sure, and had no prior sexual experience."

"My parents were very up front about nudity and sex. They were not exhibitionists, but they did not 'flip out' on the subject. I was also lucky to be in a public school system that advocated sex education. My parents were available to talk with, although the questions I asked were not so much about the sex act (the books were explicit enough) as about the reasons people wanted to be together in the first place. About love."

Positive patterns in families who *do* talk

There are some truly positive patterns which some families create, keeping the channels open and showing their love and respect for each other.

One woman describes the important discussions she had about sexuality with her mother and father at a critical time during her life:

"The only big scene was when I was eighteen. I became pregnant and had decided to have an abortion. Mom, who had guessed already, spent a whole day talking to me and helping me come to terms with my fears and my decision. She wanted to make sure I was comfortable with what I'd decided. Anyway after I had the pregnancy confirmed, Mom told Dad because he had a right to know. She told him just before I got home and he didn't have time to adjust, and everything came boiling up again when I got back. He hated the boy (said it was all his fault) and on and on.

"Next day Dad took me out for a drink and apologized and talked about the way he felt and why. He then took me through the whole abortion procedure which required signing some papers and talking with the doctor. Then making the appointment, as well as taking me to the actual operation. I got through to the real man for the first time then, the vulnerable and human side, the side that makes mistakes and gets confused. It was a bonding that continues.

"I love both my parents. They work hard at their relationship, and love and respect each other. They're far from perfect and the relationship is not perfect either but they're committed, supportive and kind. If I ever marry I think I have a good example. I can see what the ingredients are for a successful partnership."

And another girl recounts how her father and mother would have a little friendly sex play in front of them, the children—making for an affectionate, happy family atmosphere:

"I grew up in a family where we hugged and kissed each other, my sister and I cuddled in bed at times, and I often saw my parents hug and kiss. I saw my father sometimes tease my mother by feeling her breasts or hips, which she mock-protested about, only because I think she was somewhat embarrassed by his doing that in front of us."

In contrast, another girl with a family who did not talk or prepare her at all, describes her early sexual feelings and how she became pregnant at fifteen:

"I would have loved high school if I'd been more secure. I liked writing, and got good marks. But I was so afraid of the other kids—I didn't come from a 'good home', and I felt beneath them. There was a great pressure on me to dress like the other girls. We just didn't spend money on things like that. Living in the country, I couldn't do sport because of no ride back home if you missed the bus, and nobody to come and get me. I felt out of it and that was one reason I got pregnant. A baby to love and for me to be somebody special to.

"I wanted to date very early because I was pretty and the older boys in high school asked me out. This made me feel good. But I was too immature to cope with sex. I should have done things a lot differently. My parents had had two daughters pregnant already, and I guess they just expected me to follow suit. I did, but I showed everybody that I was different, that I could look after myself and my baby. That's a form of strength that won my father's respect and even my pessimistic brother-in-law's admiration.

"Today my mother and I are best friends—we can talk about anything in the world, she is so straightforward and honest with her feelings. We share poetry and stories and our hurts and happiness. We had our clashes when I was growing up, but when I got pregnant my mom never deserted me, she stood by me, as only a woman would do. I respect her and understand her."

What should parents say?
What about the double standard? Can parents rightly "encourage" girls to take pride in their growing sexuality, without also warning them that "the world" may not understand? Saying "Be a good girl" to a daughter who is dating is not saying anything useful.

It is possible to find a better way of discussing with a daughter the unfortunate existence of the crude labelling of women (the "double standard"), as well as the seduction routines of some men. By doing this, creating an awareness of the situation without distorting her developing ability to relate to others, to love, you will be taking her seriously as a person.

Opening up the topic can be done in terms of talking about what went on in your own life, the questions you had or, if you're really shy, the questions "a friend you knew" had. Before you know it, you'll be able to say all kinds of things. Or, ask her to exchange questionnaire responses to some of the questions you can find in the appendices of this book.

What is parents' fear?

Why don't many parents want to hear what is going on with their daughters? Why do they find it so threatening?

Almost all teenagers feel massive amounts of confusion about "sexual freedom", "women's sexual liberation", the double standard (Are "reputations" still important?), drugs—and especially condoms and Aids or HIV. They have learned, however, not to ask. Their parents are not so good at discussing "touchy issues". And besides getting no information, if you broach these subjects, it can lead to too many questions about "how much" you have been doing . . .

We have seen the strange attitudes and silences with which most parents greet their daughters when they begin to menstruate or develop breasts. Don't they think these events in their lives are beautiful? A wonderful part of growing up?

What is perhaps the most strange is the silence with which so many families react to their daughter starting to date. Having ignored menstruation and even breasts, many parents continue the tradition by also ignoring—or trying to ignore—dating. Once again there is very little acknowledgement given to their daughters of these new interests in her life, not to mention any feelings of joy or of opening up and sharing what happened to them when they were teenagers.

Instead of taking these chances to open up a dialogue, veiled warnings are frequently given to girls about "sex". (Rarely a word about love.) Trite phrases are used, such as, "Avoid getting a reputation," "Be a 'nice girl'," or, "Tell me if you need to see a doctor." This is the atmosphere in which girls find their growing sexuality acknowledged. And sometimes parents, especially fathers, over-react, treating the daughter as if she were already "guilty" somehow (usually related to comments about her manner of dress or her make-up).

In many families, the way girls learn first-hand about the double standard (and to "watch out", i.e., restrict their behaviour and freedom) is either from remarks their father or brothers make, or from television, magazines, and pornography. These remarks may be about other women—the brother's girlfriend(s), or a relative of the family, or a woman walking down the street. Mothers also, of course, make remarks referring to the double standard, but they are usually (almost always) oblique: "Keep your legs together, don't sit sideways in your chair, always be a lady. (Otherwise they may call you a 'tart'.)"*

By this time, a girl already knows that anything to do with her body is non-discussable (having learned this from the silence on masturbation and menstruation), so she continues to try to figure it all out by herself, and go her own way, splitting off even more from the parents' world, the "family"—while still maintaining a life (or one "identity") in it, i.e., living with an increasingly separate double identity.

Loneliness

"When were you the loneliest? Did you ever cry yourself to sleep because of problems with someone you loved? Contemplate suicide? Why?"
Being lonely is generally a condition of being left or let down by someone, or being with someone with whom you cannot be close, with whom you must pretend—not simply of being on one's own or alone. To be with oneself can be a great pleasure.

Many girls feel lonely and alienated when their sexual identity is not accepted by their parents. If they find a friend(s) to talk to, this danger point is usually passed. Without such a friend, the teenage years can be a very unhappy or distressing time.

Girls' suicidal thoughts
A serious danger point in terms of loneliness is high school or just after, perhaps the first year of college or a job, according to many young women here:

"My loneliest time was my first year in high school. For some strange reason that I will never know, I found myself with no friends. My closest friend stopped coming over (we later became friends again) and another girl I was hanging around with did the same. It was also the peak of my mother's alcoholism, which made things worse. I contemplated suicide but I knew that I couldn't because my father was depending on me to take care of the kids. I never cried, I do not cry very much."

* There will be a discussion of the various meanings of "lady", "tart" and other words applied to women in The Hite Report: Twenty Years On, to be published in 1996.

"I was loneliest in college. I had this kind of existential angst. I felt no one could ever have been as lonely as I. I have never felt that way since and I have no idea why."

"When I was thirteen, my mother was in a hospital for a 'nervous breakdown'. Father drank a lot at that period. My uncle interfered with me sexually. I was shabby, spotty and had head lice. I stole some crayons. I tried to hang myself from a strong hook on the bedroom door."

"I was the loneliest right after my parents divorced. Because of this desperate loneliness, I went out with a terrible guy who hurt me over and over again. He was awful, but I was so alone that I always took him back anyhow."

As noted, during the early school years, the parents are generally no longer physically affectionate, thinking the child "too old". The combination of not talking "about things that matter" and little physical affection can create a feeling for the child of being from Planet X. Statistically, the number of suicides of high-school students in the US, and attempted suicides in Germany and the UK, are very high.

A New Attitude, Despite Parents

Perhaps girls will take change into their own hands, even without their parents, as one letter seems to be describing:

"I am fifteen and am sexually experienced, as are many girls my age now. I have a boyfriend. I'm at boarding school. A couple of weeks ago some friends of mine and I brought a copy of *The Hite Report on Female Sexuality* to East Hall, a boys' dorm.

"We got a lot of boys to read it and tell us what they thought. There were about fifteen of us, boys and girls, and we all sat down and talked about it. The response was phenomenal. We learned that they shared a lot of similar feelings with us about lack of real affection during sex. They also learned a lot about women that they had not known before. I must tell you there is a marked difference! I also learned a lot from them about how society had 'brought them up'.

"All I can offer is the hope of a new generation, one that has bridged the gap between '50's views and those of the Me Generation. Something has to be working right if we were able to talk about it together. Your book was the perfect vehicle."

Girls As Best Friends

Fortunately, if most girls can't talk to their parents, they *do* have friends, or usually a "best friend", to whom they can confide everything.

"Did you have a best friend? Did you spend the night at each other's houses? Talk on the phone? What about? How else did you have fun together? Are you still in touch?"
Almost all girls say that they had a special relationship with another girl, a great relationship they love to describe:

"We talked on the phone every day for hours, about *everything*. Some of our most open talks were at 3 a.m. We spent hours on the phone or out on the beach under the sun, especially when the guys we had our eyes on were there. We also had lots of fun roller skating. We discussed how to ask a guy to wear a condom, and how to get out of taking drugs guys offered us without looking uncool."

"My best friend was even closer to me than my boyfriend. We talked every night on the phone about guys, sex, and being fat—although we weren't fat! We baked cookies at least three times a week and gossiped over the bowl of dough. We were inseparable: we snow-mobiled, ski'd, swam, explored the woods, drove, sunbathed and got drunk together (when we had a crisis, like flunked an exam, dented the car, had to make a trip to the dentist). It was wonderful."

"I had a best friend. We did everything together. We slept over at each other's houses. I had a boyfriend, and my boyfriend and I set her up with my boyfriend's best friend. We talked for hours about school, friends, and most of all, about our boyfriends and sex! For the really juicy parts, we kept journals and swapped them."

"We talked on the phone so much that my parents limited me to twenty minutes on the phone and twenty minutes off. We'd talk about everything—boys, school, our latest crush, shopping, brothers, parents (everything except masturbation and sexual likes and dislikes). We also went bowling, to movies, shopping, swimming. This all started in junior high. Then by high school, we went into ideas in more depth. She was pretty and "cool" and a good party-goer, also an idealist and a political

130

activist. One thing I miss about her is she was wonderfully physically affectionate (whereas I could never be physical). She spoke well and wrote beautiful poetry, trying to come to grips with her brother's death—she never could.

"We are still in touch but with a definite strain on the relationship since she has 'come out'. There's this feeling I get now of constantly being left out of the circle. It's a society setting itself apart while complaining it's not being accepted. Lesbian books, artists, musicians—fine. Some of it is well worth paying attention to. But don't let a person's sexuality be an automatic cover, don't close yourself off from the heterosexual world. Too often I hear her say, 'You can't say that . . . I have *a* friend who is straight.' I begin to feel like a token straight friend."

"I had one close girlfriend during high school. We often spent the night together, as well as being almost constantly at each other's homes. We lived just two blocks apart. (The way our telephones were at home, we couldn't talk very privately, so we just came over.)

"We double-dated a lot, and shared all our secrets. But my parents disapproved, they said she was too sexually free. She wasn't really 'sexually free', she just loved to look popular with the guys. We used to go shopping and she would find all the trendiest and crazy stuff. She had a slight weight problem, and was always dieting, fighting her weight. I believe dieting killed her. Well, it wasn't dieting, it was the being-thin syndrome that killed her. She had a massive stroke. She overdosed on diet pills and booze, they caused her death. You can't combine them. I was really torn up and can't believe she's gone. I miss her very much to this day."

Why do girls like their best friends?
"She has velvet eyes, and a very sensual voice. She is honest and fair. When we get together we sit and talk, laugh, and drink coffee. We have an intense friendship."

"I like going out with her, staying over, shopping, writing and phoning. With her, I can be *me*. I feel free and well understood."

"Dancing in the house and hugging. We get together and put on the music, and laugh, sing, talk and cry. When we are together, we show our souls to each other."

"My friend is a magnificent woman: warm, emotional and ambitious. We write letters, phone for hours, talk all night long, go on holidays, and cuddle. I feel relaxed, happy and content when I am with her."

"She is scared of no one. I love this quality. When we are together, time flies. I feel relaxed, inspired, important and that she appreciates me as a person. I'm not afraid to say anything, I can talk about my wildest dreams, and she won't laugh, she encourages me. She makes me feel enthusiastic about everything."

"With my best friend I am confident. I tell her everything."

"We discuss everything, she is my diary. I can be myself, more than at any other time. She likes to hear what I have to say, she really listens, with her eyes as well as her ears. We talk so easily with one another."

Almost all girls, describing their relationship with their best friend, say that with her they feel important, self-confident, and able to express themselves fully, express themselves more than at any other time.

Betrayal, First Gender Disloyalty and Its Consequences

Of course, girls' friendships are not always a bed of roses. Sometimes there can be painful betrayals and break-ups. Often these happen when one or both of the girls feel pressure, sometimes subtle, to choose between a "boyfriend" and the "best friend".

One woman paints a vivid picture of her complicated relationship with her best friend, its various ups and downs, and eventual demise:

"It was a strange friendship. She was my 'ideal' in looks, very dark-haired, olive-skinned and with dark-brown eyes. She was also very physically mature, though she knew nothing of sex. I think on one level she had imbibed from her mother the notion that sex was dirty, disgusting and 'boring'. Yet she was only too happy, on another level, to listen to the filthy jokes I had picked up in the street.

"I often used to stay the night with her at first. I thought it tremendously exciting. She had her own well-furnished room, with an enormous double bed in which we slept, and she always had a tin of chocolate biscuits by the side of the bed, which was a tremendous treat for me. We would lie in bed telling spooky stories and jokes, giggling until the small hours. However, after a while I began to find these overnight stays rather claustrophobic. Susan's devotion to me was intense, and in addition the house itself was oppressive. The curtains were always half down because of her mother's headaches, the house was never aired properly lest she caught a chill.

"Her mother disliked cooking, so they ate nothing but the same dreary round of convenience foods. In addition, Susan was so afraid of incurring her mother's disapproval she wouldn't do anything like drinking a beer, or taking a forbidden bus ride out of her mother's sight. If I tried to persuade her to do something, she would plead a headache—exactly like her mother.

"With her mother's inability to respond to her as a child, Susan began to adopt her mother's 'world-weary' attitude towards everything—particularly 'childish' pursuits. She affected to find Brownies boring, although she joined when she found I was a member. Playing in the street was 'boring', going swimming, riding a bike, going to children's cinema on a Saturday morning—it was all boring! What she maintained she liked most of all was playing cards (as her parents did), playing tennis (ditto), and watching TV.

"What put an end to our friendship eventually was one day when she repeated one of the dirty jokes I told her to her mother, who then complained to mine. I was outraged and disgusted with her for being so stupid and sneaky as to repeat such a joke to her mother.

"From that point on, I started making excuses not to stay overnight, and I found less and less time to spend with her. I began to travel with another set of friends who were more adventurous and exciting."

Sensuality Between Best Friends

It is notable that many of the things girls enjoy doing with their best friends are pleasurable because they are very sensual. This includes trying on clothes together and looking at each other in them, sewing and mending clothes together and talking about where they will wear them and what others will think, sampling make-up and putting make-up on each other, and fixing each other's hair, talking about their "weight" (their bodies), and their skin—almost the same things that their mothers often enjoyed doing with them during those twilight years of close physical intimacy of late childhood.

These are some of the few ways women are "allowed" to touch each other by a society that is terrified that women might "like each other too much".

In their friendships, girls in a way, too, share vicarious sex, sensuality and eroticism. That is, girls together can be sharing vicarious sex by discussing their dates, how it felt to kiss and touch a boy, how it felt when he touched them or explored their body (and "how far"), what he said and how they felt.

As one girl describes it:

"It was a wonderful time when I first began getting attention from boys. I was very happy. My friends and I spent hours talking about clothes, experimenting with make-up and going places where we knew we'd see boys . . . Those were my favourite relationships. I'm always trying to get one back."

Can girls love each other?
Should girls break off their friendships with their best friends in order to focus on boys? The assumption is that "mature" women should turn their allegiance and love towards men exclusively. Yet why should women break off these marvellous friendships with each other?

The evidence of the research presented in this book suggests that there is no "heterosexual sex drive" that asserts itself at "puberty" separately from the strong social pressures to direct one's sexual feelings and desire to have sex at members of the opposite sex. Therefore most people focus their feelings in that direction. Many times this has a happy result: it is not that these feelings are false or "bad", rather that they are a response to social pressure—sexuality is being directed in a certain way. It could have been more fluid. If we were living in a different "social order", it very well might be.

The evidence of this research demonstrates that there is a multitude of affections, sensualities and personae latent in almost all children and adults, but that to fit the social system, these feeling are directed and channelled, especially at "puberty", to fit the patriarchal (father-ownership) model of the family and world. In psychological terms, this means that all eyes must be trained to focus on the male: all emotional, psychological, and sexual attention must be fixed on the father, with one exception: boys must be made to see girls as sexual objects of desire (reproductive objects of desire).

Love Affairs Between Best Friends

Statistically it is quite rare for girls as best friends to become lovers, while it is relatively common for boys. One young woman describes having had a sexual relationship with her best friend:

"I had a best friendship in high school which turned into a sexual relationship and lasted about two years. Over the years, we have managed to keep in touch, but on rare occasions. She is a lesbian, and I am not. At one time, this part of my past disturbed me a great deal, but now I consider it a fairly usual, but private, part of growing up."

Another in her late teens describes her best friend, who is also the one she loves, with great happiness:
"My girlfriend, best friend, is blonde with beautiful eyes, very

sweet, sexy, and gentle. She can make me laugh when I am down, and she kisses me. She lives upstairs above me, so often we eat together. I like our airy, gay, chattery times. What do I like least? When she tries to be mothering. It's the most important relationship I have had with a woman in my life: being in love, making love to her."

What is a "lesbian"? Can girls be affectionate and intimate with each other, perhaps just sleeping together without having "sex", or maybe kissing and embracing, cuddling up while watching television or listening to records, without having to apply any label to their feelings, or society judging them? And without having to make any momentous decisions about "what it all means" in their lives?

Another girl, seventeen, is in love with her best friend, but will never tell her so:

"I am deeply in love with a woman, but we are not sexually involved in any way. I am closer to her than anyone.

"My mother does not know how to be affectionate. She was never endearing, gentle, or sweet. I love her, but as a fourteen year old who was very, very vulnerable, I needed a woman's touch badly and she was not there for me at all. I like my father's acceptance of me, no matter how strange I look or feel, even though I dislike his domineering attitude. For several years my hair was spiked and bright purple. Mom hated it, but Dad had the insight to smile.

"I do have a best friend of eight years. We spend many hours together, often she will sleep over at my house, or vice versa, and we go out. We talk on the phone phenomenal hours, always about horses.

"My first mature sexual experience occurred at sixteen, and I felt very ashamed, yet gratified. It was with a woman. Nobody knew it happened.

"I am deeply, richly in love now. How can I tell? Because I look in her eyes and my soul in that instant belongs to her. I want to give her everything I have, yet sex must be omitted, for she is happily married and would never dream of it. I tell her 'I love you' and into that single phrase I pour all the need, shame, gratitude, and vulnerability I have ever felt. In that one pure instant of beauty, my mind falls away into the black eternity of space, and I am released. My eyes are bright with tears at the miracle of her, and I know I have glimpsed heaven.

"I have often cried myself to sleep because of bitter fights with my parents, although I love them. Also, violent problems with a beloved horse I had caused me many nights of tears. I am happiest with my seventy-seven-year-old, delightful grandfather. He is the easiest person to relate to I've ever known. He's so sensitive.

"It is wonderful to be in love. It is a constant state of asking pertinent questions and leaving the answers open. It is music, it is intense, flamboyant joy and sharp pain. Often the pain is caused by my regrets at my failure to communicate, rather than anything she says. Love is important enough to gladly, freely die for.

"I often crave love and affection. It is a desperate need. I have an intense desire to be held and understood.

"I never talk to my mother. I know she masturbates, as I found her vibrator. I would like to talk to her about this, but feel she would never understand. She is not sensitive or caring at all, and I would need a hug and physical reassurance from her very badly to be able to talk.

"I'm ashamed to admit it, but what I like is to feel a woman's breast in my mouth. I like to masturbate her. I have never given a woman oral sex. I am afraid to try it but I would like to. I like to be masturbated, but a delicate balance must be achieved if I want to orgasm while someone other than myself is doing it to me. I like it vaginally but it is extremely sensitive.

"During masturbation, I fantasize about my coming on a woman's breasts, about a male transvestite, about oral sex on satin sheets and about Prince."

We have seen that the great majority of teenage girls have a best friend with whom they share their feelings, experiences and plans for the future. Although it is a small minority who have a physical, sexual relationship, these are usually very loving friendships and mean a lot to the girls involved.

A handful of young girls do not seem to have these close friendships—and one young woman is clearly feeling pressured by the question's "expectation":

"I do not have a best friend. Do you have to anyway?"

Of course, no one *has* to have a best friend. Approximately 10 per cent of girls who answered do not have a close or "best" woman friend. But since most girls and women seem to enjoy these friendships so much, it could definitely be something worth trying.

Chapter 5

Mothers and Daughters: Lovers and Strangers

Girls and Their Mothers: Adoration and Contempt

"I felt secure in knowing my mother loved me beyond all else; I believed she even loved me more than she loved my father, my sister or even herself. I thought she was the most beautiful mother in the world."

"She was the disciplinarian in our family, but strangely, though I see her that way, I can only remember being spanked once."

"I admire strong women, intelligent women, independent women. My mother was a wimp."

"A perpetual sense of guilt, that's what I feel about my mother."

"The woman I have loved the most in my life is my Mom. She is supportive—strong, intelligent, beautiful and creative. She taught me everything from how to make cookies to inspiring me to have a career. My mother is the greatest woman I have ever known. She did everything for me I ever needed. I can only hope to become half the woman she is."

The relationship most crucial to disrupt and destroy in patriarchy is that between mother and daughter.* Any natural feelings of physical closeness or desire, love, must be stamped out, forbidden, lest women become too strong through their belief and trust in each other.

Patriarchal ideology is emphatic on this point. Thus, through centuries of indoctrination, we have arrived at the place now where we consider it the most "unnatural" and unlikely thing that daughters would ever be emotionally or sensually attracted to their mother. Or vice versa. And yet it is considered "normal" that fathers and daughters at

---

* Why? The pre-patriarchal social system was based on this relationship, inheritance went through women, as it did in early Egyptian history. Is its existence, for example in the increasing number of single-mother families today, a threat?

137

least notice each other sexually. Mothers are the butt of jokes, and almost constantly depicted as "nagging", no fun, and too "demanding".

Father-dominant ideology severely enforces the separation of women in order to maintain its own system. Women must serve the cause of male dominance in the family, support men emotionally and physically, through housework and sometimes sexuality, or through emotional comforting. Daughters must not see mothers as Number One figures, equally powerful as men. Children in patriarchy must "belong" to the father, physically and psychologically. This is how the patriarchal family system is maintained.

Yet we are seeing a new kind of relationship emerge between mothers and daughters, especially within the last short twenty years. When I began investigating mother–daughter relationships in the 1970's, I found a large number of girls and young women absolutely despising their mother, yet all thinking that they were individually and uniquely reaching this conclusion about "her".

Today, in the 1990's, a majority of young women describe positive feelings for and experiences with their mother—even though they still have a large number of complaints! Fights are by no means a thing of the past, nor are feelings of conflict, nor is the old saying, "I hope I'm not like my mother." But there is definite, palpable change. Who has changed? The daughters? The mothers? We all have.

"I Hope I'm Not Like My Mother!"

Girls' attitudes of condescension to their mother

Things are changing between mothers and daughters, but still most daughters react almost with horror when asked the question, "Do you want to be like your mother?"

"If I grow up to be like my mother, I'll put a gun to my head"

Women of varied social classes, races and backgrounds vehemently state that they don't want to be like their mothers. Why?

"I am afraid of being anything like her—even to the point of hating myself for looking similar to her. I hate the thought of old age because I think I will get to look more and more like her. Psychologically, I am working to separate from her upbringing of me and find my own identity."

What *is* this fear we have of being like our mother? Is it fear of being second class, not important, not counting? Of developing subservient behaviour? Or is it fear of being considered "unattractive" and "old"? Or all of these?

Many girls and women muse over how much they are like their mother:

"In many ways I am very much like my mother. I worry about things like she does, and like her, I try much too often to please everyone."

"I didn't like it when my mom tolerated stupid people or went along with things they said. I worry when I see myself now being a mirror of this sometimes."

139

"Why doesn't she stand up to him? Leave him?"
The basic reason most women give for not wanting to be like their mother is, "She let my father treat her so badly, so condescendingly," "She didn't fight back enough," "She didn't have enough pride," "She was a wimp."

One woman remembers the very day when she first realized that her mother was conscious of the dominance of her father, but would do nothing about it:

"I thought she didn't understand how badly Dad treated us, but one day when I was grown she said something that made me realize that *she had known all along.* I was angry with her for years after that. I asked her *why* she hadn't done something about it—and she shrugged. That was all. She shrugged. It took me years to get over that."

According to my research for this study, the majority of women coming from two-parent families feel great ambivalence and distress in relation to their mother: 73 per cent feel a deep love and tie, but also great disappointment or anger about her subservience, "passivity", or even "cowardice" in the face of her husband's domination.

"I longed to be close to her, but she was so repressed and dominated by my father that she rarely expressed her true feelings. She was a full-time mother and housewife. I felt very protective of her when I was young, impatient at her lack of guts when I was older. She died five years ago—having devolved until she was unable to make any independent decisions and seemed extremely depressed. I feel anger at the waste."

"My mother is the world's greatest victim. She never took control of her life. But I've got to say, she is getting better. She has more self-confidence now at sixty-four than ever in the past. I am so pleased for her. Am I like my mother? I never wanted to be like her, hate it when I am . . . when I am the 'victim' of life, when I get too needy, when I have high approval needs. I resent her passing those things on to me. I mostly make it okay, but not all the time."

"My mother was a doormat for my father—very passive and mousy, very little-girlish. She gave up being a nurse to raise his four children. She spent her life searching for dirt and trying to contrive the appearance of normal, presentable children for her lord and master. For her, we were to say thank you at the right times, match the décor, and never express ourselves. My father used to make himself feel like a big man; my mother was supposed to be pleased we fitted into her fairy-tale of the nuclear family, and said thank you and smiled."

"My mom tried to argue but my dad would never respond, which to me at the time made her look foolish. My father's attitude toward Mom was not to get as 'worked up' as her, because he was 'above it'. He looked superior to me. Mother's attitude: You have to work around him in order to get what you want from him."

"My father really treated my mother like dirt. The only time I ever heard him communicate with her, it was to scold her and refuse to eat his favourite Friday-night supper, tuna fish, because it wasn't on a bulky roll, it was on bread."

Many also lament what they see as their mother's "whitewashed" or too "nice" personality.

"My mother was a good mother, stable, loving, wise, patient, soft-spoken, a hard worker, never complained. In fact, a living martyr! In other words, she was not really human, never showed any weaknesses, never was overtly sexual, and only slightly affectionate. She was responsible and dutiful. She didn't work outside the home: she was a full-time mother. She screwed me up a lot when I was a teenager. Now she is tired, resigned, slightly spaced out."

"I admire her. She always does what needs to be done, and has withstood all the hard parts of her life with intelligence and grace. Still, it would have been better for us if she had stood up to my father, had been more open, less prone to ignore our pleas for help or communication."

"The prevailing philosophy was that everything was okay if it *looked* okay. We were encouraged to hide our emotions, any strange or bad behaviour was ignored or scorned, never explained or discussed. If something bad happened to us, we were to pretend nothing had happened, and get on with life."

"I notice she is always smiling. I sometimes don't know whether it is what she really feels, or if she has been doing it all her life and just can't help it."

When daughters speak thus about their mother, their frustrated, conflict-ridden and often guilty-sounding comments all reflect one thing: the pain young women* feel on viewing the second-class status of women within the nuclear family, their desire for their mother to free herself and for themselves not to repeat the same pattern.

* Boys feel this pain too; see Part III.

Gender Roles: Still with Us

"How did your father treat your mother? Your mother treat your father?"
"My parents were not affectionate in front of me. They argued about almost everything. Dad taught me to respect my mom, but that her ideas were wrong and radical. She taught me to respect him but that he was not perfect."

"My father would call my mom 'Mother'. I always thought that was strange. He talked to her like she was *his* mother. On the surface, he was respectful, but he liked to 'get away with things' behind her back—like with a mother. And also, his attitude to her was like she was a 'tired old thing'."

"My father would occasionally slap my mother on the fanny. She would kiss him goodbye in the morning and hello at night. (My mom was a full-time mother and homemaker). My father never really reciprocated. They never hugged (except during family tragedy) or held hands. They never argued because my mother refused to argue, she would just keep silent. My father could rant and rave at my mother on a regular basis. My father's attitude towards my mother taught me that women were inferior. My mother taught me that the man was always boss and was to be served unquestioningly."

"I don't like my father's attitude toward Mom. Mom is sometimes subservient to Dad, sometimes domineering. She tells him what to do, and if he's indifferent enough, he'll do as she says. She is subservient in that she never asks him to do something just for her. If Dad comes home late and Mom is tired, she'll still make him an elaborate meal. She'll complain behind his back, but she does it."

Mother Blaming*

Should younger women blame their mother for "passivity" in the face of the limited options most women faced? Aren't many of the compromises women have been making based on economic necessity and the pressure of centuries of stereotyped attitudes? And how "perfect" are younger women, the daughters, today?

Why do so many girls and women retain such negative feelings towards their own mother? Is it fear, as one boy says, that we as women will get pulled into the same outlook and the same role if we "understand" too much?

* Terminology originated by Paula J. Caplan, Phyllis Chessler, Rachel J. Siegel, and Janet Surrey for the 1988 Godard Conference on Motherhood. (See *Woman-Defined Motherhood*, eds Jane Price Knowles and Ellen Cole (Harrington Park Press, New York and London, 1990); and The Haworth Press, *Motherhood: A Feminist Perspective*, a special issue of *Women and Therapy*.) These discussions are turned on their head in 1980's "post-feminist" "backlash" rhetoric: "Our 'feminist mothers' were too angry and militant, younger women now can be loving and pleasant!" See *Backlash: The Undeclared War Against Women*, by Susan Faludi (London, Chatto and Windus, 1992).

How Many Girls Admire Their Father More?

"I liked her but I thought her a bit lightweight beside my father." Many girls identify with their father rather than with their mother because fathers have higher status, greater freedom and independence, more right to say what they think, and greater financial power. This is not to say that fathers cannot be good fathers; despite the paradoxes, the closeness and feeling of support that some girls enjoy from their father are extremely important to them. Yet some of those who identify with their father are really identifying with the archetype, the symbol of power.

It was disconcerting to note in my earlier research that neither the majority of women (*Women and Love*) nor the majority of men (*Hite Report on Men and Male Sexuality*) felt angry with their father over the issue of their mother's status. Women's "passivity" was seen as the mother's problem, while little cognizance was given to the economic and social factors which may have made a woman accept humiliating situations at home. Very little blame or criticism was directed towards men who allowed these situations to go on, and benefited from them.

While most women in this study are very angry with their mother for not standing up for herself, they are not usually as angry with their father for treating their mother as "second-class" although, when asked, 92 per cent state that their father clearly did have condescending attitudes.

Yet according to my new research, there is now a decrease in the number of women who say they felt closer to and admired their father more as they were growing up. (See Chapter 6 for girls' attitudes to their father today.)

There is a corresponding increase in the number of girls who are angry with their father because of his attitude to their mother:

"My father had nothing to do with anything in the house. He didn't even know how to make a pot of coffee. He went to work in the morning, he came home at night . . . and he was waited on by my mother, who also went out to work. I felt a great deal of contempt for him."

How Girls Are Taught to Turn Their Attention to Men

Mothers' messages to daughters about their father: "Don't upset and contradict your father"

Girls are taught in the subtlest of ways to let men lead:

"My mother told me to try to remain in peace with my father, not to oppose him."

"I was taught that, when I was in the presence of my father, I should do what he says. Not make him angry. Later, when he was not around, I could relieve my feelings."

Though this sounds almost the same as girls being taught simple "politeness", in fact, through the guise of just learning "good breeding", or to show "ordinary sympathy and understanding", girls are being taught their "place". And that as girls they are of "secondary importance".

Girl's often feel like traitors, because while they side with their mother to some extent, they also feel that their fathers are more fun, dynamic, exciting.

How can girls have a good self-image if they think their mother is subservient, ineffectual and ultimately inconsequential? If girls are taught subtly and convincingly that women are less important—and believe it—this leaves them in a situation of either feeling self-hatred, or identifying with the father and with "male" values.

How seriously can we take ourselves as long as attitudes that "female ways" are second class are internalized and unquestioned?

1990's: Girls' New Esteem

One of the most remarkable changes seen in this research data is how in the 1990's so many women in their teens and twenties say they think being a woman is a *fine* thing—even if they still say they don't want to be like their mother, though they no longer look down on her.

Many girls and young women say they like women's range of emotional expression:

"I'm proud to be a woman. I'm more free than if I were a man. I can be myself without 'power behaviour'. Women have a lot more freedom."

"As a woman, I can do what I want, I can be both male and female. I can do 'men's jobs', and as a woman, I am allowed to look beautiful and wear make-up!"

"I like being able to express the emotions and sociability of a woman. I am more free this way than a man would be."

"I like being a woman because I understand the world better than if I were a man."

Is this a new attitude on the part of women? Ten years ago it would have been said that men had more freedom and privilege. Women were called "too emotional", and "silly" because they liked the sensual pleasures of clothing and enjoying their bodies. It was then rarely recognized that men are generally stifled in the area of emotionality.

When women say they enjoy expressing their personality and emotions freely—in ways that men rarely do or are not "allowed" to do—this points to a new pride in being female.

Another surprise is the outspoken, positive feeling so many young women now express about women's bodies; they say they like their bodies—women's bodies—and their sensuality, sexuality:

"I like my beautiful body and I have my freedom to fight for—although that's terrifying now and then."

"I like women's bodies. You have the ability to get pregnant, and I just think it is beautiful to be a woman."

"I love my body. I like to dress beautifully, use my sex appeal and enthusiasm."

"I like the feminine art of seduction. I think women are beautiful."

"I like to bask as a woman in the arms of a man, or behave like a 'vamp'. I want to get rid of the saying 'stupid blonde'."

"I am gay and I like flirting with other women, using charm as a way of managing things."

Overall, there is a lot of enthusiasm for being a woman:

"Why do I want to be a woman? I would not like to miss the women-to-women sphere. Being a woman is the most beautiful thing on earth."

What's wrong with it?

"I pity the fact that you are not taken as seriously by other people, and the fact that you are seen as a woman and not a person."

146

"What are women's best qualities?"
A full 85 per cent of the women in this study under twenty-five speak highly of women's qualities, describing them thus:

"Warmth, emotionality, social abilities; they are not as tough and egotistical as men. Women are more honest and loving."

"Their friendliness, ordinariness, braveness, elegance."

"Organizing, listening, adjusting, appreciating. I think a woman is more of a human being than a man."

"Sparkling, playful, considerate, creative."

"Emotional adultness, emotional independence, concern for other people's emotional state, talent for organization. Their insight into themselves is more clear than men's, less one-sided."

"Women have developed better emotionally. They have intuition, ability to see things the way someone else does."

"Women are emotionally rich. They can empathize, think the way someone else does."

"Their energy, humour, frankness. Their ability to talk, their non-violence."

"Women are more beautiful, sensitive, and understanding than men."

The Thatcher versus "femininity" debate
But despite this, issues related to their feelings about their mother not standing up to their father are raised again about female politicians. Several comment, with regard to Margaret Thatcher, that to have power like this, a woman has to become "male" in her thinking and behaviour:

"Thatcher types are powerful, women who conform to the male world."

"When a woman wants to get a powerful position in politics, she has to become like a man (Thatcher). I don't think many women want to lower themselves to that."

One twenty-three year old seems to be debating with herself about whether it might be worth it, at least to get some space, some respect:

"I did not always agree with Thatcher, but she was listened to, she was respected."

A new power: feminine power

But some young women declare that women today *can* have power, and this is how:

"Who has power? Independent women, with power over their own lives."

"Power appears when women make choices in favour of themselves and stand up for what they are doing."

Women's New Positive Feelings for Their Mother

In the 1990's, there is now an emerging spirit of respect and understanding between mothers and daughters: most women still describe their mother as "giver" but 30 per cent see this as positive rather than "wimpy":

"Mom was a full-time mom and home manager. I liked her a lot. I admired her beauty and sociability until I was teenager. Like her I can't concentrate on my own pleasures until I clear the table, so to speak, get home duties out of the way; I feel I have to help everyone (less than she does)."

"What I like most about my mother is her giving, loving nature. She's never cross. She's seldom unfair. She's always there to give encouragement unless my father interferes. Like when I was pregnant, my mother had to go along with my father's decisions. She always accepted her role as second-class citizen. It wasn't until my father had a big love affair with a woman he'd gone with for years earlier that my mother got the courage to leave him."

"My mother is kind, generous, funny, beautiful, and easy-going. Perhaps it was her gentle, giving nature that made her a victim, but all she ever showed us was her courage."

"My mother was perfect: always patient, always giving, caring, understanding, supportive, always on my side no matter what."

"My mother is the person I've loved most in my life. I'm very close to her, both physically and emotionally, still. She is warm, understanding, stable and dependable. She's much the same now, except she seems increasingly dissatisfied with her life and my father."

"My mother's affection was verbal endearment and facial understanding when my father was very angry and unreasonable. She was a dedicated caretaker of others. She was always tired, but could really be there when needed. Like when one of us was sick, she could be very tender and nurturing."

148

"She is a great listener and should have been a therapist, she's so good at supporting. She's too traditional in that she does the cooking and cleaning while he does the lawn, but she's always growing and can always see the bright side. I only hope I can be half the woman she is. She also has her head on her shoulders. She was a homemaker, then she went out to work when Dad went bankrupt in the early 1970's."

One woman explains how she and her mother have a relationship based on mutual respect, each understanding that their lives have been and are different, but that this does not matter:

"I am and always was emotionally and physically close to my mum. She had always shared the emotional and practical details of her life with me. We were a team, though now that she lives away, our lives are separate. Mum was a housewife while my sister and I were young. She nursed her mum (whose house we lived in) until I was eight. By the time I was hitting adolescence, she had really established her own personality and will and was determined to live her own life. She took little jobs which my dad tried to persuade her were against her own interest, but she persistently held out and eventually got a responsible job with a large firm.

"Throughout my teens, we spent a lot of time together, as friends and companions. My dad worked shifts and so we often used to have the house to ourselves in the evenings. We'd watch TV programmes we wanted and then discuss the issues together. We grew politically aware and educated each other. Today her life with my father is as emotionally unsatisfying as ever and she misses our special closeness, but she also knows I have to go my own way.

"I think I am like her in terms of being a person who responds in a loving, caring way, but I'm also aware of how life has treated her and have learned not to be manipulated in the same ways, i.e., not to be as forgiving, and self-sacrificing, and hopefully not as dissatisfied on a personal level. I know I couldn't live my life through other people the way she has done."

Three women whose lives have changed enormously from their mother's more restricted situation, describe their complicated feelings for their mother:

"My mother worked full time as long as I can remember. She was my mother *and* father. My father drank his money away, so she had to work to survive. I remember how I used to cry when my mother would go to work at night. I never let her know though, I used to just cry to myself. She worked from about 6 p.m. to 3 a.m., cocktail waitress.

149

"I used to fantasize how, someday, I could just hide in the back seat of our car and wait for her to finish work. I was very afraid of my father and hated being home alone with him. He abused my brother physically; he was terribly, terribly abused. I was not spanked a lot, by luck, but mentally abused and brainwashed. I was extremely close to my brother. He was my friend and my provider, when there was no one there. He tried to protect me and took me under his guidance.

"My mother had many jobs later, secretary, fashion show co-ordinator, real estate agent, school teacher (Sunday), and switchboard operator. I remember as a child, my mother applying for jobs that called for a 'male', and her arguing why she couldn't at least try! Although you won't see her go out of the house without lipstick on and she never wore trousers before I turned twenty-five, she knew her stuff. So there were never any sexist roles as far as she was concerned.

"Now I think she's wonderful. She had a very difficult life and tried in vain to find happiness. She is still looking, I think, for the 'ultimate' happiness."

"I have never been really close to my mother, we are worlds apart. She's been working in the restaurant since I was in the 7th grade (part time) along with full-time housewife duties. I get the feeling that she resents the fact that I have more options about my future than she had. She was raised to believe that she should get married and have a family, period. Nothing else. I think that she resents the fact that I have the option of choosing my own career, that I'm going to college and she never did. I love my mother, but it's hard for me to find qualities in her that I admire."

Ambivalence—understanding, yet pain:

"My mother was a farm wife, she worked farm-wife work, from dawn to dark. She was curious about human nature and read the semi-psychological articles in women's magazines and *Reader's Digest* and talked to me of her dissatisfactions. She never supported me in any of my career aims, and laughed at my plans. Now, I have been away from home over twenty years. When we are together there are long, long silences. She waits until immediately before I am to leave before bringing up any subject (my divorce, for example) that particularly bothers her, so that she will have just enough time to state her opinion and I won't have time enough to refute it.

"Every few months she will write an accusatory letter (we write once a week each, as we have since I went to college) about whatever my current situation is. I try to explain with a ten-page letter in response, to which she often does not reply, or she might respond that she ought to know better than try to give me any advice or voice her opinion anyway since I've never really paid attention to her. Still, I have finally come to believe that she really wanted me to get away from the farm (as I think she wished she could have), but couldn't help feeling envious. My climb into the middle class was always a reminder of what she didn't do. I think she is now totally unable to understand my relative contentment with my life as it is. I do not think she can begin to understand that a woman can live alone, do her work, and have warm and close relationships with her daughters. (This too is possibly a kind of accusation about what she doesn't have.)

"My most pained little moments are when I glance in a mirror and see myself making a facial expression like hers. I try very hard not to have that same bitterness she had. When I catch it in a comment, or seem to echo her, I stop myself. Then feel upset for hours or days as I think about it and fear having her attitude when I grow older. This long description seems to me to barely skim the surface of this relationship."

Another young woman expresses pity and contempt, all mixed up with rage and love, for her mother:

"When I was fourteen I had a pretty good idea that she was 'sneaking around' behind my father's back. That made me feel strange. I wasn't really mad at her, but I felt like I should tell my dad. I didn't, though, which in turn made me feel guilty for not telling him. So, instead of trying to do anything about something which wasn't even my business, I ran away.

"I was close to my father in a way, but we never talked about anything that was really important to me. He did try to talk to me a few times after I ran away. By then it was too late.

"I guess I have felt sorry for my mother all my life. I do not like to spend time with her, she is constantly complaining about how fat she's become or how her hair looks or how she wants to divorce my dad and marry the guy she has been seeing since I was fourteen.

"Actually, it is more like I am the mother and she is the daughter. I do love my mother a great deal; I just wish she would 'grow up'. Still, I respect her for working so hard at her job all these years, and not really complaining that much.

"Now, we have not communicated at all since before my son was born. She was apparently disgusted and horrified that I could have a baby without being married. She seemed unhappy with her life the last time I saw her, she drinks a lot of beer and smokes packs of cigarettes a day. I feel I cannot communicate with her because of the alcohol. I haven't seen her in almost two years; when I am with her I feel sort of bored and depressed, she doesn't like to talk about things—issues, or philosophy, or new ideas or anything. When I left the last time, we both had tears in our eyes, like so much was left unsaid, and never could be said."

Girls Cheer Their Mother's Revolt

"I admire my mother very much. It does my heart good to see her standing up to my dad after years of her waiting on him hand and foot. She is much more her own person now. She thinks about herself while taking care of her family."

Girls with single mothers—whatever other problems there may (or may not) have been—almost always report a different picture of their mothers than that of a "wimp":

"Without a father around was a great way to grow up. There were no male or female roles in our house. Mom taught both my brother and me how to do housework, then he and I would have 'trades'. I liked to iron so I did all the ironing, he liked to vacuum so he did that."

Of course, some women are growing up with good family relationships all around:

"As a child I was very close to both of my parents. They both did and still do love me. I loved the way that my mother made me feel special, being the only girl in the family. The thing that I didn't like was that she was always busy, and sometimes I felt forgotten. My father was always one to encourage family outings at the weekends, which seemed an imposition on my free time as a teenager, but looking back on it now I realize he wanted us to know that, despite the fact that he worked six days a week and travelled a lot, he loved us all and wanted to spend time with us. Many of my friends never had this type of close, warm family relationship; it is only now that I am away from them that I can appreciate how much they did for me, and how happy we were."

"My folks were always polite to each other and friendly. I don't remember *ever* seeing them argue. They always presented a united front. Each instilled a sense of the importance of the other and backed up the other's authority—no chance of, 'But Dad said I could . . .' I believe very strongly that they were very happy together."

Mothers tell their side of it

A mother (aged seventy-two, "and finally single!") explains, from her point of view, why women stay in poor marriages and behave like "victims":

"Children are such a deciding factor in what a woman can or cannot do—or at least, they were in the past.

"My experience of marriage from 1945 to 1990 with four children hampered my self-expression. My husband was mean with money and drank a little too much, but any anger I had subsided by the time he got home, the children were in bed and I could express it. Often I felt glad of this, but over time I also built up deep resentments, which possibly damaged the children too.

"One thing he did was give away our savings. Having saved four years at my expense, my husband then started handing out sums of money (wildly beyond my dreams) to his three sisters and two young daughters. I raged at him and tried to oppose it. Finding that that didn't change anything, when my youngest was eight I started a four-year, part-time teacher training course. Eventually I taught for eight years until I was sixty, retirement age.

"What happened during those years? Well, it is something like my mother's marriage. As a child, my father's dominance and ill temper disgusted me, but in retrospect I assume that my mother's acceptance of it was due to an unwillingness to fight in front of three children. Also, he suffered from asthma quite badly, so she probably 'made allowances'.

"Now, after years of caring for my husband in his last illness, I am happy, healthy (I hope) and enjoying a freedom I have never before experienced. It is good. At the same time I adore my four children, their spouses and eight grandchildren."

"Surrogate mothers"★

Of course, not all these mothers are biological mothers; many girls are close to a "surrogate mother". It is the *relationship* that is important, the mother doesn't have to be the biological mother in order for the whole spectrum of feelings to be there:

"I was closest to my maternal grandmother. My grandmother doted on me, listened to me, wasn't critical, was always supportive, and I always

---

★ Here and throughout this book, the term "mother" or "father" refers to the *relationship* with the child, whether or not there are biological ties.

felt that she loved me no matter what I did and would never turn away from me. She was sweet and funny and absent-minded—one of those people who always had to be busy. I felt closer to her than to my own mother."

Why Do Teenage Girls Fight With Their Mother?

Most girls remember a very special intimacy and warmth with their mother when they were small children:

"Mom told me I was 'a very nice girl', and showed me she loved me by romping with me, cuddling me, and making sure I could go to the school I wished to go to. Giving me a lot of freedom."

"Between us there was lots of warmth, embracing, saying sweet things, calling each other darling."

"She told me she was proud of me, she backed me up."

And yet, around the age of twelve–thirteen, just after "tomboyhood", girls begin to resent their mother, fights break out:

"My mother told me she loved me, we cuddled a lot when I was small. Later, when I was about fourteen, we had clashes about my appearance and about my father."

"When I was a child, I had a lot of freedom. I liked it very much. Then from my tenth birthday, they became more strict and allowed me less. I felt imprisoned, their prisoner."

"When I was a child, she made me feel secure, she cuddled me and told me I was sweet. Then, especially from my fourteenth birthday, we had conflicts about school reports, my behaviour, my friends. She did not like most of my friends and got angry when I started to get what she called 'unruly'."

"They Took Away My Freedom"

Why does this early closeness change? How does the intimacy of earlier years get lost, so that eventually most girls reach a stage at which they feel their mothers are "wimps" who don't "stand up for themselves"?

Fights between mothers and daughters come about because, as we have seen in Chapter 3, the "family" (the society) is trying to tame girls' rebelliousness, in a way that isn't done/wouldn't be done with boys, and mothers are delegated to the role of family "policeman" to carry out this job.

In the code of "feminine" behaviour which most mothers believe they should teach their daughters, to "prepare them properly" for the society that awaits them, boys are allowed much more leeway: "Boys will be boys", but girls must not "throw tantrums", must smile and "calm down", not "go out and make a spectacle of themselves" by doing daring things. Boys are encouraged to be more adventurous, not docile.

Further, a mother may believe that she does not have the right to tell the boy what to feel or how to behave, that he is already becoming her superior (and to "interrupt his development" will "damage his manhood"), whereas with the daughter there is more a feeling that if a daughter "has her own mind", this "rebelliousness" is not a sign of growth, but an indication that she is "uppity". Her thoughts are not so important.

Most mothers (and of course fathers are participating heavily in this genderizing system, frequently in covert ways, in the role of "good policeman", as seen in the following chapter) do not realize they are participating in the genderizing of girls. Like mothers in Africa who force clitoridectomy on their daughters, these Western mothers truly believe they are bringing up a proper, charming and socially acceptable individual. Girls who fight back are simply "rebellious", and need even more to be "tamed".

The family system disrupts mother–daughter relationships

The family system gives women in families two mutually incompatible roles: to be the nurturing provider of love (for the children and father), and to be the family's/system's police. This is hardly fair; how can one person be both? It means she will be distrusted, disrespected, and, worst, maybe not really loved, even after all the love and care she is supposed to provide.

Mothers as the Family Police

Mother "understands" but gently represses . . .

Mothers are caught—or have frequently been—in an impossible bind. The archetypal mother role means being, in most cases, the mediator between the father and the children. Not only is this an untenable position for the usual reasons (such as those union arbitrators feel), but also because the mother is mediating between two cultures, and feeling such torn loyalties inside herself.

On the one hand, she has to be a "good" mother (i.e., asexual in front of the children, in patriarchal households), and also represent the father and teach the girl(s) the rules of propriety, how they must be "different" from boys, and somehow make them accept "as a privilege" that they face more restrictions. On the other hand, she knows in her heart what it is like to be a girl, and she knows (probably) the secrets of female sexuality, and that it is unfair for her girls to grow up, as they probably will, to be considered second-class citizens by many, having to fight much harder for their rights and respect than men.

But she must deny herself, her own female life experience, if she wants to be loyal, or help her daughter "fit into the system". She must teach the daughter that "reality" is "male" reality. This means that the girl must accept a split identity and learn to believe/behave/know that men are more entitled to run the world, or that their power cannot be effectively challenged (!), or to do so would be incredibly dangerous.

This is to betray oneself, as a woman, but she feels she must do it to be a "good mother". No wonder so many daughters come to see their mother as a "wimp", and despise her, at the same time knowing that their mother loves them, no matter what.

What are the fights about?
Girls explain the multitude of little ways clashes come about:

"Things my mother did not like about me: puberty, school, disco. In other words, my 'wild', independent life. She told me it would get me into trouble. But she never told my brother that, he had freedom."

"She criticized what she termed my sassiness and love of ease. The fights always started when I was disobedient."

"She says I am too noisy, telephone too much, talk too loud, spend too much money, learn too little. When I use the telephone more than a quarter of an hour, she says I have to be more serious. She also said this when I went on a winter sport holiday, despite the fact that I had no money!"

"We argue about her being a lesbian, and my coming home late, where have I been?"

"We began fighting about sex, when I began the pill."

"We argued whenever I was critical of her, or when I told her I thought she was too dependent."

"When I made love to my boyfriend in her house without asking."

"She was always giving me a talking to: for being late, my clothes, eating, cleaning up, too many purchases."

"When I was dating a 'dark' boyfriend."

"When I was thirteen, I had to wear certain shoes. Ugly brown shoes, such as boys wore. I felt embarrassed when wearing those shoes. I rebelled, but she insisted on me obeying her. I ended up leaving the house, wearing the most ugly shoes in the world. I think she needs help, she's been unhappy for years."

"When she offered me a party and I did not thank her, and even told her she was not allowed to come."

"My mother was very caring and loving, but not able to change the situation at home for us children. My father used to beat her up. The worst part of it was that I was the one with the shoulder to cry on."

"When I was young, I didn't think she dressed well enough. She wasn't classy enough. Always wore polyester."

However, as adults, most women come to like their mother again:

"When I was twelve, I did not like her touching me. Now she treats me as her equal, she respects me as a person. In fact, she is my best friend."

"Today I like her and respect her. She lives her own life and is not an extension of her husband."

"As a child, she would pull me to her, and 'ask' for compliments and love. Now I appreciate her more, because of what she made of the life she had, and she is very happy that I am kind to her and love her again."

Some girls can mistakenly believe that the cause of the fights is a generation gap. This is a common misconception which can be quite insulting to the mother:

"We argue about anything, about money, boys, my way of life, alcohol, sex. Once in particular when we fought, I hit her in the face (one time, never again). I really love her very much, but she is from another generation—which may be the cause of our problems. What does my father say about this? He disagrees with my talking back to her, but he thinks I will be all right. He is very modern, he knows what is happening nowadays."

"My parents say about the way I have my hair that it is not feminine, a boy would never want to put his hands through my hair. I just want to be strong, not sweet.

"I admire my mother, but I see her limitations. I do not know why she stays with my father, it must be partly a question of the difference in our ages that I cannot understand."

But when daughters are angry with their mother, what are they really angry about? They are, in fact, angry with the institution of the family, the feeling of pressure that is coming down on them, denying them their very inner existence or any discussion of the confusing reality they are facing, refusing to hear their ideas and questions. (How ironic that most parents remind their children from time to time that they owe their very existence to them—that without them, they would not "be there".)

In patriarchy, a girl's role is to be a "dutiful daughter", to be quiet and smiling and to take a back seat. Most mothers don't see that they're enforcing a taboo against assertiveness, or if they do, don't understand the momentous political significance of this taboo. They just think they are teaching their daughters politeness!

Hair: the Last Area of Control and Physical Intimacy

One of the main foci of conflict between daughters and their mothers from around the age of twelve and during the teenage years, is the daughter's hair:

"When I was twelve, I wanted to do things for myself. It seemed to centre on my hair; I wanted to control how I'd wear my hair. This didn't go down well. My mother always said my hair looked terrible 'that way'. Things just went downhill from there."

"She always nagged me to do something with my hair. I refused to get a permanent and threw a hell of a tantrum whenever they tried to touch my hair!"

"I had very long hair until I was about thirteen. Mom loved to brush it and fix it, but I hardly ever let her because she brushed it so hard it hurt—a lot. She insisted it got my circulation going."

"Once she gave me a home permanent, which made me look like a goose and caused great social embarrassment. But I kept my thoughts and feelings securely underground, so there were few clashes. They eventually sent me to a child psychologist in the 10th grade because I never spoke to them."

"My mother wrung out my hair so hard it hurt. She took me to a beautician to have my hair styled so my face would look better ('Don't smile so widely for the pictures, Lynne, your gums show' and he cut it all off in a pixie that made my ears stick out and people tease me. And when it grew out, she took me to him *again*."

Why is it that sex and hair go together? Is it because this is one of the last outposts of touch or caress possible between mother and daughter? (See Chapter 1.) The last gesture of the mother towards the daughter that is permissible? After girls are no longer babies, most mothers feel that they cannot touch their daughter in any sensual or intimate way; mothers often take to brushing their daughter's hair, or "doing her hair".

Hair is also a last area of "control", the last vestige of the physical contact that was once much more intimate. Being able to tell your daughter how to wear her hair is one of the last ways of touching her. Are frequent admonitions to girls to "fix your hair", "do something with your hair" a kind of displaced anger that some mothers feel about the loss of intimacy, the anger that now they can't be close and touch their daughters any more?

Of course, hair has stood for sexual development since Biblical times, if not longer. Neat hair symbolizes being "in control", not sensual or "sexually loose". (In boys, this is true too; just think of the "military", cropped cuts that men are given in armies all around the world.) Hair in the Bible symbolized sexuality and sexual power: Samson loses his "power" when Delilah secretly cuts off his hair while he sleeps.

On another level, hair and dress are the symbols of "being respectable" within a system that many mothers feel they have a duty to impart to their daughters. Clothing, hair and make-up are especially complicated symbols for girls since, unlike boys, they have to deal with the double standard of being perhaps seen as "too sexual" and, if so, "cheap". To guard against this unfair labelling, mothers want their daughters' hair to look "neat" because "taken-care-of" hair is a mark of "respectability" and "ladyhood"—the opposite of long, "wild" or flowing locks, which stand for nature, sexuality and freedom. Thus, mothers groom their daughters for social position.

Clothes and Make-Up
("Don't be sexy, otherwise, you're a tramp . . .")

The constant undercurrent of the double standard in our society—the "prostitute" or sexual woman versus the Madonna, Mary the Virgin Mother—makes it difficult for any happy resolution of the "two sides" to take place. Mothers, seeing their daughters become sexual, feel that this is dangerous. And so the "mother" is pitted against the "sexual daughter".

Since "sex" in the family is always hidden, even masturbation, girls must live with a secret self, as we have seen. Part of them may long to talk to their mother about it, tell her their feelings, what's going on; yet another part resents her so much for never having opened up to them or shared her own sexual identity or secrets (was the mother too "loyal" to the father to do so?) that now most daughters distrust any questions which try to "pry" into their lives. They prefer to talk to their friends, with whom they can be totally honest.

Still, there are many mothers who try to be positive and encourage their daughters to enjoy "dating" and their physical lives and selves. The stereotype, however, depicts mothers as being against make-up, dating, and grown-up "female" behaviour with its sexual implications. Is this true?

In this study, 81 per cent of girls say they had to fight these attitudes coming from their mother, and 63 per cent say they felt them coming from fathers (see Chapter 6):

"I was not allowed to wear make-up, because only 'loose' girls did that."

"I hemmed my dresses to get them short enough when my mother wasn't home."

"One of my biggest adolescent fights was to wear make-up. I remember having my face scrubbed clean when I wore make-up at thirteen."

"She kept telling me, when I was looking at fashion magazines, that the clean, natural look is the look of girls who are nice."

"I remember putting on my mother's make-up, looking ridiculous. I could never 'get it right'—my stockings were always crooked, my hair wrong, my clothes never fitted."

"They always wanted me to dress conservatively, like the nerd next door."

"It seemed, if anything, my mother was trying to hold me back from becoming a woman. Not wanting me to shave my armpits, wear a bra, not telling me about menstruation until absolutely necessary, never telling me about sex, not wanting me to wear stockings when my friends were allowed to."

Clashes Over Sex

"My mother doesn't know I'm having sex. She occasionally asks me if I'm still a virgin—or some similar question. I tell her I still am! She'd have a fit if I told her the truth. I'm sure she couldn't handle it."

"I've been very close to my mother in all aspects of my life except one: men. I saw early on that we totally disagreed. When I tried to discuss anything, we ended up arguing. I couldn't stand it. My love life is one aspect of my life where I can absolutely not tolerate a second opinion."

"There were clashes between us, mostly about my boyfriend. When I was sixteen, she 'grounded' me for two months and wouldn't let me go to Junior Prom with him because I came home two hours

161

late from an 'under-twenty-one' disco. I felt unjustly punished and decided to disregard her every command. She was furious. It was a frustrating time."

"The worst clash was the summer before I left for college when she somehow discovered I was taking the pill. At the time, I was working as a teaching assistant in a sex education project, a job which *she* got for me. When she found out I was on the pill, she threatened not to let me go to college if that's all I was going to do there, and she said she would make me stay home until I learned a few things.

"I told her that there was no way I would stay there, that I would leave whether it was college or not on my eighteenth birthday, so she might as well send me to college because at least she would know where I was. That was a bloody time. Awful.

"Today it's still bad. We never speak on the phone. Visits are rare. About once a month I get a letter. Upon seeing it and touching it I feel contaminated. I am filled with dread and loathing at the prospect of answering it, which I feel somehow obliged to do, before I even open it."

One nineteen-year-old woman is pressured in just the opposite direction:

"My mother is a neo-Freudian shrink, always very liberal with me. In fact there is a lot of pressure, 'Where are the men?' My parents know I have had sex. They're probably thrilled, sure I am not asexual or something. They pressure me a lot to find men."

But for most girls, the mother's silence and guarding of her sexual knowledge to herself leaves the daughter to believe, when she does dress or act or feel sexual, that she is disloyal, since she never had permission.

She may feel that she "can't" have sex because that is her mother's territory; therefore when she does have sex or express herself sexually, she can feel even more confused, ashamed and/or proud and defiant. This may make it harder to identify her true sexual desires and feelings.

Fathers as "Mr Popular"
"My dad left all the discussions of this nature to my mom—plus all the disciplining. He was Mr Popular. When he came home, it was fun time. He was the fun one."

When a father is silent, while the mother metes out discipline, he may be supporting the mother. However, according to a large number of both men and women here, the father's silence may be accompanied by sadness as he empathizes with the child. A majority felt he was not really being "silent". As one boy, perhaps flippantly, put it, "Were those who were silent while they watched Louis XVI go to the gallows innocent? What about those who watched the Jews put into cattle trucks and herded off to the concentration camps? Were they 'innocent' because they were silent? They didn't actively 'do it'?"

What a father is "saying" in such a case, as many children here interpret it, is, "I agree with you and not your mother; I just can't say so."

The father's "silence" in a case like this is a betrayal of the mother, and gender divisive: the silence and averted eyes of the father *tell* the child that she or he doesn't have to respect the mother—and also tell her or him, as a subtext, to take sides. Fathers *should* speak up, take responsibility too, not continue the "traditional family" pattern of mother as "duty policeman", responsible for daily discipline.

"Don't talk back!"
"She was angriest when we talked back, especially if we used certain words, like 'bitch'. It really flipped her out when I said that."

"When I'd say she didn't know what she was talking about, or something she did was stupid, she got furious."

Signs of lack of respect are a special irritant for most mothers, because even though contempt for women is built into the culture, and mothers feel it acutely all around them every day, to hear it come back at them from their very own children is especially painful and infuriating.

Under the surface, a mother experiences "smart remarks" as her daughter's real contempt for her "power", a reminder that it is not real, like the father's power. A reminder of her lower status in the "family" hierarchy.

Beauty and Age: The Politics of Personal Appearance Between Mothers and Daughters

"I carried with me a perception of being very close to my mother. My mother always said we were more like friends. Now I wonder if it was said to hide her uneasiness in being a mother, instead of still 'an attractive young thing'. She was, until recently, very attractive to men but her inner image might have been at stake. Anyway, I thought she was the most beautiful mother in the world, and that she could sing better than anyone. I used to think she should compete in the Mrs America thing and she'd win for sure."

Traditionally, one of women's few powers in society has been based on "looks". How much is this still true?* Misogynist writers for centuries have focused malevolently on women's "ageing", and the supposed waning of women's appeal and attractiveness—from D.H. Lawrence, to Tennessee Williams, to Shakespeare.† While most assume this "waning" to be "natural"—an objective, if lamentable, reality—could it not be that younger women are seen as "beautiful" because they can reproduce and are valuable to a society which has made reproduction women's main function, above all else, for centuries?

Power in society based on looks
Is there sexual rivalry between mothers and daughters? Do mothers feel jealous of daughters, and do they feel guilty for feeling this? Do daughters sometimes feel a mixture of shame and pride for being "prettier" than their mother?

The topics of beauty and age seem to be forbidden ones for most mothers and daughters, something rarely discussed or acknowledged between the two. Nevertheless, there is often a hidden agenda, a war, that goes on between mothers and daughters in this area.

The cultural scenario is all around us, with advice on "how to retain our looks". Or, as Marilyn Monroe warns in a famous song in the film *Gentlemen Prefer Blondes*, "We all lose our looks in the end." What women should do for insurance, according to the song, is get men to give them diamonds!

In patriarchal societies, age and appearance are two of the most competitive areas for women, who are encouraged to see each other as rivals, never as "objects" of pleasure for each other. Between mothers and daughters, this cultural alienation can take the form of rivalry for the father's attention, or rivalry over "power-looks" and status in society.

Ageism: Mothers' and Daughters' Reflections

"When I am in a store with my mother, and her hair is kind of straggling—she's worked hard all week and hasn't had time to take

---

* See *The Beauty Myth* by Naomi Wolf (London, Chatto and Windus, 1990).
† See Germaine Greer and Simone de Beauvoir for a different approach to ageing.

care of it—and she looks a little beat up, just dressed for messing around doing grocery shopping, somehow I know that I get the nod of approval from shopkeepers, like men. They want to talk to me, they want to help me. I often find myself in the position of getting them to wait on us, help us—just in little ways, like a little eye contact, looking 'cute' or 'needing help'. It's nothing I do, really, just letting them see me, letting them know I see them. They don't 'see' my mother."

Some mothers write of their "looks" *vis-à-vis* the daughter's:

"I'm already out of the game, I'm forty-three—almost fifty! As a younger woman, I used to feel guilty, that I was prettier than older women. And I felt sorry for them! I wonder if there's a way for older women to be sexier than younger women? Anyway, men make the rules of this game. So, if they glorify girls' looks, that means there's no way out. No matter what you do, the game is going to go against you at some point. We women can take advantage of our looks when we are young—it doesn't guarantee anything with men in the long run, of course, I can tell you. But it's more fun than being invisible—which I am getting to be."

"I am trying hard not to resent my daughter's increasingly interesting-to-men appearance. She seems both unaware and aware of it. Doesn't care much about it, but of course enjoys it when she gets attention and interest and approval. Who doesn't? The main thing I have to do is find other sources of happiness for myself. (This doesn't necessarily mean men, it can mean anything that makes me happy. Baths. Walks. My dog. My lover?)

"Anyway, she's a sweetie. I don't want to lose her or my love for her in my problems over my own identity, my own situation. She's too good to lose."

One daughter describes her father's provocation of intense rivalry between her and her mother, as he compared their looks on a regular basis:

"My family situation was the usual mess. My father was very violent. My mother's role was to make everybody believe that my father had no problem, that he was fine and everything was fine. (All women in families are 'supposed to', she believes, validate the reality and importance of the men, like Nancy Reagan for example.)

"With my parents, I used to say during the violence, 'Stop treating her like that,' and it would help for a while. My mother tolerated my father's violence and this told us all (non-verbally), 'Your mother is a martyr.'

"She also taught me that you must never be flustered and always dress just right, never be too sexy or too outrageous, if you're a woman. My father has discouraged every feminine impulse in her making her wear tailored clothes, not too much lipstick, etc. My mother used to go to the beauty parlour—she got a lot of pleasure out of it, it was her way of relaxing and also exalting herself.

"But my father would say, 'Oh, I see you have your warpaint on,' when she would come home, all done up, with more colour on her face than usual. 'Ginette (that's me) spends nothing on her hair and yet it looks good, while you spend all my money and don't look as good!' You can imagine how that made me feel, I wanted to crawl under the table. And it didn't make me very popular with my mother, I can tell you.

"She wore her hair lacquered, but I wore mine loose, Brigitte Bardot style, long loose locks piled up on top of my head. After his comments, she started not to like make-up or special clothes on me either. Every sign of femininity or sexuality, she wanted to cut off. She refused to acknowledge I was growing breasts. I wanted a bra, but she insisted I didn't need one. I used to see my chest wobble as I walked to school. At school, I tried not to walk too fast, to keep still or not call attention to it . . .

"Sometimes I would challenge her, or talk back to her, and this would make my mother furious! That made me laugh, I enjoyed it.* The result of all this is that even today I am still conflicted about my appearance. For example, I have a lot of clothes—looking at all those clothes in my closet makes me feel like a selfish bitch—the Kurds are dying and I'm looking at my clothes . . . What is the solution? Not to care about anything?"

If this is a society in which younger women are supposed to be more beautiful than older women, does the daughter more or less automatically push her mother into second place in the family in terms of power? Whether or not it is fair, or even always "reality" (and certainly not a true assessment of women's worth), is this the *realpolitik* of popular culture? *And*, in the nuclear families of most women?

In the world's terms (that is, the current social order's terms), girls are usually seen as "prettier", "younger" and more attractive as sexual objects than their mother, by the beginning of their teenage years. A daughter's "power status" can then zoom ahead of her mother's.

---

* Why is this? The phrase "How furious he was!", about our fathers, does not usually make us laugh. Is it because a mother's rage is impotent, and therefore ridiculous? Is this why her rage is funny?

Is this changed power imbalance (and some daughters' condescension because of it) what some mother–daughter fights are about? To many girls, when the mother tries to maintain the double standard (or prevent a "sleazy-sexy" appearance in their daughters) it is as though the mother doesn't want them to grow up or be sexual. "Is my mother just jealous?" many girls wonder, pitying the mother for being "older" and "not as young and pretty anymore". But, as we have seen, this may not be the mother's motive at all.

Is this competition lessening, and admiration taking its place?
Despite the impact of feminism, and the fact that, as we have seen, girls are identifying more with their mothers, not looking down on them but regarding them with more appreciation and admiration, the issue of "looks" is still a forbidden topic of discussion, as if avoiding it will make it disappear.

Hidden Eroticism between Mothers and Daughters

Denied sexual attraction?
"I remember a sweet but critical affection in my mother's way of treating me, and I am pained to see it come again in me towards my twelve-year-old daughter. Even as I braid her hair or caress her, I poke at a scab or tell her to wash her hair or hold her tummy in. I remember well that mixed criticism from my mother, and it hurt me and hurts my daughter."

Are these mothers and daughters denying their impulses towards expressing sensuous or "erotic" feelings?

My research here suggests that there *is* a repressed desire for intimacy between daughter and mother, and that the denial of the existence of these feelings causes resentment and mistrust. A girl at puberty can understand, even if she feels guilty, that society expects there to be some attraction between her and her father; but there is nothing to help her accept a similar denial of her feelings of desire for physical intimacy with her mother.

Girls' Crushes on Their Mother

Sometimes the hidden eroticism and/or denied need to feel the body of the other close to them seems to come from mothers as no touch at all, a jerky prohibition on all touching:

"My mother was brought up by a strict family and treated roughly, so maybe she found it hard to express affection. Even today, the only times my mom and I hug or kiss each other are when I come home or leave. And even then, she doesn't really kiss me, but turns her cheek for me to kiss. I live quite far away."

Can girls have crushes on their mother, as well as their father? Yes, but this is hardly recognized, not "seen" or legitimized by the culture, although it is accepted that boys have a period of erotic feeling for the mother (the so-called Oedipal stage). Of course there is nothing "wrong" with these feelings. In fact, they can be quite beautiful:

"My mother was very kind and loving. I loved it when she played cards with me, or when she took me with her to the hairdresser's—we would always stop and get a doughnut or ice-cream. I thought we had a 'special' relationship. I was the youngest of five, and my mother was the youngest of her family (of thirteen). People always told me I looked a lot like her, and I felt a special connection to her. I was her special 'helper'. I loved helping her do things (like clean and sweep). She died of lung cancer when I was seven and I missed her."

"My mother was so affectionate with me, she used to stroke my hands and play with my hair. I would hold still and forget all else to enjoy it. She and I spent a lot of time together before I started school. When I went to school, I think she was lonely during the day. She used to cuddle me when I was sad. She supervised my baths on Sunday nights before *Disney World*, and I remember very clearly when I had to begin bathing myself. In 2nd grade, she didn't play with my hair anymore. In fact, she took me to get my long hair cut and I cried because then it was shorter than my brother's. She said as it grew back and she saw I was taking care of it, she would let me keep it long."

Another young woman describes her mother and their relationship, shyly, almost as a hidden love, a lost intimacy:

"As a little girl I remember the pleasure of hugging her and the smell of Ivory soap she always seemed to have. As I got older we stopped having physical contact, but she was still good at taking care of me. For example, making toys or clothes for me, and waiting on me when I was sick. I felt it, but would have been embarrassed to say, 'I love you,' as we never said that. Once in a great while I would make her a card that said 'I love you'.

"The only time I remember her saying she loved me to me directly was when we were having a 'mother–daughter' talk—about some bad feelings, I guess. Then she said, 'I *love* my kids,' as if I had denied it. Maybe I had, somehow."

Sexist Discrimination in the Family

A major cause of fights between some mothers and daughters is perhaps the most obvious: sexist prejudice. Even mothers can unknowingly adopt "girls-are-worth-less" stereotypes.

One way mothers sometimes unconsciously (but accurately) give the impression that this is their opinion of girls is in the frequent message that the mother feels burdened by them. The feeling is that daughters "create extra work", and should do more housework than boys to "make up" for this extra work. (Sons are different, they can be depended on to eventually bring in an income, and provide status.) The message to girls is, "Clean up after yourself, don't be a bother!"

One woman relates the story of how her parents financed her brother's education, not hers; not only her mother, but also her father, made this decision:

"I remember watching my father beat my mother when I was a child. My parents married when my mother became pregnant. Not much love, but always 'duty', and a very big effort to be socially acceptable and keep up appearances.

"Did they love me? There was always attention paid to the superficials and how I looked, but never to what I felt, thought or wanted. I remember being excited about the space programme and discussing rocket propulsion. My mother was embarrassed that I would discuss those 'intelligent things' in front of other people.

"Intelligence in a woman was clearly not considered an asset. 'Intellectual' was not considered a feminine trait. Thus, in the 5th grade I was accused of cheating on an IQ test as teachers knew it wasn't possible for me to do that well. In high school, I was told to take home economics, that I didn't have the ability to study foreign languages or academics! (Later, for my undergraduate degree, I graduated with honours in Spanish, secular education and minors in French and German. I also know Portuguese, Italian, Norwegian, Russian!)

"My brother is a brain surgeon. He had his education financed by my parents; I got a scholarship. My mother actually said, 'She is so sweet, you'd never know she was educated.' Also, I got a reputation as a slut because I enjoyed travelling around the world on my own and refused to be sheltered. (There was more to life than the world I grew up in.) It was assumed that women on their own and away from their families were ignorant and would inevitably 'get into trouble'. 'Nice girls' were chaperoned.

"In 1970, I desperately wanted to accept a job gassing jets at the airport, but 'nice' girls didn't do that. Various insinuations were made about my being kicked out of the house, so I ended up taking a 'respectable' job at minimum wage. I always regretted it."

How common *is* this? Is sexism still so much of a problem in families today?

Unfortunately, 83 per cent of girls with brothers say their mother was often "nicer", granted more freedom and privileges to their brothers than to them. Three-quarters of young women now in their teens and twenties say their mother gave their brothers the right not to do dishes, more rights to go out of the house, more privacy and freedom ("You can't force him, he's a man, after all!").

One young woman describes her anguish in a triangle of "love" with her mother and brother:

"She is just a channel, I know that . . . but she even told me I emasculated my brother! Why? How did I do this emasculating? Because I'm too smart (smarter, this was the sin), I achieved more, I'm too successful! *And* she said I was 'verbally abusive' to him when we were children—never mind that my brother used to actually beat me up! And now he gets an apartment bought for him (by our mother—who never thought of buying me one), just so he can have a place to live with his pregnant girlfriend (whom he cannot support). Well, you know, men and boys have a right to 'spread their seed'! We all have to pay homage to the inevitability of male sexuality! Even including having an apartment bought for him so he can lord it over everyone. Yet I am told not to complain and not to be 'jealous'!

"My mother either doesn't or can't see the different treatment she is giving to my brother and me, or its relation to gender; to her it's just 'natural'. She really doesn't *see* she's giving my brother preferential treatment. I've brought it up and tried to talk to her about it (screaming, I guess it was, actually), and on several occasions, but she could never, never see it.

"Even with very small children, I mean, I went with my mother the other day to visit some of our cousins and their families. It was amazing the way she treated the children, even tiny ones, differently because of their gender. It was sort of an attitude like, boys are straightforward, you treat them that way, but little girls have guile, you're not as direct with them. Or you don't trust them somehow.

"But maybe this is women's guilt coming out; you can't look another woman or even a little girl directly in the face, because you know you despise her, you know she is worthless, an object of scorn and contempt, you know you feel these things but you can't help it, you can't change it. You can't look her directly in the eye because you know she will be 'competing', you are jealous, she will try to take the attention and affection *you* want."

"At nine, it got so bad I used to cry in bed every night. I believed my mom preferred my brother, I thought she was going to give me away. My mom won't believe it now when I tell her this. I also thought that since I was not a Third World child, I had no right to cry. Then by the time I was fourteen, I felt okay, I felt I could fight back, because I knew I could make it out in the world, somehow, if I had to. I can't even today tell her that she preferred my brother, she won't discuss it.

"My father preferred me, but he wasn't home very much—so it didn't help. And he was more loyal to her, my mother, out of a sense of duty . . .

"I remember when my mother was pregnant with her third child, my brother and I both asked her desperately over and over again, 'Which do you want, a boy or a girl? Which do you *want*?' We wanted to know which of *us* she wanted.

"Children are just the most powerless, disenfranchised group in society. When she favoured my brother, I thought there was something wrong with *me*, not that she just liked him better, but that there was something dislikeable about me myself. I tried to figure out what it was. I thought I had to just *try harder* to make myself likeable or perfect.

"My brother didn't have to do anything around the house, I had to do *all* the housework. He was just considered charming for being there. He was sent to an expensive private school, I had to cope with the state school—even though I always achieved more at school. But funny, I never noticed I was doing well at school, it was rather 'I wasn't causing any trouble' by not doing badly."

The same girl goes on to describe how this sexism (perceived) on the part of her mother seriously undermined her health and her pride in her own body, as she tried to get rid of parts of her body that were "feminine":

"I remember dreading the moment my mother would discover I had breasts. Intimacy between me and my mother was acutely embarrassing!

172

And later I remember I was disgusted when I had hips. I thought frantically that I'd better diet to get them off, to get back to my real shape, my boy shape, my normal shape before.

"At my all-girls' school, we used to run around feeling down each other's backs to see if the other one was wearing a bra. This was between the ages of eleven and thirteen. Boys were never discussed, it was all breasts. Big breasts were tarty, small were better. Having your period later was better. I got mine at sixteen; we were part of the anorexia cult so we were all so thin, we began menstruating very late. Fashion/fascism magazines were our Bible. *Cosmopolitan* was the biggest influence of my teens. All my friends and I had big blow-up photos of the models all over our walls.

"What we worried about was, how to tell our mums when we started our periods. This was the constant question, I suppose we were worried because we thought she would think we were dirty! And this was during the '70's, this wasn't so long ago. My mum kept asking if I'd started mine and I took this to mean she was voyeuristic!

"I didn't want to become like my mother, I wanted to stay a child—or preppy, not one of those hated 'women'—for ever."

Girls' Guilt (For Not Being "The Boy Jesus")

Some girls believe that their mother doesn't really love them—she only pretends to love them out of duty:

"I was close to Mom until I was about eight years old. I think she had us kids because she was expected to, but then resented her choice. I think Dad decided to have kids for the same reason, but he doesn't resent me. I don't know if my mom ever loved me—probably only when I was young, cute and controllable. I dislike her martyr-like self-denial of any joy."

"I was just an accident and a responsibility."

One young woman describes how she felt seeing the frequent look of disgust on her mother's face, which she now believes reflects her mother's dislike of her for being a girl:

"When I was teenager, I couldn't believe it. The way she *looked* at me sometimes! I used to ask myself, 'Does she despise me?' Even when she smiled at me, it was kind of sneering, I thought, mixed with some kind of revulsion. I was always looking for the fault in *myself*. I thought it couldn't be prejudice or even less, what she really *felt*. No, it had to be me! Something I was doing or saying—or looking like—I was disgusting.

"Now, since I have discussed this with friends of mine and they had something like the same experiences, I think it is just such a mother thing to look at their daughters with disgust. Mothers like that have a lot of self-loathing. But they don't know it."

Just as daughters are socially trained to respect women and their mothers less than men, aren't mothers also influenced by these same social pressures and attitudes, to value their daughters less—simply because they are girls? Many women try hard not to feel this, but a bit of this massive social prejudice can still creep in, as mothers freely acknowledge, when talking about their own inner struggles. After all, the model of the family has a boy baby, Jesus. Thus, a girl is never "quite right". There is always "something" wrong with her, for some parents.

A Burden and a Joy

How many mothers resent their children, especially their female children? It is true that, contrary to archetype,* mothers sometimes have children because they feel they "should" have children; then they resent the duties and restrictions that come into their lives, as well as the unequal burden of childcare they bear, doing more than their partner, who has more freedom. This is understandable, but many children feel that this anger is taken out on them, since the mother "cannot" show it to the father.

On the other hand, some women find their children are the light of their lives, the delight of their lives and a great source of strength and joy. This of course is the best of all possible situations.

Many women say very positive things about their daughters:

"I have a ten-year-old daughter. I think she is one of the most pure and beautiful people I know. I feel closer to her than anyone, and yet further from her at other times. It's strange. It may be because she's a girl and I think I should know her so completely, yet she is a separate person so I can't."

"My daughter is a ray of light in my life. I love her dearly, dearly, dearly, she is a beautiful human being. Have I talked to her about menstruation? Oh yes, years ago, she's older now. I told her that she

---

* But in Giotto's painting of the Annunciation, Mary looks anything but happy about the impending "happy event" that the angel is describing to her. She is frowning and her head is turned aside, as if she wishes she were not hearing what she is hearing.

is a human and her body is hers and that she should always take pleasure in her body and never feel guilty about it. She thanked me profoundly, and she still thanks me, she still remembers that."

"I talk openly to my lovely two-year-old daughter about sex, at a level she can understand. I want her to like her body, particularly her crotch—so I began telling her she had a pretty crotch as soon as she could understand. She occasionally touches herself and I do not stop her unless it is in front of people, which is rare. I want her to have a different attitude about herself than I did and I want her to feel pretty as well as smart, which she is!"

But 43 per cent of mothers, including those who love being mothers (the majority), also voice (some) resentment:

"When my children were little, I felt the need to work to get away from them. I married at eighteen, had a child just after I was twenty and had the third by the time I was twenty-three. I gained a certain amount of fulfilment from having children, but honestly, I don't particularly like having children.

"Giving birth wasn't bad at all, but raising them was hell. I once answered a poll by Ann Landers and said I'd never do it again. Now that they're grown, I enjoy them. Raising three children so close together was hectic. My life would have been more serene and I could have enjoyed my husband more if I hadn't had children.

"Having children changed my relationship with my husband. They took time from him and we disagreed about how to treat them. He never knew love or affection while growing up, it was always hitting and yelling, so he didn't know how to treat his own children either. He alienated them and therefore put me on the defensive. I wanted my daughters to have the close relationship with their father that I had with mine. They never did, so our oldest daughter now looks to older men for attention."

"I was happy to be pregnant and now I enjoy being a mother. I gained three more people who love me. A family, I always wanted a family and it's great. Not always fun or easy, or even sane, but I'm not sorry.

"Our relationship survived children. They put a terrible strain on our marriage. There's no privacy because they're all in their teens and always around. Makes casual sex next to impossible. But this too will pass and then I'll have him to myself again and I'll have them too. Still, I also dislike the economic strain of children. They take away from the marriage not only money, privacy and space but some days I swear they also take my sanity.

"How can I be a loving, adoring, caring wife when I'm being the

175

mother, PTA chairman, holding a job, keeping house, disciplining children and cooking dinner? My husband has only recently taken part in household chores and child raising. He's much more helpful than he used to be since I've been working full time. But he is not as helpful as he could be. I think we'll both be happier when the kids are grown."

"My daughter is now seventeen; I think the early years of night feedings, diapering, chasing toddlers, childhood illnesses were not nearly as trying as the teen years. It is so many-faceted, the raising of a teenager. On one side, it is exciting to see your 'child' becoming a woman and forming opinions, seeing their independence develop. But I think the hardest part of parenting for me has been stepping aside and letting my daughter take on her own responsibilities, even when I am much better qualified (through experience) to make the 'right' decision. And then there's the difficulty of knowing when to step in and when not to.

"Keeping open communication lines between me and her is very important. This usually means when she's talking to me I have to remember not to be judgemental or give advice where it isn't pertinent.

"I think it is important to let your child know that you love her but not necessarily like her one hundred per cent of the time. It is good for kids to know that they don't always have to like you either, and there are times when a parent will be wrong and that all you can hope to do is your best. Making a mistake is natural and everyone is allowed to do it!"

Are Mothers Angry with Daughters—or with the "Mother Role"?

Are mothers more irritable than fathers? Or is it just that the stereotypes lead us to believe it? These stereotypes insist that mothers do a lot of nagging and "bitching" when it comes to daughters. But they are not angrier than fathers; in fact, mothers often advise daughters how to "stay out of his way", not to incite his wrath, approach him the right way. And, if mothers are angry, it may not be with daughters in particular, but with the situation in which they find themselves, e.g., doing all the housework, both physical and emotional.

In short, frequently it's not anything a girl is doing that makes her mother irritable, but the woman's increasing feeling that the family is trapping her, that her husband is not doing his share, that somehow her time is always eaten up, that she has no time for herself, *her* life, *her* dreams, *her* work.

In other words, if some mothers have become *more* angry by the time girls are teenagers, it is usually not because of the girls or anything the girls do as teenagers, but because their role in "the family" is getting to them.* They may begin to see no future for themselves and to feel they have sacrificed everything to the family, to their children, while other goals are placed out of reach. They may also feel they face some major decisions as to whether they should stay with the family, or leave before it is "too late" to change their work or career, or perhaps find a partner who loves them better. Sometimes, mothers' "ups and downs" relate also to their private romantic lives, but then, how could their daughters know about that, since mothers do not tell them?

Many girls describe seeing their mother go through various stages: first, a happy selfhood, gradually turning into anger (daughter's teenage

---

* For more on women's perceptions of their married lives and their emotional decisions therein, with or without children, see *Women and Love*. There, mothers give a full account of their lives within the family, and especially the "hidden" experiences of emotional and sexual relationships with husbands.

177

years or puberty), and finally either a martyred withdrawal or the stereo-typical "happy" and "loving" blank look of the Stepford wives. Some girls understand what the problems behind this are, others do not.

One woman talks about how, now that she is married herself, she understands her mother much better:

"I can remember my mother holding me and kissing me. She also sang, as I do to my children. She bathed me and washed and set my hair. Then she was critical of my appearance as I grew up and yelled at me a lot for being sloppy. I think she went through a very difficult time in her marriage to my father and a lot showed up in her relationship with me and my brother and sister. Until I had gone through marital stress myself, I don't think I appreciated the pain and anguish that this can cause. I enjoy spending time with her now because she seems to understand what I am going through. She really seems to be able to relate to it, although I don't think she has approved of all the decisions I have had to make."

Freedom for Mothers?

If we remember that mothers and daughters don't usually start out with animosity—things are usually warm and loving when girls are very young babies and children—why do they so often degenerate?

This happens for two reasons: (1) the mother needs more freedom.★ She's carrying too much of the load at home, and usually working outside the home as well now, and (2) the daughter feels the social clamps coming down on her (more than they are on her brother or boys in the world around her) and tries to fight back.

At times, both women feel angry, and they see each other as the cause of their lack of freedom, or part of it. Neither sees the "father-family" system as responsible for the situation—or their position in that system. The problem to each seems to be the "idiosyncrasies" or personality of the other.

★ The current "single mother" controversy in the UK is a case in point here: single mothers are being blamed in the press for not being "good" mothers—and yet, few are asking where the "bad" fathers are, who left these women alone to take care of the child(ren) on their own. Women are expected (and expect themselves) always to stay with children, to care for them (despite the gnawing poverty of many woman-headed households). Yet there is no similar expectation of men: a man who doesn't stay at home is often seen as an interesting "man about town".

The Future of Mother–Daughter Relationships

Are these patterns still being handed down from generation to generation? Not so much now! There has been a big difference in twenty years.

However, a counter-revolution has arisen to try to stop the change. Fundamentalists insist that only a return to "traditional family values" will restore all that is "good" about family life. But what is so good about these "family values", if one result is that many or most girls still feel that their mother is not a model they could follow ("I don't want to be like her!")? This hurts and pains mothers.

Girls now do not see their mother in the same way that girls in the 1970's saw their mother. They see her as a much more exciting person, not someone they have to "understand", while desperately hoping they will never be like her. They admire and like her, most of the time. Of course, this is not true in every family; but there is a definite trend towards change since the findings of my 1970's research.

In the 1970's, girls were angry with their mother, considered her "useless", because the mother could not help the daughter out of the role of being a female and into a career and life of respect and power, the new life she wanted. The life she wondered why her mother had never demanded, or gone after. On the other hand, girls thought that their father had a lot to teach them, show them, that the father could help them join the world, that he was a much better model.

In a way, it was difficult for mothers to be good role models for their daughters during the 1970's: almost all girls and young women wanted to have jobs and careers as well as families, and they looked at their mother, who did not have job or career, and thought her inadequate. Daughters thought they would never accept the inequality around the house—housework, emotional housework, love—that they observed in their mother's marriage. In a way they were right, and now that they have come of age, they *have* indeed changed the family structure—yet they have also learned to understand the historical moment of their mother's situation, and the advances that women of so many previous generations have made for us.

179

Chapter 6

Girls and Fathers

"I idolized Daddy but never understood him"

Friendship: The Future Model for Father–Daughter Relationships

Girls very often describe their father and their feelings for him in extreme ways: either he was the most wonderful father ever, or he was a monster—rarely anything in between. Why?

There is an atmosphere hanging over many father–daughter relationships: "Warning! Heterosexual Impulses Possible!" This "unacknowledged" but ever-present (socially constructed) message makes a spontaneous relationship almost impossible. It is a "red light" which subtly distracts most families, making them slightly nervous and distorting their feelings. This distortion is increased by the taboo on talking about sexuality. Family members must pretend that they don't think about or experience any of these feelings; for fear of incrimination. Better to abstain from trying to become friends, lest too close a relationship looks "sexual". The outcome of this is painful alienation. In father–daughter relationships distance, anger, disappointment, misunderstanding and hostility are common. The majority of fathers who replied to my questionnaire do not feel sexual attraction for their daughters, but they remain terrified at the possibility.

Of course, there is frequently a large element of sexism also interfering with these potential friendships: when fathers see their daughters as "mere females", "not important", and thus trivialize them.

Potential friendships between fathers and daughters can also be hampered by family politics, i.e., the position of the mother at the bottom of the family hierarchy, and girls' consequent fear of betraying the mother by befriending the father. Many girls feel they're involved in a constant balancing act. They want to "play fair" and not offend "either side". Boys also, as we will see in Part III, have their own problems *vis-à-vis* the gender split in the patriarchal family. But much of girls' perplexity can be seen in their relationship with their father.

What needs to develop is a new friendship between fathers and daughters—and there are some excellent examples of this here, break-throughs in relationships in which fathers are able to reach out a hand to their daughters, provide a real relationship that does not exclude the mother, does not compete with her, but stands on its own as a testament to what could and should be the relationship of the future:

"Physically my father wasn't affectionate, but he said and did loving things, like leaving a book on my pillow that was pertinent to a talk we had had. We talked about all my problems, from the practical, daily ones, to emotional or major life decisions. We went zillions of places together every weekend and had lots of vacations jammed with fun activities and travelling. He was relaxed, sometimes even funny, on these excursions. I always liked him and respected him a lot, even though I feared making him angry or disappointing him—or worst, looking silly to him.

"We didn't argue much since, when I disagreed, he would just lay down the law. He was so good at logical arguments and confusing me with making his side seem the best, that I would give up in despair or frustration or humiliation. Later, I learned to ignore his air of superiority, and became good at logical arguments myself, asserting my preferences as if in court. We'd argue about studying, bra or no bra (guess which side I was on) and how much freedom I could have and what I could do with my friends.

"Today I see his vulnerabilities, which were hidden to me before, and sympathize acutely with his difficulties in expressing them. I love and care for him deeply, and respect his intelligence."

Love and Longing: Girls' Feelings for Their Father

Most girls feel a strange mixture of emotions for their father: closeness and distance, fear and longing, joy and fury:

"As a child, I learned from my mother that the best way to handle my father was to ignore him. I learned from my father that the 'proper' attitude towards my mother was ridicule. She was treated as if she were stupid, even though she was a college graduate. She eventually divorced him, and he never forgave her for leaving him. It hurt his pride.

"I was close to my father until he remarried—when I was about eleven. His wife was jealous and possessive and wouldn't let me be alone with him. She especially disliked his being affectionate with me. Before that, we'd been affectionate and had talked alone a lot. I was afraid of her and I lost respect for him.

"As I developed physically, I seemed to remind him of my mother. He made remarks about my body, so that I felt ashamed and covered up. He forced his affection on me while I tried to get away and my stepmother fumed at me.

"Thirty years later I learned from my mother that he had treated her the same way and had even spoken to her the same way. I don't know what it means, but it was an awful way for a girl to grow up. I was afraid of him, mainly because he hurt me with the mean things he said. He wouldn't let me argue or think for myself. He didn't want me to date or marry. When I was thirty-five, he told me I wasn't old enough to talk back to him!

"My father and his second wife fought for ten years before they settled down. After my brother and I left, their family consisted of themselves and their two children. They all got along fine. She's been a wonderful wife to him and I've learned a lot about marriage from her. She's now one of my best friends, believe it or not. It just proves that anything is possible."

"My father and I spent our lifetime together fighting. Although I was his favourite child, my relationship with him was always one of conflict. I wanted to please him but could never do anything well enough to merit a word of praise from him. Oh, how I wanted that! Eventually, I just quit trying and felt more hate than love.

"My father was very authoritarian, whereas my mother was gentle, loving and warm. He never praised us to our faces, but he did to others. Maybe pride and love are the same thing.

"Despite everything, I was aware that the love was there, especially for me. I sensed that I was my father's favourite. He was always scrupulously fair with us all, but this special love for me was confirmed when he died this year; my mother told me of things from my childhood (letters, drawings, compositions) that he had kept hidden away and she had only now found.

"Throughout my adult life, I had avoided him as much as possible, until I heard that he had contracted a fatal illness. Then, all that suppressed love for him came flooding back, and I managed to tell him that I loved him before he died. He never said the words to me (not once in my whole life!), but I knew he wanted to from the expression in his eyes and from the way he held me so tightly one day when I went to visit him. I feel sad that he was never able to express love through words and touch. How much easier that would have been for his children and his wife, and himself."

A hallmark of most girls' statements about their father is their frequently self-contradictory nature; almost three-quarters of girls' replies contain contradictory, even disjointed, statements:

"We went places together. I never feared him. He is a lot like me. I have a hard time accepting him and I love him a lot."

"My father was the meany of the neighbourhood. We were scared of him. In our house, we never argued: he screamed, we listened. But when we went on family vacations, it was entirely different. Those are very fond memories for me, he seemed relaxed and friendly."

"My father was not affectionate, but he was playful, carrying me on his shoulders and tickling me. He was a strict disciplinarian and I feared him when he was angry. He would let me come with him when he went to work on the farm, and teach me about nature and old customs. He seemed to know everything. I respected him very much, and did what he said. Today I am frustrated with him because he is so stubborn about what he thinks is correct. But he did raise a large family of two girls and three boys, and gave us all a strong set of values to live by."

"My father is affectionate by nature, but was somewhat inhibited from expressing it, except in a good, firm hug and a rather wet kiss. He was quite busy as a doctor when I was growing up, so I only remember in detail our time together on the two-week vacations in Maine every summer, where things were done a certain way (his way).

"He talks freely with me now, and there have been some important talks in the past which gave me permission to be sexual, to adopt a child if I wanted to, to live with a woman, etc. Only once did we tangle seriously, when I wished to return to a relationship with a man that was, indeed, destructive for me.

"One good thing about my father, he was always stubborn and opinionated but also very fond, strong, and steady in his affections. Very willing to listen. He is now eighty-six and deaf, but still willing to listen. I admire the way he continues to be zestful, enjoying small pleasures, taking pride in his bread-baking, his flower garden, and keeping abreast of all of our lives."

What is the reason for these confusing jumbles of emotions? One is that the archetype (including fear of "sexual motives") makes it difficult for family members to *see* one another realistically, since the icons keep getting in the way; the facts of the relationship are only "seen" and experienced through the mythological gauze of the "should's" and "shouldn't's" of the archetype. Thus individuals have difficulty forming valid relationships, based on their unique feelings and experiences. This is as true of mother–daughter relationships as it is of father–daughter relationships.

Affection—and Later Betrayal?—from the Father

Many girls report that while their fathers are affectionate when they are children, there is a complete change, sometimes an abrupt change, later.

Some girls remember a wonderful degree of affection in their early years:

"My father would give me rides on wall board (he designed and built much of our home and we always had pieces of building materials around the house) up to bed—where he would hold the board above my bed and shake me. That movement would cause the board to break in two and I would fall into bed with giggles. Sometimes when we played, I was afraid he would let me fall, but of course he never did. I am told that I was his pride and joy, and I was the only female child that he had anything to do with raising."

"He called me his 'Little Princess' for years, and I loved him. We were frequently together as a family at weekends. I didn't fear Dad—when my mother died, he came to fill the roles of both parents. We have remained close, even though both he and I have married since then."

"I adored my father. My father was so affectionate—he would hold my hand when we went out, he put his arm around me lots of times, and scratched my back every night."

Girls' warm, early memories of physical affection with their father—although not as numerous as memories of mothers—are clearly very happy reminiscences:

"How was he close to me? By reading me bedtime stories, singing for me, taking me out to the park, the cinema, buying things for me, teaching me to fish, play chess, football and wrestling, letting me laugh, and bathing me. I was his 'underella'."

"He used to wake me up from my naps in the most shy way—by patting me on the head just very softly, stroking my hair for a minute. I loved the feeling of his hands, and the expression of tenderness on his face. As soon as I woke up he would stop—as though I shouldn't see his expression, as though this kind of touch between us was forbidden."

185

But just as many girls say that their father never expressed his affection or love for them, but that they 'knew' he loved them anyway:

"My father was not so affectionate. I knew he loved me, but we were not very physical about it. I liked him and respected him immensely. Today I respect him even more seeing how hard he works. He is one of the sweetest persons on earth."

"I adored my father. We didn't do much together. He was always working or playing cards, but he sure did let me know that he loved me a lot. I respected him and feared him as a child."

"My father did not show affection. He didn't talk with me very much. The way he shows affection is to say things that tease people."

"My father always kissed me goodnight, but that was about all the physical affection there was. But he was the one who helped me with my homework, and the one who drove me and my friends everywhere. He was very patient."

"My father loved me, I instinctively knew that, although he never showed me."

However, most fathers stopped all physically affectionate touching with their daughters soon after early childhood, usually for fear of "provoking" incestuous ideas or appearances.

One father offered his daughter an explanation, years later, for his withdrawal of affection—as his daughter describes:

"Until I was in my twenties, I thought my father didn't love me, because he wasn't affectionate. Then he confessed before he died that he never showed his love for me because he didn't know how to without losing control of his male desires for females. We never talked much until this one time."

As other girls describe their father's emotional and physical withdrawal:

"We used to play games before bed, like him throwing us in the air and giving us piggy-back rides when we went walking. But when we were too old for that, nothing else took its place. With my mother, we kept on by talking, and doing things around the house together. But with my father—nothing. The last time we were close (touching) was hugging goodbye at the airport."

"When I was young, he was affectionate with me (not with my brothers). He would hold me, and speak softly. He wouldn't spank me as hard as he would my brothers. Then we started to argue, when I was twelve. Now I avoid controversial opinions in front of him. I think he's confused and trying to find peace with God. He is not the father I remember."

"I spent lots of time with my father as a child, usually doing outdoorsy things. But from the age of thirteen on, we didn't spend much time together—I don't think he could begin to understand an adolescent girl. We didn't get along again until several years after my parents were divorced and I'd been living at college."

"I loved him as a child, hated him as an adolescent (he became very critical), and now I have mixed feelings of love, respect, and bitterness. We communicate best by mail. After three days in person I want to strangle him because he has to have his way all of the time. It may get better now that I've established myself in a profession (his), since he understands and respects the demands it makes."

Of course, not only mothers, but also fathers can have their own life-cycle problems to deal with—problems that have nothing directly to do with the children. The anger that many teenage girls are seeing in their father correlates with feelings about their lives that many men in *The Hite Report on Men and Male Sexuality* describe having in their forties and fifties. Many feel that although they do almost everything they "should" do as a man, taking care of the family, being there, earning a living, somehow they aren't satisfied. Many of them feel empty.

Another girl describes how her relationship with her father went through the basic stages, the same basic stages described by many other girls:

"I felt closer to my father. He wasn't extremely affectionate, but I could hug him (not my mom). And he would rock me to sleep in his lap. He was my protector from my older sister. I loved him. We did quite a few things together, like skiing, skating and fishing. He would take me to the beach, even though he didn't know how to swim.

"It was he that woke me in the morning for school, got me ready, and made breakfast. If I had a problem or was hurt I went to him. He expected me to treat him as I wanted him to treat me. If it took me three days to mow the lawn, it took him three days to fix my bike. Seemed fair. I never feared him, I only feared his disappointment.

"But when I was a teenager, our relationship became more strained. Major disagreements arose when I started camping in mixed groups. He never forbade my going, but he would ask me if I 'thought that was the best thing to do' (one of his classic lines). I got used to not quite telling the whole story.

"He didn't want me to go away to college either. I felt as if I was going to university against his wishes. He wanted me to do secretarial work. Told me I could get far with it! My mother said well, at the university maybe she'll marry a professor. My dad had these discriminatory, sexist attitudes I didn't like—also about my mother. He actually did use the words 'women's work' every once in a while. He also didn't like it when my mother went to work outside the home.

"Later, when I lived with a guy for a year when I was twenty-two, Dad didn't speak to me for at least a month, and never came to visit us, or called. I received messages through my sister, though, and he was still sociable when I visited him. But what he didn't realize was that after learning to love someone else (my boyfriend), I found I could love my father much more. He wasn't the loser.

"Then, later when my father became very ill and was going to have an operation, we became close again. I had just broken up with my long-time boyfriend (the same one). I was afraid that my father was going to die and not know how much I loved him, and so I started sharing more with him. Showing him the more private side of me. It is amazing how little my father and I knew about each other's feelings at that time. When I first told him I loved him (it was just before his operation), he cried. I felt that I had given him the biggest piece of love I ever had. Now I hug or kiss him whenever I feel like giving him love, and he's giving it back to me."

Betrayal
Many of the girls who recall early affection from their father also bitterly describe how they felt they were betrayed by him later:

"After the divorce, my father let us down. He never called. It was as if we had never been born."

"My father let me down when I told him that my brother had sexually abused me. He didn't take it seriously. He never punished my brother at all."

"I used to love him but he is authoritarian. He hit my mom."

"I couldn't get over his not telling me that he had married for the second time."

"He sold my pony without telling me."

"My father is a married bachelor. He has a girlfriend, he wants his freedom, and he wants to show off his children—us, when we come for the weekend."

"He calls me unjustified names, just because I wear lipstick and short skirts."

Fathers' right to be "free" of the children?
Many girls, of course, do not live with their father—since, statistically, in most divorced families the children stay with the mother:

"I saw my father only on Sundays, but he called home every day of the week and spoke to my brother and myself, how's school, etc. Mother made me ask him for more money every time. It is now twenty years later and he still sends her money through me. I don't know how I feel about him. He has a common-law wife."

"My mother divorced my father when I was five. He remarried soon after and didn't keep in touch."

An unwritten rule in society seems to say: if a man divorces, it is socially acceptable for him rarely or even never to see his "former" children; whereas, if a mother were to do this, she would be considered extremely disreputable or a pariah. The archetypal role of the mother implies that a mother must stay with her child, be loving and nurturing, no matter what—while the archetype of the "father" is much more remote and independent.

Should fathers see their relationships with their children more in the way mothers have traditionally seen theirs? That is, should they feel they must stay with the child, no matter what? Of course, some men do feel they should do this, and want to do this, even if divorced. However, child-support statistics in most countries, and girls' testimony here, demonstrate overwhelmingly that a large number of men do not.

A daughter leaves her father
On the other hand, many girls "leave" their father, whom they loved when they were younger, because of the "betrayal" or bad relationship that develops.

One young woman writes a very moving letter to her parents, and especially her father, in which she expresses this sense of outraged betrayal and her anger, and says goodbye:

"Dear Mom and Dad:

"Relations between Dad and myself have reached an end-point for me and I want you to know this in writing, where I can say what I have to say calmly and completely.

"Dad and I have had extremely poor relations for a long time now, and I guess that can go on for years of unhappiness and tension . . . But years of your terrible temper, Dad, and your unhappiness and frustration have worn away at not only you but also me. I really want no part of that anymore. You try to efface other people constantly, and I resent you for that. You totally ignore the feelings of others, and that is too bad, because every situation in life doesn't hinge on you. It is constantly necessary to 'escape' you to have peace of mind. Years of this negative contact between us have extinguished my desire to know you.

"You treated me terribly and were cruel to me for years, although there was a time when things were good between us. I can remember several exceptional events here that have led to this end point for me—but I won't—but the way you treated me the morning before I left for Montana was 'the end' for me. You did one of the lowest things a person can do to another. You tried to make me hate Grandpa. When you knew I was vulnerable, you said something incredibly shitty. But it didn't make me hate Grandpa to hear it, because even if he said it, you knew it could hurt me and also him, and so that bit of information should never have gone past you. Instead, you violated both Grandpa and me by telling me. You saw I was upset when I was on the phone. You wouldn't leave me alone when I nicely asked you several times and you saw I was upset.

"You knew Mom, who unfortunately always has to act as a 'buffer', wasn't home, and you took advantage of the fact that the doors don't lock in this house to violate my need to be alone by simply running around after me yelling at me. Yelling at me about how I have been trying to tear you and Mom apart for years . . . when I am in a crisis of my own that is very important and upsetting for me, all you can think of is yourself. The disgust I feel for you really sickens me even now, and I am past the point of a few years ago when I felt it was important to know you.

"Quite frankly, I am sorry that I did not make out a police report on you when the highway patrolman made you pull over because he saw you hitting me so hard while you were driving that the car was not in control. But people who are victimized are often the scared defenders of those who are hurting them. Maybe if I had said yes to him when he asked me if I wanted him to book you, I would actually have helped you. You would have been forced into some kind of therapy, and you need it and should get it.

"I still would like to see Mom, although I realize that that may no longer be possible. I love her very much. I never did understand why two people with such strained relations would either a) do nothing in order to better things if they loved one another and wanted to stay together, or b) split up. I have always wondered why you stay together, although it is also true that I never knew the two of you well and I'm sure things exist between you as a couple that I'm not aware of. But it is precisely because I respect your private relationship and wish the best for it, that I can say that I do realize that in making this decision I may also be closing off seeing Mom, who I love dearly.

"I lived in your house for a long time and you had a great chance to make our actual relationship grow. Instead, you created a chasm of huge tensions and unhappiness, and a great loss, you lost the possibility of knowing someone and having a real relationship—it grew dimmer and dimmer the longer it went on. I hear from other people what nice things you say all the time about me—and I think it's sad that you can never show me care or human respect when we are around each other.

"I was in fear of you and imprisoned until I left home for school. Until then I was a 'captive audience' (I always did see living with you that way) but you never understood that after I left home you would eventually have to start treating me like a human being in order to earn my respect and desire to know you; otherwise I would not choose to be 'captive'.

"It is possible that you will keep this letter, like things that have affected you deeply, like my 'joint' when I was thirteen . . . Although you hit me for hours in your shop, screaming that I tell you the 'whole story', the story was already complete, it was actually a very simple story. I never forget how you beat me with a bamboo for a couple of hours, trying to force a confession out of me for some 'sordid' story that didn't even exist and which I refused to invent because I had always been taught not to lie. Well, I hope that you keep it with whatever else you may have kept over the years (I still remember how I wanted to laugh when, years after the 'drug' event, you pulled out the joint to demonstrate how this event—which was negative for you and 'showed you' how shitty I was at age thirteen—was so important to you, you had kept the joint to remind yourself of it and to remember it always!).

"I really do hope you keep this particular letter and that, instead of approaching it defensively, you find the capacity somehow to open yourself to what I have said and to admit to yourself that you should seek some inner change. It has been for the purpose of making you 'take a look' that I have mentioned a few painful events in this letter. Do not think for a moment that I have ever forgotten either of these events, or the countless others. If you love people, you shouldn't act like you hate them and treat them with lack of regard to their character, needs, and wants. I say that because even though it is over for you and me and that can no longer change, I am only one person. You still have other people in your life and you can make your relationships with them different. It's not too late. Change, which is always possible, could help you to be closer to them and I truly believe this would help them and you to be happier. Anne."

How do things get to this point?

The change in fathers' behaviour towards daughters: from affection to silent withdrawal, or nagging criticism

By the time a girl is twelve or so, her relationship with her father has often become quite distant and alienated, sometimes entailing violent or angry outbursts: "I remember being very young and loving my father dearly. He smelled good, he read to me, and was warm and cosy. Then he just completely withdrew. He became very aloof, critical, and stopped all interaction. When I was in high school, he became very violent."

Girls feel confused and ask themselves, "What happened? What did I do?"

Sometimes after the withdrawal of affection a girl longs for the "good father" to come back, for "special affection" to be shown again. This "waiting for a lost love to return" can become a lifelong emotional pattern as far as her future relationships with men are concerned.

Living with so much longing and hope for approval from a distant father, a woman may later pick "distant" men, hoping to make them "see" her, love her. She may believe, as she did about her father, that no matter how cold or heartless, the man loves her underneath it all—since in the case of her father, her mother kept reassuring her: "Yes, he loves you really."

This is not such an unusual pattern. Many fathers develop attitudes of alienation and cynicism, becoming known for their cutting remarks and potential violence. Why? This pattern has everything to do with the training for masculinity which boys undergo, as seen in Part III. But what kind of relationship does this leave the father and daughter with?

The Archetype of the Father

What Kind of Love?

"I feared his displeasure but respected him greatly."
The majority of girls (and boys) say something very much like this in answer to questions about their feelings for their father.

The word "respect" is used in 59 per cent of replies, and in combination with the word "fear", in 41 per cent of replies. (In other words, 41 per cent of girls say they both respected and feared their father.) It is interesting to note that the word "respect" is used ten times more frequently in replies about fathers than in replies about mothers, and "fear" is used in 81 per cent of answers about fathers, but only 7 per cent answers about mothers.

One of the first things one notices about children's statements about their father is that most are far less effusive than the answers to similar questions about their mother. There is a different, more remote tone. Most answers, from girls or boys, whether in the 1970's or the 1990's, describe a person who is much less well known to them; indeed, the answers often specifically state this: "He was a quiet person, hard to know," or, "We rarely saw him, he didn't talk much."

How well do these children understand their father? Are they responding to an archetype or a real father? What characteristics do they admire?

61 per cent of girls say they feel love for their father, but what do they mean? This girl's statement is typical:

"Although I don't remember talking to him about important things (except on a few occasions), still, I love him and respect him today."

Why does she love and respect him? She doesn't say. Does she know? Is this the "duty" of a "good daughter"? Or an example of the confusion children absorb about the word "love" in the context of the "family"? Do

193

they repeat it as a kind of talisman to ward off the father-god's anger and punishment?

In another girl's statement, it is unclear whether—or how—her father loves her, or whether she believes herself to be loved:

"He is not very affectionate—he's not a kisser or hugger. His way of showing his affection is a big joke in our family: on birthdays he buys the mushiest, most expensive cards he can get his hands on. It's a riot. He never says or does anything to express his feelings, so when he buys these gushy cards, we all think it's just a scream! He really means what the cards say, I'm sure."

And what are we to make of this:

"I am not close to either parent. When I was younger, my father beat my mom and he on occasion beat me too. My father was (and still is) an alcoholic. Yeah, I guess they love me. My mother was rarely affectionate and neither was my father, they were always arguing. He was the one who was home (drunk) while she went out to work."

A few girls explicitly state that their father didn't love them:

"I was not close to my father, I knew he didn't love me. My mother kept on saying, 'He loves you, Lynne. He just doesn't know how to show it.' I answered, 'Then he ought to learn how.' I felt he didn't care about me or understand me, I never got the kind of praise that meant anything to me, or even talked to him about things. The relationship was almost formal."

"At one point, when I thought I might expire from TB, he came to visit me at the hospital. I thought that since I was dying, I would erase all past sins, and said, 'Dad, I love you.' He said, 'I think a lot of you, too.' Can you imagine that? I was dying and he couldn't even tell me he loved me. I've since stopped trying to get the kind of love and approval from my father that I once thought one should have. I'm freer now, in a way, it's like a weight lifted from my shoulders."

Girls' principal complaint about their father is that he is too critical of them:

"I didn't like him. He was always so critical of me. He *said* he was trying to help—it was always 'for my own good'."

"I lost my father and I miss him terrifically. But because he was so sure what was right all the time about my life, a small part of me is glad I don't have to worry about pleasing him anymore."

"My father was never affectionate (perhaps rarely). He always

194

used to put me down, but in subtle, intellectually disguised ways. Emotionally, he was totally non-supportive and destructive. I have not seen him since a year after my mother and he divorced when I was sixteen. I have no desire to see him, yet I harbour no anger or resentment against him. He is just a weak loser, unable to really care for anyone but himself."

A Special Closeness with Fathers

Icons of Male Love

"My mother doesn't generally know my deepest, darkest secrets, whereas my father does."
A large number of other girls say they felt there was a "special relationship" between them and their father, that they had been "his favourite", and, "He was the one I really loved":

"I was crazy about my father, I think I was his favourite of three girls, although I caused him all kinds of pain by rebelling, running away, and getting kicked out of school! He wasn't impatient like my mother. He was wonderful to me. Even after I got kicked out of school, he helped me to get into another very good school. I think my mother resented me. I don't blame her. What a hard time she had—three daughters and we all adored my father and disliked her."

"I was closer to my father than to my mother. He was much more demonstrative, affectionate and emotional, even if that meant being capable of great anger at times. I always felt sorry for my mother. My father ruled the family with a strong hand, and this included her. He insisted on total obedience. My mother indirectly taught us to fear him by her example of waiting on him hand and foot, and acquiescing to him on every matter."

"I loved my grandfather. (I lived with my grandparents.) He was the sweetest man I ever knew. He always wrote me little notes, and left me surprises, and I know he loved me. My grandmother would often scream and shout at me, and at him too . . . I guess she had good reasons, and as a feminist now, I know I probably could have felt the same in her position, but there was just something great about my grandfather, he made me happy, terribly happy."

"My father and I have a secret bond, a true understanding. He believes I should have more independence, but since he thinks my mother knows more about kids, he lets her overrule him. He can't contradict my mother. But he understands."

196

"The closeness I had with my father was more of an unspoken understanding. My father was never affectionate with anyone, he came from a family of ten kids and was taught that it was wrong to show emotion or affection."

This special relationship was almost never acknowledged in words between father and daughter. 36 per cent of girls in this study say they felt closer to their father than to their mother, while 41 per cent felt closer to their mother. 23 per cent didn't feel close to either parent.

Anger and Conflict Between Fathers and Daughters

Other daughters, 38 per cent in fact, are very angry with their father. Usually the anger is the result of final frustration at what a daughter feels is a lack of understanding, her father's not seeing her as a real person—and exhaustion at playing the father–daughter game:

"I fear and dislike him. He never listens to my point of view, and we all have to do what he decides."

"My dad and I argue mostly about men. He's always said and still maintains that I'm living my life only in search of a man. That drives me crazy. I tried to strangle him once—grabbed him by the throat in such rage—I've never got over my anger with him. He refuses to listen to me or see me as an individual human being with dignity."

32 per cent of girls (and 41 per cent of boys) say that their father had a violent temper which they feared, some also describing punishment by their father:

"I feared him most of the time, he has a terrible temper and reacts irrationally. Due to his paranoid view of the world, he always hears something other than what is meant, and draws bizarre conclusions."

"My father was a violent overbearing man whom I hated as a child. If I had argued with him, I wouldn't have lived this long. He was a nutcase when it came to 'punishing the children', especially when drunk. Today I think he's a sober version of his former self, but just as mean."

"I was very afraid of my father, and still am. He was a violent alcoholic with a terrible temper, he abused my mother terribly, mentally and physically, and my brother was terribly, terribly abused. He was beaten a lot. By luck, I was mentally abused and brainwashed, but not physically."

"When my father and I got along, we got along great, but when we didn't (which was much more often, especially in my early teens) things exploded. Then I hated him. I hated his temper and domineering manners, I hated the way my mother served him all the time, and the way he considered us property because we were dependent on him for support."

★   ★   ★

One girl describes her father suddenly making a scene about her nakedness and whipping her, when she was twelve:

"When I was about twelve years old, I remember my father punishing me for not wanting to take a shower. If I recall well, this is the first and last time my father in any way hurt me physically. We were in our weekend house, and I didn't want to take a shower. I think I was just too lazy, and didn't like the shower; the water came out in droplets. My father told me to take a shower and I said I wouldn't. I remember that I was naked, as I always used to walk around the house this way. After several attempts to make me take a shower, my father, angry at this point, went outside and cut a long branch from a tree, he came back and he whipped me. I remember crying a lot and ending up having to take a shower.

"Maybe it had something to do with my father being an alcoholic at the time (now it's been over ten years since he's had a drink. The weekends would be horrible, my father drunk and arguing with my mother and physically hurting her. My sister and I would always run to my mother's aid, crying, telling her to shut up, not to talk back to him because he was drunk. We were always on the point of calling the police. My mother would always cry, and later would come to our room asking us who we would want to live with when they divorced."

Almost every girl who reports being physically punished or "disciplined" by a non-drinking father says that he only did it when she "really deserved it" (boys, on the other hand, were almost always angry about being punished).

"What I liked most about him was that he was strict, but not overly strict. When we were spanked we knew we deserved it. What I liked least about him was his quiet moodiness—which I've inherited, and his inability to show affection."

"I really started hating him over one incident. I always wanted a dog, it was a family 'joke'. But I couldn't have one till we moved to the suburbs when I was ten. I loved the Labrador we got. Then one day she bit the paper boy and Dad made us have her put to sleep. That contributed to my hate for him.

"My dad has mellowed a lot since my mother died, he is less authoritative and uncompromising. We have learned to hug each other (on my instigation), mainly on hello and goodbye."

Can Girls Criticize Their Father—or Is This "Disrespectful"?

It is difficult for girls to criticize their father—despite some of their criticism quoted in the previous statements. Many children, both boys and girls, fear openly criticizing their father, because they have learned to fear the father's punishment. This fear of male authority figures can last throughout life.

The strange jumble of feelings seen earlier in girls' statements about their father represents not only lack of clarity but also fear. Our society almost forbids the examination of our feelings for the "sacred icons" of mother and father. Feelings of anger towards fathers in particular are rarely explored. They are the most taboo, especially for females. Much more acceptable is to hate (or be angry with) the mother, to whom all the anger can be directed.

Painful and Distant Relationships

28 per cent of girls describe relationships with their fathers in which they do not even have the memory of an early, affectionate time:

"My father was so unaffectionate that after the age of five or so I remember him hugging me only once, when I was eleven. I hung like a limp rag doll because I didn't know how to hug him back. We rarely did things together alone, but occasionally I would ride in the car with him if he asked me to. I felt kind of sorry for him, afraid that he would think I didn't like him if I said no, and feel rejected. I loved him, but it was quite difficult living without any affection."

"My father—I remember him doing things like pinching my cheek too hard, giving funny quick kisses, or pounding my arm playfully till it hurt, and then complaining that I wasn't tough enough to take it. We never talked, it seemed like he dreaded being alone with me. I did not like him, I feared him. He was unyielding. He had no conception of respect. It was his house and he made the rules.

"He had many ridiculous rules that pain me to describe today. For example, he went so far as to put intercoms in the bedrooms, so he could tune into us from a central control panel in the living room; we were unable to turn them off. And many times he rammed into my bedroom when my mother and I were talking privately together. Or if I said some swear word, whether he understood the conversation or not, or just heard the 'shit' or 'damn', he screamed at me for talking snotty to my mother."

"When my father died (I was eleven), I was glad, because the arguing was over, finally. I prayed a great deal of this time, as my mother was distant as Mars, and I felt some guilt in being glad about my father's death. But I knew he was happier too."

"What I remember most about my dad was the smell of his shirts. I disliked everything about him. He used to hit my mother. Even after she had been battered by him, she would be able to hold me and tell me it would be all right.

"My father was not affectionate, he and I did not talk. I hated him. I feared him and had no respect for him. I spent much of my time thinking of ways to kill him. I remember one day all five of us kids put our heads together to think of how we could do it (kill him). We never argued with him because his word was law. He is dead today, and I am glad, because I don't have to check over my shoulder anymore for him, or go out and look for him on street corners. He killed himself with booze and abuse."

"No friends ever visited my house during the day, let alone over night. Once I spent the night at another girl's house and we giggled till late, but her father was like mine. He was pretty scary. I remember seeing bruises on Judy's mother's face. I knew what they were. Once I was there overnight when they fought, and I was able to hold Judy and tell her that I had this kind of thing happening at my home too. We cried together. We never talked about it much after that.

Sexual Politics in the Parents' Relationship

Gender Inequality and Its Effect on Children

How children are forced to take sides inside the family
"Most of the emotional energy of the house was focused on my father."

Why do families fight? The biggest problem in "the family", ironically, is gender. Lack of equality between parents creates unstable conditions for many children. We see constant mentions in the press of "divorce statistics on the rise", read hysterical warnings about "families collapsing", and so on.

The underlying cause of this "collapse"—which is really a process of democratization and diversification of families, something which will benefit us all—is the traditional "emotional contract" between men and women. (See Chapter 5 and *Women and Love*.)

Feeling torn between the parents
When asked to describe their families, most girls focus on the gender-power difference between their father and mother, the tensions this creates, and how they felt strongly that they were called on emotionally to "take sides", not necessarily by the parents themselves, but by the stress of the situation, the set-up. 73 per cent of boys and girls say parents showed very little or no affection to each other. 64 per cent say they felt torn, forced to take sides or juggle the two sides much of the time they were children. 38 per cent say they tried to be a "peacemaker" and bring the two sides together.

The dilemma of feeling emotionally torn between her two parents is painted vividly by one young woman:

"I can remember lying in bed between my parents when I was about six. I would give one leg to each of them, my mother and my father. I wanted to support each of them, not let either one of them think I loved them less. This was very hard, because there was a terrible crack in the middle of the mattress between them where I would lie!"

★　　★　　★

Feeling this tension, which is built into the patriarchal structure, makes children uneasy, as they try to understand and wrestle with the problem, usually for several *years*, while they are growing up. Which side is morally correct? What do parents really feel for each other?

Another girl describes her feelings of confusion in the midst of the struggle her parents were waging:

"I felt very close to my mother as a child. I thought she could protect me from anything. She was always there to talk to or to fix my bruises. Basically, my father brought home the pay and drank at weekends. I loved and respected my mother for being strong (she ran the house, raised us, and put up with my father's drinking).

"I hated the fact that my father drank, because it made my mother sad, plus he would act very stupid. However, he was affectionate with me, which was beneficial because my mother did not like to be affectionate. At times he was too roughly affectionate, but not intentionally. He could not express himself very well verbally, so he let his hugs do the talking. My father was big, heavy and loud, but he always had a big heart. I felt bad that my father and I could not have been closer when I was young, but he never learned how to express himself well. I also think he was too busy going to work every day to relate to me emotionally.

"I respect my father because he went to work every day to a job he hated, in order to give his family what they wanted. I feel he got as rotten a deal as any woman who couldn't satisfy her dreams because she went along with what society told her was the 'right' thing to do."

A twenty-two-year-old woman describes her mother and father and their relationship, and tries to come to terms with her feelings about them:

"My mother does not demonstrate her feelings (very rarely anyway) by touching or cuddling, more in the way she speaks to you and defends you with words. I like to spend time totally alone with her, like when my dad goes out and it is just her and me, and I have her full attention to tell her my feelings and thoughts.

"My parents were very affectionate towards each other—although it was always my dad who initiated it—holding my mum's hand, telling her he loved her, hugging her first. They argued openly only a few times. My dad would argue and my mum would calm him, and then tell me and my sisters how she would leave him if she could! But never tell *him* how she was really feeling about things. Instead she'd keep the peace and tell *us* her feelings (I never agreed with that).

"My father was more affectionate to me than my mum in the way of kissing or hugging, but he never really talked to me like my mum did. He and I never really talked much (and still don't) so he never really understood me. He is quite a moody person. One day he will be in a foul temper about something, then the next be all right again, so as a child I feared him. We very rarely went places on our own, but when we did it was special to me, these have stuck in my head as 'special times'.

"I find it difficult to express how I feel for him today. I still fear him, although not as much, but I do respect his values (well, some of them) and I love him a lot."

Divided Loyalties: Love as Guilt

"What did you learn from your mother was the proper attitude to have towards your father? What attitude did you learn from your father was the proper attitude to have towards your mother?"
Almost every child was vividly aware of the subtle (or not so subtle) gender politics going on between her or his parents.

"I learned from my mom that the attitude to have with my dad was not to be too much of a nag. If I wanted to ask him something, just to ask and not beat around the bush, but not badger him for an immediate response. My dad taught me to handle my mom via 'calling her bluff' to keep her from getting irrational. My parents respect each other and treat each other well. They were affectionate, my parents taught us that showing love and telling another person that you love them is a natural part of life in a family."

"We would all scramble when Dad's car pulled up at night and scurry to finish setting the table, so that dinner would be on the table when he walked in. Whatever we were talking about, we would stop. I don't remember him ever being late for dinner. My father was very demanding of my mother, and we all feared him. He was very distant. I loved him, but I didn't like him."

"Mom told us to be quiet in front of Dad. When he napped in the afternoon at weekends, we tip-toed around. My father taught me that my mother was to stay home and not work, that she should be happy to be home with us and free to do the housework and call her friends on the phone to chat. My mother taught me that my father was always going to be like he was and not to fight him about it."

"From him I learned obedience to my mother, to avoid getting her upset, and not to take her too seriously; from my mother, I learned to treat my father with deference, seriousness, caution—to avoid getting

204

him upset. Also I learned unquestioning obedience, that he could be approached with any problem, but not bothered with too much silliness that wasn't direct play that he initiated."

"Daddy is the leader and the head of our household. He treats Mama very nicely, gives her nice gifts, and seems to enjoy her company. Mama defers to Daddy. But she is definitely not an 'extension'."

"My father loved my mother and thought she was the cutest thing on two feet and showed it. He insisted that we show respect to her. She felt that, since he worked hard all day, sometimes for at least twelve hours a day, that when he was home, he should be 'king' of the house. He got the best chair, best piece of meat, and his choice of radio shows. She showed that she thought he was the most attractive man that she knew, and it's still a good system for keeping a husband happy, women's lib or no."

"I grew up in a family of nine children. My mother was head prefect at a school in England where the motto of the school was 'My joy is in serving others'. Mum lived that, and is still doing so. She dotes on her husband and children and grandchildren and has, outside the family, no life of her own. According to her this does not bother her in the least.

"My father had a rough childhood in India, he was sent to boarding school, which was brutal. He always had servants at home and now my mother is his servant. He does no housework, except when he feels like cooking. He never cleans up after himself or anyone else.

"Dad will eulogize Mum—her determination, dedication to the family, her tireless work, but in daily life he often belittles her or lectures her for things he feels she hasn't done, or has done inadequately. I grew up thinking that a woman's love meant submission, i.e., if you love someone, then anything goes."

"As a child, I learned that my mother was a servant. 'Don't say anything, keep the peace at all costs,' was what she taught me. She tried to make her life an example for my sister and me, and wanted us desperately to buy into it. My parents were never affectionate in front of me."

"From my mother I learned that my father should favoured, even though she made more money; she informed me that she put herself down on the tax statement as the dependant, because men must be put first.

"My mother and I went food and clothes shopping, leaving my father waiting for us for hours in the parking lot while we shopped. My father was not affectionate physically; but if I asked for money, he always gave me more than I asked for. He shared with us his very strong ethical sense of how people should be treated. We didn't talk much, but I liked him. We never argued. I now like him more than I did then, since he seems more giving, quite needy emotionally, but impotent in terms of getting his needs met by others."

Love and Domestic Violence:
How Are Children to Reconcile These?

Is observing domestic violence worse than feeling the gender tension, never seeing a display of affection, or violence, between the parents, but being told everything is all right? Being told this is "love", that, "We stayed together because we love each other."

Girls describe their reactions to seeing their father hit their mother:
"In the beginning of their relationship my stepfather treated her well, but it deteriorated in the course of the seven years they were married into a nightmare of domestic violence against her. We, my sister and I, grew angry and disgusted with him—and finally with her too, in the end, because she was putting up with him."

"All I remember about my father is that I was scared of him. I do not like or respect him, and would never see him if my mother was not alive. I think she was a fool to have stayed with him, but it was what she believed to be proper. I do not like to spend time with her but sometimes I have to, to be polite."

As we have seen, 32 per cent of girls and 41 per cent of boys were "scared of" their fathers.

Growing up being scared of the father, or seeing one's mother tiptoe around him, creates a habit of acceding to males, especially males in power. This can create enormous problems for women in later life.

Changing the Emotional Contract Between Mothers and Fathers

Here we are talking about the subtle second-class citizenship of the woman as it is built into most mother–father families. This genderized atmosphere is carried on in subtle psychological ways, as women describe in detail in *Women and Love*.

We need to work out the subtle patterns of the "emotional contract", to name the standard forms of "emotional violence", and include in our analysis not only the individual personalities of the people involved, but also the disruptive social patterns of the traditional nuclear family/the

206

"love relationship/couple". We do not have to go on using that authoritarian emotional contract to shape our relationships, nor to define "love". We can build new and different emotional contracts and different lives.

If men have more status in the world, so they also do in love relationships and the family. This is true, independently of whether they are happy in their relationship/family or not. There is a tendency for some men to say, "She makes my life impossible, I have to keep trying to please her, it's really a matriarchy around our house." Being unhappy with a relationship does not mean that the other person has the power. These are the problems of the old, authoritarian "emotional contract".

This gender tension may have something to do with the level of hostility developed by many teenagers against their parents, as soon as they are old enough not to feel quite as vulnerable, quite as "hopelessly" dependent. They often say, "Why couldn't they just work it out? I mean break up or work it out!"

Of course, there are cases which are uniquely terrible:

"My mother subtly tried to get me to dislike my father and I did. I think they both loved me, but they and I lost sight of that love a lot because of their personal war. I was a pawn used between them."

In fact, all the conflicts in the traditional hierarchical family could be seen as loyalty conflicts. The mother is angry and hurt because the children are not really loyal to her, but to the father and "to all their friends" (society, school, the father). The daughter and son are angry because the mother is not loyal first to them but to the father and society. They are disappointed. They had expected the father to represent society, but they are surprised when the mother turns out also to do so, although not to have the power to intercede between society and them the way she used to intercede between them and the father.

All loyalty is focused towards "the Top", the father, in this authoritarian family system, the hierarchy of allegiances, and this is very disappointing. Because in this system, how can you have any real, balanced relationships? Relationships based on feeling, and not on "marketability", status or power.

Fathers and Sexuality

Daughters as Their Father's Girlfriend

Are some fathers flirtatious with their daughters for lack of knowing any
other way to relate to women?

One girl describes her frustration and fury about an intense
closeness she felt she shared with her father, which was cut off by
the father's death:

"My father passed away two years ago. My idol, my most admired
person, a war veteran, only sixty-seven years old. He died from a heart
attack. Part of myself died with him.

"I was not close to him but we loved each other. They say his eyes
would light up whenever he saw me. He used to brag about me and was
so proud when I won a beauty contest and trip to the Bahamas. It was
a highlight of his life, too. He taught me to be strong and self-sufficient
and I will always be grateful to him for that. He was a man of honour
and paid his debts. I have adopted his ways in honour of his memory,
I try to be just like him.

"When he was younger my father based almost all his confidence
on his personality and good looks, and he taught me to do the same. I
excelled in my looks, and they were an asset rarely wasted. I used them
to get my own way in relationships with men, to succeed in business
deals, purchases, wherever and whenever I could sense it would work.
I also had my father's smile and used it. My mother was appalled at
such shallowness, yet proud of my good looks. I was so confident in
being blonde, blue-eyed and beautiful that I didn't even notice brown- or
black-haired people! I can't believe I was so shallow.

"I loved my father more than anything. I admired his strength and
honour and personality, the good and the bad about him. His pride in
me and mine in him. It went without words. We knew.

"My father's death evoked a deep feeling of anger in me: Why did
you leave me, when I need you? I am you and you are me!"

Being the father's favourite

"My mother accused me of being flirtatious with my father. I was really very close to him, but that's not the same thing. Didn't I have the right to be close to him? I loved him, and he loved me, he understood me like no one else in that family."

Girls' feelings when they are their father's "favourite" can be quite hard for them to deal with. On the one hand, the girl can feel she is betraying the mother, as the mother is supposed to be the love object, his loved one, not the daughter. Also, the daughter may feel shame for the hidden sexual implications, whether she feels them or not.

Even smiles exchanged with the father sometimes become guilt-laden in our society, which is so self-conscious about heterosexuality. (This is also true about a mother and son having a social life together—they can't even go out to the theatre without causing a stir.)

The daughter can wonder, Am I being flirtatious? Am I just irresistible? Therefore superior to my mother? How will my mother feel about this? How will she feel about me? She must hate me . . . And so on. (Although one woman had the theory that her mother colluded in her father's liking for taking the daughter out. Why? Because it gave the mother some time alone; in effect, the daughter thought the mother saw her as sort of "babysitting" the father, who could not chase after other women, because he was, after all, with the daughter!)

A promise of sexuality

Is it possible that girls could have a desire, in their heart of hearts, to "seduce" the father, emotionally at least, because this would mean having more power in the family, more power than the mother *or* the father? *And* this would take the daughter out of the hated category of the powerless, the "child". Thus, a slight impulse in this direction might be "natural"; however, to interpret this as a kind of perversity on the part of girls would be to make the mistake Freud did when he interpreted girls' desire for the rights of men in society as "penis envy".

To understand what is going on, we must not neglect to take into consideration the gender and ageist power constructions enmeshed in the structure of the "traditional family". These feelings and behaviour on the part of the family members certainly do not imply that there is a "natural heterosexual attraction" or urge between father and daughter. The society is busy obliquely whispering suggestively to the father and daughter that they "might" feel this sexual attraction; but without this social suggestion or tension, would the thoughts occur so easily? Without it, fathers and daughters could have much better relationships. They could be friends.

The family system as we know it is set up for trouble. Because of the way that the social order is constructed, most girls soon learn that their one basic power is their sexuality (whereas boys' might be through athletic prowess or good marks, or being leaders of groups of boys, etc.).

Some girls think they are "guilty" of having sexual feelings for their father, when they are not. For example, a girl who receives gifts from her father—money, dresses, shoes, etc.—could naturally feel pleasure and excitement, which might cause her body, including her genitals, to flush with a heated, happy feeling. This flush could be confused with, or interpreted as, guilty "sexual arousal".

It could also be interpreted as general emotional arousal, happiness. That is how it probably would be interpreted if the gift were coming from the mother. However, behind every interchange between a father and daughter lurks the "danger of heterosexuality".

This sexual self-consciousness lends a sexual atmosphere even where there is none. Films like *Lolita* and *Gigi* reinforce the idea of sexual "danger", especially between older men and young girls. Further, there are very few models of men and women being "just friends" in our society; usually "friends" are of the same gender, and so almost all opposite gender contacts are presumed to be sexual.

Complicated Scenarios of Love and Power in Family Triangles

Flirtation with Fathers for Special Treatment

Why girls learn that "female sexuality" is power, their only real weapon, has to do with our society's construction of "women's place", not with girls themselves, or with whether a girl is a "good girl" or a "bad girl". When one has so little of it, it is a natural temptation to use power. This does not "prove" that "heterosexual impulses between father and daughter are natural" or any such thing; it merely proves that fathers have the power in the hierarchical family, and that sometimes girls see that one way to get to that power and approval is through sexual flirtatiousness, cuteness or "innocence".

To look at it another way, it is, after all, "normal" in life that individuals prefer some people over others. For example, even though all of several children may be "born to" us, they are not alike, by any means. It is only natural for a parent to like some more than others, or feel they have more in common. This works, too, in reverse: children's feelings for parents are similarly influenced by personality traits.

Should we assume that all relationships should be equal within a family? Should we accept "family favourites" within a family? Crushes between family members?

Fathers Over-React

Fathers Make Sexual Remarks to Their Teenage Daughters

Fathers, often without fully realizing what they are doing, respond to their daughters' new sexuality with misogynistic, "double-standard" comments:

"Don't wear that lipstick! You look like a prostitute."

"You used to be my sweet little girl. What happened?" (on being "confronted" with a daughter with breasts and/or a boyfriend)

Or, daughters report instances of fathers not respecting them:

"My father was very abusive. I grew to hate and fear him. He always thought of me as a whore. I was pretty and friendly, and in his psychotic mind that meant slut. Now, he has stopped drinking and is more amiable, but he is still ungiving."

"I may as well have been raised by a robot. I was molested right in front of him, and he didn't even try to protect me. But I guess since I was eighteen years old with big boobs, the excessive attentions of a twenty-eight year old seemed natural (I'm being sarcastic). What do I feel for him? It's a confusing topic. Love-hate-hate-love."

"Don't be provocative"

Another message girls often hear around this time:

"Rule number one around the house during our teens, I always remember my mother saying, 'Cover your body! Don't go around naked! You don't want your father to see you, do you?'"

Girls are supposed to hide their menstruation, never mention it in mixed company, and not "show" their bodies (i.e., have the pleasure of the freedom of movement they enjoyed when younger) because this would be provocative to men, "asking for it", meaning "sex" . . .

How Should a Father Discuss Sexuality with His Daughter?

There must be a way for a father to speak with his daughter about sexuality that is more direct; to express a comradely and affectionate notice that she is growing up, and indicate that he is trying to find a way to relate to this new aspect of her with respect without being provocative. Could they work it out together?

Mothers, grandmothers and other relatives frequently point out or make references to a boy's masculinity or sexuality with pride and/or awe—or a feeling of, "That's his, there's nothing I can do about it, it's part of the male world, which is stronger than I am, and it's his self-identity, it's pretty great, huh! Yeah, he'll be a man, have a penis, have all the machismo and rights of a man!"

Fathers, however, in their sexual references to their daughters, too often shame girls about their sexuality.—Why? It is time to change all this, and for fathers to congratulate girls and become their friends, to give them pride! This would be the best protection (if any were needed in the kind of a world we hope to build) from the degradation or exploitation she might expect from other men in her future life. Furthermore, it would end the double standard.

How could a father respectfully recognize his daughter's new sexuality, her sexual persona? There should be an honest recognition that she looks female and bright and attractive, focusing on her good points. Not, of course, a rapacious, leering encouragement to have sex or to copy men—nor a "dominatrix" model—but "permission" for her to have a happy, positive, assertive, explorative yet self-contained identity which makes its own individual sexual signature, its own expression, with pride.

A male teacher shares his observations on girls' developing sexuality and suggests society should change its gender attitudes:

"Childhood sexuality is a complex phenomenon. It is repressed because it is a threat to adults. As a teacher I have been closely acquainted with hundreds of children and have had ample opportunity to observe their sexuality and adults' reaction to it. Children of course are vitally

213

curious about sex—it is the great grown-up mystery. So much adult behaviour is patterned in response to sex needs and sex roles. Trying to understand grown-ups without understanding sex is like astronomy without Copernicus. Children are moulded into socially approved sex roles before they even get to school. They never have a chance to ask: How did I learn to be a boy? Or, How did I get to be a girl?

"Parents, peer groups and the mass media teach children to 'use their sexuality' long before they grasp the meaning of it all. Girls very early in life learn to use their bodies to manipulate people. Parents force a kind of sexuality on children simply by the clothes they choose for them. For example, even in the primary grades, girls tend to wear clothes that reveal as much skin as possible whereas boys are more commonly dressed for play. Girls are constantly encouraged to be aware of their bodies and to make others aware of their bodies. A girl's body is a valuable asset, a social tool, to be displayed, admired, and desired. Boys are encouraged to use their bodies in a completely different way—not as something to look at, but as something to use to manipulate people with directly through strength or aggression. Yet even though girls are groomed from infancy to exhibit their sexuality and to elicit sexual response, society is not prepared to accept it when the response takes some overt form.

"If I had my way, both as a parent and a teacher, I would like to see boys and girls remain sexually undifferentiated for as long as possible, up to the onset of puberty. It is unfair to make sex objects out of them while at the same time denying them any real sexuality of their own."

Girls Describe Their Father's Sexual Behaviour Towards Them

"You learn from your father it's okay to be cute, sexy, and flirtatious when your mother isn't around; the two codes of behaviour."

"My father gave me *Lolita* to read when I was twelve. It was 'our' story. He knew I knew it, that's why he gave me the book. I was so disgusted, but I didn't do or say anything. My mother was right there. It was so unfair of him, he used to put her down and praise me. I did like him, and I thought my mother was a real nerd to put up with it. I didn't like her, but that didn't mean I approved of his behaviour either. Still, I liked him better than her. So I had to pretend to love them both for years and years. I pity them."

Sometimes the father seems like a long-lost love object—his silence, his distance make boys and girls long for closer contact. This can be reinforced by the inconsistency of the father's contact, the unpredictable nature of his availability, and the unreliability of his attention.

In some cases, a father's sexual molestation (see also Part I) is associated for the child with emotionally intensity. The closest this type of father may get to the daughter is when he is angry, or sexually or physically abusing her. So, part of her may "want it" too because it is a relief from the waiting, waiting for him to speak, to reveal himself and the mystery of his power. Finally, to show some *feeling*.

Sexual Abuse and Molestation

31 per cent of girls and young women describe having had to deal with sexual abuse, either from a father (or stepfather), a brother, an uncle or a grandfather—sometimes "just" sexual harassment, sometimes forced coitus:

"When I was a child, I was constantly molested by my grandfather. That was an emotional crisis that will always leave a scar. I was terrified

215

of telling anyone. I hated myself for letting someone use my body for his pleasure. This went on for eight years. It went on from when I was eight until I was sixteen. No one said anything. Everything went under the rug. I never forgave myself until recently.

"I hated my family for not knowing or helping. I was afraid to tell. I felt cheap, dirty. Unworthy, not normal. I couldn't talk to anyone. The guilt overrode my life. Then with the help of therapy I decided to stop punishing myself for something I didn't do.

"After I learned to talk about it, I found out that three of my friends and even my mother had had similar experiences. Only one of them had anything done and the man was sent to jail. Everyone else would rather not talk about it. I'd really be interested to hear how other women coped with sexual abuse. It is a shame but it is there in our society. I know it isn't something every woman can relate to, but something everyone should face up to. No one wants to talk about these things, but they won't go away. I don't know exactly how many sexually abused children there are, but it is a lot."

"My stepfather came on to me a few times when I was about twelve. If I was washing my hair over the sink, he'd look up my dress, or if I was lying down, he'd try to see if he could catch a 'glance' up my dress. After that, I wore trousers a lot."

Sexual abuse or provocation and suggestion is more likely to take place between stepfathers and daughters than between fathers and daughters. In any event, out of all cases of abuse and incest, fathers or male relatives are the perpetrators 99 per cent of the time, not mothers or female relatives. This doesn't, however, prove that "heterosexuality is normal".

One woman, about to be married, describes how she is able to integrate in her mind the experience of a sexual relationship with her father, and her sexuality now:

"I am a twenty-year-old woman, engaged to be married. I love my fiancé, but I don't feel romantically 'in love'. I never have been romantic or sentimental. I am happy, but my happiness springs from far-reaching and indestructible values, not being romantic. I want most to act as an agent for change, improvement, enlightenment. I want to contribute and create—whether through a freshly expressed idea, a hand extended in need, or a new life. I am angered tremendously by cruelty, injustice, greed, and the destruction of innocence.

"When I was twelve, my father made sexual advances to me. It started out almost innocently, but gradually progressed to French kissing and his manual stimulation of me to orgasm. He encouraged me then to feel him, and that led to masturbation of each other. Later on, this graduated to fellatio, and once, cunnilingus at his insistence. I remember that with particular horror as I felt so ashamed and so vulnerable. Finally, at about seventeen, the unnaturalness of our relationship became unbearable to me and we stopped.

"The question of course is, *why*? It's deceptively simple: my father, I know, had mental difficulties which led him to 'demonstrate his love' in this way. I, on the other hand, accepted his will as right and good. I loved my dad, and if this was what he wanted/needed, then by God, I would do it. To compound the problem, he would tell me he would someday kill himself, and so I tried all the harder to please him in an effort to prevent this.

"Unbelievably, we never had intercourse. Once he came close, but something stopped him (I don't know what). Nonetheless, I identify the whole five years as an emotional manipulation not unlike rape. He had me believe that our closeness was the result of physical intimacy: I was so sensitively attuned to his feelings that I compromised my body and better judgement for his emotional well-being (so I thought!). When I see in flashes the nights my door would open when everyone else was asleep, the time I knelt down on the bathroom floor to give him head, the afternoons I watched the digital clock, knowing how many minutes I'd have to endure before he got off, the moments of confused embarrassment when he kissed me or touched me in front of friends—I could cry. But I don't, because he must have been sick. Physically, he never hurt me, and he has never used our relationship as any type of blackmail. He acted selfishly, thoughtlessly, and very immaturely, but even the worst situations spawn some good.

"My closest friend is an older male, probably a father-figure, whom I met at eighteen. This man is the antithesis of your cold, non-communicative, insensitive American male who only uses one hemisphere of his brain. Through almost a spiritual, non-verbal understanding, we knew each other from the start. I had never even considered confiding in a person about the relationship my dad and I had had. My psychological immunity system had sealed it off in the lower reaches of my memory for ever. But this man somehow knew, and he drew it out; he cared for me sincerely, and while he could have had wholeheartedly and joyfully everything my father had forced, he never succumbed to my 'innocent' eyes and trusting demeanour. And this was as much psychological as moral: although he was married and would have refrained anyway, he taught me that making love is the physical manifestation of deep, underlying, eternal love and care.

"After confiding in this person, I was able to live with myself and tackle the problem of mending an abused father–daughter relationship. I remember it being the most remarkable feeling to kiss my friend, knowing that he knew everything else that mouth had done—to my own father. I had thought he might find it disgusting, but this man loved me. And I love him, in a beautiful sense, for ever.

"Despite everything, I was very close to my parents; both loved me and I them. Thankfully, my mother is blindly naive, and she didn't know about my father and me. I respected but pitied my mom. Many times I mothered her. She's been burdened with an immature, lazy, unambitious husband, while she is the opposite. Both, however, are making progress in their middle age.

"In high school, I played football and swore a lot. I needed to think I was tough. I also masturbated quite a bit (yes my father knew; he taught me how!). I saw nothing wrong with it, so sometimes three times a day I got off.

"My parents know that my fiancé and I now are reserving my (technical) virginity for marriage, and I believe they feel it's unwise. I do not. It's very hard to do, as we are sexually attracted to each other, but I have committed myself to chastity until marriage because, to me, making love is so special, so sacred in its potential to give life, that its rightful context is only in the sacrament of marriage.

"I am a sensual and a sexual person, but I no longer masturbate and I discourage my husband-to-be from too much physical closeness. I experience orgasm very quickly and I respond readily to him, but as I said, I hold our sexuality in high esteem and reserve it for our spiritual union in marriage."

Another young woman explains the effect her father's sexual abuse had on her dating during high school and after:

"I dated from age thirteen on. I had no trouble separating my incestuous sex life from my social dates, although I was slow to warm up to a boy, and, other than with my fiancé, I have always (except once) stopped short of the boy's orgasm. And never, except with my fiancé, has this been coupled with true emotional feelings. It was great to leave for college. I badly needed to get the hell away from my father's threats, depression, and fits of anger."

Having to live such a false life, with intensely mixed feelings on so many different levels at once (one life with the mother, another with the father, a third inside herself, and probably also two or more separate realities or identities with the father), may contribute to an inability to

218

have relationships with true feelings as their base. If you act within the expected role, if you are just "nice", relationships can be managed. However, where does the individual exist in all of this? Does the real person become lost in order to cope?

Another woman, though happy in her marriage now, tells how she had to overcome her feelings about her sexual molestation by her brother when she was a child and teenager:

"I recall being closest to my father. Mom found it harder to express love. I liked the way my dad would get right down on the floor and romp with us. He could hug you or play on the floor without worrying about losing dignity. I really liked him. He died when I was eight.

"I liked most about Mom the fact that she would do things for you, that you felt taken care of. I disliked the way she would punish out of her anger, not according to the wrong-doing's importance. She was not physically affectionate. She did things *for* you rather than hugging or showing affection. She did my hair for years; I hated it because I had braids and boy, were they tight and did they hurt. She was angriest if you disobeyed a direct order. I love and respect Mom today because I realize now what she went through when my father died and she was left to raise four kids alone.

"In high school, there was a lot of pressure to date boys, but I was very afraid of boys, because after my father died my brother turned from being just a bully to molesting me on a fairly regular basis. I knew if I told Mom it would somehow be my fault, and there was no one else to tell. I felt guilty about it and worried about getting pregnant (shows my ignorance—we never had intercourse and I hadn't started menstruating). I finally refused to continue when I did begin my periods and that was when he started on my little sister. More guilt. This began his beating me instead of molesting me. I took the beating as preferable to being used. I became more and more withdrawn from the age of eight to after high school. There was no one I could talk to about the major disasters in my life—my father's death and the following abuse. I was most bitter over Mom's failure to protect us.

"Because of the problem with my brother I didn't have anything to do with boys until I was nineteen. Then I went out on a date—just one single date—because when he kissed me, I froze. He thought I didn't like him, so that was that. When I finally had sex with a man, it was to prove that I wasn't a lesbian. My brother had taunted me with this label since I fought his advances and his beatings. He said a real woman would submit. I had doubts myself because I couldn't be close physically to a man without feeling sick with fear and the only person I was close to emotionally was my younger sister. But I have never felt any physical attraction for a woman. I discussed my sexual experience with no one.

"I was most 'in love' with the first man I slept with. The whole relationship was agony. It didn't last and couldn't last. I was trying to be 'normal', i.e. have a relationship with a man, and I had no guidelines. He was totally unsuited to me. I very seldom cry but I did over that affair, because to fail meant I would never be 'normal'. I thought of suicide. In fact I made an attempt at it and my realizations after that attempt changed my life for the better. I was never lonelier than the night I tried to kill myself. I view my life as starting again after that night. I put the past behind me as much as possible and started to live.

"I'm not 'in love' now (being 'in love' means agony to me), but I do love my husband. I think of being 'in love' as a fantasy state where you think someone is perfectly wonderful, then you hit hard when you finally fall back to earth. The real loving is when you see them as they really are and still love them. Also, I am very attracted to my husband. That is important to me. I couldn't be sexual with someone who repulsed me no matter how much I liked him as a person!"

Mothers Face the Sexual Molestation of Their Daughters

Women describe their feelings when they discovered that their daughters were being sexually abused:

"We had a bad time when Jim's father propositioned my daughter (then thirteen). He believed his father, who claimed there had been a 'misunderstanding'. We confronted his parents; it was me against the three of them. I am convinced that he (Jim's father) was guilty, but couldn't admit it. Somehow the confrontation cleared the air; my relationship with his parents has improved since then. My relationship with Jim weathered the storm."

"As a child, I was molested and raped by a gang of guys. I suppressed the emotions all these years and seemed to be doing quite well.

"But at the age of twenty-nine I've found out that my stepdaughter was raped at four by her stepfather. In my own way, I've been trying to be supportive to her through her trauma, but I am having sexual difficulties myself. I'm remembering more and more about my past and having nightmares, reliving the whole ordeal all over again. My husband and I have a very strong, secure marriage and I've talked to him in detail about what's happened in my past. He's very understanding and I thoroughly enjoy making love with him, but at times it's a reminder of what happened to me a long time ago. How can I get over these feelings and get my intimate life with my husband back to normal? Your books have helped me and were something I could identify with.

"I am in the process of setting up a self-help therapy group here in my town, for victims of sexual assault and their families. We have gone from one agency to another trying to find help; after one referral after another and still no help, I've become determined to form this group to let people in the community know that they are not alone in this and that they do have somewhere they can go and someone they can turn to who knows exactly what they are going through. Also to let them know that people who have problem children may be children who are victims of this."

Here is a rare instance of a girl being able to tell her mother straight away about her father's unwelcome sexual behaviour:

"During my early adolescence, he started playfully tapping my rump. I told my mother and he quit. Except for a few jokes, we never communicated much."

A Father's Desire for His Daughter?

One father angrily explains his sexual feelings and thoughts about his daughter:

"Adults want children to suppress their sexuality because otherwise they, the adults, would have to deal with their own repressed feelings. It's simple. Sort of a chain reaction:

"A teenage girl becomes pregnant and her father is outraged, her mother 'hurt'. What is her father really mad about? Maybe he's jealous that his daughter has been sexually active with someone else, and not him? Ridiculous, you say? What about Mother? Maybe she is remembering her own pregnancy and how she felt? Who the hell knows? I've seen too much parental jealousy, especially from fathers towards daughters.

"Why does every society have some sort of taboo against parent–child incest? Why is Greek mythology (and Shakespeare) so full of it? Because it's there!

"Damn it, when a man raises a daughter from birth, sees her, bathes her, feeds her, comforts her bee stings—and all that, when her breasts begin to develop and pubic hair begins to grow, and suddenly he is excluded because of 'modesty', he is relegated to 'little-boy' status, something he has fought to overcome—what does he do now? She's still his daughter, his 'little girl', and he's always going to remember her that way!! This whole thing gets complicated as hell as time goes on. I'm not in the least surprised when a 'middle-aged' man has an affair with somebody 'young enough to be his daughter'!

"Case in point: my own experience. My stepdaughter, I raised her from the age of four. I loved that little girl (still do, only she's not little) and, because her mother was out of town, would have 'Tampax-trained' her had it come to that, but she trusted me, and she still does. I don't see her much because she lives far away, but we get along very well. There is a sexual attraction; I know it and so does she. I wouldn't hurt that girl for the whole universe, because she trusts me not to! She's going to be one helluva woman! Sexual activity can take a back seat in this one. Would I go to bed with her if I could? I'll be damned if I know! But I would still like to comb her hair, soothe her bee stings, bathe her, and have her asleep in my lap!

"How does she feel about me? She cries when we meet, laughs a lot later, and cries when we part, both of us cry. She'll tell me anything about herself that I ask, no hesitation, clear-eyed, straightforward. Last time we spent a few hours together, I asked her about her menstrual periods. (Her mother and *her* mother both had hysterectomies at young ages.) I just wanted to know how she was faring. She's now fifteen with no menstrual problems yet. Do you know how many boys and men are just plain ignorant of menstrual physiology, have never seen menstrual blood or even taken a close look at a tampon or pad? It's just appalling! Adolescent boys are curious; they want to know, and their mother and sisters are their best bets. But try laying this on Protestant, Jewish and Catholic America!"

And another father:

"I try not to repress the sexuality of my daughters. I recognize my own attraction to my attractive twelve-year-old pubescent daughter. When we are nude in the house, we make no attempt to disguise it. (In fact we all go nude bathing every summer on a public nude beach.) Both my children are, as far as I can tell, uninhibited about their sexual feelings, however incipient. (I would never have thought of discussing anything with *my* father, after several rejections of the subject.)

"Nudity was not an absolute no-no in my parents' house, but it certainly wasn't natural or frequent. My daughters have seen me erect in the bathroom, for instance, after I've emerged from the shower with my wife, and they have commented several times on my erections—often visible in the morning when they come in. I must admit I'm shocked by their simplicity and naturalness and slightly bashful curiosity. After some confusion, though, I just explained to them what it was. I don't believe, though, in 'show me' explanations!

222

"My wife has explained everything to them, especially the twelve year old. She has several books, excellent ones, obtained from our paediatrician. She even knows about oral sex ('Yes, a man and woman use their mouths, too'). No problems. We don't parade it. It's there, that's all. I do, however, believe in restraint. I love a lovely rare steak, but I don't elevate it to an altar. You know what I mean.

"Childhood, my own, was repressed, yes. But it was also filled with lots of mystery—not all bad. Maybe some sort of mystery needs to be cultivated, so I don't discuss sex with the girls unless they ask me. I don't hide my body from them, even if I am taken by surprise when aroused. And, of course, there is some pleasure in that, for me and them. I just don't make a big deal out of it."

Incest: a Statement to the Mother

Cases of incest almost always take place while a daughter is still living at home. Why? Is incest only fun if it occurs while the daughter is still living at home with the mother? Otherwise, why is it not usually continued when it is easier, i.e., when the daughter moves out? Because now that she is not a girl/child anymore, the thrill is gone?

This is not, in itself, enough of an explanation. Why the sudden end? Surely, a sexual partnership might be continued, as affairs are, for some years?

Incest is a triangle through which to achieve contact with the mother. It is virtually meaningless without the "presence" or figure of the "mother". Thus, incest is a way of saying something to the mother.

Incest is a means by which the man dominates the mother still further, reminiscent of the droit de seigneur of feudal times. This might explain why more stepfathers are incest perpetrators. The new father in this way desires to "show dominance" over the woman's previous life. It is not a sexual act in the sense of being caused by desire. Like rape, it is an act of aggression—against the daughter, but also very strongly against the mother.

Just as when two men fall in love with the same woman, and they are using this as a subterfuge for loving or hurting each other, so, the woman is the necessary third party in the erotic triangle. It is the mother who is being "fucked"—the husband and daughter feel the additional erotic (?) overtone of this; they are cheating on the mother, "doing it" to her. It wouldn't mean nearly as much without this feeling of a hidden, second reality, in the house.

How Does the Daughter Feel?

On one level, as noted, some girls may feel grateful for receiving some attention, irrespective of type, rather than none at all. There is such a sense of powerlessness in children. They are so completely dependent on adults (and forced to be dependent by not only the social order, but also their physical need), and can guiltily experience a wide-ranging mixture of emotions.

Some of these emotions may include feeling, for example: "I am more desirable than the mother if he wants *me*." Power!

Or other feelings, like, "I want to have sex! I want my sexuality to be celebrated! I am turned on and have been turned on by you both for years—*see*! Feel my power . . . I will be like my mother, take on my mother's identity—and feel my father inside me. I will *be* you, *be* your sexuality, *feel your sensuality* through the only acceptable way there is to feel it—through a man, through intercourse, the great mystery, the grand secret you have shared behind closed doors for all these years."

It is also very difficult for girls, especially girls who are taught to be "good girls" (almost all!), to resist their father's (or boyfriend's, for that matter) advances. The continual denial of the child's sexuality by the family, this silence on the topic in the family, makes her afraid to tell anyone else what is happening, because in her experience, there is nowhere to talk about sex, and if she talks about sex, she will be told she is a bad girl. The phrase, "Be a good girl" should be abolished.

A New Kind of Friendship

One of the most politically hot, touchy and difficult subjects—one rarely talked about—is the daughter–father relationship, its emotional and sensual overtones. To leave this undiscussed seems simplest, for this denies that any close or erotic possibility exists.

Yet, as we have seen here, fathers do not need to stop being physically affectionate with their daughters. It is not physical affection with a child that causes the idea of a sexual relationship to occur. Men should clean up their act, and not see their role as one of seduction and trying to "score". Boys can learn not to define their sexuality as coitus, as "penetration" alone; learn how to enjoy their sexuality and their feelings in more diverse and interesting ways.

While men and boys in several Hite Research studies, including this one, have had distant and unsatisfying relationships with their father, they seem more emotionally unsettled or unresolved about their relationship with their mother.

Strangely, girls would say, *vis-à-vis* their father, that either he had been terrible (distant, uncommunicative, violent) or that he had been great (wonderful, best friend, special, lots of fun, smart). There rarely seemed to be an in-between.

Girls, like boys, were in more conflict about their relationship with their mother than their father. Even if they felt that either he or they had been flirtatious, they were more guilty about the betrayal of loyalty to their mother (and angry that "she" should put them in this position) than about breaking a taboo (even if just emotionally).

Generally, instead of feeling guilty or worried, daughters enjoyed their relationship with their father. After all, they were giving him their true love, he was an appropriate symbol to admire, and his liking the daughter, seeing her as "special", sometimes preferring her to the mother, was their secret understanding. She was thus lifted out of the class "woman" and into his own world of the chosen élite. (It is interesting to wonder whether this phenomenon of girls' admiration for the father, and semi-girlfriend status is more prevalent in middle- and

226

upper-income households, since in lower-income homes, girls might not see the father as so admirable?)

It is also not surprising that girls would, of their own free will, add erotic overtones to their time with/view of their father, since the whole of society (their mother's behaviour, and every magazine they see, not to mention men's own messages and reward-and-punishment system) tells them that heterosexual relationships are never just friendships, they are always sexual . . . Then there is the constant saying, "If you want something from a man, being pretty and acting sweet and nice helps, never hurts . . ." and so on.

It can be extremely difficult for fathers and daughters to talk about these subjects. However, if fathers and daughters shared their thoughts about this chapter of the book, using some of its paragraphs as a point of departure—or even wrote each other letters about them—this could be an excellent way to start a real relationship, a real friendship. Or, readers could go through the chapter and mark or make a list of the characteristics that are like their own relationships—the good and the bad, what they would like to change, and what they would like to keep and encourage, the new directions they would like to go.

PART III

Growing up male:
The mysterious meaning
of the game

Oedipus Revisited: The Emotional and Spiritual Construction of Boys' Identity

Conforming to the Male Icons

Boys feel under tremendous pressure, around the age of puberty, to "leave" the mother, detach themselves from emotional involvement with her—and at the same time, begin to "act like a man"—conform to one of the "male" icons*—as peer pressure taunts teach them. The new spectrum of emotions a "man" must have, boys learn, includes anger and aggression, but not empathy or "softness".

This pressure to "toughen up" happens at the same time that boys are experiencing a wonderful new surge of exquisite physical sensations in their bodies—"sex". Boys' testimony here shows that these new erotic impulses become inextricably entwined with the psychological trauma of leaving behind their primary connection with their mother, learning to identify with cultural notions of male identity.

"Male sexuality", boys' psycho-sexual identity, is formed in this atmosphere. The powerful emotions boys undergo when denying the mother—yet loving her—are experienced traumatically at the same time as first full orgasms for boys, creating in many men a sort of love/hate relationship with their sexuality, with women's sexuality, with women, and with love. This is one of the most important and unexpected findings of this research.

Renouncing All Things Female: Loving a Woman is "Dangerous"

This social pressure on boys to form an allegiance to the "male group" at puberty creates many problems for men later on, especially in love

---

* Which icon to choose—the "holy father" or "rebel son" (as Jesus grew up to be)? Usually the "rebel son", as only "older men" are fathers. Are Clint Eastwood, Arnold Schwarzenegger, and James Dean, even Elvis, the contemporary versions of the Jesus-boy-grows-up-to-be-tortured-rebel version of the icon? These might be more faithful to the original Christ story. What about more "female icons"; boys admiring and copying women? After all, girls are expected to admire male icons, try to "be tough", like them; why not the reverse?

231

relationships with women, but even with men. Since most boys learn that their primary allegiance must be to other males, and that "identification" with a woman makes them somehow "less than men", later in life when they are in love, they can sense a terrible inner identity conflict, *danger*, when they again feel "that close" to a woman—since through this identification, they are breaking the code they have been so brutally taught.

Many men, sadly, cannot really enjoy being in love with a woman, it feels frightening, rather than pleasurable. *The Hite Report on Men and Male Sexuality* showed that most men do not marry the women they most passionately love—and furthermore, most are proud of this, since it proves that they did not let their feelings overcome them(!), but "chose rationally". That is, they passed the "test", and retained their primary loyalty to the larger male group.

How many women and men have suffered from this hidden block? Men (and women) could be so much happier if men would only give up their allegiance to patriarchy as a social and political system. Women (and some men) are their friends, not the system! At least, not the ways boys describe it here.

Chapter 7

Boys Learn To Be "Men"

"Don't Be Like A Girl!"

Confusing and Harassing Taunts to Boys

Male "emotional identity"—such a phrase is almost never used in discussions about men, although similar phrases are constantly used when talking of women. Do males have an identity that is emotional? Yes; however, the spectrum of emotions assigned to men and boys is quite different from that assigned to women, i.e., men are encouraged to be "angry" and "active" while women must be "loving" and "passive".

The training boys undergo to learn "male" identity is quite harsh, as their testimony here amply demonstrates. It strips them of their "natural" emotional colouration, the full spectrum of emotional feeling. This "socialization" applied to boys is perhaps much harsher and more scorching than that girls receive: being plucked of all the tender emotions and alienated from half of humanity. Is this worse than what happens to girls, i.e., being forbidden action and anger? Both are terrible. Girls, "at least", are not asked to "leave" the father, show their utter hostility and contempt for him—although there is pressure on girls to show contempt for their mother.

Boys undergoing this process of emotional stripping find it extremely painful but, later, they "forget" and glorify the system, thinking of it as *theirs*, that it benefits them. But does it? Or is it their suffering in joining it that has bound them to it?

It is often said, "It's women who bring up boys; it's women's fault if men are too 'macho'." This is not borne out by my research. According to boys' statements here, it is not women but men and other boys who teach them their emotional identity. The remarks and taunts of other boys and men, even their own father, are what boys say "bullies them into shape" during these years—quite painfully so.

Most men and boys say that they were taunted (or they taunted others) with phrases like, "Don't be a sissy!" or "He's a mamma's boy—gonna tell your mother?" and told, "Act like a man," "Prove you are a real man!" "What's the matter with you? Stand up and take it like a man!"*:

"My father told me this stuff about being tough—a man can '*take* it'—during one of my emotional onslaughts when I was a teenager. I kind of agreed at the time. Now I think he should have at least asked me what was wrong. I didn't have anyone I could talk to."

"My father frequently exhorted me to be a man, calling me a sissy when I had difficulties physically mustering up to his ideal. I felt deeply hurt and bitter, and pushed myself even harder to gain the nod of approval. I was doing men's work full measure side by side with him from the age of nine. In the process I got three permanent physical injuries."

"I cried during a very violent quarrel between my father and stepmother. They interpreted my crying to be weakness and told me to stop being a baby, and refused to hear of my frustration and fright at having seen their physical cruelty to each other."

"I remember sissy-baiting. I got it, then when someone relatively more of a sissy came along, I gave it to them, you may be sure. One of the boys on our block, a fat one, we often called a sissy. We looked down on him. I once asked him if he took this very badly, and he insisted he did not. But I think he really did."

"When I was in boarding school riding alone on my horse by the football field, the team was out for practice, and they started calling 'Fairy' and 'Isn't she sweet' at me. I don't recall being affected by them, as they were not my friends, so I couldn't care less. But I remember the incident, that must mean something."

"I underwent humiliating ceremonies when I was drafted into the US Army. Men who are drafted are treated like dirt in the Army by sadistic officers and sergeants. They are called 'sissies' in training. It was very dehumanizing and degrading both in basic training and after."

"When my mother died, and I saw her in the casket, I started to cry and bawl almost like a baby. One of my sisters said something like,

* During the 1980's, these taunts began to be used against adult women seeking jobs in the workforce. Now they too were supposed to "take it like a man", or this would prove that they weren't able to "handle their job", not really mature people. Thus, the macho taunts, the "male model", had come to define what a "good person", and an adult, meant.

'Why don't you shut up! You're acting like a baby.' I felt resentment at not being able to cry for my own mother's death. Is that what 'being a man' means?"

"My peers considered me a sissy in grade school because I played the piano. I felt bad but held in my anger."

"Once I ran to my father because one of the kids picked on me. Afterwards I felt inferior to the rest of my friends for having told him. It made me think that before the incident took place I was one of the gang, but afterwards I was an outsider—maybe a coward too."

"Have I been called a sissy? Yes often, at the bus stop. On my block, the fellows my age went to parochial school. The public-school fellows were a year older, and bigger and cockier. When we were all let off the bus in the afternoon, I was the only one who had to go the same direction as those older kids. Their houses were beyond mine, and they used to taunt me, 'You should be somebody's sister, not brother,' 'You weak coward, you haven't the manhood to stand up to me,' 'Look at him trembling! Ain't it a laugh!' I walked that gauntlet for several years. In the spring of my 8th grade year I took to walking home from school, a little over a mile, just to avoid it."

Fathers' Messages

Most boys get a particularly negative indoctrination into "masculinity" from their father; the majority complain that their father did not explain in any clear or positive way how to "be a man" (an adult), but only criticized them for doing the wrong things, e.g., "Stop acting like a girl":

"My father was very concerned that I didn't grow up to be a sissy. He reacted hysterically to signs of weakness (e.g., crying) or femininity (e.g., wiping my ass from the front instead of the rear). His behaviour is astonishing to me now, but at the time, I felt very deep shame."

"My father said, 'Don't take shit from anybody.' That was about it."

"Father didn't really 'tell' me much, except he gave me the idea that women were just for sex."

"He seemed to have the attitude that my mother was helpless and he was supposed to tolerate her."

"He made fun of me when I was beaten up. Lots of disapproval."

235

Creation of "The Destroyer"

The Cult of Team Sport

Sport is a hotbed of "male" pressure, according to most boys:

"I was called a 'sissy' by a PE teacher when I didn't want to play football with boys older and heavier than I. When I was forced to participate, I was kicked in the face and then called 'sissy' when I cried. I was humiliated and angry."

"In grade school I was called a sissy because I didn't like baseball. I felt very hurt, defensive and confused."

"In gym class in junior high (the toiling ground of many) I was called a sissy by the gym teacher when I failed to run a mile."

"I was told, 'Be a "man", not a "sissy"!' during sports, and many times by my father. It hurt because I always wanted to please my dad. My violent dislike of athletics and strong lack of competitive spirit left me open to these charges. I felt like a traitor."

"I never liked football, but when I was growing up my brothers used to get me to play to make up a team. I never wanted to, but because of being afraid of being called a sissy, I did. I was a cruddy player and usually after every game would end up fighting with someone. I hated it."

"At about ten I was relegated to an inferior place in our group and looked down on by the other boys because I didn't like sport."

Team sport is supposedly especially "manly", i.e., playing with the group is better than "proving yourself" as an individual:

"In 10th grade, when I was injured in football and had to sit out most of the season, I realized that I liked not playing better than playing. But I didn't have the internal strength to quit sports teams, even though I grew to dislike them."

"I did not go out for sports. I didn't feel less manly about not making teams, but I took a beating emotionally when I would get chosen very close to last when teams were being picked for street games."

"I was an intellectual kid who always had his nose in a book. I was

236

driven into a lot of isolation by demands to be a jock and good at sport—I couldn't handle them at the time."

"In high school I used to get beaten up quite often for having no interest in sport or fighting, and for being a 'closet fag'. In essence, I was ostracized by my peers during much of my high-school education."

Told Not to Have Girls as Friends

Boys also describe a lot of pressure not to associate with girls ("You're a sissy if you play with girls"), not to have girls as friends ("Girls are for 'sex'"), and to spend their time with other boys.

"I was always being criticized for playing with girls. I felt that playing with girls was just as much fun as playing with boys, but this attitude bothered my parents."

"At about eleven my father criticized me for wanting to play with the next-door neighbour, who was younger than me, because she was a girl. Another time he blew up at me for spending the afternoon at a girl's house rather than doing something like being out playing football."

"I used to help my mother cook. But my uncle started making fun of me. One day he even 'explained' to me pointedly, '*Boys* like to do things with their mothers, but as they get older, they find that *men* are the ones they want to do things with. Why don't you try getting involved with some of the other boys who have hobbies, like fixing up their cars?'"

Sex: Another Sports Arena for Some—Learning the Seduction Scenario

Boys also say they are taunted as to whether they have 'made it' sexually:

"My friends in high school called another guy a sissy when he said he was afraid to ask his girl to go all the way. I hadn't either, but I didn't say anything. The idea was that we were all 'men' because we could brazen our way through any girl's defences—make the tackle and complete the pass, so to speak. What she felt didn't matter (or what we felt either, as far as that goes), so long as we scored. We listened to these stories from each other, secure in our knowledge that we were all being men. The others were sissies."

"The pressure to 'score' with girls began when I was about thirteen. It seemed that all the other guys were 'dating' someone; girls were a regular topic of conversation among the boys in our grammar school (a Catholic school). How did I feel? I enjoyed being with girls, but I did not like being

237

told what I was supposed to 'do' with them. I have always had a strong 'romantic' streak, and idealized notions of 'love' played a very important role in my life.

"All through high school, whenever I went out with a 'girl', I never felt it necessary to try to act out the fantasies of others (e.g., locker-room discussions about women). I just enjoyed being with the individual and doing things together, whether it was going to movies, school dances, or concerts. I never forced myself physically on a 'girl' I might be dating, even for a kiss."

Already in junior school, boys are hearing talk about "good girls" and "bad girls", i.e, the ones who "do it with everybody", and the ones who won't "do it":

"At about eleven I remember discussions about girls and those who were willing to 'make out'. There was pressure to have a girlfriend and we all wanted at least to date a girl who wouldn't mind having her vagina felt or her breast squeezed. This, however, was not the girlfriend that we wanted to have as a steady. When I was in 10th grade, I remember notes being passed in class about the availability of certain girls. There was pressure on the guys to have sexual relations with these girls."

One man describes his initiation into the bizarre world of "male sexuality", as defined by his military superior:

"Oral sex exercised a peculiar fascination over NCO military instructors where I was stationed. I was lined up in some formation five or six times or more and asked, 'How many of you guys eat pussy?' I thought it was gross."

Hunting: Learning to Be "Mean"

"Hunting" is another testing ground of toughness—even torturing dogs and cats, or dissecting animals in biology class, boys are expected to show that they can dispense violence, pain and even death* without flinching, not showing tenderness but pleasure.

Some boys object to these activities, but others develop a real taste for them and grow to enjoy them:

"One time a friend of mine and I trapped a wildcat and beat it to death with clubs. Even now my stomach turns when I think of it. I regretted doing it almost immediately after it happened."

"Dissect animals? They are beautiful and fascinating—I did it in high school, but I did feel a bit guilty about it. There was some competition among the guys along the lines of seeing who could be the grossest."

"I went hunting a few times with other men, with a .22 rifle, when I was eighteen to twenty-two. It was, admittedly, a fun game, feeling the surge of power."

"I used to go hunting with my dad for four or five years, during my boyhood. Unfortunately, I have always been a very poor marksman (my hands shake too much). I gave up hunting after an incident in which my dad and I were duck hunting in a boat with some other men. I had just brought down a duck, and we paddled the boat over to pick it up. As we reached it, I was astonished and delighted to find it still alive and looking well. It seemed so cute and attractive I imagined taking it home with me, nursing it back to health, and keeping it for a pet. One of the men picked it up and proceeded to beat its brains out over the side of the boat."

"I grew up hunting and fishing. Most hunters pretend to hunt for something called 'sport'. But I know that what makes hunting game attractive is the killing of the animal. I like to kill things. The very real sense of power over life and death projected through space. A

* Boys learn it is "manly" to kill cockroaches with pride; girls learn they should not have such "aggressive", "bloodthirsty" attitudes.

239

high-calibre rifle is what makes the sport so popular. Otherwise, why not undertake the hunt with a camera? You have to be even more skilful to get that close to the animal you are tracking. Violence is part of the thing."

Watching "the Game" Together:
Learning "Male" Psychology★

Participating in sport is one of the few ways fathers and sons spend time together.

According to my research, it seems that by bonding together against the opposing "team" or "dangerous animal", men achieve the maximum emotional contact that they are able to have under the male "family system". Here, they are allowed to feel excitement together (but not directly towards each other); sharing emotions in a "team" makes emotional sharing "legitimate", since the emotions are directed (ostensibly) at something other than each other. Thus, the two have an emotional interchange, an emotional climax, that is sanctioned by the society because it is channelled through a third party.

"The game" and its meaning

This is also what makes the *watching* of sport together such an important activity for boys and men. Through sport viewing, men are seeing "the game", their game, and learning about men in groups. The appropriate etiquette to use with other men is crucially important for men in their business and work lives, as well as their social relationships with other men. Lack of emotion (except for outbursts of anger), and "staying in control" while still "showing power", are the watchwords.

Thus, large parts of "male psychology" are learned through sport. It is an intense and essential part of the genderizing process, learning the proper way of behaving, the correct mode of comportment, in the World of Men.

When asked how they spent time with their father, most boys said

★ Is there such a thing as "male" psychology? How do male readers feel about these descriptions of their socialization, illustrating the cultural construction of masculinity? Men often see themselves as "free agents", while women are the "unfortunate prisoners of social conditioning". Yet men are imprisoning themselves through their self-imposed cultural restrictions. Their lives could be so much more fulfilling, if only they would leave behind the outdated and violent attitudes of the hierarchical world.

241

that the only way they had spent time together was watching sport on television, and as one added, "He always seemed to sleep on the couch when a sports programme appeared on TV."

Many women too have commented that men often sleep contentedly in front of a television which has an extended sports programme—baseball or soccer. Why? Do they sleep because the bonding is mandatory, but nevertheless slightly boring? Or is watching "the game" restful because TV presents an escape from personal relationships?

Mass group bonding through the watching of football, soccer and hockey games, brings to mind the spectre of mass psychology, crowds watching bullfights, the safety of being one of the group.

What have men endured that has made them want to watch such bloody sports, to need so much the safety of so many other males? Is this "male bonding", as is so often asserted, something in the hormonal make-up of men? Or due to the traumas of early childhood—for example, circumcision? Or is this need to participate in the male group a compensation for the father's distance and silent rejection when they were children? His physical punishments?

None of these, although most are commonly cited as "obviously true", is the basic reason. The reason for "male psychology" as we know it is not hormones or anything mysterious like that; the reason is the "family" structure and the way it is imprinted on the boy through men's and older boys' harassment and bullying.

Individualism versus Conformity: Fathers Who Encourage Their Sons to Think for Themselves

A few boys report quite a different experience with their father:

"'Think, don't conform,' he always told me, when I would say I wanted to do something because all my friends were doing it. That advice has helped me so many times in life."

"My father never pressured me to 'make something of myself'. He encouraged me to *think*."

"In 2nd grade I won a reading contest and was allowed to pick a book as a prize. I chose one about a nurse. Well, believe it or not, that caused quite a commotion. It was decided that the teacher could not give me that one. Not masculine enough! My parents stood up for me and I finally got the book."

★　★　★

One boy escaped (temporarily) the conformist pressure:
"I played with dolls at my cousin's sometimes, and also played with toy cars and building blocks, creating complex cities. My closest friends were girls. We would invent imaginary worlds away from everyone."

Men in groups: the male club

A young man in his twenties explains how the male group's games are played where he works on a construction site:

"It is really sickening to be a man sometimes, because the group always tries to find out if you're a 'cool guy' (macho) or a reject (fag, college set, disco set, hippie, or sissy). It is such a drag to have to spend energy and time worrying and thinking and dealing with other men on this level, but in order to survive in the job world one must either conform or be a super-macho different. It is pathetic that this is an economic fact. If I don't have a lot of juicy sex stories to tell about all the women I've fucked, I won't be accepted into many groups of men, regardless of my abilities in the field. This was true in sports too, in high school, particularly football. The idea being once again how much physical pain you can absorb and dish out. The spectators participate vicariously, with cheers like, 'Hit him again, hit him again, harder, harder!'

"Men in groups I know are hostile, edgy, and like to show that they don't have feelings—feelings of tenderness, caring, or friendship (except under the rules of bonding), or pain, be it emotional or physical.

"Many jobs we do involve exposure to dangerous live wires, or require us to work at dangerous heights, but most macho men won't wear safety equipment unless it is required or the situation is extremely dangerous, because macho men like to show each other that they don't feel any pain.

"Macho men comment to each other about female passers-by, and if you don't have a comment to support the group's opinion, you are considered (1) a fag (2) a mama's boy (3) a prude (4) a real jerk (5) a jerk-off. Then you draw the next round of insults from the group, and become the victim of their further abuses and hostile comments. It's very childish, like the way children ostracize and tease the kid with glasses or a stutter or any physical weakness.

"The thing is, this whole macho group-bonding thing is actually taught in the high schools and trade schools, as the students who are studying skilled trades like plumbing and electricity and carpentry must also withstand the nonstop group harassment and teasing that goes on in the classroom. Even the instructors do it, and humiliate and abuse slow or weak students. 'You gotta be a real man to get into the Brotherhood of the Plumbers Union!'

"To keep a job one must deal with this horrible social system. The foreman is typically the most macho, grouchy, cursing, angry-looking person on the site. There is never any positive reinforcement for good work, only criticism for bad or slow work. One never admits ignorance in one's job just as one never does about women, because that would bring the roof down on your head and all the humiliation that goes with it. Men behave very different among themselves than they do in groups with women.

"Since I don't like to tell macho sex-exploit stories, I have to impress men in other ways—by excelling in my work, for instance. I would hate to be rejected and ostracized, even though I basically don't like what I have to put up with to be accepted by other men. I wish I could just relax my mind when I work or do anything with other men. I'm constantly worrying that they will think I am weak or not a man, and then treat me like a reject. The worst part of it is that I don't do anything to change it really. I just put up with it because I want the money. And to be perfectly honest, I also want to be accepted."

Initiations

"I occasionally enjoyed teasing or trying to humiliate weaker boys—such as one of my classmates in junior high school who was somewhat effeminate. Also later in college in my fraternity we had 'pledge week' during which we were supposed to do, and did, humiliate the new guys as much as possible. If they broke down, sometimes we kicked them out. They didn't have what it takes. I remember once when we lowered a German boy out of a second-storey window by his heels. He became so frightened that he urinated all over himself."

What are "initiations" all about? The point of these initiations is, once again, for boys to answer the following "tests": "Can you take pain? Inflict pain? Will you bond with us through dishing out pain and cruelty?" The joiners must demonstrate that no matter what unethical acts the members perpetrate on "outsiders", they will not betray the group but still be "loyal" and take the side of the members as "right".

This can have murderously disastrous consequences for society—consequences seen in political parties, in corporate politics, as well as on every street corner—because the "man's duty" is to uphold not "the right thing" but his group, right or wrong. To justify and "understand" its actions and put the best light on them. This characteristic is, in part, an outcome of the boy's forced, unethical decision to "betray" his mother and join his "father" at puberty, which strips him of some of his moral courage. (See Chapter 8.)

The Price Boys Pay

"Gaining membership of the male group is so painful, you never want to lose it later, once you've got it. You must observe absolute unconditional loyalty, no matter what."

245

GROWING UP MALE

There is an enormous pool of resentment on the part of boys towards their sisters; over and over again they say that their sisters had things easier as children. At first this seems surprising, as the discrimination against girls is so well known. (See Part II.) Girls describe so vividly how their brothers were favoured, encouraged intellectually, given special dating privileges and more freedom (no dishes, housework) in the family. Money was often set aside for brothers.

And yet, from boys' point of view, girls may have had it better:

"They can cry and get sympathy, they are told they are pretty, they get cuddled and loved."

Proving you're really *bad*: funky tests of manhood for boys

Teasing, cruelty, showing they can compete with other boys for "grossness" by doing things like blinding dogs or cats and not flinching, not showing any emotion except pleasure—cutting off their own feelings of empathy—this is the world boys are being asked to join.

We are so used to all the subliminal messages about "toughness" put over by advertising that we accept these male attitudes as the way of the world. But they aren't inevitable, they represent in fact a terrible form of emotional cruelty carried out by patriarchy to frighten boys into compliance and loyalty.

Michael Jackson's video *I'm Bad* speaks eloquently to those issues. He starts out as a black-leather-jacketed motor-cycle gang leader, and ends up laughing and smiling as he sings, "I'm bad, I'm bad, I'm bad!" Clearly, he wants to take the machismo out of the term "bad", and change the male bonding-as-aggression-to-others definition of masculinity.★ What *is* "bad"? The term is the opposite of what "Be a good girl" means to girls. (See Part II.)

It is not mothers but fathers and other boys who teach boys their emotional identity

It is often said, "Women bring up boys, so why don't they bring them up to be less macho, if that's what they want?"

Is this true? No. As we have seen, it is actually men—fathers and other boys—who "teach" boys their emotional identities. Mothers only "bring up" the children when they are younger—they spend more time with them, talk more with them, as well as having part of the disciplining role. The brutality comes from peer pressure, the system's pressure on boys to join it.

★ Fortunately, Martin Luther King, Gandhi and some of the men who speak in this book also believe men—and the social system—can be changed, and are not afraid to try.

The cult of "masculinity" demands obedience

Many people feel they can do nothing to change this brutal process. They say this process is "normal". Or that it would be like swimming against the tide—all the television programmes, books, friends' prejudices and stereotypes—where would you start?

We *can* change this process. After all, women have de-constructed and re-constructed their lives in the last twenty years, and are still in process of debating further de-constructions and personae (still changing after all these years!). Men can too. It only requires stopping and thinking about how ludicrous, destructive and unnecessary the whole process is, and having the courage not to conform to an obsolete agenda.

One reason why men find it difficult to start this process is that the cult of "masculinity" demands unthinking obedience to its basic values. This same "unthinking" quality makes it hard for individuals to begin a critical process of disassociating from "masculinity", the icon of supposed male privilege and safety. Also, when men try to change, they are ridiculed as "non-masculine", called the grown-up version of "sissy", i.e., "wimp".

So it may not be that men couldn't change their minds if they wanted to, but that the price for doing so, being expelled from the male club, is too high.

One young man describes what it was like for him growing up trying to "be tough" at all costs in a ghetto in the US:

"I am nineteen and black. I write to you because I am lost, in terms of living and understanding life. I don't know where to begin really. I was an only child. In the ghetto, where I was born, I always got beat up. I never won any fights, I was a sissy. When I was about five, I remember being raped (anally) by some playmates. I still don't know why they did it.

"Anyway I continued being a pushover (you might say) till one day when I was thirteen (I used to be fat) I decided to build myself up. A friend who knew of my problems showed me his results (physically). After lifting weights for about a month, I was hooked. I continued at it for two years even though at times the exercises hurt so much I felt like crying.

"During these two years I gained strength and more respect than I ever had before in my life. My enemies feared me but I felt I still hadn't increased in confidence like I should have.

"I felt my ego needed satisfaction. I felt twisted after being pushed around so much. I turned to things that represented power, manhood, I used to dig Bruce Lee, and went into Martial Arts, and continued muscle building. (Yes, it all seems kind of crazy, but I must go on.)

"My mother and I lived with my grandparents, under their rule of thumb. Even when she was thirty, my sixty-year-old grandfather would beat her like she was still a little child. I would stand by and watch it, afraid to help, and because somewhere I despised my mother for the way she had halfway raised me to be a weakling. These beatings, he said, were to punish her for her 'disrespect' to him.

"One day I realized there was a certain madness to the way my family was organized. I felt I could take no more. I was fifteen then, and I thought that I was man enough to make a living for myself—but I didn't know where to turn. There was another argument with my mother, and my grandfather told me if I continued to yell at my mother, I could get out.

"I left to spend the night with my friend, who together with his mom talked me into going back to live with my grandparents. This was like giving up all my beliefs and morals, that's how much it meant to me. I went back, but this was the start of my problems, from that moment on, I felt as though I had lost. I felt my world slipping. I felt as though my proud spirit had been broken. (I think I should note that I had a great fear of my grandfather, which must've been subconscious, for he was an old, weasly man, who believed he could still outdo me in anything—but this had been put in my head for years as a child, like a barrier slowly building up over years and years.)

"Also, one day at that time my friend beat me in a wrestling match ten times in a row. He beat three other guys, too. But none of them got beaten repeatedly like I did.

"This affected my ego so badly that overnight I lost the desire to have sex with a woman. When I went to school, I would associate with girls, but wouldn't be sexually interested in them as I was only two days before. At first I didn't pay much attention to it, I thought I would overcome it. But I must have felt so much shame from being beaten that I wouldn't even get hard when I thought about sex—or looked at a picture—or anything.

"To this day I am still like this. I believe that no one can give my sex desire back to me—except myself. But I don't know how, I can't afford a psychiatrist or psychologist, or whatever you call them, anyway I don't believe they can help me.

"This all seems crazy, doesn't it? But it's true. My solution is that I have now joined the US Marine Corps, to get out of there and get a new life.

"PS. There was something I left out. I was going to try to commit suicide, but I decided not to. I look at it like this, I didn't bring myself here, something else did, and if I leave my life before this 'something' wants me to, I may suffer again, in the spirit world or whatever."

The male code he describes is very brutal. Where were the welcoming arms of liberal establishments helping boys with intellectual leanings in his neighbourhood? A good school system could have meant everything to him.

The Death of Empathy

Some boys can suppress their "inappropriate" feelings better than others, who suffer terribly—the sensitive ones. They are the ones who cannot stand watching as other schoolboys blind a dog's eyes, for example.

To them, and many others, joining the "male world" full time seems about the same as jumping into a black hole where one can only survive by distrusting everyone else, being prepared to fight at all times. To enter the male world is thus to "leave behind the things of childhood", i.e., their mother, and the world where one can expect harmony.

Feminists have asked, "Why don't more men feel bad, or do something about it, when they see the unequal treatment of women? Why don't they feel more uncomfortable? Fight *with* us instead of against us?" After all, many whites participated in the black civil rights movement of the 1960's in the US, people all over Britain campaigned for black rights in South Africa even though they were not black, and so on.

One answer is that men are so focused on the rules of their own system that they just can't "see" the problem. They have become blinded/they have blinded themselves (as they may have blinded the dog in the schoolyard) to half the world. *The Misfits*, Arthur Miller's film with Marilyn Monroe, expresses this very well: in man's cruelty to animals is the destruction of his own spirit.

When man after man, or boy after boy, says here,* describing his mother, "Why didn't she stand up for herself more?" they are overlooking the power of their own system and what it does to people. When I asked men, in a special sample in 1992, "If women ran things, would you be better off? Worse?" men puzzled over their answers, and some finally stated, "Well, I would have to start a revolutionary group. I would be a revolutionary leader."

Consider Oedipus blinding himself to what his mother represents, i.e., the matrilineal social order—learning to "accept" the injustice of dominating another, even someone he loves as much and is as much a part of as his mother. Patriarchy as a system creates fear and hatred of women by forcing boys to leave or "desert" their mothers, and

* See Chapter 8.

250

bond with their often more distant fathers. So they end up watching "the game" on television together, both trying, straining to decipher, the rules of their game—that is, to understand each other—and taking comfort in the droning on of the rules which never change, the system which is always there to tell them what to do. Men choose the father, prefer the father, but secretly love women in the night, go to them for light, emotion and warmth.

Welcome to the void! Who is a "typical" male?
Interestingly, most men do not feel that they are "typically" male. When asked their opinion, they usually state that they do not know if it will be valid because they are "not typical"; in fact, the great majority respond in just this way. Is this because most men are living a lie, so to speak? Because they know, deep down, that they are "different", that they (thankfully) do not "measure up" to all the "male" criteria, i.e., they are *not* dehumanized and insensitive to pain?

Why do men feel powerless?
Yes, but also, most men do not feel that they are powerful. In fact, they feel that they are relatively powerless. They often say they do not have the power to change things, whether in their personal lives or in the larger world.

Why do so many men feel "powerless"? Perhaps it is because true power comes from not being afraid to express yourself. And this is the reverse of male power: men's power comes from *not* expressing themselves, staying loyal to "the group" point of view. They must conform to the group to have "power". But do they have power?

Perhaps they are right when they say they have no power. For a man to be pushed out of the system means to lose all power. Most men live in fear of other men's rejection. This is the poverty of the system for men: they feel very little power, but they also experience much less love and emotion than they could if they did not fear losing or betraying the system that is exploiting them.

For many boys, then, learning to join the "male club" means losing their innocence, their ability to feel, or fully express joy or spontaneous pleasure. Boys may *know* this and feel that they are losing their emotions, part of their *selves*, but they are promised that submission to the system will bring them long-term rewards.

The Icons of Masculinity: Joseph and Jesus

Fathers and Sons

As we have seen, there is no "masculinity" for a boy without bonding with the male group.

The alternative is to be a heroic loner, a rebel. Examples of this are the hero of the film *Shane* in the 1950's, or James Dean, or even the Marlborough Man or Moses on the Mount—but most of these "rebels" are the mirror images of the authority figure of the father, they are the son, Oedipus, fighting his father.

Joseph and Jesus are the two basic archetypes of masculinity in the family. In most men's psyches, there is no recognition of other roles to be played, no grappling with the world outside the symbolism of the son's struggle with the father: all ethical battles take place within this inner circle. Relationships with women are in another sphere, and do not have the same rules.

The father defines everything, as does the heavenly archetype of the Father,* who is the only one the son must "fear".

This can lead to a very cold, painful and alienated emotional state. Boys describe enormous distance in their relationships with their father, and also a feeling of longing, trying to reach the father emotionally. Yet most men, according to my research, look to women when they need someone to talk to and for real emotional support: most married men in my research say it is their wives who are their best friends. However, women do not say this about their husbands. (See *Women and Love*.)

One man describes his private feelings, including quasi-sexual fantasies of longings for his father:

"During adolescence I had erotic fantasies of being caressed and approved of by my father. I was well into my twenties before I began to work on these feelings. What I realized was that I had very powerful urges for love and confirmation to flow between us. It makes sense to

---

* Who is the basis of our social system, our ideological construction of "reality"?

me, now, that my needs for approval expressed themselves in sexual ways because I wanted some reinforcement for puberty's confusions. I haven't felt sexual desire for my mother because we are very close, and we know how much we love each other."

A Male Backlash?

Some men today are in fact engaged in a debate about their tradition and power. They no longer believe male dominance is a matter of biological inevitability or superiority, but an historical circumstance that should be changed. That current definitions of masculinity hurt not only women but also themselves.

How far has this discussion come? Are "femininity" and dolls okay for boys now? As okay as they are for girls? No. There is a long way to go: the vast majority of boys are still suffering the painful adolescent traumas of initiation rites documented here.

Other men do not see the benefit of feminist critiques of patriarchy, and instead cling to the old system. There is a strong movement now to "return to traditional values", that is, to "protect the family". This does not mean, as it would sound, keeping the world safe for loving values. Rather it means maintaining the traditional family hierarchy: women in the home and subservient, and men "in power", but impoverished emotionally.

This reactionary backlash movement, or "counter-reformation", is reimposing an authoritarian system in the name of religion, opposing the movement to democratize the family, to bring justice to the relationships within families and between men and women.

Chapter 8

Leaving the Mother

Leaving the mother—children switching allegiance from the mother to the father, to men and the system the *father* represents—is the linchpin of the social system of patriarchy. This basic political message has been obscured and trivialized by the placing of this event in a solely emotional context by psychoanalytic theory. But the issue is not only one of emotions, but of ethics and morality as well. Is the domination of women by men, continued via the family system as we have known it, morally sound? Defensible? And if not, how are boys to develop true moral character, when they are asked to compromise their honour so early in life?

Pressure to Leave the Mother and Her Value System Age Ten–Thirteen

Boys' newfound contempt for their mothers

There are hundreds of messages given to boys, increasingly intense at puberty, that command "Don't be like your mother, don't cry—leave the girls behind, don't hang around women★."

Having to deny the mother, make their disdain and separation known, is one of the "tests" of "manhood" in patriarchal societies. A boy can "love" his mother, yes, but he *cannot* hang out with her, socialize with her, or be like her. To denounce her ways, show his difference, proves his full-fledged loyalty to the male group or father.

The effect this has on boys is to create a sort of emotional rape—which would be terrible enough—but worse is the effect on men's relationships with women later, as documented over many years of my research: most men carry away with them feelings of "guilt",

★ It is no coincidence that one of the most insulting things a man can call another man is "woman" as Andrea Dworkin has pointed out.

love, loathing and disdain, erotic attraction and suppression of that attraction, as well as confusion over whether love and sex really mix. This confusing combination of feelings, which is rarely fully examined or understood, tends to cloud men's reactions when they fall in love with a woman as adults.

Leaving sisters behind too

A young man from my earlier research tells a poignant story of having to leave his sister behind, in order to be accepted by the guys:

"My father told me very little about being a man, but he expected the women in the family to do certain daily things, like clean the house, cook, take care of the children, and the boys and men to shovel snow, fix cars, clean the garage. My mother always listened to me, even though we never talked heart to heart about how we really felt, or about sexuality ever, and we were never really physically close. I never kissed her or held her after about five. But I love my mother. She gave a lot and always makes me feel cared for.

"It was my sister I was really close to (one year older). She was my 'best friend' in 2nd, 3rd and 4th grades. We did things together as equals with no role barriers. We were *friends*. As a child I remember that boys were supposed to play with boys' toys, and girls with girls' toys. Girls played 'house', 'dolls', and 'shopping', and boys played army men, fort games, snowball fights, and more strenuous games. Boys could run faster and were tougher than girls. But there were some things that boys and girls could do together, like play cards and table games, ride bikes (though later on that became more segregated—trikes were co-ed, bikes were segregated).

"There were times when I felt torn between playing with my sister, who was my best friend, and playing with the boys. Especially skating: the girls did figure skating, and boys played hockey. Of course, it was an honour to be accepted into the group of boys as a hockey player; I remember feeling like I had betrayed my sister a little when I went to the rink with her but didn't play with her once we were there. I didn't want to be a sissy, so I let her play with her girlfriends and I played with the boys.

"One summer before that we were best friends, we shared secrets. It was never the same after I left her to play hockey, and we took off into our respective masculine and feminine roles, which were enforced more and more until we became adults. Now it is almost impossible for a man to be 'friends' with a woman or 'best friends'. The roles we are assigned don't allow it. Men have their wives, and their friends (other men). Men don't see women as equals: perhaps they did as children, but when they follow their roles, they begin to feel guilty for leaving women behind, and later feel contempt for women who are not their equals, since they didn't let them be. Society tends to emphasize the differences between men and women, rather than the common things. Men show contempt for women, because they consider themselves superior."

Boys' Opinions of Their Mother

Boys with Good Opinions of Their Mother

During the last fifteen years, I find a difference in men's attitudes towards their mother emerging in my research. Most boys and younger men, still today, face awesome pressure to disassociate themselves from mothers and show contempt for all things female.

But many more boys and men now have positive attitudes: 24 per cent express extremely positive feelings, as compared to only 11 per cent in the late 1970's and early 1980's. It is refreshing to hear them:

"Mother confided in me, believed in me, supported me, loved me, respected me."

"She was an understanding confidante and adviser, and she provided the important things in my life. I loved her deeply."

"We're quite close. I like and admire her a lot. She's generous with her affection, honest about her feelings, willing to stand up for herself, and has a good sense of humour. We share a similar passion for music and metaphysical ideas. Lately we've been helping each other with our various struggles. Like me, she has trouble releasing anger."

"My parents almost always got along very well and worked together, though I never saw or imagined any great passion. I was always closer to my mother and respected her much more than my father. I think she is tremendously strong and intelligent. I envy her moral and social judgement and her impressive collection of friends. I also think she has much more passion and drama than my father, and she and I have always had an understanding beyond words. I really know her as a person, her romanticisms and frustrations."

"When my mother was having hassles with her boyfriend, she would just hold me and cry and cry. She was always open and honest. I give her credit for making me what I am today."

"She's intelligent and independent and I admire her."

"I know my mother loves me, she shows it every day. My dad is very distant and emotionally detached."

"My mother is totally loving and giving. She is almost always happy. I want to be as emotional and strong as she is. She is beautiful. My father has never been affectionate or listened to what I say. He only talks about himself and his financial duty to me."

Mothers as "Wimps"

"She is too weak, and refuses to assert herself. She lets my father treat her like dirt."

And a woman describes her encounter with a ten-year-old boy:

"Today on my way home, I saw a boy sitting on the kerb stroking his dog (I think he had been crying). I smiled and he looked shy, then called after me, 'Wow! Look at that!' making sexual innuendoes. This must have been the only way he could relate to a woman, to reaffirm his 'dominance' after being caught crying. Maybe there was no language for starting a friendship. I could only be his 'mother' or a 'sex object'."

Still, patriarchy's message about mothers and the attitudes it expects from boys is strong, and takes its toll. Of course, not all mothers are perfect, and neither are fathers, but the amount of contempt and hostility in so many men's and boys' statements about their mother is stunning. The interpretation of women's care and concern is often to define it as weakness. Boys seem to feel they must emotionally and psychologically dominate their mother, or lose self-respect.

Status of Mothers Versus Status of Fathers

Where do these attitudes come from?

There is a second powerful way in which boys are taught "masculinity": from the example of the father's attitudes to the mother.

Boys in two-parent homes have usually witnessed an attitude of superiority by the father towards their mother (79 per cent of father–mother homes). Earlier in life, boys may have felt that the father's attitude was unfair to the mother; but now most come to feel, "Why doesn't my mother *fight* it? Her problem is her own fault."

"What did you learn from your father was the proper attitude towards your mother?"

The majority of boys* say that there was a double message: their father told them to respect their mother, but their father did not respect her himself:

"There was a dual attitude. He always taught me to love, respect, obey and protect my mother. However, my father behaves in a pitying and superior way towards her. He is fairly careful about this but it has increased over time."

"A mixture of love (because it's the Catholic duty), pity, looking down on her (because my mother is *not* an intellectual and has no personality), helping her sometimes (kitchen and so on), but also expecting many sacrifices and a lot of support from her. My father told me once never to marry a woman like my mother. This I will never forget."

"My father punished me if I did not listen to her or if I talked back, but he himself treated her in a very verbally abusive way. I never believed that that was the proper way to treat her or any other human being."

"Occasionally I was encouraged to help her out or obey her when I was a child. Today, my father sometimes ridicules her for nagging, mismanagement, and general foolishness."

"If he ridiculed or talked down to her, it was not to be a model for how I was to behave to her."

"Sometimes she'd be moody and annoyed, but he would sort of keep on going to work every day, and wait for the problem to go away. His attitude was that she was being silly and over-emotional, childish, and that he would wait until she came to her senses. That he as a man was above these kinds of things."†

"From my father, I learned the only way to deal with my mother was to humour her and get the hell out at the first opportunity."

"Gradually I Came to Despise Her"

As we saw in Chapter 1, both boys and girls have warm and happy memories of their mother in early childhood. Yet listen to how boys' attitudes change:

"I felt so close to my mother when I was little. She would sing to

* And girls; see Chapter 5 for girls' descriptions of the same gender set-up.
† See *Women and Love*.

me and help me do my homework. Gradually I came to despise her. I saw that what she was really doing was making me like her, binding me to her, more like a girl than a boy—she didn't want to let me go. I rebelled. She seemed hurt, and this only made her seem more stupid to me, like a big, sad, needy cow. She still wanted me to love her the way I did as a baby. I couldn't help growing up and leaving her behind. I'm sorry for her, but she should go out and find another life for herself."

This is a standard psychological interpretation of a mother who loves too much—but is it accurate?

"I guess I don't think much of my mother. She is a very narrow person who has made most of her life's decisions, and all the important ones, out of fear. I know she loves me, and gave up a lot for me, but I would rather have had her be her own person.'

Some boys sound almost proud of being angry with their mother, of not being close: dislike and distance seem to represent the height of personal achievement, status, and success. Once again they have "proved" their own identity by showing distance from "things female". Is this so surprising? After all of the taunts "not to be a sissy" or "like a girl", it isn't so strange that boys begin to see their mother as not up to much.

Sadly, although boys sometimes express anger towards their father, they do not fault him for the unequal gender situation at home, although most men do say that they saw his attitude towards their mother as negative and condescending, something like a bully's. Nevertheless, like the girls in Chapter 5, they think it is the mother who should change (or leave).

Why is this anti-woman behaviour encouraged so much at puberty? Could it be because, to paraphrase Mernissi,* boys have to learn to be

---

* Fatima Mernissi, *Beyond the Veil: Male–Female Dynamics in Muslim Society* (Al Saqi Books), page 8: "I am not concerned with contrasting the way women are treated in the Muslim East with the way they are treated in the Christian West. I believe that sexual inequality is the basis of both systems. My aim is not to clarify which situation is better, but to understand the sexual dynamics of the Muslim world . . .

"Nor am I concerned with analysing women as an entity separate from men; rather, I try to explore the male–female relation as a component of the Muslim system, a basic element of its structure. It appears to me that the Muslim system is not so much opposed to women as to the heterosexual unit. What is feared is the growth of the involvement between a man and a woman into an all-encompassing love satisfying the sexual, emotional and intellectual needs of both partners. Such an involvement constitutes a direct threat to man's allegiance to Allah, which requires the unconditional investment of all his energies, thoughts and feeling in his God."

more loyal to Allah and his system than to a woman they love? So that, if at puberty (or later) they are in "danger" of becoming too enamoured of a female, this socialization will keep them mentally and emotionally aloof?

The Moral Dilemma of "Leaving" the Mother

One boy, in the middle of the distancing process, expresses his mixed feelings of love, hate, and confusion about how he really feels for his mother:

"I'm still in high school, I still live at home with my mother. I like to define a strong sense of personal masculinity for myself, and this has led to a very distancing effect from my mother. We're sort of close and sort of distant. It seems like whatever I do, she finds something wrong with it. It seems to serve as an escape valve for her own frustrations. I think she is mad because she was never able to carry herself as far as she sees other people carrying themselves in the world.

"She had kids when she was young (I have sisters), so she had to stay at home and take care of the family, then especially after she got divorced, and especially after my father died, she always had to work, she always had to take care of the family and provide, so she was never able to expand her horizons or go to school or establish a career. I can see that that's a legitimate, logical frustration, so I really don't blame her. I can see how she could feel angry and frustrated.

"Sometimes that makes me feel guilty for being a burden to her, but I don't let it get me down. Anyway, I think if you have some sort of goal, you should be able to achieve it and not let obstacles stand in your way."

Under the guise of "analysing his mother", he is really saying that he strongly disapproves of her behaviour and life. Most boys don't similarly delve into their father's psyches.

Another man describes his change in attitude to his mother, and the reasons he sees for it:

"My mother was always nice, and always listened to my problems when I was very young, in grade school. I didn't see my dad much, he was always working, but my mother was always home. I thought my parents were the greatest and had a great marriage. As I grew older, I realized I didn't know my father very well, and later, I realized I didn't

262

know my mother either. I thought I knew her, but it was more like she knew me, or, at least, I used to talk to her a lot.

"At a certain point, I began to feel angry with my mother because I realized that in our long conversations I would be the only one talking. She would listen, and act interested, but I began to feel strange talking to someone who didn't really talk back to me. So I stopped talking to her pretty much. I withdrew and became very reserved and unemotional.

"I tried to sympathize with my parents, as they were really struggling with a large family, money troubles, and life's hardships. But I felt like baggage to them. The only things that made me feel good were rock-and-roll, pinball, fishing, candy and building things with my tool set. I hated school, life and the future. When I went away to school, I didn't really miss them, because I didn't really know them.

"I thought my father was an idiot, and my mother even more of one for not asking more out of life. All she ever did was passively listen to the rest of the family and my father's complaints, and act like a maid around the house for us. I think she originally wanted to be a lawyer, and she was always reading books about law, but she never did anything about it. After a while, I couldn't sympathize or identify with her anymore. About this time in my life, I realized that my problems were my own."

Another feels that his mother's loving behaviour is irritating and "weak", yet does not characterize his father's behaviour in a similarly angry or emotional way:

"My father does only what *he* wants, and my mother lets him get away with it. She won't do things or say things that might provoke him, get him angry, or create problems. Once I said to her, 'Why don't you stand up to him?' She said, 'You can't change an old horse.'

"Although my mother was always loving, concerned and considerate, she was also overbearing: 'You gotta eat,' 'What are you wearing, it's cold outside.' But she's still a weak person. She never stands up to people and things that are stronger than she is, but she's overbearing when it comes to people who are weaker than she is. I wish this weren't true, but it is."

Another describes the same characteristics in his mother, but with much more empathy and understanding, a more tender, insightful and respectful attitude:

"I was closer to my mother than my father. My mother took me to a lot of places before I started school, while my father was working, then, as I got older, my mother was easier to talk to than my father;

she is just more verbal than he is, more eager to converse. I remember my father would come home from work, say hello, then go out to the garage where he had a shop, his world, and spend his time out there until dinner was ready.

"My mother never complained, she wanted to please him. She could be very aggressive and ambitious where her children were concerned, but she was not outspoken when it came to him. During high school, she helped research and write papers for me and my brothers, it was her way of being connected to the larger world, growing, I think. Looking back now, I wish that she had had more outlets for her intellectual ambitions. I feel she's in a relationship where she is not with a peer. She is an avid reader, but her education was cut off too early in a really awful way. She also has an outlet through the church where she uses some of her intellectual abilities, but I wonder if it's enough.

"I think there's a kind of unhappiness that she masks by going through all the motions of being a good wife and so forth. She's hungry for meaningful talk, and she doesn't get this kind of companionship from the man she lives with. If I could have changed her, I would have made her more able to reach out and get what she needed, more active somehow for herself, not just in the traditional areas like children or church work.

"Many times when I was growing up I looked down on her for this. At times I felt a deep aversion, even a physical aversion: I was afraid I could become passive and false like her, and I didn't want to."

Fear of becoming "like her"
Is his last sentence a key to understanding other men's fears too?

Do most daughters and sons fear that, if they sympathize with and "understand" their mothers too much, they may be pulled down and become "a wimp" as well?

Guilt Creates Hate

Many of these boys' answers about mothers contain a great deal of anger, anger not seen in men's descriptions of their father. Why? After all, most boys got much less love from their father. Is the anger because of the greater love for their mother in the beginning, later "betrayed"? Is this the reason for the passion in men's statements about their mother?

Or, do so many of these answers contain a great deal of anger not seen in men's descriptions of their father because, in terms of emotional support and understanding, not as much is expected of men? Is it anger with mothers for not perfectly playing the archetypal woman's role of Mary, endlessly loving and giving? Or, are we just looking at plain old everyday prejudice against women?

Is it a question of boys feeling guilty about the whole situation? In other words, boys feel forced into a decision to conform to the "male" rules—in a brutalization process that leaves behind a great, enduring anger, which they mistakenly direct at women. They come to feel that *she*, the mother, deserted *them*, rather than vice versa.

Stereotypes of "Mothers"

Blaming mother for everything

One man points with self-righteous anger to the "nagging" mother stereotype, as the source of his problems:

"Women I go out with do get upset and angry with me. Why? Damned if I know. Women are always upset and angry. Should I try to reason with them? I'm too lousy an ad-libber for any of that. And damned if I'd know what to say, after a long list of chores and struggles—most of which, as far as I'm concerned, they don't have to do if they don't want to—followed by, 'What thanks do I get?'

"Leaving won't help; it'll never blow over. And as for listening to her and being silent, there's a name for such men: Henpecked.

"No thanks. I got more than enough of that shit for seventeen years from my mother, to which—that's right, which—I haven't spoken for years. And from my sister (three years older), to which I haven't spoken either. Hey, if we're all alike, then you're all alike, too. Or do you believe in equality only when it's convenient?!"

Another man accuses his mother of being reponsible for his lack of sexual activity:

"I might say that my sexuality with women is retarded, because of the attitude implanted by my mother, without mentioning it, that women are not sexual beings. Therefore, I feel most confident when the woman makes the first move, otherwise I doubt that she is sexual. I feel the need to have permission for sex."

New Interpretations of Old Psychological Clichés

Political or personal stages of child development?

Parents for millennia have noted that their children go through several stages; mothers often note how "sweet" and loving their boys are when quite young, then how distant and irritable they become.

What is the meaning of these stages? Are they a biological unfolding of personality?

No; they are, in fact, various stages of coming to terms with the social system and the family power structure. These stages are not a consequence of some kind of universal "human nature", they are *reactions* to the power and gender structures the child is facing, structures created by our society, not "structures" inside the child.

Boys around ten to thirteen do "turn" on their mother, begin to be surly, disrespectful and aggressive, as reported in many standard child psychology textbooks. This aggression has sometimes been held to be a function of hormones, especially male hormones, so that it is more or less concluded that this "aggression" in males is "normal". After all, "boys will be boys"!

In fact, this hostility in boys is created by all the factors just mentioned.

Single Mothers and Lesbian Mothers

(Why do we almost never hear the phrase, "single fathers"? Need we say "single" mothers; why don't we just refer to "mothers"?)

Most boys who grew up with single mothers have positive opinions of them. They are likely to have "experienced" the process of disassociation from women much less strongly than boys from father–mother households:

"My father died in the war when I was four. My mother and I were very close. She told me her troubles and I told her mine. She worked as a stenographer. She had an enormous enjoyment of life, an ability to be truly joyful, and a great sense of caring for people. I wasn't jealous of the other boys who had a father, I felt lucky not to have one, because I had no one to tell me off! I couldn't understand why the other boys stood for their father telling them off. I always asked them why they put up with it!

"When I lived with my mother, she didn't go out much, but now she goes out almost every night—she has lots of friends and has a lot of fun. All in all, she's one of my favourite people."

* * *

LEAVING THE MOTHER

An overwhelming number of boys and men under thirty who like and admire their mother are those who grew up, for most of their childhood years, with their mother as the sole head of the household.

According to my findings this is equally true statistically whether the mothers are lesbian mothers or heterosexual mothers. There may be, of course, differences too to be found here, but the numbers of examples are not yet great enough in this data to draw further conclusions.

It is increasingly clear that the great majority of these boys also grow up to have better relationships with women, a different sexual persona, from boys/men from most mother–father families. They are usually more free in conversational style, listen with more interest to what women say, and see women as individuals first rather than "women" first. In short, they are more comfortable with women, and identify much more. They are not afraid of solidarity with a woman, or of trusting her.

This is not because—must we say it?—there is something wrong with "men", or heterosexual reproduction, but because we live in a society which still has feudalistic ideas of "family": Joseph "owns" Mary and Jesus.

Reconstructing Boys' "Puberty": Towards a New Society

Boys are traumatized at around ten–thirteen when they have to decide whether to identify with their mother or their father, women or men. A clear choice has to be made: a boy learns he must turn his back on his mother, "desert" her, if he wants to be accepted into male society. This can include making fun of her, ridiculing her, and thus "siding" with boys.

Many men develop a guilty conscience about this betrayal of their early tie and bond with the mother; many had sympathized with her as a young child (even envisaging growing up to defend her).

The process of "becoming a man" is a spiritual and *political* crisis in boys' lives. It is a very problematic period which challenges boys both psychologically and morally. Yet this problem, or moral dilemma, goes totally unrecognized by society, and unnamed by general psychological theory. Thus boys and their families have little help in thinking this process through.

The process of acculturation is traumatic. Lucky is the man who can go through this and find himself on the other side, who manages to keep a sense of real individual identity and direction, in the face of this cultural onslaught, this change in gender identification and allegiance that is so roughly imposed.

If this moral challenge is not resolved in an honourable way, problems are created for men's ethics with women later. For example, what men mean when they tell a woman in a love relationship that they want to be free is that they are terrified that other men will reject them, because by identifying with a woman and taking her as their primary relationship they are betraying the "masculine", betraying male bonding, betraying male society.

Most men make a compromise of sorts; they do not marry the women they most intensely love*; they marry women they can feel

---

* See *The Hite Report on Men and Male Sexuality*. This was a major finding of that research.

268

somewhat separate from, and thus perhaps superior to, in order not to have to make this terrible choice between satisfying love in personal life and acceptance by male society.

And for many gay men, does real love, an allegiance to one man, still seem "female", still a denial of the supremacy of the overall male world, or an abdication from it? Is this a reason for the high incidence of multiple sexual partners in the gay world?

The much-discussed changes going on today in the composition of families, as well as the high divorce rate, indicate that many people—especially women—are trying to form truly moral and ethical family units and relationships. Far from representing "the decline of society", these statistics indicate a new vitality: a decline in hierarchical and women-exploitative families, and an increase in human rights and democracy in families. This more just social infrastructure will make society stronger.

Chapter 9

Eroticism and Betrayal of the Mother

Why Do Some Men Associate Eroticism with Hurting Women?

At the same time that boys learn to reject the mother, they learn to focus their sexual feelings on women. They learn that women's sexuality is to be desired, but that women are to be rejected, that women are lowly and scorned but objects of desire.

Sexual Energy and Emotional Turmoil

It has not been sufficiently recognized that at the same time as boys' emotional and moral landscape is darkening, there is a sudden flowering of sexual feeling—and this combination of sexual energy and emotional turmoil has lifelong consequences.

Think of this: a boy is lying in bed in his room, masturbating, hearing his mother in the kitchen making dinner. He is thinking of his sexual feelings, the images he has seen of "male" sexuality, i.e., that "men" desire "sex" with "women". He "knows" that he should desire women so he masturbates thinking of women's bodies . . .

Between the age of ten and twelve, the changes in boys' bodies make full orgasm possible for the first time. (See Chapter 10.) This is different from the changes at puberty in girls, which are a question not of orgasmic capacity, but of reproductive ability: the onset of menstruation and the growth of breasts and body hair. Orgasm has been a part of girls' lives for much longer: 45 per cent of girls in this study began masturbating to orgasm by the age of seven; over 60 per cent by the age of eleven or twelve. (See Chapter 3.)

A time of secrets
"I remember it as a time of secrets. It seemed a whole and complete second world was opening up around me. My father started explaining sex to me, and my mother told me about menstruation, that girls sometimes bled between their legs when they got older. At this time I was also using pornographic pictures and magazines in my masturbation routines, and I began to incorporate the girls in my class into my fantasies."

The eroticization of the world: fantasies and masturbation
Fantasies, pornography, feelings of love and attachment, hearing about "sex", slight touches and smiles from someone one "likes"—everything seems sexual—even parents' silence about sex seems sexually charged. The whole context of boys' lives at puberty is erotically flooded.

Between the age of ten and twelve, most boys begin a very heavy masturbation life, in secret, although over one half of boys soon after share masturbation, and perhaps other sexual acts, with other boys. (Kinsey, 1948; Hite, 1981; see Chapters 3 and 10.) This is just the same age at which boys receive the genderizing treatment of being told to "get tough", behave "like a man", "stop hanging around your mother". They learn that a major part of masculinity entails differentiating themselves from women, and proving that differentiation in front of other males by ridiculing, and ostentatiously avoiding, "women's ways".

Sexually, most boys' early sex lives are subliminally yet potently associated with feelings for the mother. As noted, she is the woman they are most intimate with, they know sex is part of her life, or part of the hidden things they cannot know about her life.

The frequent citation of an Oedipal period in boys' lives is confirmed in the data here which shows that boys are thinking of their mother during their initial years of sexuality and orgasm. However, the Oedipal theory as we know it does not go far enough: the connection is not made between this and the violent psychological disassociation from women and "things female", which results in the negative (and pain-inflicting) eroticization* of women—a lifelong psycho-erotic script played out in love affairs with women.

A pattern for life
The mother's continued nurturing of the boy during puberty is seen as the mother humiliating herself (rather than being loyal), and this affects how boys learn to define the "love" given to them by a woman. Some

* Consider the prevalence of male sadism towards women in pornographic literature.

boys begin to think, Let's see how far I can go and whether she will still come back for me. Unfortunately, in many cases this becomes an unexamined erotic/love package which some men take with them throughout their lives, leading to emotional and physical violence against women they may even indeed be trying to let themselves love.

For other boys the hurt is uppermost: it is painful when you cannot be "proud" of your mother, someone you love and are close to, simply because the social context is telling you to see her behaviour as "stupid" and/or second class (she is "just a woman", after all).

For some, the combination of these anguished feelings, resentment yet also need, results in relating to love as to an eating disorder: wanting it, and bingeing, then rejecting the woman and her love, in a confused mixture of passion and denial.

By the age of fifty or so, according to *The Hite Report on Men and Male Sexuality*, many men express a great feeling of emptiness and anger: "I did what I was supposed to do, I denied myself all of my life, kept my feelings in check, provided for a family, worked at my job. Now, where is my reward? Why don't I feel more fulfilled? Why do I feel ripped off? What does life mean, anyway?"

This "midlife crisis" or despair that many men express (often as cynicism) is created by the patriarchal family system: while supposedly giving men "ownership" of the family/society, and therefore privilege, in reality it often causes them great psychological pain, and can even amputate them sexually, erotically, and emotionally.

Erotic Feelings for the Mother

Many men have erotic or sensuous memories about their mother, as we saw in Chapter 1.

Interestingly, most people react guardedly to the idea that boys may find their mother erotic; they may react even with outrage when asked, "Do most men—or do you—have erotic memories or sensuous feelings about your mother?"

Do men find women "erotic" who "look and behave like their mother"?

Vladimir Nabokov once published a short story in *Playboy* in which a male character is sexually attracted to a "dumpy, middle-aged" woman carrying shopping bags. One day in the street, he starts following her, becoming more and more physically aroused as he does so. He keeps asking himself why he is feeling these things. After all, he reminds himself, she is not the proper "sexual object"—there is nothing about her that is like the stereotyped sexual images of "attractive women". But his feeling persists, as does he.

How many men feel attraction for "sexual objects" who are like their mothers, of which they never speak. Probably more than a few.* In fact, in my research, a majority of boys and young men in their twenties say they want to marry women who are like their mother.

It is rarely or never stated that boys find their mother erotic. It is much more common to hear that boys find their mother "goody-goody" and "a pain in the neck", always restricting their movements and "telling them what to do". Yet, when they are younger, many boys feel other things, interest, curiosity—they are drawn to their mother's company. It is society that tells them, over and over again, that this is "wrong" and should be ended, at least by the age of twelve.

Most boys/men also want to marry women whom their mother will like, according to my sample of young, never-married men in *The Hite Report on Men and Male Sexuality*, i.e., women who are like their mother.

Is this because they want to "play safe" and marry "asexual good girls", the Mary icon, or because they find these women long-term sexual objects?

In any case, this "rational" choice of marriage partner tends to continue the pattern inside marriage of seeing the wife as "mother", and having a girlfriend (lover, or daughter) as the focus of their actual sexual (mechanical) behaviour. Just as when they were living at home as a teenager, they dated outside the house.

* There is no reason to think this a "bad thing". It is a pleasure to see middle-aged couples holding hands and kissing in public. Yet this sight is rare because of the social pressure to hide erotic feelings after a certain age. Only "the young" have the right to show off their love in public. (See also *The Hite Report on Men and Male Sexuality*.)

The Definition of the Mother as Asexual in the "Family"

Does This Inevitably Create the Double Standard?

Men's belief in the double standard comes from their belief that their mother (a "good woman", after all, since she had *them*) was non-sexual. Just as Mary, the icon of the "holy mother", is asexual.

This asexualization of their concept of the mother/"good woman" means that men's sexual identity can be dangerously distorted—loving and hating the mother, women, is confused in such a way that a man can feel perfectly justified, when sexually attracted, in striking out—engaging in emotional "resistance" or psychological or even physical attack. Thus, the stereotype: a sexual woman represents danger, a "femme fatale" can lead you to death! as in *The Blue Angel*, the famous German film of the 1920's starring Marlene Dietrich, and many others since.

The idea that a sexual woman is a "bad woman", and "dangerous" is not fading, but gaining currency. The 1980's film *Fatal Attraction*—and its depiction of a supposed "good woman" versus a "bad woman"—is a sign of the strength of the old, medieval double standard, and the new force of the political movement known as "fundamentalism". (See Part IV.) The double standard is being revived as part of the fundamentalist attack on the gains of women for equality.

If the belief in the double standard is created by the taboo on the mother appearing sexual (even being seen as sexual with the father, as she must be "pure" like the Virgin Mary), is the solution sexual relations in the family? Is this the only option we have for breaking this vicious circle? No, of course not. The total denial of the existence of the mother's sexuality is not necessary, it is simply dictated by the patriarchal family's attempt to own women's bodies. And—one interpretation of the Oedipus myth goes—if the son ever looks, he will be very sorry!

The consequence of this "purity" imposed on women is that most boys experience deep conflict when they fall in love or feel strongly physically attracted to a woman. They often think that she must be "the

274

other kind", a "slut", not right for marrying! And so this pattern goes on and on: as demonstrated in my previous research and noted here, most men do not marry the women they most passionately love.

Children—not only boys, but also girls—are learning this lesson over and over again: since the mother cannot offer sex to her children, or admit them into the mysteries of the world of sex, she must be seen as asexual★. Any woman who does have sex can then be viewed as an outsider, not a potential member of the sacred family system, not a "holy mother"—but as "no good", shameful, and dispensable, as all too many young women have experienced.

Two boys describe how confusing and disorientating this "female asexuality" was and is for them:

"I am twenty years old, white, in my second year at university. I am somewhat confused about what my sexual feelings really are. My attraction to men is just as strong as my attraction to women, but different. Physically, I am aroused more by attractive men in a sexual way.

"For women it is different: emotionally I become aroused. I have been aroused by fantasies of sex with a beautiful lady, but I feel that there would have to be much more emotional involvement than in a homosexual context."

"To make love with a woman, I first had to demystify women and eliminate the mother picture which was so omnipresent for me. How could I make love to my mother? That was a hard feeling to suppress—though I guess it's never gone completely. And after that, I had to learn how to make sure she was enjoying it too, not just take my fun, period. I was always ejaculating too soon, I felt I never satisfied girls. I was very preoccupied by this, very ill at ease."

★ Fathers are "asexual" too, but not as much so; they do not "show" their sexuality, but neither does their icon insist that they are "pure".

What Men Feel Towards Women During Coitus

Men want to marry someone their mother likes, or who is like their mother, according to their statements in my research. Why? On one level, is this a way of getting back to her? And to that comfortable, warm and intimate relationship as a child?

To touch her at last, penetrate her, dominate/have her . . . is this part of the feeling? Over and over again, men in *The Hite Report on Men and Male Sexuality* say that by "penetrating" a woman vaginally, "giving her my come", they are showing her their love.

They do not feel anything like as strongly that giving the woman an orgasm* shows their love. And if the sexuality is forced, many men in my research say it "still shows my love". Is this attitude a reflection of how upset they have been, ever since the "denial of the mother", all that love–hate feeling bottled up, ever since they were forced to "betray" the mother?

Sons as Lovers

What kind of erotic feelings do mothers have for sons?

The social atmosphere makes it "unseemly" for mothers to express delight in their little boys in the same way that fathers can express delight in their daughters. It is considered "really male" and "natural" when Louis Jourdain falls in love with Gigi, in that internationally famous film of the 1960's, but it would be considered "ugly" and "weird" if an older woman were to fall in love with a teenage boy.

Why? Because women do not have the same "legitimate" sexual status as men do, especially older women, who are generally treated as sexual outcasts. As we have seen, only women of reproductive age are considered desirable. The actress Delphine Seyrig once remarked, "I can't think of a single actress over fifty who is working regularly."†

* Whether by hand, mouth or during coitus.
† See archives, Centre Audio-Visuel Simone de Beauvoir, Palais de Tokyo, Paris.

EROTICISM AND BETRAYAL OF THE MOTHER

Of course, mother–son "incest" can be emotional rather than physical—the son can be a stand-in partner for the mother. Certainly, some boys say that they are afraid to arouse the mother's jealousy, particularly when it comes to bringing girlfriends home, especially the first one.

How much of this "emotional" incest occurs? In a minority of cases, according to my research here. Relationships between "single" mothers and sons seem to be more "comradely". Situations in which the boy is pressured into being the mother's psychological "lover", taking the place of the husband, are much more likely to happen in "intact" families. The reason for this is, as women voice in the Hite Report *Women and Love*, that women often feel more lonely in a bad or inadequate couple relationship than when on their own. Single women have the freedom to develop other friendships; in a couple, they feel more constrained.

Why Men Kill Love

Many men project the ending of love from the beginning: they cannot seem to imagine a passionate emotional relationship with a woman that does not end. Why?

Having had to kill their love for the mother (as she earlier killed their physical intimacy), men learn the fatal love scenario: it must always end. They, the boys, learn that the emotional script for intense love always has an ending, often tragic, and that it is they who must end it. As we have seen, men do not end their relationships with their wives (it is wives who initiate most cases of divorce); they connect their wives with the role of the mother (whether or not they have children). But they almost always end strong love affairs, both before and during marriage.

Thus, men project the ending of "romantic" love from the beginning: "You can't go home again." This is the cause of so many men's negativity, cynicism and pessimism in the face of love: "You can't change private life, the battle of the sexes is inevitable—it's impossible to conceive of another type of marriage or family," and so on.

The tragedy scenario . . . one must "pay for" happiness. During the 1940's, almost the entire US male population of reproductive age was massively de-individualized and militarized, e.g., films and popular magazines "proved" men's "killer instincts". The government poured money into the Hollywood film industry for the making of films encouraging men to fight and further exaggerating their distance from women. This implanted the real-men-put-duty-before-love-and-family scenario even more deeply, and the love/passion/break-up script was now fixed firmly, as this generation "passed on" its psychologically damaging tradition—against which some 1960's sons tried to rebel.

Also, perhaps fathers coming home from World War II were more violent towards their sons than the previous generation of fathers. Disciplinarian fathers may have forced boys to leave "the mother" in much more traumatic ways than previously. The sons of that generation are now the men in power in the fundamentalist '90's.

Interestingly, boys who grow up with no father sometimes escape this it-must-end scenario altogether.

278

Must Passion End?

Must intense love end? Does passionate love create "an unbearable tension" that causes many men to feel, This can't go on for ever? Is the tension because the man is being false to himself, doesn't really love the woman? Or because his life, he feels, is in disequilibrium, he is too identified with the woman, with things female, for which he will eventually be punished by the "father", i.e., male society?

Many women report a pattern in men which they find extraordinarily confusing and irrational. The man behaves with undeniably real and intense passion towards them (not only sexually, but also emotionally), only to turn around and close down his feelings almost in the middle of love (almost in mid-orgasm, it seems to some women; see *Women and Love*). Then, the same man may return again, showing passion but also muttering cynically about "paying a price later" for "all this". Of course, this is followed yet later by another break-up and goodbye. Many women say they are being "left", when they are *sure* he really loves them, whilst the man maintains he's "not sure", and doesn't want to "make a commitment".

Falling in Love—A Loyalty Conflict

When a boy who has experienced a "normal boyhood" in the patriarchal family system has grown up, and he first falls seriously in love—he can experience it as a bomb, overwhelming, totally unexpected in its power. And negative. Differing from women, men often find these feelings too intense for comfort. At first, love feels "natural" and good, men report, but soon something inside tells them that it can't be good, that they are letting a woman dominate their every action and feeling, and that this is not proper behaviour. Many feel instinctively that they are in danger when "in love", and that they must get out of the situation somehow, no matter how pleasurable the feelings are.

Leaving the mother causes a paralysis in boys, a trauma of guilt, which can make it hard for them to love and accept love later, and creates conflict in almost all relationships with women (including those at work), because it brings up feelings of guilt and fear of "entrapment" in the women's/mother's world. Men as boys have had to learn and accept the gender class system and their place in it, i.e., their "right" to dominate women, and compete with men.

This knowledge and the memories of the feelings become blurred as the years pass, their origins lost to the conscious mind. However, "too close" an identification with a woman easily raises all the old alarm bells, and the result is confused feelings and behaviour for men in love.

Chapter 10

Boys Discover Sexuality
Age Ten–Nineteen

Circumcision: Many Boys' First Sexual Experience

Is the world that boys meet at birth a happy and warm place? How much are boys allowed the pleasures of discovering the physical world, and how much is a violent world foisted upon them?

Boys in many countries and cultures experience one major life situation that girls as infants in the West* do not: circumcision. Not all boys in the world are circumcised, but many are. For example, in the United States, almost all boys are circumcised, usually just a few days after birth, without anaesthesia.

What effect can this have on the new child? It must have a major effect, but one that is lost to conscious memory, integrated into the child's psyche at a very deep level. After all, another human (almost always male, whether or not this is clear to the baby) causes a wound on an area of his body that he is sure to consider very special after this experience, for all of his life, and yet perhaps not remember why. This wound heals only gradually, remaining painful for some days. The baby must be keenly aware of this feeling and injury for much of this time.

Once grown up, most men who are circumcised say they don't

---

* Girls in some Arab countries undergo the barbaric practice of clitoridectomy and/or infibulation, i.e., removal of clitoral tissue and/or sewing together of the vaginal lips. These practices—performed not at birth but during early or later childhood, up to puberty—are extremely painful and dangerous. They take much longer than circumcision to heal, and have much worse lifelong psychological and physical consequences—for example, they usually make it impossible for the woman to have an orgasm in any way, ever—with all the implications for one's self-concept and outlook that this implies. Also, infibulation makes intercourse (coitus) extremely painful, as with first intercourse the skin which has now grown together must be broken and penetrated in order for the man to reach the vagina. This can be a health hazard for the woman.

regret it—they like the way the penis looks—though some express doubts about whether or not "the operation" may have made them slightly less sexually sensitive:

"I am circumcised, and I think it's great. I think it makes my penis look much better, more attractive. Guys that are not circumcised don't look as appealing (to me anyway). If I had a son, I would have him circumcised, I think that I would be doing him a favour, and that he would appreciate it when he gets older, just like I do."

Although most circumcisions of boys are done almost immediately after birth, one man explains the story of his circumcision when he was twelve:

"I am Muslim, born in India. I am circumcised. I like the way my genitals look to me, easier to clean as well. But I miss the smell. I can still remember the smell I had before circumcision.

"I have had my son circumcised, within a week of his birth. All Muslim are circumcised during their childhood, but I was not, till I was twelve years old, which was quite embarrassing for me. I wanted to get it done with. However the experience was very embarrassing, as two of my relatives who were about ten years older than me were watching the operation, which I resented very much, but could not tell them to get away. Then the cleaning was done so roughly there were subsequent infections. I still get painful sensations in my genitals whenever I hear someone talking about circumcision, or think about it, and the penis and testicles shrink to their smallest size. The physical reaction lasts for about a minute or so.

"I do not think it has affected my attitude towards exposing my penis to others. Of course I do get pleasure if someone gives a look of appreciation. I think that after circumcision the exposed glans penis becomes slightly less sensitive with constant friction, and may help to prolong the intercourse to some extent, but I am not sure."

How much is men's oft-mentioned worry about the penis, its shape, size and state (tumescent or not), related to the early trauma of circumcision? A lot of it is to do with the exaltation of the penis by male-dominated society. ("You're not a member if you don't have one!") The penis is a symbol of male power, as well as a symbol of men's reproductive ability.*

Nevertheless, a case can also be made that circumcision should be

---

* See *The Hite Report on Female Sexuality*, *The Hite Report on Men and Male Sexuality*, and feminist classics such as Kate Millett's *Sexual Politics* or Andrea Dworkin's *Intercourse*.

eliminated and is a severe trauma; there is, in fact, an organization of men in the United States trying to have the practice banned.

Visions of the Penis
"I think I have a very nice cock."

One young man gives a very clear picture of his semi-obsession with his penis, its size and appearance:

"I consider that the male organ is the most erotic, powerful, sexy, grotesque, good-looking, fantastic part of the man's body. Of the sexual organs of the sexes, I feel it is the most erotic.

"Speaking frankly, I am happy that I have been born male and that I have a penis. I wouldn't change it for a vagina under any circumstances. Only men know the fantastic power their penis generates to the whole of their body.

"While it is true that without a woman to turn the man's sperm into a baby and a man to deposit the sperm to create the baby, the world would end . . . I do feel that without the huge feeling of power created by the penis and the need for a man to expose it to the opposite sex the sperm would be useless.

"I am amazed at the construction of the male organ. For years nobody would answer my question as to what the 'knob' was for. I assumed that the glans was there so as to not hurt the woman during the thrusting action of the pelvis as the penis goes in and out."

And another is self-conscious about his penis:

"One aspect that used to cause me worry and a great deal of embarrassment was having to expose myself to other men, daily, in the showers or locker room at school and the workplace urinal.

"Men are forced to expose their cock, knobs, bollocks—the whole thing—at urinals. This causes embarrassment for these reasons:
1) The fear of showing an erection.
2) Not having a big enough cock compared to the guys standing next to you.

"Well, now I never feel ashamed to look or to know that guys are looking at me, in my view it's all a part of being a man.

"The problem when using a urinal is knowing where to look. I can't help but notice other men's penises when they are standing on either side of me. I don't consider myself perverted, but I feel that under the right circumstances a urinal slab full of young sexy guys is a very powerful place.

"I am happy with the way my penis looks. I am 7^1/2 inches—my only wish is that I could be circumcised.

"When I get my cock out of my pants at the urinal, I feel very powerful: I hold my penis in my hand, then shake it until all the urine has gone. I feel erotic power. I think it's because you are showing others that you can hold back from any homosexual advances such as gaining an erection or starting to wank it off. It's like getting a gun out and knowing you can pull the trigger."

Despite the violence of the last sentence, his point that boys have an opportunity (that girls do not have with each other) to see other boys' and men's penises and sexual anatomy "first-hand", and that this can be awkward or embarrassing, also has a positive side: perhaps this makes men feel more comfortable, more sure they are like other men, like each other, more related somehow, more "normal".

Girls rarely see other girls' genitals. They often wonder if "their" clitoris is in the same place as others', the "right place", or looks the same, or if their vulva lips are longer or shorter, darker red or paler pink, than other girls'. Do their vulvas smell the same? Is their vagina larger or deeper than other girls', or tighter? Wetter? More or less muscular? The vulva and female sexual anatomy remain a mystery to many women all their lives.

Boys sometimes play games together to see each other's bodies, not to have "sex" but just to have a good time:

"In camp, at the age of twelve or thirteen, our group had a ceremony called a washbah in which a group of boys grabbed one of their friends, pulled down his pants, and poured all kinds of shaving cream, aftershave, deodorants, etc., on his genitals.* The idea was to make them burn."

---

* Does this game have overtones of re-enacting a kind of mock circumcision?

Boys Discover the Magic of Masturbation

Boys' Early Feelings About Masturbation and Orgasm

"How old were you when you first masturbated to orgasm? How did you feel, and what did you think about it?"*

"When I first began masturbating at eleven or twelve, I had no idea of its connection with 'sex', I simply thought I was a unique human who had been given this special ability to have pleasure, which seemed mystically connected with ladies and flying."

"I was in 7th grade when I first masturbated (eleven or twelve years old). It was to orgasm. I learned by myself. I had an erection and it felt good to touch and rub it, so I went into the bathroom (which was the only place where I could have privacy), sat on the toilet, and rubbed my erect penis because it felt good. I didn't know that it would lead to an orgasm (ejaculation), but it did and that felt great, too. After that, I went to the bathroom nearly every day after I got home from school and sat on the toilet and masturbated."

"I had my first orgasm before I was aware of sex in any form (at about twelve, I led a very sheltered life), as I was climbing a tree. For almost two years I 'made love to trees'. I would climb trees just to get that good feeling. I was about thirteen before any juice would come out. To avoid staining my pants, I would go into the woods where no one was around and take off my clothes and climb around trees until the juice came. I didn't know what the juice was, but I knew I wasn't just leaking pee."

"I was thirteen and had been having wet dreams for about four months before learning how to masturbate. I was daydreaming one afternoon, absent-mindedly massaging an erection, when I had an orgasm. It completely blew my mind. I felt expanded, wonderful, and very secretive. It was the first time I felt *adult*, as if I'd been invested with responsibility. Briefly, I thought about babies. I kept

* See also the *Hite Report on Men and Male Sexuality*; some of the data here is also reported in that volume.

285

all these feelings to myself because I was certain that I shouldn't speak to anyone about this."

"At one point, my normal washing of my genitals (which I had been doing for a long time) caused a 'good' feeling in my penis which then proceeded to erect itself with repeated washing strokes. So I continued, and after a short while the 'unbearable' and ever mounting pressure resolved itself into bursts of ejaculating semen. The sensation was incredibly pleasurable. After that, I'd rush home from school at least three days a week, dash to the bathroom, turn the water on in the sink, drop my trousers, grab the soap, and jerk off wildly."

"My first ejaculation, masturbating in bed at night, was a wonderful feeling and I wanted to tell my friends all about it the next day."

Some boys can orgasm before they can ejaculate, as this boy describes:

"I remember my first masturbation was at seven, because my mother caught me in the act and forbade me to do it again. In those days I would always masturbate in bed by lying on my stomach with a pillow under my penis and moving back and forth until I reached orgasm. I say orgasm, rather than ejaculation, because I was masturbating for three years before I could physically ejaculate. I still occasionally masturbate in this fashion."

A minority of boys are alarmed and terrified by the ejaculation, as nothing had prepared them for such an occurrence:

"I had heard about 'jacking off' but didn't know quite what to expect. I was horrified when this thick fluid came out of my penis in spurts. I thought I had harmed myself and was very distraught. I felt very evil and promised God I'd never do it again, a promise frequently remade and broken."

"Age twelve. I was riding my bike and I came. I thought I had damaged myself. I went to a doctor who diagnosed me as 'getting old'."

"I remember fondling, rubbing, and stroking my penis under the covers for quite a while, until one day I orgasmed. It felt like something breaking, but nothing was broken. I hadn't ejaculated yet. And then one night when everything was going as usual, I orgasmed, and this sticky gooey whitish stuff spurted all over me and the bedclothes, I thought I'd broken something. I'd ruined it for ever. I was scared and felt guilty and sinful. Plus I had to clean it up or my mother would find out. I swore to all the powers that be, if only it would be all right, and no one would find out, I'd never do it again."

"I was quite shaken the very first time. I thought I had unloosed something that was hitherto unknown to mankind. I thought I was losing my mind, and so reported the sensation to a friend, who thought I was a riot."

The majority of boys, prepared for ejaculation by other boys or by magazines and widespread sexual information, feel they had achieved a new status as a man:

"I felt that I had arrived—now I was one of the 'big guys'."

"With my first ejaculation at fifteen, I thought of it as a big thing, quite macho. Something to brag about to the guys."

"One day I was masturbating and noticed hair around my cock. Instead of just climaxing, I shot a wad—a totally new experience for a fourteen year old, I tell you. I felt like a man, heh-heh."

A surprising number of boys, according to this study, have their first masturbation with other boys or learn to masturbate by watching other boys:

"A boy two years older showed me how to masturbate by having me stroke his penis until he ejaculated. I was horrified. A short time later I tried it out on myself with some timidity. It was a revelation."

"I shared a bed with my brother, who was twelve years old when I was six. We used to stimulate each other manually. I reached what I remember as a terribly hot pulsating feeling."

"I was twelve when I began to masturbate. Boys from school, groups of six to twelve, used to go to one guy's house after school; his parents worked and didn't get home until about 6 p.m. We had jack-off contests like: who could squirt the farthest, who could last the longest, the tempo of the stroke being followed set by following the beat of a song on a record. Who could come with the most quantity into a Mason jar; who could come the most number of repeat climaxes in measured time. There was mild homosexual contact: touching another guy, never actually stroking another guy to climax; checking out each other's equipment. Group nudity and checking out asses."

"Around thirteen, at Boy Scout camp after taps, the guys used to talk about fucking, blowing your guts, etc. I didn't know what they were talking about. Then one afternoon when we were supposed to be writing letters home or resting (the counsellors were off swimming) two of the guys had a contest to see who could 'come' the fastest. They took their pants off and started working their limp pricks up to a boner. (That's what they called it; beats me!) Well, that was the first time I'd ever seen a boner or anyone 'come'. It was amazing. I started playing with myself and have masturbated ever since."

Sexual Experiences Between Boys: 59 per cent of Boys

One of the most startling findings of my current research is the increase in the number of boys who, as teenagers and older children, are having sexual experiences with other boys.

This number has increased substantially since my research done between 1974 and 1981, and since Kinsey's research in the '40's.*

To hear how easily and naturally many boys share sexual activities with each other is truly surprising. Though some boys worry a little, for most, these activities seem to be remarkably free of guilt and conflict. Indeed, most boys do not wonder if they are "gay", they don't seem to worry much about anything, they simply enjoy the pleasure and camaraderie. The biggest worry is HIV.

In the 1940's, Kinsey reported that 48 per cent of the men in his sample either masturbated or had sex with other boys as adolescents or in their early teens. In my own work for *The Hite Report on Men and Male Sexuality*, I found that 43 per cent of the sample were doing this. Now, in the 1990's, the figure in my sample has increased to almost 60 per cent. Does this mean that the number of boys masturbating together is increasing, or are these percentages all in a range hovering around the 50's percentiles? On average then, approximately 55 per cent of boys?'

Girls, on the other hand, rarely learn about sex together. However, girls form intensely emotional and sometimes romantic friendships around the same age, in an atmosphere of strong feeling. They create great intimacy verbally, in a way that boys almost never do, despite boys' greater physical intimacy.

The spread of pornography and explicit television programmes has probably encouraged boys not to hide their sexual feelings and bodies from each other; is this what is responsible for the increase in shared sexual activities?

* Alfred Kinsey, *Sexual Behavior in the Human Male* (Philadelphia, W.B. Saunders Co, 1948).

However, many boys who feel they are "homosexual" (as opposed to those who just feel they are having sex with other boys for fun) still report feeling very isolated with regard to their sexual desires for other boys, especially if they live in very small towns:

"All through junior high and high school I was frightened. I was not aware of anyone else who was gay. I saw my sexual feelings as a barrier between me and everyone else, and felt completely alone with these feelings. I would hear the ordinary ugly innuendoes or jokes that every kid hears about gays. This deepened my isolation: I was frightened of having any of that scorn or hatred directed at me."

"I cried a lot when I was thirteen, because I decided I was homosexual. I thought of killing myself rather than admitting to it. I was afraid to tell anyone, and I felt very alone. I didn't know where to find anyone to talk to. This lasted until I was almost nineteen."

"Even at five or six, I knew that men were fascinating to me—and that if I could survive my growing up I could find a more acceptable world for myself elsewhere. I kept my sexual feelings private and waited."

What Do Boys Do Together Sexually?

"One day during the school holidays, three of us were together at my pal's house when we began talking about sex. After a while we decided to compare our pricks in both limp and erect states. We dropped our pants. I was the only one who wasn't circumcised. Although we didn't have a ruler to measure the organs, my pal was the smallest, then came myself and finally the other guy."

"I was twelve years old when I had my first sexual experience. It was with my best friend and another boy, age twelve. I will always remember him. I continued to have sex with him until he moved to another state at twenty."

"When did I have my best sex? When my cousin came over to spend the night and we went up to my bedroom and locked the door. He started talking about sex with boys and what to do, how to do it. I was only thirteen and he was seventeen. We were on the bed and he took out his cock, it was huge, it was about three inches longer than mine. He started masturbating, his dick was really hard, and all of a sudden this white stuff came out.

"We decided to go to bed, he told me to put my cock into his asshole, so I put it in, it felt so good. He took it out and he said roll over on your stomach and then he slid it in and he went up and down and he came and it felt good."

★　　★　　★

What is really surprising is the kind of sex boys are now having together. According to my 1970's data, this contact was mostly mutual masturbation, often without touching each other. Now, it is much more common for boys to touch each other, masturbate the other boy, and 36 per cent of boys also perform fellatio together. 19 per cent have experienced anal penetration, or penetrated another boy. Very few kiss.

Still, less than half of these boys consider themselves "gay". Are they worried about whether this form of sex and enjoying it could make them gay? The majority do not seem concerned, they do not seem to worry about whether they are "homosexual" or not, or whether they will be "hetero" later in life. Most seem to assume they will be, although others say that they are so happy they hope nothing ever changes—though they still do not use the label of "homosexuality" to apply to themselves or their activities.

The mention of this sexual activity can be remarkably nonchalant. One boy remarks:
"I like it up the ass, but it's not safe anymore. A rubber should always be used and nobody's fluids should be exchanged."

Unfortunately, only half of those boys who here express such delight about anal intercourse seem to be as aware as this boy that anal intercourse has a higher risk of HIV/Aids, and so, therefore, it is most important to use a condom.

Some boys, though a seeming minority, do worry about "being gay":
"At first, I was frightened about being attracted to both sexes. I felt so different. I know now that many of my friends went through the same trauma. Although I enjoyed all my experiences, with each one I had a nagging doubt in the back of my mind. I regard myself as lucky, I wasn't effeminate so I could 'get away' with it, unlike others in my year who were taunted. I wasn't picked on, but I didn't stick up for the ones who were. Why? Because like everyone, I wanted to be accepted. I feel guilty about it now (I'm nineteen)."

Another boy, however, has no doubt that he is "straight":
"I come from an upper-middle-class home. My father was extremely religious and strict. I had a terrible childhood because of my father. My parents are finally getting a divorce.
"I have had sexual relations with four men, mostly while I was still

living at home. I don't consider myself gay, because I like women. I've just never been in a position to, as they say, put the moves on yet.

"I have a male friend who I kiss in a friendly way on the cheek and maybe the lips. But I have French kissed men before. I really don't like just a peck on the cheek. If it is a sex partner, I like tongue kissing. I also enjoy hugging men in friendship and during sex.

"Sex with males starts with kissing and touching. Maybe some games like strip poker or just, let's get these clothes off and down to business. There is kissing and fondling of breasts. Kissing and sucking the nipples and breasts, the navel, the penis and balls, the ass. The 69 position is good, also lying on top of one another, kissing and thrusting our penises together. Having oral sex and anal sex. Nothing very far out or kinky. I don't know if giving a person a blow job or receiving is better.

"If I can recall my first experience, it was when I was twelve years old. I was camping with a friend and we started by you show me yours and I'll show you mine, and you suck mine, I'll suck yours. No orgasm into the mouth though. It started like that and I just built and widened my activities. I must have been young when I had orgasm, because I did not discharge. I masturbated a lot and for a long time until I had discharges, everything. It was fun. Finally, I was masturbating with my brother one night and I had semen with my orgasm. I was shocked and pleased I had reached the age."

Judging from these replies, it is almost as if shared sexual activity is a secret reality for men, part of the bonding process. Or perhaps it is a new way in which men, and especially boys, are beginning to open up to each other. Is a more "female" style of intimate conversation still "off limits" to men, whilst "sex" is not?

On the other hand, this increase in the incidence of boys loving boys could imply an impending denial of women, part of the current backlash against women's rights. Is men's politeness towards women a charade, a pose, in a hypocritical world where men know they are closer to each other than to women? Is this a revival of the completely male-dominated world of societies like classical Greece?

Some "Homosexual" Autobiographies

This trend of increasing physical intimacy between boys is so striking that it is worth hearing more about the lives of boys who are having such experiences. Are they "bisexual" or "homosexual", or simply passing through a "stage"? Is this the "new man" to come?

Boys together seem to have a wonderful time; most sound as if they find their activities quite natural, and many also think about or have sex with girls:

"When I was seven, this fourteen-year-old boy next door gave me a dollar to masturbate him to orgasm. I had my first dry orgasm soon after. I learnt from the older boy. I had my first orgasm when I ejaculated at about eleven. Now I masturbate once a day, sometimes in privacy, sometimes with a friend.

"I love to masturbate with my friends. I hold my hand tight around my penis and move it up and down until I come. I like the way my genitals look, but I liked them better when I didn't have any pubic hairs. I don't like pubic hairs around my balls. I liked them better when they were smooth. I am not circumcised.

"I saw my first porno magazine when I was ten at an older friend's house; he was thirteen and a half and had some magazines on young boys. Kid porno. My parents think pornography is all sin. I like the magazines on boys my age and older.

"When I was twelve, this twenty-year-old guy penetrated me with his penis. It hurt at first, but soon began to feel better. Since then I have been penetrated several times by some of my schoolfriends with their finger or their penis.

"My older friend (who first did it to me when I was twelve) still does it to me even today. He likes to do it to me and have me masturbate myself at the same time so we can orgasm together. At times he will masturbate me while he has intercourse with me. I enjoy having anal intercourse with a younger friend, with me doing it to him.

"Although I prefer to masturbate with another boy, when I get older I would like to try sex with a girl. Right now, I have more male friends. I don't like girls."

"I'm fifteen. Right now I'm sexually confused, but I'm leaning towards homosexuality. I get very aroused when seeing other guys' dicks, especially in physical education, and I love anal sex. To be penetrated by your partner, and knowing that something of him has entered your body, brings much delight and pleasure. I also love fellatio, and swallowing semen is great.

"I believe in monogamy, but for now and the next five or ten years, I'm going to experience many sexual relationships with men. I'm curious to see how many kinds of dicks I can find to blow off.

"I'm quite satisfied with my genitals for my age, but I hope my reproductive organs haven't stopped growing yet. At fullest, my erection can reach seven inches. I might add that my balls should be bigger, but most men wish that, from what I have read.

"I was sexually active with my cousin throughout my childhood until last year when he moved. I was always aroused when I was close to him. Supposedly, I was the more feminine and he was the more masculine. He and I were very good at oral sex. (I should say I am.) Caressing and fellatio was what we liked best. I even French kissed him. I asked him many times to penetrate me anally, but he said it was too soon for that. I very much wanted his penis to enter my rectum, that is, to see how it would feel, and if it was pleasurable.

"The last time I had sex with him, I made him very aware of homosexuality, and that we were having gay sex. The next few nights he wasn't keen to have sex with me. (We hardly did anything exciting.) I've been writing to him lately. He still hasn't written back; I've even sent him a birthday card. Evidently, he hates me. I must confess that what I wrote in those letters must have been upsetting to him (telling him how important homosexuality is).

"Still, there is another young man that I just fell in love with. He is a fellow student in 9th grade. There were many nights when he wanted to go down on me, but I told him I wasn't ready. Honestly, I wanted it bad, but something was holding me back. Four months after that occasion, he asked me to spend the night at his house. I was so pleased that he asked me. Finally I said to myself, I can have some meaningful sex.

"Finally, I asked him to turn off the lights, and we began with oral sex, and ended with anal sex. I was more experienced, so therefore I didn't penetrate him anally.

"Right now, I know he hates me for what we've done and for making him identify his sexuality. Teenagers just have sexual needs so they'll do anything to have sex. The best thing about being with a guy is that you can't make him pregnant.

"At present, I go to a psychiatrist for help in deciding my sexuality. I'm very grateful to have someone to talk to—he helps sort out my feelings. My parents have acknowledged that I have homosexual feelings. I have read many books on homosexuality.

"Masturbation is a big part of my non-sexual life. Sometimes pornography helps to arouse me. I would love to be in a pornographic movie, specifically a gay one. If it was up to me, I would go to a store and buy as many smut magazines as I want, but I'm under age.

"Every once in a while I realize that I have a reputation for being very effeminate. I must admit I am effeminate. To follow a homosexual life will bring many lonely nights and hardships, I know that. And because of the small community I live in, I'll have to move to a larger town in order to have gay friends. So I'll have to think carefully, weigh it up."

293

"My first sexual experience was at the age of twelve at my friend's house and for some reason we started to touch each other. It felt wonderful, I wasn't bothered that my first sexual experience was with a male—I was just happy to have my first ejaculation.

"I have masturbated since I was eight (i.e., stroked, pulled my penis because it felt good), and I had a lovely feeling by pressing my erect penis against something hard, like a bed, but I didn't have my first 'proper' orgasm until I was twelve years old, a couple of months before my first ejaculation.

"Although I am only nineteen, I have never wanted children. Indeed I am not the type, but about a year ago, a woman at work became pregnant. She was single and had no contact with the father. I volunteered to go to classes with her. We were bonded by this and are so close now, it's lovely. Then, the baby arrived. My mind was blown. The whole thing was just so incredible. I sat there crying, laughing. My emotions flooded out. The baby is now three months old and one of the most fulfilling parts of my life is seeing him, playing with him. The idea of being a father is one that will definitely be in my thoughts now when I meet the right lady.

"My upbringing? I did not have a strict upbringing. It was full of love and kindness. I come from a working-class background. My father is brilliant (funny, intelligent, witty and generous). We talk about everything. We share all our secrets. I love him more than I do anyone. I couldn't be without him. We are very close. He's a super man. I'm very lucky to have him.

"My best friend (not my lover!) and I do everything together. We go out whenever we can. He's my closest ally. He supported me through my stage in life when I wasn't sure about my sexuality. He gets on brilliantly with my boyfriend and never judges. We kiss when we see each other and hug. We sleep in the same bed and are just 'together'. I cannot describe our love. It is not sexual but at times we are more like lovers than friends. I would recommend homosexuality (or at least bisexuality) to anyone. Personally, I prefer oral sex and anal masturbation to penetration.

"I'm very close to my mother. We talk, go out together, hug; I like her as a person as well as a mother. I don't understand how people could not like anything about women. They are half of society. Without them there would be no human race. I'm all for the women's movement.

"I had a girlfriend but we split up recently. She was great, fun to be with, and very sexy, but I fell in love with my boyfriend so we split up. We still see each other. She makes me laugh.

"It was this summer that I fell so in love. It was at a concert

294

in London. I saw this man and was instantly attracted. He had drop-down-dead good looks. He saw me staring and walked over. As he made his way towards me I prayed, 'Please, please, let me like him, let him have nice teeth, a great personality, be kind, a sense of humour.' He spoke and I passed out (very nearly)! I felt sick. I could hardly talk. He spoke to me softly and said, 'So, you like Madonna?' and that was it. Two hours of marvellous Madonna and then eight hours of talking, stroking, kissing, hugging. Fantastic.

"I don't prefer sex with either men or women. I have an equal share of friends of both sexes. If I am in love with them then the sex will be good because we will try to fulfil each other's needs. Sex is not about orgasms, it's about love, closeness, sharing. If you have them, fine, but it doesn't mean you can't enjoy sex without them. But I show my emotions. It's a natural thing to do.

"I masturbate perhaps three or four times a week. I like it, you can enjoy your fantasies. I usually move my hand up and down my penis but sometimes I like to move. I'm actually simulating sex. I like the wetness. I like how it charges. I like seeing it. It amazes me that babies come from something so small and strange. My thoughts during masturbation depend on what I have done that day. If I see a beautiful person (a woman) then I will masturbate about her. I have never masturbated about a man even though I am attracted to them. I can't explain it.

"When I was twelve or thirteen I looked at pornography. My father does not read pornography as he believes it degrades women. I now share that view. I saw my first magazine at a friend's house.

"Once I had a lover who was eight years older and knew what she liked, so told me. I was grateful as I knew barely nothing. My girlfriend also showed me what to do. It was very erotic to see her wank herself off. She used a vibrator.

"When I was fifteen I first had sex with a girl. She did orgasm and I try to get all my partners to orgasm this way. I felt happy that I could fulfil her. I read my sister's magazines and there was an article in it about female orgasm. When I discovered how many men don't care, I felt ashamed and sad. Why should we have all the joy?

"Oral sex? It's lovely. I like the taste, the juices. I like it stuck on my face. Also, seeing my partner aroused arouses me.

"Even if the woman uses some kind of birth control I always use a condom, due to my own past, and with Aids and other diseases always around.

"At college my friend became pregnant. Abortion was the only answer. I drew out the money needed from my bank account and went with her to the clinic. It's the most upsetting experience I can remember. We both cried for days afterwards. It had to be done, but I must admit I didn't like being a party to it. It wasn't my baby. I supported a friend when she needed it. I still believe in abortion, without question.

"I have never had violent sex. Sex is a loving experience which violence has no part in. Rape is sex when the woman (or man) has stated that she or he does not want to take part. Rape is something I will never be a part of."

In some cases it seems that older boys may be exploiting younger boys:

"I am sixteen years old, I work in a grocery store, and attend a small-town high school. I plan to go on to college. My parents were divorced when I was six years old, and since then I have never been truly close to my father. I'm considered good-looking by most people and therefore I guess I consider myself handsome as well.

"When I was about nine years old, some new neighbours moved in next door, and they had a seven- or eight-year-old son. Every day he would have some friends over, one his age and one my age, and they would walk out and hide in the bean field. They said that I could come along so I did. They began sucking each other's cocks and asked if I wanted to participate. At first I didn't want to, but then I gave in and found that I really enjoyed it. That's when I discovered that I preferred sex with my own sex to sex with a girl.

"About seven years ago, my Mom remarried. We moved to their home and I became acquainted with my stepfather's grandson. He is about three years younger than me. I was upset about being taken away from my other sex partner and I finally got up the nerve to introduce Shane, the boy, to sex between two boys. I found that he enjoyed it. After about a year, whenever he would suck my cock, I would ejaculate. I always remembered how it felt and couldn't wait for the next time. He would stay all night so he could make me come like that again.

"I have had sexual relationships with boys for about nine years. Shane has been my lasting sex partner for about six years. When we have sex it usually happens like this: we watch television upstairs in my bedroom. Every now and then I glance at his crotch and imagine his cock. Then I start rubbing and caressing him there until he starts to respond. When it is time to go to bed we both get undressed and climb into bed. We then lie on top of each other and I start to caress his ass. He starts kissing me, a French kiss, and we do this for a few minutes. Then he moves down and starts sucking my nipples. Then he'll start licking my chest, neck and around my cock. Finally he takes my cock into his mouth and sucks on it until I come. He will then suck my balls and lick between my legs. Then he will lie on his back and let me go down on him. I start off by kissing him, then sucking his tits, his small but tasty cock, swallow what little preseminal fluid he has, suck his balls, lick in between his legs, and lick his asshole.

"Though I enjoy sex with Shane, I really want to have sex with a man. I have not found the warmth and closeness that I want. I keep saying that sometime I will but I can't work up the nerve to find another homosexual who wants the same thing I do.

"I have sent Donnie, one of my classmates that I dream of as being my sex partner when I masturbate, letters letting him know that there is someone that desperately wants to give him a blowjob, but never signed them. He has replied that he wants a blowjob, but I can't find the nerve to tell him I'm the one and therefore let him know that I'm gay.

"I definitely would love to be penetrated rectally by a dick. Shane already penetrates me with his finger and it feels very good, him moving his finger back and forth inside my asshole.

"I greatly enjoy talking to my male friends, especially those that I wish I could have sex with. They help me ease my tensions and allow me to discuss my problems openly. I have never expressed how much my friends truly mean to me because I'm afraid I may make a fool of them or let them know that I'm gay. I don't think they would accept that fact too well—nobody knows I'm gay.

"My best male friend is approximately six foot tall, sandy brown hair, hairy legs, arms, massive amounts of hair around his belly button, a serious acne problem, but very good-looking. He is very intelligent, has a large cock, and sexy ass. I love to gaze at his crotch and wonder if he masturbates and if so, how often?

"I am part of our high-school basketball team, a manager. I belong to it so I will have an even better chance of seeing some of our sexier whiteball players naked—though I do enjoying watching basketball.

"I would very much like to be a father someday. I truly want to be married and have children and for that reason you would probably have to call me bisexual. I have discovered, though, that every time I masturbate, my imaginary sex partner is always male. I have often tried to jack off with a girl in mind but I can't. Whenever I see a nude picture of a woman, I don't get excited, but I do when I see a nude picture of a man. I have bought several homosexual books and have thoroughly enjoyed them.

"My mom has never said anything about sex to me. I think she is afraid to discuss the topic. My friends talk about wanting to fuck a girl and eat her pussy out. I was never interested in such things.

"My parents do not know I'm gay and I hope that they never find out. But I would take an open stand on gay issues because I feel that the discrimination against someone because of his or her sexual preference is just as bad as the discrimination against blacks, minorities, and women.

"I am very close to my mother. She was the only one that was there for me when she divorced my father. I admire women for their beauty, gracefulness, and their determination over equal rights. I dislike the fact that they do not have hairy bodies, cocks, and balls. They contribute much to our society, things that are so numerous I cannot list them all."

Where Do Boys Get Their Sexual Information?

One might think that parents were more likely to be open with boys, since society praises males for being "sexual" (while casting a suspicious eye on girls). Yet the vast majority of boys say they were not told anything about sex by their parents. Those who were told something found the information inadequate.

This is quite remarkable, given the openness our society is supposed to have achieved. And given the fact that the Aids virus is spreading amongst the heterosexual, as well as the gay population, one would think that parents could take more trouble, overcome their bashfulness, *talk* about things with their children.

"Were you told about sex by your parents? What did they tell you?"

"I was told almost nothing. One day my father and I were down in the basement and he asked me if I knew what masturbation was: I was nervous and sweating, told him yes. He asked then what it was, so I said playing with yourself, and he went on to ask, 'Till what happens?' I was really uneasy now and just hemmed and hawed. Then he said, 'Till something comes out, right?' I said, 'Yeah right,' and was relieved that the episode was over."

"My parents to this day have never discussed sex with me. I used to spy on my sisters bathing and undressing, and I was caught by them a few times, and they were furious. Once my mother caught me looking at my little sister's genitals and she became hysterical. I was always very curious but didn't feel much guilt. I was very angry with my parents about this, but still haven't discussed it with them. The situation is tense."

"My father explained heterosexuality when I was about four. At about six, he got me a book. There was no mention of homosexuality (no knowledge) and none of masturbation until I read a letter in a newspaper at about eleven."

299

"I was told to 'be careful' (by my family), and learned to brag about my cock being the biggest and my conquests the best (from friends)."

"I had very little sex education from my parents. What they did tell me about was the threat of HIV and Aids if I had sex outside marriage."

"My mother told my sister and me about sex when we were still in grade school. She simply said, 'When Daddy's loving Mother very much, his penis goes into her vagina.' It wasn't very detailed, and I remember my sister and I trying not to laugh."

"I remember my dad sitting down with me, telling me about sex. He seemed reluctant. From what I can remember he told me very limited things about what boys have and what girls have. It seemed a very safe discussion. But I learned a great deal from my friends."

"I'm twenty-four, raised in a puritanical family where sex was never talked about, where love for the opposite sex was never discussed. In fact only last summer when my mother went to the hospital for a hysterectomy, she wouldn't admit to my face what was going on ('female problems' was all she said). It's not very sexually open here!"

"I wasn't sure about the difference between a woman's anus and her vagina. I had never seen one. A friend used to say that if we didn't have sex when we were children (sex with boys) we wouldn't be able to have children during our adult married life. I didn't believe him but I was confused. There were other silly stories like this."

"My father told me the rubbers in his night-table drawer were available, and were to be used. That was the first time sex was mentioned. My mother has never said anything about it. My friends, however, introduced me to masturbation, anal sex, fellatio. I give them credit for my bad habits which I took to very readily."

"If my parents ever told me anything about sex I don't remember it. I eventually learned from friends and from my father's medical books, at a disturbingly late age. At thirteen I was still trying to get my father (a doctor!) to tell me how babies came out. Friends at camp had tried to tell me about sex, but I was such a nauseatingly good Catholic boy that I refused to believe them!"

"Don't get any girls into trouble. That was the extent of my sex education at home. They were too uptight to discuss it. In fact I can't even imagine my parents fucking each other (but they must have)! My friends told me about it, and it sounded dirty. I said, 'My parents wouldn't do that.' I thought that husband and wife went into a little cabin in the woods to fuck, something hidden because it was so dirty."

"When I was about eleven, my mother sat me and my younger sister down and read us a book about sperms and eggs and related paraphernalia. As you can imagine it was cold facts without any beauty. Hence I became nauseous just thinking about sex. The street terms were 'fuck', 'screw' etc., but everyone was really short on facts. I recall my older sister going through 'cramp', all of which was alien to me. I was content to climb trees, make rafts and be a little boy rather than deal with this sex stuff."

"My mother never told me anything about sex, but I remember her scolding me, when I was about five, for leaving the bathroom door open while I was urinating. She said she and her friend could hear me. To this day I am still a bit embarrassed making those noises in the bathroom."

What About Love and Crushes?

Even though parents don't tell boys much, most boys seem good at getting information about the mechanics of sex for themselves. What they can't get information about, however, is the emotional context of sexuality. Many express great confusion about the *feelings* they have when they have a crush on someone. Is it love? What does it mean? Boys want to know.

Don't parents at least want to listen, open up a space to make it possible for kids to talk? As it is they often give the impression that somehow these feelings are "silly", "meaningless", "kids' stuff"—or worse, that somehow sexual thoughts and feelings are not legitimate.

Parents may not realize they are doing this or be aware that what comes across is the impression that they disapprove of sex:

"In response to my question, 'How are babies made?' (I was in 5th or 6th grade), my mother told me the basic rudimentary facts: the penis becomes hard, is inserted in the vagina, sperm comes out of the penis and perhaps fertilizes an egg in the womb of the woman. She showed me photos from the *Encyclopaedia Britannica* of sperm and an egg. But she didn't tell me about sexual feelings—like, what about love? Perhaps that would have made adolescence a little easier to understand. From some of my peers—not necessarily friends!—I heard about masturbation, the pleasure of intercourse, finger-fucking, and what the word 'fuck' meant."

"For sex education I was basically told: 'There are two holes. Stick it in the top one.'"

Books and Sex Education Classes

Books and sex education classes are very popular with some parents, but this is no real substitute for a human acknowledgement of the place of sex in life:

"My father gave me a booklet: 'On Becoming a Man.'"

"My parents had an old medical obstetrics book they left on a bookshelf. We used to look at it. They later told us that was why they left it on the shelf."

"My dad tried to explain it all to me one day with the aid of an illustrated anatomy book, but he was so nervous and I was so young that he got no information across. What he said (I can remember it to this day) made no sense."

"My father, a psychiatrist, took all five of us children and our mother to his office one night and showed us a film on the developmental stages of a foetus. Not a word about love, warmth, or affection—and we knew better than to ask questions. This is all that I can remember from my father on the subject. My mother would answer sexual questions without obvious embarrassment but without ever amplifying the discussion past specific answers. My brothers and friends taught me all the 'dirty' stuff. I read about menstruation in the dictionary, my father's medical books and ads and articles in magazines."

"My mother did give me a book about it. I guess she felt I should be told, but was a little backward about how to discuss it with me. I picked up some information from friends which wasn't right and went blindly through life not knowing what really turned a woman on until I read *The Hite Report on Female Sexuality*. I wish I could have read something like that years sooner."

"My father sent away for a book because his father died when he was eleven, and all that he knew was from 'the street' or from armed forces' films. We sort of learned the stuff in the book together, he a chapter or so ahead of me. The book was a cheery sort of 'healthy approach to Manhood'. The only valuable stuff in it dealt with physiology."

Finally, it is curious to note that it is almost always the same-sex parent who gives the book to the child, i.e. the father is supposed to educate the son, and the mother is supposed to talk to the daughter. This is understandable in a family system that is so nervous about the possibility of starting a heterosexual relationship between parents and children. But it would be nice to see the whole family talk about these things together. This would also help to counter the attitude, "We're boys together and we can discuss all this, don't talk to Mom about it, she thinks sex is dirty."

How Do Gay Boys Feel in This Atmosphere?

One sixteen year old, who believes he is gay, makes the following appeal—since he cannot talk to his parents at all:

"My family doesn't talk to me about sex. My parents don't know anything about my two sex relationships. If they knew, they would kill me. I am worried my parents will find out I'm gay. I am also worried about HIV.

"I have never had sex with a woman, I never wanted to. I always dream and fantasize about boys. I also enjoy masturbating and playing with myself like putting Vaseline in my asshole and putting things in my ass. It feels good. I would love to have anal sex with a man! Orgasm is wonderful, my whole body tingles and shakes. Nothing comes before the joys of orgasm.

"I'm always in love when I see my good-looking classmates. It sends quivers through my whole body when I look at them and dream. What I'd like, to be together alone for about a week and let out all our fantasies. I've only had 'one-night stands' so far. It was a good feeling, but there was no holding each other. I think holding and kissing is important.

"I never discuss sex with my friends. I am afraid that they will find out that I am gay. But I want to live with guys when I leave home. I want to live with guys! I like swimming with them, I like to see men in little shorts. Their dicks really look good in them."

Nothing at all is said about homosexuality by most parents, except once in a rare while as a dire warning:

"My father never talked about sex, but he did talk about homosexuality just before I went into the Navy. He referred to the 'meat eaters'. It was silly, but I didn't tell him that."

"My parents told me about the reproductive system and bought a book for me to read. They encouraged me to come to them and not to discuss sex with other boys. They warned me about getting someone pregnant. They didn't seem to be talking about what I was experiencing, but anyway I inherited their homophobia, and desisted for many years from interpersonal sex. They were affectionate towards me and towards each other, but clearly they were not able to communicate well with a child who was gay—different in a way that they didn't have room even to imagine."

"It is hard when you are growing up and there is no one around to explain how you feel or, when you finally find a reference to it, it is called a perversion. People are ignorant about gayness. It will take years before this changes. It should be taught that these things exist, that people have these feelings and that they are okay. Parents have to change. It's a long way off."

Fathers' "Information" to Boys via Sexist Remarks

Some fathers say things about "sex", but the context is misogynistic, one of sly smiles, jokes and winks:

"My father always pointed out women's figures. He said to me, 'A man never grows too old to look, admire, and think about it! When you lose interest in looking at women, you might as well be dead!'"

"At nine, Angela and I were playing house. Somehow we wound up in a closet, we took our clothes off (she wanted to, I didn't force her). I got on top of her, we didn't fuck, just rubbed on each other. All of a sudden her mom came into the closet. I got spanked and went through all kinds of shit. Funny though, my dad laughed about it."

"Once, when I was in law school, my father found a credit card bill of mine: I had rented a motel room as 'Mr and Mrs Smith'. He thought it was humorous. (So did I.)"

"How did you first hear about menstruation?"

"When I was fourteen at a church retreat, another fourteen-year-old boy showed me and some other boys a peep hole into the girls' bathroom. He said we might be able to see them change their Kotex. Someone said, 'What's Kotex?' and he said, 'Something they wear to catch their blood.'"

"From my friend. Something about dried blood."

"My first information about menstruation came from overhearing conversations about being sick, between my mother and her friends."

"I first heard that menstruation was a painful experience. I had to find out what it really was by reading books."

"My father told me about menstruation. The way he told me, it disgusted me and kind of turned me against women."

"I first learned of menstruation by reading a folder from a pack of Tampax. I didn't realize the Tampax were inserted in the vagina until about a month later when I happened to find a sex magazine under my parents' bed. Somehow I put the vagina and sex together."

"I naively asked about my mom's sanitary napkins in the bathroom closet when I was about eleven. She referred the question to my dad, and they decided I was ready to learn about sex. My father very nervously told me a little limited information (he did not know much, as I look back on his 'facts'), and fortunately gave me a book on how birds and bees conceive, including a few details about humans. I learned that women lose blood each month, and that the blood stops and goes to nourish the foetus when a woman becomes pregnant. My friends didn't know much about sex at that age. We all knew something was going on, but we were unsure and rather ashamed to reveal our lack of knowledge. Intercourse was considered 'dirty' and 'gross', although we knew people did it. It seemed unbelievable that all our parents did it."

"What did your friends tell you about sex?"
"'Stick your dick in,' they said."

"My cousin Eddy told me that if you rubbed 'your balls', this white stuff would come out and that is where babies come from."

"Girls had three holes. All sorts of wild stuff, all false of course. No one knew anything."

"My friend told me in school that men in the locker room 'freak off'."

"My initial source of information was the boy next door. He was remarkably well informed. He gave me the basic information about the physical differences between men and women, the act of intercourse, fellatio and cunnilingus and the use of condoms. It wasn't until I was in my later teens and having my first 'heavy dating' that I learned about menstruation, the existence of the clitoris, and other esoteric things."

Strangely, few men or boys say they got information from their girlfriends:

"I have only discussed sex realistically with one person, my present girlfriend. I have known her since I was seventeen and I am almost nineteen now. Friends had only given me distorted information—crude jokes mainly."

Boys learn from all this that "sex" is a behaviour separate from feeling. (Of course they would "have" to be taught this in patriarchy, where they learn to love and respect other men more than women.) Although, if they only had sex with those they loved and respected (men), there would be no reproduction. Was this an early problem that patriarchy had to solve for itself? How did the classical Greek democracy evolve into a culture a few centuries later in which heterosexuality was considered "normal", in which all "real" men were supposed to have a wild "sex drive" directed at women?

Pornographic Depictions of Sexuality

Since parents say so little about sex to their children, one of the main sources of information is pornography:

"I first saw porno magazines in my brother's room. I was twelve. Shocking! It made me *sick*. My dad read those magazines too. Now, I don't see anything wrong with it so long as a child does not look at it under fourteen. Well, I guess I did."

As this man's statement implies, many boys look at pornography with other boys around, it is one of the accoutrements of "living", teenage style. Like carrying a condom in your wallet.

Many boys now are clearly very influenced by pornography. This seventeen-year-old boy has a very detailed, sophisticated scenario for his fantasy when he masturbates, a fantasy of sex with a woman:

"I'm just seventeen, I am a virgin, but hoping to lose my virginity soon. I'm looking forward to my first blowjob. I have never participated in foreplay, but I am interested. The closest I ever came (no pun intended) to having sex was at my pool when a bunch of friends, boys and girls, went skinny dipping. It was lots of fun, this year I am hoping to do it a lot more.

"My whole sex life right now is masturbation. I enjoy it a lot more than when I was younger. I take two pillows and fold them, next I insert my cock in the opening and move my hips up and down, in and out, until I reach orgasm, or I wear a pair of boxer shorts and lie down on a hard flat surface (bathroom floor) and move my hips until I climax. If I am tired, I just use my hand.

"When I was younger my friend and I used to compare our cocks, they were about the same. When I had my first orgasm, I didn't ejaculate, my cock just bobbed up and down in the air, I was really scared!! I didn't realize what was happening.

"Once a friend and I were playing cops and robbers, I was the cop and he was the robber, and as the cop, I was tied up by the robber in the basement of my house. I got a rock-hard erection that wouldn't go. I guess I like to be dominated a little. I like the helpless feeling.

"I lift weights at the 'Y' and often girls, women, stand at the window and watch. My fantasy is: I've been working out for about an hour and I'm all hot and sweaty. I wear a pair of white gym shorts, T-shirt and just a jock strap, because underwear is uncomfortable. While I'm lifting, this girl with beautiful jet-black hair, blue eyes and moist red lips is staring at me, and my growing crotch. She licks her lips and walks in.

"I'm trying to lift 135 lb. and really straining. She walks over and says, 'You look very tense.' I say, 'Yeah, it's been one of those days.' Then she pats my ever-increasing crotch and says, 'I know just what you need to loosen you up.' She takes me by the hand, we leave the weight room and enter a smaller room, about nine feet square.

"In the room I see a pair of handcuffs suspended from the ceiling. In one corner is a small gym mat that I suspect we will be using shortly. She shuts and locks the door and tells me to relax. She pulls the T-shirt over my head and cuffs one hand and, before I know what has happened, I am cuffed to the ceiling. She then says, 'You're going to love this.'

"And she next pulls my shorts down and off, leaving me standing there with just my jock on and my hands stretched above my head. My cock is really pulling against the snug-fitting strap. Next she begins to undress slowly with grand gestures. She takes off her shirt, and she isn't wearing a bra so her large breasts are now in my full view. She walks over to me and begins to rub her blossoming breasts in my face, on my chest and down to my ass and around my thighs and finally to my rock-hard organ. She begins to lick my inner thighs and cock, still confined in the jock. She brings me to the point of coming many times.

"After a while of this torment she pulls off the jock and releases my aching cock. It bounces out as she frees it, then off come her panties, and she unchains my wrists. I pick her up and carry her over to the mat and gently place her down. She pulls me onto her as she spreads her legs, making me enter her steaming pussy. She moans with pleasure, me too, as we both come to a shuddering climax."

In view of the resounding silence of parents, perhaps there is a kernel of truth in the idea that at least pornography gives people the information that other people do "do it".

But the increase in sexual violence towards women may very well be linked to the increase in pornography depicting women as being degraded, and "liking it". To show images of women bound and being beaten indicates to boys that this attitude of violence to women is permitted. (See Chapters 3 and 9.)

Condoms and Aids/HIV

"Nobody uses condoms in films or videos or sex magazines,
so why should I?"
If condoms are not seen in use in the movies or on television, given
the power of the visual media, why should boys (or girls) think that
condoms are something they should use? It wouldn't seem "natural"
or necessary suddenly to pull one out during sex, since "nobody else
does it".

Although, statistically, worldwide sales of condoms have only
increased by about 10 per cent in the last few years,* the world's
population is increasing by much more than that every day.

Resistance to condoms

The current governmental and condom manufacturers' public relations
seem intended in large part to try to get women to take responsibility
for the use of condoms. Ads imply that the "modern woman" would
carry one in her handbag. In the UK now, the "Femidom" has been
introduced, a plastic insert for women to put inside the vagina.

The problem with this is that women (despite the unfairness of
being expected to "take care of things") who do supply condoms are
apt to be seen by men in the light of the "double standard", i.e., as
"girls who do it with everybody": "You seem so experienced!" This
belief that "nice girls" don't carry condoms is widespread: a woman
stopped by the police and found to be carrying condoms is likely to
have this used against her, she might be cautioned or arrested as a
"common prostitute", the condoms in her possession being the only
necessary evidence.

Many boys and men are afraid of losing their erection as they
put the condom on. This is more of a status worry than a real
one, for in fact, even if a man did begin to lose his erection, he
could get it back again by simply rubbing his penis for a minute or two. This would not create a problem at all, but the per-
formance pressures inside the boy's or man's head may leave him
unconvinced.

Do men resist using condoms because they feel it is an "emas-
culation", a denial of the penis? They often say that the feelings
during coitus are not quite as good when using a condom. With a
condom on, do they feel somehow less accepted? No matter what
the feelings are, it is unfair of men to expect women to take the

---

* According to international manufacturers of condoms.

responsibility for HIV prevention, the way they did for birth control.

It would be better if more boys and men today felt like the man who said condoms really turned him on, ever since he was a teenager during the 1950's, when condoms were *the thing*.

Positive Parent–Child Discussions

Only a handful of boys in this study say they received complete information or were presented with a positive attitude towards sex:

"I was well informed about sex by my parents, especially the biological aspects. The first time was when I was five. I was told the names of all the parts and how babies were conceived and born.

"I was told about sex in a very natural way. Mother talked about love in relation to sex; she explained but never tried to push opinions on me. I was shown pictures, and once I started reading I was given books about sex. It was a very open subject. Sexual play with my friends was not discouraged. I often saw my parents nude."

"I learned very little about sex until I was about seventeen. But before that I always had the impression that it was good, and related to love. I guess it was the way my mother and father held hands sometimes, and the way they were so happy for my older sister when she got engaged. They explained to me that she would now have someone to be close to, to kiss and sleep next to, and that someday I would too."

Sexual Experiences of a "Street Child"

Of course, there is something we are leaving out in this discussion: not all boys live with their parents. One boy who has lived "on the street", or made his living there, explains what his life has been like:

"I am now in a home for abused children. I am eighteen. So far my life has been as a male prostitute. I have worked the streets since I was a little boy. That's all I knew until I was seventeen.

"The first time I had sex willingly I was seven, it was with a man who used to take me for ice-cream. Before that, when I was four years old I was raped by my babysitter.

"I don't have a specific lover, just clients that hire me for the nights. I don't get emotionally involved, I just want their money. (I am at a point where I try not to care, because I am tired of getting hurt.)

"I really can't say I am a bisexual, I'm gay, but I have sex with women as much as I do with men. People at work know I am gay, that's what they hire me for. I don't have parents, so I don't have to wonder what they think. When I was ten, I was forced by my foster parents to go to bed with my sister and brother. It was strange. It still hurts me now to think about it.

"I don't have friends. Who has time to think of yourself when you sleep with everybody that pays you to?

"Sex is very overrated—*I know!* Sex has no spiritual significance for me. It gets me money for my needs. At the time there is no guilt. I enjoy sex with men and women equally. Sex is economic. I do what they want, they give me money for what they want.

"I'm not interested in violence, but my clients are, so violent sex is always in my sex life. I sometimes like to struggle with the man or woman, it gives me some sense of pride. But I have had the hell knocked out of me. I have been tied up, beaten. I like it if it's not too rough. I like the feeling of being forced to have sex.

"Being gay is great. You don't have to put on an act of being Mister Tough Guy. To feel your lover inside you is a great feeling. Disadvantages, well if you get one too big, it hurts like hell, but once you relax it feels even better.

"I love anal intercourse, it feels like you become one with that man. To feel it slide in and out is the best feeling you could ever get! I orgasm two or three times at least. I also enjoy fellatio very much. I swallow the seminal fluid—I love it.

"I first had an orgasm when I was about eleven. I really enjoyed it. It felt strange but great. The way I masturbate is to sit down and give slow but firm strokes to the whole penis until I ejaculate. I think about being raped by a gang of girls and guys at the same time. I do this to relieve tension about work and other things.

"Even though I don't have a family, I am happy the way I am. I like all sport, it keeps me in good physical condition. I like to swim. I enjoy children a lot because I know they don't want anything from me except my love, not sex!

"I would like to be a father. I would use my experience to help him/her grow up right. I think parents should tell their children about sex so they can make their own decisions when the time comes.

"I someday want to find somebody that I can learn to love. But I don't at this point in time like people. I have been abused so much that I am paranoid with everybody!"

"There is No Sex in This House!"

Sex is outlawed

Most boys keep both masturbation and any sexual activity strictly hidden from their parents. Since most parents give the impression that they don't have a sex life of their own, they are hardly likely to encourage the boy to be open about his:

"If you are still living at home, what does your sex life consist of?"

"I live with my family. I spend the night at my girlfriend's house but don't tell my parents where I've been. I'm pretty sure they know I spend it with a girl, but if I told them, they would not approve. So I skirt around the issue. I don't believe in flaunting it by bringing the girl to my room."

"I am still living at home with my mother, but I have a 'sex' life of sorts. Solely masturbation, although several of my thoughtful neighbours did tell my mother when she returned from her vacation about the one night Ann slept over at my house."

"I live in a house trailer off campus at school with a straight room-mate who doesn't know I'm gay. During the summer I live at home with my parents who don't know either. It is difficult to have a sex life that you must hide, but I usually manage by either going to a gay bar or theatre."

"I have a sparse one with whores and girlfriends. My parents don't know. They'd die. Or throw me out."

"It is hard if you live at home. I'm getting a van to do it in. You have a hard time if you want privacy to masturbate too."

"I still live at home. My sex life consists of masturbation and, occasionally, having sex with my woman friend when the house is vacant. These are rare times, as are those at her home. We are both in the same fix. We have also taken a motel room and used a friend's apartment a couple of times. They know about the motel stops and my friend's apartment but they don't react. As far as openly discussing it goes, this can of worms has been left closed."

"I have no sex life except masturbation, which no one knows about. When my parents found out that I was having intercourse at seventeen, my father had a long talk with me, sum total: 'Don't get her pregnant.' My mother said nothing, but was upset."

313

"It is very secretive, we make love any chance that we get. They don't know anything about it and would take it really poorly."

"I assume they know that I have a sex life, as I told them I intended to move in with my 'girlfriend' at college, at which time we had quite a telling battle and they threatened to stop paying for school and to disown me. The former I could have lived with but the latter I couldn't, so the matter was dropped and I lived with her secretly."

"I go to a massage parlour if my girlfriend is not available, or call on the phone any of the numbers listed in the daily paper in the personal columns. My mother more or less knows some hanky-panky is going on, but as I say, what she don't know won't hurt her."

In these stories, quite a few mentions of mothers crop up—many more than of fathers—often in the context of the laundry and "come" stains. Boys wonder if their mother knows, or else they are "sure" that she *does* know:

"My mother, as far as I know, has never found out about my masturbation, although I've done it occasionally when she's actually in the house (though obviously not in front of her; even I have limits). However, we do the laundry together most of the time. Since I can see the dry crusty stains of my come on my underpants and T-shirt bottoms, I imagine she sees them as well but just doesn't say anything."

"My sex life at home consists of masturbation. My parents know about it and accept it as normal. When my mother first found out, I had just taken a shower and had left a small picture of a nude female in the bathroom. She said, 'What's that?' then looked at it again and said, 'Oh, a masturbation picture.'"

"My mom found my sex magazines last year when I was seventeen; she was upset. Then when I stopped going to church, she damn near died. Three months ago she found a Durex. My dad, who supports me, threatened to cut me off if he caught me having sex.

"I'm from a strict Roman Catholic family and I live at home. My dad gave me a book about sex when I was younger, called *A Christian Father Talks to His Son*. Damn near turned me into a monk. I came to hate my father immensely.

"When I'm worried or in tension my first orgasm is quick (one thrust). I feel terrible! However, if we have time, the second cures all ills, and usually it's excellent. (When they are at church, that's when I have my girlfriend over.)

"Usually my parents think I'm at a friend's studying. They would probably kick me out of the house if they found out. Same with hers. That's why we're so careful about her not getting pregnant, because

314

neither of us would agree to an abortion (we both consider it murder), and both our parents would have to find out if she did get pregnant."

As discussed in Chapter 8, many boys during these years are making connections unconsciously between their sexuality and their relationship with their mother, and we can feel some of that in the answers throughout this section.

Some boys describe being attracted by their sisters, or curious about them:

"Some of my first wet dreams involved my older sister, but that was a largely subconscious thing, as she was also just beginning to consolidate her sexual maturity (physically, not emotionally)."

"My younger sister turned out to be a very attractive girl, and for a while I toyed with the idea of having incestuous feelings for her, but that was a morbid self-created trip."

"I guess feelings vaguely described as sexual have kept on cropping up for my mother and sister. My father has never come close to being a desirable sexual object."

"I have an older sister who was voluptuously beautiful and well-developed, but she is married and has been gone for ten years. Besides, she doesn't love me anymore. She is thirty-eight and I'm twenty-two. Anyway, I never wanted sex with her, really, but one time when I was about eight or nine, while she was talking on the phone I laid my penis on her leg without her noticing it. She thought it was funny. I thought it was funny, but I was mad, too. I wanted her attention."

"I remember when I was about ten, I and a friend were curious about what girls were like, and I was supposed to try to find out because I had an older sister. I reported back that they looked sort of like a funnel."

Being accepted at home
For the minority of boys who feel their sexual selves are accepted at home, even in theory, there is a great feeling of contentment:

"My first really meaningful relationship with a girl culminated in my own bedroom in my own bed, when my parents weren't home. But they know. I feel that was one fact that kept me from having a lot of backseat fucks and traumatic experiences. Those came later and I really felt secure knowing what sex was like earlier."

"Once I established a 'sex life' in high school, I was given more respect at home and left alone."

"There is no problem with parental disapproval mainly because my mother is great. Women I sleep with usually have an opportunity to meet her first, and without exception seem to feel comfortable afterwards. My mother just turned sixty-four. She's a fantastic lady!"

"I do have a sex life living at home. A gay one at that. They accept it. If they didn't, I would simply leave."

"I lived at home last year after being away at school for years. My parents' only comment has been, 'If you do it in our house, don't do it in our bed.' They are very liberal about sex but only because I'm a male. They've admitted that they'd be stricter with and more worried about my sister."

"I have a private room of my own. That makes it easy for me to have a sex life at home. I can keep things hidden. I bring my friend home and go straight to my room—and lock the door. I guess they do suspect when they see us coming out. But that's okay."

"My girlfriend and I both lived at home up to three years ago and still had a sex life. Once we were necking in my bed and my mother walked in and saw us. She turned away and said, 'None of that in this house.' But she wasn't serious!"

Sex is only for when you're out
More commonly, if parents accept that a boy has a sex life, he has to practise it outside the home: "Not under this roof!" This attitude can continue during marriage: home is where the "wife" is, outside is where the "girlfriends" are.

"When I lived at home, my sex life was always elsewhere. My mother told me that if I didn't get into trouble or hurt anyone, I could do anything I wanted away from the house."

"On my twentieth birthday, I went to stay with a girl for two weeks. My mother was kind of glad, just to get me out of the house!"

A Question of Loyalty

When parents find out
Since most boys feel they have to conceal their sex lives from their parents, there is inevitably an unhappy reaction if parents *do* find out:

"When my mom found out, she began to cry. She doesn't believe in premarital sex. She said she and my father were virgins when they got married and everything had turned out alright for them. When I said it wasn't right to repress such strong drives, she said that a person should exercise self-control and that 'illicit' sex was immoral."

"When they found out I'd made it with a girl, at first my father didn't do anything. That's his style, he broods. Mom behaved as though

I'd deserted or something. It didn't bother me too much, I just thought it was all part of separating from parents. I was the oldest, so I gave them the shock first."

Surprisingly often, parents make the boy feel that his having sex is an act of disloyalty to them:

"At home now I have a sex life that's very frustrating, compared to the time I was living with my girlfriend. At home, I have no sex life at all. My parents wouldn't approve, and I think they would be hurt. I don't know why, it's just a feeling."

Does it mean a boy is being disloyal to the family if he has sex? Or is parents' unhappiness due to the boy breaking the "family" mould of asexuality? Is it a matter of jealousy?

One father, walking in on his son having sex, describes his shocked surprise:

"I think of myself as being pretty sexually liberated, but it was a jolt when I walked in on my teenage son having intercourse with a girl. I really didn't know what to do, so I didn't do anything. I never talked to him about it. Our kids have had books about sex, but I sense they're embarrassed about discussing sex with either me or their mother. I only talk to them about sex when I think they've picked up distorted facts."

To whom is the boy being disloyal? The "family"? The mother? The father?

"Single" Mothers and "Sex"

Single mothers are on the whole more liberal with their sons, actually having conversations and *accepting* the boy's sexual activity as a reality. This creates better relationships:

"When I was in high school, my girlfriend and I had been making love together for some time, sneaking into our converted garage when Mom was gone. One afternoon she came back unexpectedly and went into the house. We emerged after dressing and joined her. Mom said, 'I want to talk to you two. I don't mind if you have sex, just be careful, I don't want to be a grandmother yet.'"

"My mother brings me home rubbers that she gets from the drugstore, where she works. She gives them to me and tells me to wear my 'raincoats' when I 'visit' any girls so I won't die of Aids and so that the girls won't be pregnant and unmarried like she was when she had me. She also says that if I'm going to 'do' anything with girls that's perfectly all right as long as I do it outside our apartment. I am nineteen.'"

Who Are These Boys? Split-Level Reality

It is difficult to comprehend that the boys who are not able to show their sexuality at home are some of the same boys who are having, from early ages, such open and unselfconscious sex with other boys.

This makes the fact that their parents never talk to them about sex even more ludicrous, as if the children are much more sexual than the parents. In many cases they probably are but this doesn't fit the myth of "angelic childhood" our society is so fond of, nor the archetype of Jesus, the son, as asexual.

What Should Parents Be Saying?

Parents should *acknowledge* sex, love and affection, and physical pleasure. Parental silence about sex and sexuality becomes more and more ludicrous in a society where sex is in every magazine and every television programme.

What message do boys get about sex and love from their parents' silence? They conclude that sex doesn't belong in "true" love relationships, or marriage and "family": "true" love is asexual.

Why don't parents talk to boys about sexual politics and the "double standard"? Why don't they warn them of the dangers of exploiting girls and women in their quest to prove their "manhood"?

A note about the social construction of "male" sexuality

Boys undergo indoctrination into the idea that the only "real" sexual activity is penetration, and that it is natural for men to desire coitus with any woman they find attractive, whether they are interested in her as a person or not. As the Hite Reports have shown, sexual identity is socially constructed, and not a simple matter of "hormones" and "inevitable" behaviour. Since the culture teaches that "sex" means coitus and is "reproductive", shouldn't parents counter this by giving their sons an awareness of the wide variety of sexual activities that are

319

equally acceptable and desirable—not to say pleasurable? This would reduce the incidence of date rape and teenage pregnancy, and make it possible to have "safe sex" without always needing to use a condom, since there would not always be penetration.

Chapter 11

Boys and Their Father: Distance and Longing

While there is a revolution in the family taking place, relationships between fathers and sons are slow to change. The picture presented here of fathers and sons is bleak—though there are some extremely valuable exceptions, roadmaps for the future.

Changing allegiance from the mother to the father, boys often feel alone and insecure, suddenly in a new, colder and more competitive world, a world they say over and over again that their distant father did not explain to them. This world is one in which the mother can no longer protect or save them, increasing their newfound anger and scorn for the mother, and rage at her powerlessness.

Did Michelangelo Understand the Male World of Longing and Fear?

Like the Michelangelo fresco of Adam reaching for God's hand in the Creation, in which their fingers never quite touch, men feel that tantalizing sense of almost . . . almost. They can almost touch their fathers, and yet, there is a distance that is unbridgeable. They are left with a feeling that he is unattainable, other, outside, and that this is how it must be.

This incomplete relationship affects many men for ever. They attempt to reach the "father", try to make him recognize and see them, the son. This is the same struggle that women have with men in love relationships, essentially, trying to get men to "open up", be more communicative, relate fully to them, "see" them. A cycle persists of the woman not being able to get through to the perfectly contained, controlled, closed (and dying inside) man. She consequently feels less and less loved, and neither is able to understand the other. Boys (like these women) become fascinated by the power of this emotionally silent and mysterious man. It is interesting to note that the archetype of Joseph is more blank and remote than Mary or Jesus.

Men of Mystery: The Attraction of Silence and Aloofness

Boys' Early Memories of Their Father

We have seen in Part 1 how intense and close many men's and boys' contacts with their mother were, and how important to them these memories are.

Although there are some wonderful early memories of fathers, for the most part boys do not offer the kind of warm descriptions of their father that they do of their mother.

Only a few men remember receiving affectionate physical closeness from their father when they were young. Even among those who do, their answers are quite brief and with little sense of the pleasure in remembering:

"My father hugged me. My grandfathers hugged me."

"I was cuddled by my father as a baby."

"I have few memories, but I remember my father would, when I was pre-school age, teasingly cover my head with his jacket while holding me."

"I remember being tucked in. My daddy did it a lot."

Poignantly, many of those who don't remember getting any affection at all from their father still sometimes assert that it *must* have existed anyway, so much do they want to believe that their father was affectionate with them. Their answers sound plaintive, almost desperate, "explaining" that even though they remember nothing, the reason must be just that they have "forgotten":

"I guess my father carried me and kissed me goodnight when I was a baby. But I don't remember it."

"He must have done what fathers do—walked the floor with me when I couldn't sleep, kissed me and held me. But he has never talked of it, and there are no photos of us together like this. Still, I feel sure he must have."

★　　★　　★

323

When boys don't get cuddling from their fathers, does this leave them with an inability to feel (or do they focus their emotions on their mother)? Or do they grow up angry and distrustful of their father?

As they get older, as we shall see, boys struggle to find a relationship with their father. Even to understand what their own emotions are for their father is difficult, most say: as he does not talk to them, thus they cannot talk to him either.

Many boys between five and fifteen, commenting on their relationship (non-relationship?) with their father, say that there is almost no disclosure of himself, nothing that enables the son to get to know the father better, and by extension, get to know what he himself should be as an "adult". Does this just leave a void, or create resentment? Perhaps longing?

While some members of the men's movement have insisted that feminists' theories and "proposed world order" treats fathers like "second-class citizens", jealously guarding women's closeness to children, it is not "feminists" who are creating the situation. In reality, fathers don't take as much part in the intimate daily details of care of their children as mothers do.

Women have stated in poll after poll that they are still doing most of the childcare and housework. They wish desperately that their husbands would become more involved.

Fathers and Physical Intimacy with Children

Fathers Describe Cuddling and Playing with Their Children

Do fathers want to touch their sons, and be affectionate?
A minority of fathers taking part in my research here speak of actively enjoying affectionate contact with their sons. The rest just left the question blank or answered no.

The following answers represent under 24 per cent of replies; they are reproduced here for their enthusiasm and beauty:

"We snuggle, wrestle (known as 'huggling' and 'rough and tumble' respectively in our house). I used to enjoy giving them baths, but they are older now and look after themselves mainly. I still enjoy drying the younger one (the older does it himself most of the time). In fact, I was always better with them as infants than my wife. With a colicky kid, I was the magic daddy, who would walk with them curled against my neck until they fell asleep. I still seem to have some talent for calming infants by touching them (thus now with infant nephews). Also for getting poor feeders to suck well. Don't know how I do it. Maybe some throwback to my grandmother."

"One of my greatest joys was sitting in a chair or on a couch and holding them for hours as they slept. This way I could look at them, I could feel their soft cheeks, listen to their gentle breathing. Today I am their Superstar, their number one. I would take over night feedings whenever my wife was either too tired or too sick to do it. The love and affection I have for my children is deep and very gratifying. They were born out of an act of love and I love them. No matter how busy I am, I find time for my family. Another job I can find tomorrow. Another family is impossible to find."

"The happiest time of my life was the first three or four years of my younger son. As one of those child-rearing books says, 'At two years of age, some of them can be a real joy.' I think that this was true for me because my own father had set me the example."

"I enjoyed cuddling and rocking and playing with our children.

325

When I used to bathe them, sometimes all four of them were in the same tub (three boys, one girl), while my wife did the dishes. I held them and fed them as babies, I changed their diapers when I couldn't gracefully get out of it. Dressed them on plenty of occasions. Fed them and cleaned up their burps and spills. Had all the fun and part of the work."

"I like to hold my daughter face to face and talk to her. My wife and I used to let her come into bed with us. We all loved it."

"I have two kids, a boy and a girl. We used to have 'barfoling', that's a made-up word we had for a game of about ten minutes of tummy and back rubbing several times a day. Also we'd play a word game—I'd touch their noses and say 'nose', and then they'd do it to me. I carried my kids on my shoulders constantly till they weighed 35 pounds. Also, we played 'Boom chicka boom', a lap-bouncing song game where I had them lean sideways and backwards while bouncing.

"I must admit I was very keen on developing their body awareness and co-ordination, as I'd read a lot about how stimulation increases intelligence and stuff like that (in college I majored in psychology). We also played games like their blindfolding me and *talking* me through threading a bodkin, or their shaving me."

A very rare man describes some tender and private moments, comforting his sick son:

"When my son's not well, I enjoy putting my hand on his forehead, stroking his hair, saying things like, 'Poor David, oh, I know it doesn't feel good, does it, I know it hurts. Would you like me to turn on the TV? Would you like to play basketball? Come on, let's go shoot a few!' (The latter in a tone of voice that I use when we do little comedy routines together, he always the straight man.) I hold his hand, rub his arm, kiss him on the forehead. Sometimes do baby talk."

Men and Childcare

In some of the families beginning to emerge now, men are at home much of the day with their children:

"I am home for more of the time than my wife. In fact, she's the main bread winner. I enjoy snuggling and holding my sons. I like playing with them and making them laugh, especially when they are tense. I enjoyed feeding them up to the age of three—after that it became monotonous and demanding. Now I enjoy getting them involved in outdoor activities.

"I had no difficulty in reversing roles with my wife—who went back to teaching when our younger son was three months old. She got thoroughly fed up with being in the house and my long working and travelling hours. The walls seemed to stifle her enthusiasm for living, while I felt that my participation in family life was too little. It seemed a useless and tense grind—we felt we were living more like robots—so my wife found a teaching position not far from home, I changed to a part-time sales job, thus we immediately gained more time together as a family."

Fathers who have daughters rather than sons, have been equally involved in childcare:
"With my two girls, now twelve and seven, I bathed, dressed, fed, made formula, changed diapers, washed diapers and bottles. I loved to hold them both. After their bath, sometimes in the tub with me or their mother, I liked to dry them and talk to them, kissing them. I liked to lie on the bed and put them on my chest (no shirt on). They were very soft and warm, and I took great pleasure in feeling them wiggle and squirm and look up at me and smile. It was a very special way of being close with my children when they were young."

"When she was newborn I'd get up for her in the night, every night for three months. Her mother almost never did. But I loved it. I loved raising her from a little baby. Watching her growth, holding her, feeding her, taking care to see that she got the best food, changing her—I liked it all."

"My nine-year-old daughter and I are best friends. I'm divorced, see her twice a week. She asks me about sex, like you would a friend. But physically she's my baby girl. Cuddles up, snuggles and goes to sleep like a kitten. It was hard for me to relate to her fully until she was about three and truly verbally responsive, though I always held and cuddled her in infancy."

Interestingly, a substantial group of men who speak of enjoying looking after their children never mention gender:
"I loved—repeat, *loved*—touching and holding my children, and walking with them in my arms, up and down the floor on a cold winter night. I was always reaching out to stroke their hair, their cheeks, or put my arms around their shoulders, lift them up, or carry them all over the house, the yard, town, everywhere. I used to love to mow the lawn carrying one of them on my shoulders! I changed them, fed them after they left their mother's breast, cared for them when they were sick, spent hours and hours with them, neglecting other work."

"I cuddle them a lot. We kiss constantly. I confess to enjoying their wonderful bodies. We play a lot of games. On the nude beach, we wrestle, and with my nephew and two nieces, friends' kids, too. No problem. I used to love giving them baths when they were smaller, rocking and feeding them. My wife and I always shared all the pleasures and duties of taking care and playing with them. She worked for years at her profession when I was a student, so I spent lots of time with them at home. I would often break from work to play with them."

"I love babies. Like in a Russian movie I saw, I kiss their bottoms after baby oil and powder. I love to draw cartoons for them and hold them while I read. And kiss and take them piggy-back on my shoulders."

"They're too damn big now. However, all their young years, both my wife and I gave them lots of physical affection, and that's a happy memory. I loved to hold 'em, feed 'em, fight 'em, bathe 'em, rock 'em, occasionally sock 'em, and haul 'em everywhere. The oldest is twenty, the youngest thirteen and we still hug each other, wrestle and mess around. 'I love you' is heard every day—from them and us—and we all mean it."

Some of these sound more nostalgic than real, unfortunately. Are they sincere or just enthusiastic about their own pictures of themselves as great fathers? Perhaps some think the "new man" *should* say he is affectionate and involved. But some fathers *are* changing in their relationship with their children.

Partial and problematic as many father–child relationships are, the strong feelings of real love and even sadness some fathers express ring true and are genuinely heartrending and moving:

"I had a little girl who I loved very much, but her mother and I separated. I enjoyed her feeding and baths. I used to buy her a new dress every week."

"I enjoyed hugging, wrestling and general tomfoolery. Now I am separated—these experiences were long ago and cherished still—though memory is dimmed by time."

"It's a beautiful thing when a child hugs you."

"When my children were younger and we were together as a family, I enjoyed holding them, but we live apart now and they are fourteen and seventeen and we just don't do it anymore. More's the pity."

How Close Is Too Close?

In relation to very young children, some men wonder if there can be too much physical intimacy. For example, should a father wash the child's genitals in the bathtub?

"I like to hug my five-year-old daughter. I love her so much. We are very close, maybe too close. But I have no sexual feelings towards her. When I bathe her I usually ask her to wash her own vagina. I love to hold her, rock her, sing her lullabies. I rarely sleep in the same bed with her, but when I do, I really like it. I rarely do it because she is so dependent as it is (abnormally so, I fear). I don't want her to have to sleep with someone every night."

"Recently my eight-year-old son asked if we could get into bed together naked and cuddle, so we did. It was really fine. We both had erections, but that just seemed a natural thing to happen. There was no sexual activity, it was just a warm happy time."

"I am the father of a five-year-old and live alone with him. I would like to mention areas that have caused concern for me. When playing with a child in situations where both I and the child were nude, my erection has worried me. If the child played with it, I would feel guilty even though I might enjoy it. If I told the child not to play with it I would be making an issue out of it and somehow reinforce the idea that there was something wrong with an erection.

"I eventually discussed this with a close friend and came to this conclusion. It was not acceptable for me to involve the child in a sexual situation, even though he appeared to enjoy it, any more than I would permit him access to a knife. It was my responsibility to alter the game in a subtle way so that the sexual element was removed without the need to mention it."

What about this man's closeness to his son?:

"I enjoy everything about my seven-year-old son. I have never been able to leave him alone, we are always holding hands, leaning on one another and going to sleep together. We still have goodnight kisses (on the lips), and there isn't anyone who can tell me that this will 'turn him into a queer'! I have had very intimate contact with him ever since he was born, and hope that we can continue like this for ever."

But not all fathers are as enthusiastic and affectionate with their children as those we have just heard; the above examples represent a minority of men in this sample.

Most do not enjoy intimate contact with young children. They're happier playing boisterous games and being "male":

"Holding children makes me nervous, but wrestling is fun."

"I don't enjoy physical contact with children as much as talking to them. I like being a pal, giving them leadership."

"I don't like holding small children for very long. They can't talk much so they can't tell you what they want—it makes me feel uneasy."

"You Can't Touch Anymore After a Certain Age"

Fathers confirm here what men and women say in Chapter 1—that physical contact reaches a cut-off point when children reach five or at least by adolescence:

"Since they are now young adults I do not hold or snuggle with them as much as when they were children, but I enjoyed it, especially with my daughter when she was a little girl."

"I have three boys and we did a lot of wrestling when they were young, up to eleven, and we took baths together. Also, up till eleven or so, I told them bedtime stories. Then I had to stop. But this, I feel, has 'paid off' handsomely as they are struggling through their middle and late teens, a difficult time. We have a closer relationship due to these many hours of story time."

One father is trying very hard to go against the cultural tide:

"I enjoy touching and holding my children. Snuggling, wrestling, too! We have a seven-year-old girl, eight-year-old boy and fourteen-year-old boy. I am still very comfortable doing all these things with the younger two, but it's more difficult with the teenager, although I try hard to touch and hold him. We both sense that in our culture it's not done often; but I try to hug and kiss him on the cheeks as much as possible without embarrassing either of us."

And some fathers describe, regretfully, the end of touching and affection:

"It seems unfortunate (at least for me) that as my children grow up, and acquire lives of their own, there is less and less physical contact, almost as if by mutual consent. Thus I can still wrestle with and hug my twelve-year-old son, but with my eighteen year old, it seems inappropriate; with my seventeen-year-old daughter there's an additional puritanical element in operation."

"I love my children more than anyone, apart from my wife. When they were younger, it was natural for me to hold and kiss them, and give them baths. They are older now so I do not do as many of these things as I used to but I have a tremendous amount of fond memories."

"I enjoyed holding my children, loving them, rocking them, feeding them. But I severely limited it as they reached adolescence, as I felt it might adversely affect their lives. My only physical contact now is when they return after an extended absence."

How does the child interpret this end of demonstrative physical affection? Do these fathers think anyone should explain this change in behaviour to the child? Or is this just something the child 'will understand in time'? Doesn't it upset and confuse the child, and cause a feeling of rejection?

Some fathers explain that they do not touch their daughters after puberty:

"I have two daughters, now married. I enjoyed holding, hugging and touching them when they were younger, but as they began to mature, I was somewhat afraid of arousing myself by too much physical contact. Now, I really enjoy their kisses and embraces and do not feel aroused."

"I have two girls, aged sixteen and seventeen. We never touch or hold one another, although I think it would be nice if we did. All such physical contact ended when they were small, about eight."

A few men still touch their older children—but it is rare:

"My children are now grown and in college, but when they were young I enjoyed cuddling them. As our first son grew older he was less inclined to be held, but our younger son has always been more affectionate and enjoys touching. In fact, even now, I frequently put my arm round his shoulder when we are together."

"I love hugging my boys still. But they're at the age now where my attempts to feed or bathe them would be resented."

Fear of Homosexuality

Many fathers say you cannot cuddle boys or they'll become "gay":
"I have five sons, between two and eleven, and God should strike me dead if I ever touch them. I would prefer them dead, that would guarantee them heterosexuality. My sexual life with my wife is completely hidden in the bedroom."

"I liked a certain amount of snuggling with our two sons, but like most men, I wanted them to be all boy, as I was, so I cut it off."

"I have a daughter. It is easy to be close to her but I could never be close to a son, for fear I would render him gay."

"I didn't cuddle them as much as I should have. They were boys and later young men, and I am so strongly heterosexual by nature that I presume this was the ground for my 'keeping my distance'. Had they been little girls, things might have been otherwise. With men, I don't care to go beyond a hearty handshake. With women these things are all fine with me. As for doing all this with babies, I have left that to my wife."

There is no evidence whatsoever that cuddling children causes homosexuality; in fact, a case can be made that just the opposite, a lack of fatherly affection, could "cause" homosexuality.

Our culture has a very strong taboo against affectionate male physical contact. Many men are afraid to touch and cuddle with their sons after the early years, or even altogether. Most of society finds male affection shocking. For example, two male friends walking arm in arm or holding hands would be seen as dangerously strange, especially if the men were not "gay" or having a love affair. The handshake is a Western invention used as a greeting between men. Originally it was designed to show that no one was carrying concealed weapons.

Fathers of the Future

Some men who don't have children of their own express pleasure and sometimes surprise at the delight other people's children can be:

"I like the way small kids just kind of curl up on you. I guess they feel safe and cared for. That's fun."

"Children, in my limited experience, are magical, as they have not been socialized into thinking that touch is an invasion of self and so they react naturally to the touch, as we once did."

"Caring for my girlfriend's little boy: babysitting, feeding, making sure he's okay, cheering him up when he's hurt and answering any questions to the best of my ability is really fun. I didn't know it would be."

"I have no children of my own but I have a cousin who has a one-year-old boy. I like to hold him and play with him very much. I wish he were my own. I love it when he says my name or touches me."

"I have never been married and have no children. However, I have taken care of my sisters' children and children of my friends, and loved it. I used to imagine they were mine."

"I don't have any children, but I worked in a day-care centre at my high school for a while and I enjoyed playing with them. Fascinating, too, to watch human beings in their formative stages, exploring the world around them. I find children beautiful. I enjoy snuggling with them. Feeding them can be fun (but corn in my hair isn't). Even changing diapers has its good points."

This man is consciously working to develop childcare skills:

"I used to be clumsy with children. I couldn't deal with them till they were old enough for me to relate to intellectually. However, the women's movement made me think about parenting and I knew I didn't want to imitate my father, so I started spending time doing childcare at retreats. I now enjoy it and people comment on how well I get along with children. I still have two problems: it's hard for me to act as an authority figure (I tend to play with them) and I get frustrated when they cry and I don't know what to do. But being with children is an important source of intimacy which lets me bring out a more childlike part of myself. You too can learn to like children!"

Fathers Remain Distant Throughout Childhood

"Are you (or were you) close to your father? . . . What do you think of him? Can you talk to him? What was your relationship when you were a child?"

The main problem most boys describe in their relationship with their father is his distance, his aloofness—not being able to talk:

"I have never been close to my father nor have I ever talked to him about anything that was really bothering me. My father believes in the Catholic commandments, and expects everyone in the family to follow them. If you don't, you pay by having problems. The answer apparently is not to discuss the problems, but to mend your ways and return to the fold. In spite of all this, I do like my father, as he is very loyal and kind, even if he doesn't talk to me about things that bother me."

"We used to go fishing and crabbing together, but we never talked much when we went. Even today I have a hard time talking to him. My father keeps a lot to himself, he is a loner in his own family, although he seems happy enough."

Some boys long for more affection:

"I remember my mother always holding my hand or putting her arms round me. This gave me a strong sense of security. After she died, I tried to get my father to hold me but he wasn't interested."

Another boy describes life with his single father:

"My mother died when I was ten years old, so when I was young, my dad spent more time with other women than me. He got me interested in baseball but just dropped me off at the game and picked me up when it was over. He was passive with me, but acted very masculine among his friends."

Boys' Fear of Their Father's Anger and Punishment

41 per cent of boys say their father had an "explosive temper" that "you had to watch out for", as do 32 per cent of girls. (See Chapter 6.) It is interesting to note that boys seem to fear their father's anger more, while girls seem to fear their mother's anger more. Is this because these same-sex relationships are in some ways the most troubled in the traditional family?

The majority of boys say that they "respected" their fathers—as do girls. This is the word they use most often to describe their main emotion for him:

"I respected him. We worked together on the ranch during my teens. He was considerate of others and honest. But we could only talk about light matters."

"My respect for him bordered on fear. He was a person not easy to know."

Respect—or fear?
What does the word "respect" mean for these men and boys when they use it to describe their father? Is "respect" the same thing as fear for many men? Are they denying, as girls might be, other emotions—rage and alienation?

Do all children believe "respect" is an attitude one should have towards power? This is clearly one way fathers teach boys "male emotional identity".

Punishment of Boys: Physical Discipline

When asked whether they had been close to their fathers as children, many men remembered being physically punished.

"At least once Daddy tied me to a porch pole when I wouldn't stay in the backyard where he could keep an eye on me. A lot of people think that was terrible, but it didn't bother me then and doesn't bother me

335

now. I don't remember being held that much but I'm sure I was never shunned when I really needed to be held."

"Dad was very severe about discipline. The Black Belt loomed in our minds like the Rack in the Inquisition. And he applied psychology that he learned in the military. He would draw back for the first lick, then not deliver. He would repeat that until we were almost relieved to get hit. I don't bear him any ill over it (I usually had the punishment coming), but I am unable to tell him I love him. I do him favours and give him stuff, but I'll never be able to say the words."

Is the punishment psychological and emotional as well as physical? (See Chapter 2.) How can fathers punish boys emotionally if they are already distant and silent to begin with?

In 20 per cent of families in which children live with both parents, boys are punished by their mother, in 80 per cent they are punished by their father.

The child's impotence in the face of the stronger physical and psychological power of the father brings up strong emotions: rage, powerlessness, fascination. Are these softened, depending on whether the child feels the punishment was "just" and "deserved" or not? What *is* "just"? Does one later come to accept and rationalize the punishment? Identifying with the one in power, the punisher?

One young man is trying to come to terms with his feelings about his relationship with his father, and the physical punishment he received from him. His struggle now is to understand and shake off the effects of what this did to him, and not let it interfere with his relationships in his life now:

"I'm the oldest of three boys and two girls. I had no role model to follow, other than my father. I wouldn't exactly call my mother a dominant personality.

"My father was himself abused as a child by his strict father back in the Ukraine in the 1930's and 1940's. I can't blame my father totally for passing these attitudes on to me, even though he is a macho, stubborn hypocrite. I don't have any respect for him, which is kind of funny because that was one of the things he drilled into us. 'Respect your elders! When you grow up you'll understand why I've done these things and you will thank me.'

"After all, he was our father and so naturally he knew what was best for us. It sounds like a broken record, doesn't it? It makes me sick. I guess I just feel pity for him and sadness for my mother. She put up with

336

a lot of bullshit and abuse over the years. I wonder how many times she considered leaving him and how close she came to actually doing it?

"My mother is meek and self-effacing on the whole. This rubbed off on me as a child. It's rough to live life like this, because people tend to walk all over you. On the other hand I have seen my mother lose control of her temper and it's not a pretty sight. It takes a lot out of her, it isn't good for her. She has recently started to discuss some of her experiences during her first years of marriage. I get this information through my sister.

"Slowly I'm getting a better idea of what it was like for her. I feel so sad and shocked sometimes. Example: when my mother immigrated to Canada she didn't know any English. My father was not waiting at the airport to welcome her. Already this shows a lack of concern on his part. She had to get an interpreter and then call to announce she had arrived. After waiting for several more hours she eagerly rushed forward to embrace my father when he finally did arrive. Imagine her shock when she felt him rudely brush her arms aside and proceed to sign some documents.

"She said the Customs and Immigration man's jaw just dropped when he saw this. My father later admitted to her that she did not deserve to be treated like this, but he lamely claimed that he did the best job he could as a father and a husband.

"I rarely see my parents, and when I do see them, the conversation centres around religion. They want to know if I've been reading my Bible and going to church. They say they pray for me (because of all the sinning I'm doing) and they worry about my soul. When I began living with my girlfriend they were hurt and basically disowned me. This was a strange feeling; sort of like being cut off from your roots."

The same young man describes his longing to "love" his parents but he can't connect:

"I have never really been able to discuss with them what they are feeling, what their hopes and dreams are, or what some of their failures were. There has never been any real communication. To me it feels like they are living in another world. I keep reaching out to them, but I never get anywhere.

"I've finally given up and written them off. It's not a pleasant feeling. This, coupled with my recent divorce, has left me feeling very lonely at times. I look around (sometimes in a cold sweat) to see who is left in my life."

He also has the classic problem associated with the "stern father" model with its insistence on the son's total rejection of the mother as he grows up and becomes a "man". In his relationships with women he is uncomfortable:

"Another problem that I'm working on is my fear of falling under the control of a woman. I don't know where I picked this fear up. It's not as overwhelming as it used to be. I have kept a journal since I was about fourteen, but I never wrote down any of my innermost feelings and thoughts, for fear that they might be used to blackmail me! Writing this letter to you, for example, would not have even been a remote possibility two years ago. It's a paranoia, I suppose.

"I hate taking risks with what I consider to be important aspects of my life. I believe this cautious attitude eventually leads to a kind of sterility or numbness; at least in some areas. I feel like I have missed out on something, or that life has at times passed me by. However, the more I talk about it, the more I realize that I'm not the only one who feels like this."

To be blunt, this shows clearly "how macho attitudes fuck up love later", i.e., how the pressure to leave the mother, repudiate her emotionally, leaves a residual ambivalence towards women—a mixture of attraction and contempt in love relationships with women, as discussed in Chapter 8.

Revolt, Revolution or Acceptance of the Father as He Is?

Many men and boys, while they may "respect" their father, also feel angry and disappointed.

And yet revolt is rare; acquiescence is standard, learning to accept, fit in, not "react like a girl". After all, a "man" should admire strength and not cry: if a boy's father is "unemotional", this represents "strength" and is to be accepted, emulated. If a boy's father hits him, this too is to be accepted "like a man", not rebelled against. Thus, the power of the father is all-inclusive; to rebel at maltreatment is to be a "wimp". This is a catch-22 system.

One man describes a rare rejection of his father:

"I loved him very much as a boy; now I am ambivalent. He is a weak man, dominated by my mother, dependent. I am angry with him because he was not a good model for me. He does not know himself and so taught me to be someone that can't exist, macho."

Boys Who Have a Close Relationship with Their Father

18 per cent of boys say they have or had a close relationship with their father:

"We are emotionally and intellectually distant. We very rarely do anything together. But we are close. The key to our closeness is our mutual support and honesty. We can talk about anything and there are no judgements, just real concern and support. He's given me a model of a man who is very masculine (he is a construction worker), but can still be gentle. I recently had a problem with one of my lovers, and while he wouldn't pry, he was willing to talk with me when I was ready."

★   ★   ★

339

These boys were encouraged by their father to be individuals, listened to and taken seriously, and not treated as stereotypes.

A Sense of Loss

The male emotional world can be a hard one:

"I feel 'on guard' all the time around other men. To inflict pain on weaker, slower individuals is the tough, macho way to show your superiority. Men justify cruelty by emphasizing that the victim is a 'weak' person, who deserves it. And this mentality also says, 'Why not? I deserve everything I got, I earned it. The slobs deserve everything they get too (punishment).' I don't understand this competition fully, except I do know it is prevalent in every aspect of my life, and I do it myself too. But I hate it."

"I still feel very angry with my father. He never approved of my career choice or seemed proud of me for what I am. When I got accepted to the most prestigious graduate programme in the country he said *seriously*, 'You're not going, are you?' I think he always tried to break me down, break my idealism, get me to accept reality, like money, responsibility, mortgages, and family life.

"I've had lots of dreams where I scream and yell at my father and tell him I hate him, why did he do this to me. But I feel extremely guilty for harbouring this anger towards him, because he did, after all, always support the lot of us without complaint. He always did his duty. But he didn't really know who any of us were—myself, my brothers and sisters, or my mother. Weird."

The feeling of loss and isolation evident in so many men's relationships is hauntingly portrayed by another:

"When my brother came to visit me (we hadn't seen each other for four years, although we were very close when we were growing up), we had a good time, as though we had never been apart. When it was time to go, I took him to the airport. He never said if he had a good time, and I never said I was sorry to see him go, we just said, 'See ya.' But I felt really sad to see him go. I felt very lonely watching him walk away."

It is extremely upsetting to men to be told that they are the group in power, they have the "best of all possible worlds", when most of them don't feel very happy or content. The backlash against the feminist movement is partially fuelled by this feeling of being misunderstood.

340

However, some men *do* see that it is not "women" at whom they should direct their anger, but a problematic system, the hierarchical psychological system born in the "family":

"I didn't know my father really. I didn't know what went on in his head. He went to work, he came home, he got angry at odd moments and everybody seemed to have to help arrange things so his anger would go away and he, the god, would be pacified. I used to ask my mother what I was supposed to be like—him?

"I always identified with the son in *Death of a Salesman**. I didn't want to be that salesman either. So I tried to go along outwardly with the behaviour they all expected of men, damn it, say as little as possible to avoid conflict (or discovery that I was not all I was supposed to be, I wasn't a 'typical' man). Funny thing, one day my little son said to his mother (when they thought I wasn't around), 'Why doesn't Daddy say anything?' I had managed to behave just like my dad.

"I felt a sharp pain, almost a stabbing blow, as if someone had put a knife in me. I went and sat down on the sofa and hid my face in my arm, I was crying. And my wife had said to my son, 'Oh, your father's like that. He's in his own world, he can't help it,' as if she were alienated too. It was then I knew I had to change, I had to make a different life, for myself and everyone around me."

What form should this change take? A rapprochement between father and son that merely entails bonding between men and does not address the relationship of both with the mother and daughter will only solidify old male bonding attachments and reinforce antiquated ideas of power. After all, classical Greek society was based on exclusively male power: it was a status symbol for older men to have sex with younger men. Women were primarily for reproduction: Greek law reminded men to have sex with their wives at least three times a month.

The New Male Revolution

Boys who grow up with "only" their mothers are better off

It is a surprising conclusion of this study that boys who are closer to their mother throughout their teens, or perhaps grow up without a father altogether, are emotionally and psychologically better off. According to my research, they have a head start, they are not so fearful, not as

* The play by Arthur Miller.

closely bound to patriarchal stereotypes, and are more comfortable with change. They feel more sure of themselves conversationally and make better relationships with both men and women.

Boys should join the girls

Boys and men should throw off patriarchy, and take women as their friends, allies, and comrades. Make alliances with women, join them. If men think about their real lives, and not the "male" models, they may notice how often it is that women are their friends and aides, or how often it is that women around them have bright ideas and show leadership in situations both at home and at work. Men should drop their notion that they would look silly "following a woman", and *help* women (and men too, of course—as if it needed saying)—who will then support them in return.*

The institutions of both personal and political life will be vastly improved when men no longer feel terrified of the father—of not putting other men first. When they forget the archetypes, and see others for what they really are.

* The men cheering Margaret Thatcher but not voting for her in the recent UK Parliamentary vote on ratifying EEC membership is a case in point: the Tory rebels agreed with Thatcher, but ended up voting for Major, "the father" icon, and the party system.

PART IV

Democratization of the family: a renaissance for the West

A Democratic Revolution in the Family

What we are witnessing now—and participating in—is a revolution in the family. The way we live our personal lives, with whom and how, is being questioned and debated in a ground-breaking and important revolution. The fundamentalist reactionary forces that are calling for the "preservation of family values", opposing this democratization, are wrong to insist that the revolution is causing harm, and have no statistical base for such claims.

One constantly hears that the family is in trouble, that it doesn't work anymore, that we must find ways to help it. But does it matter if the family is in trouble, if it doesn't work anymore? If the family doesn't work, maybe there is something wrong with its structure. Why assume that humans are flawed, and that the family structure is fine and good? People must have reasons for fleeing the nuclear family: human rights abuses and the battering of women are well documented in many governments' statistics.

Are people "happy" in the traditional family? "Unhappy" with these changes? Most people are happier with their personal lives today than they were fifty years ago: women especially have more choices and freedom than they did in the past. A "golden age" of family bliss exists more in people's imaginations than in their experience.

What is happening is that finally democracy is catching up with the old, hierarchical, father-dominated family: the family is being democratized. No one wants to go back to the days before women had (at least in theory) equal rights in the home, before there were laws against the battering of women, before the freedom of men and women to divorce if they could no longer sustain a loving unit . . . All these things are advances, signs of the development of a more ethical and "true" sense of family and human community.

And there are many more advances we are on the threshold of achieving: naming and eliminating emotional violence, redefining love and friendship, progressing in the area of children's rights and in men's questioning of their lives.

This book salutes the gentler and more diverse family system that

345

seems to be arising—one that does not keep its members in terror: fathers in terror lest they not be "manly" and able to support it all; mothers in terror lest they be beaten in their own bedrooms and ridiculed by their children; children in terror of being forced to do things against their will and having absolutely no recourse, no door open to them for exit.

Towards a New Theory of the Psycho-Sexual Development of Children

"To understand women and the family, it is necessary to leave Freudian theory behind completely."
                                        Simone de Beauvoir

What I am offering in this report is a new interpretation of relationships between parents and children: a new theory of the family.

Some of the elements of this come from the body of feminist works which sociologist Jesse Bernard has named the Feminist Enlightenment. Other elements have grown out of the statements of those who answered my questionnaire about their childhood. Though in themselves these statements may not be "unusual" or "unexpected", here they are presented through a new lens—one that may seem disturbing to some.

What is that lens? My interpretation of this data takes into account not only the individual's unique experiences, as is done in psychology, but also the cultural backdrop—the canvas of social "approval" or "disapproval" against which children's lives are lived. This interdisciplinary theory also takes into account the historical ideology of the family: those who took part in my research are clearly living in a world whose perception of "family" is filtered through the model of the "holy family" with its reproductive icons of Jesus, Mary and Joseph.

The "Holy Family" of Jesus, Mary and Joseph

Surely, you might comment, in this day and age people no longer think like that. The modern family is not a religious one, most people are not Catholics, and so on. In fact, the icons of the "holy family"—the only type we are supposed to admire—are all around us. Their message comes to us through some of the most glorious art of Western history.*

---

* Alternative bodies of "great art" are the classical Egyptian and classical Greek (including its eighteenth-century French revival) traditions, each of which depicts its own sacred and political (religious) pantheon; others are the Persian and Chinese. Then there is the art of the Creation Religion and culture of pre-history, whose main symbols are female reproduction, sacred plant and animal life.

347

In the sumptuous images and colours of great painting, in architecture and music, the story of the "holy family" is told and retold. Artists such as Titian, Raphael and Michelangelo were commissioned by the Church to create art out of Biblical themes, as were composers such as Bach and Handel.

No matter how beautiful (especially in its promise of "true love"), this family model is an essentially repressive one, teaching authoritarian psychological patterns and a belief in the unchanging rightness of male power. In this hierarchical family, love and power are inextricably linked, a pattern that has damaging effects not only on all family members but on the politics of the wider society. How can there be successful democracy in public life if there is an authoritarian model in private life?

Why do the icons hold our hearts?
So used have we become to these symbols,* that we continue to believe—no matter what statistics we see in the newspapers about divorce, violence in the home, mental breakdown—that the icons and the system they represent are right, fair and just. After all, we are told, the "holy family" is a religious symbol, so who can criticize it? We assume without thinking that this model is the *only* "natural" form of family, and that if there are problems it must be the individual who is at fault, not the institution. We cannot even begin to imagine that our beautiful family system, the object of all those magnificent paintings and symbols, might not at heart be good or right. What is "reality", we wonder—the icons or the violence in marriage we read about? And who is to "blame"?

What we need is a new interpretation of what is going on: what is happening is a *transformation* of the culture, not a collapse. It may be one of the most important turning points of the Western world, the creation of a new social base that will engender an advanced and improved democratic political structure.

The Psyche of Patriarchy: A New Way of Seeing How We Grow Up: Results of This Study

In the twentieth century, we have conceptualized children and "family" through Freudian and "holy family" constructs of childhood.

This book refutes those categories, and offers a new theoretical view:

* And to the emotional patterns they create: we call them "human nature".

348

A DEMOCRATIC REVOLUTION IN THE FAMILY

1. Is "puberty" a real stage for girls?

Since girls can masturbate to orgasm from the age of five or so, while boys reach full orgasmic capacity (with ejaculation) only at puberty, is puberty really misnamed when applied to girls? Has Freud made too much of it, basing it on a male model? It is the beginning of girls' reproductive capacity, not their sexuality.

Puberty is the stage at which patriarchy demands that children shift their allegiance from their mother to their father and the system of father-right. This ideological baggage is superimposed upon the biological events of "puberty", the acquiring of reproductive capacity.

2. Oedipus in love (Oedipus revisited)
Oedipus's eroticism after leaving his mother

The major crisis in boys' lives is created during boys' puberty (when boys are flooded with sexual feelings, first masturbate to full orgasm, and often play sex games with other boys). At the same time boys are pressured heavily by the culture to demonstrate "toughness" in sport, stay away from girls, told not to hang around at home with mother: "Don't be a sissy or a wimp," i.e., "Don't be female or feminine."

Thus boys are taught that women are the proper objects of desire, but also the objects of contempt, leading to a love-hate relationship with women/the mother. This is Oedipus in torment, not an Oedipus complex. Oedipus wants to love, but must disassociate from all things female.

If men learn as boys that they should demonstrate contempt for the female world (and the mother they love) men can grow up to feel extreme ambivalence towards women. Men often desire power and control in a sexual relationship with a woman in order to avoid these feelings of confusion and "danger": loving and identifying with the mother.

The Oedipus complex is a relatively recent concept (i.e., "Don't trust your mother") and this allegiance shift has become more imperative during the twentieth century, and especially since World War II.

Psychological theory for a century has held that boys pass through two "Oedipal" stages, loving and desiring the mother, age three to six, and then age thirteen to sixteen. Freud based his analysis of men on his self-analysis. Is it a valid theory? No. What causes pain for boys is society's imposition of "masculinity"—not the mother's betrayal of the son for the father, as Freud surmised.

349

3. Democratization of the family—or the "family in crisis"?

The current slogan "preservation of family values" really means not preservation of love in the family, but preservation of the hierarchical family, with the father as its head, instead of the new egalitarian family.

The current "crisis" in the family is really a sign of transformation, not a collapse of "civilization as we know it". This transformation is the democratization of an institution that was never democratized, even though we have believed in equality in the political sphere for two centuries. This revolution in the infrastructure of society is for the better, and can make for a new, more advanced form of political democracy, one less aggressive–defensive in its impulses, and thus more suited to the twenty-first-century multi-racial global community.

4. Why do girls fight with their mother?

The relationship most essential to disrupt in order for patriarchy to work is the relationship between mother and daughter. Mothers and daughters are not "natural enemies" (competing for the father as Freud egotistically imagined), but "natural" friends, as they have many things in common. If this relationship were unbroken, however, patriarchy could not continue, since all power would not be in the hands of men. Women would vote for other women as often as for men. Distrust of women, and the double standard, are hallmarks of patriarchal psychology.

5. The mother is central

The relationship with the mother, and the social system's demand that boys and girls deny this relationship's meaning when they grow up, is at the heart of boys' and girls' psycho-sexual identities.

6. There is no daughter icon

There is no daughter in the "holy family" archetype—which is our basic role model for what the reproductive family should be. Should we choose a role model for the left-out icon, such as a character from *Little Women*, or perhaps Dorothy from *The Wonderful Wizard of Oz*, or even Alice from *Alice in Wonderland*? These are all active, inquisitive little girls. Is the lack of such an icon one reason for our fascination with such young women in popular literature?

A DEMOCRATIC REVOLUTION IN THE FAMILY

7. Torn loyalties of children in two-parent families

A crisis of loyalty is the unseen psycho-sexual drama for children. Most parents' relationships, according to children here and many government statistics, still reflect gender stereotypes: most men don't do housework, and condescend to women at home, while many women are psychologically and emotionally dominated by men. Children are sometimes better off with a single parent, than with two who are unequal and thus present the child with an insoluble loyalty conflict. Children in my research for this book document over and over again feeling pressure to "choose", "take sides", or help the weaker one—or else be left feeling cowardly and self-hating, confused.

8. Sensuality is natural between parents and children

Why must affection be ended so abruptly? Affectionate touching is not always "sexual", and "erotic" components are not necessarily "bad" and to be feared. Body closeness should not be cut off so soon, and more in-between ways of touching and caressing should be developed.

9. Construction of girls' double identity

Girls learn very early to connect their sexual identities with shame and not pride. Menstruation is not celebrated, and they cannot discuss sexual matters such as masturbation, not to mention asking to see their mother's anatomy to reassure themselves that theirs is the same. Girls' sexual anatomy, like Eve's, is still linked to shame, so that to ask questions is "shameful". ("Keep your legs together!" is a command most girls hear frequently between the ages of three and thirteen.)

Thus girls develop a double identity, one a "good girl", and the other a private sexual identity. (This must be hidden and is not something one can be publicly proud of. Women are "whores" or "madonnas"; there's a mind–body split.)

This is a social crime against girls, which is carried out in the name of "love" in the family (the social enforcement arm of patriarchy).

"Tomboyhood" is a real part of girls' identity, not a "stage" they should grow out of. Friendship between girls is important, and represents the underground "self" of the girl.

As we continue in Part IV, we will explore the larger ideological and political ramifications of this style of "upbringing".

History and Theory of the Family: Personal and Political

An Authoritarian Family Does Not Support a Democratic Political System

The family is an institution that has until now been left out of the democratization process. Although John Stuart Mill wrote clearly in favour of women's rights in new egalitarian democratic theory, much later the family and women's role in the world were left out of most discussions of democracy, left in the religious "sacred" domain. Also, women and non-property owners, as well as "minorities", did not have the vote when democracy first began.

Thus men made a fatal mistake: the democracy they thought they could make work in one sphere could not really work without democracy in the other. That it has worked as well as it has, in a jerky, stop-start fashion (despite presidential assassinations in the US, from Lincoln to Kennedy), is a sign that it is potentially an excellent political system—despite its critics.

Democracy could work even better if we changed the aggressive kind of personality that we are imparting to the world through the family system. Children brought up with choice about whether to accept their parents' power are more likely (according to this research) to be confident about believing in themselves and their own ideas, less docile or habituated to bending to power. Such a population would create and participate in public debate very differently.

Creating new families with more democracy means taking a clear and rational look at our institutions. It is our right to re-shape and improve them, throw out the unjust and dysfunctional parts. If we believe the scare tactics of those who want to keep the family unchanged, keep it based on the tenets of patriarchal and feudal structures, we will be promoting the idea that independent thinking is followed by punishment.

Habituation of the acceptance of power in the nuclear family
If there is any truth in the statement that democracy doesn't work, i.e., that the majority often seem not to be making wise decisions, or do not vote in their own interest (for example, it is often asked why, if women have had the vote since the 1920's in most Western countries, they have not voted into power other women who would implement women's rights), then perhaps this can be explained by lack of democracy in the traditional family.

People vote not for themselves, but for "fathers", or "father" icons, it seems. This loyalty to the father is because of an ingrained fear of male power, the fear of punishment if they disregard or disrespect "the system" instilled in most people as children.

The founders of our constitutions were right: democracy is a great form of government. But they didn't realize that the personal and the political go together: that without democratizing personal life, including securing equal rights for women and children, political democracy cannot flourish and reach full maturity.

The Political History of the Family

The family in patriarchal religious tradition has always been a hierarchical family, one headed by the father. Just as "God rules the Earth", and "God loves his children", so the father was supposed to rule over the family and provide for its welfare. The heavenly father, just like the father in the family, was also the dispenser of justice and punishment.

However, the democratizing ideas of the Enlightenment and even of Christianity itself (which after all emphasizes the importance of each individual human soul's relationship to God) have meant that now, at the end of the twentieth century, not only racism but also sexism is considered something that should be eradicated. This sexism has its deepest roots in the family.

The family as an institution was overlooked when, two centuries or so ago, governments began to change over to a democratic system: no longer would the idea be that there should be a "sun king" or one central power, but indeed "the people" should have the right to strive for fulfilment and happiness. They should have an equal right to education, health, and a voice in their own government (although as we have seen this did not at first include women, or men without property).

At the same time, the right to religious freedom was guaranteed to each and every person. Yet this meant that—since religion was filled with feudalistic ideas of family relationships—the god-like idea of the authority of "the father" in the house remained absolute.

Where did the 1950's family come from?
Before the industrial revolution, most societies in the West were made up of rural, farming families. Not only were these extended families, but they were groups of people who worked together, the labour was shared. When the workplace was moved to the towns, and most people began to work in factories instead of on farms (that is, men "went out to work"), men were displaced from the home, while women were left there. At the same time, the extended family was evaporating, leaving the woman isolated except for the children. When the children were old enough to go to school, she would do "housework" and "beauty work". It is interesting to note that the beginning of the massive spread of women's and "fashion" magazines took place around the turn of the century, not long (in historical terms) after the industrial revolution began.

Women too decided they wanted not only the vote, but also jobs. By 1939, in the US and elsewhere in the West, a minority of women had jobs, mostly as teachers, nurses and in service industries (beautician, housekeeper, etc.), but the War changed that. With men away, women were needed in all sorts of jobs, as well as in the military services. Women made a great success of it, but after the War, in the US, for example, the government cut day-care programmes for children and took other measures to convince women to give up their jobs and go home, leaving the employment for returning men (who "deserved the jobs more"). This policy in the US decreased the number of women working, but a few short years later, by the early 1950's, women found a new job market and moved *en masse* into the secretarial positions opening up in new corporations.

Even though the 1950's were the time of the greatest advertising hysteria over the "happy family" (or is ours greater today?), the family had already changed: it wasn't only young, single women who were working in office jobs. It was married women too.

"No sex before marriage!"
Women (and men) in the 1950's were enticed into marriage by a complete prohibition on sex before marriage: shame came upon a woman, public humiliation, if she was "found out". A ban on abortion and birth control, except for condoms, kept women afraid of expressing their sexuality with men and pushed them towards marriage. Gays were completely in the closet and their existence unmentionable: being gay was considered an even bigger "shame" or "sin" than being "found out" as a woman who had "done it", i.e., "had sex", before marriage.

In the 1960's, this repression broke open in the joyful "flower child" movement, and the civil rights movement in the US started with the activism of Martin Luther King and a group of black churchwomen. This began a refreshing current in American society which looked at its own ideals of equality and condemned racial segregation. Soon after came the Vietnam War and the pressures of the draft, leading to the anti-war movement and the politics of peace and love. The peace and love movement saw the family as a repressive anachronism, something destined to fade away into history—as were nationalism, war and aggression. In many countries divorce laws were liberalized, although just as many people got married during these years as before. At the same time the gay and lesbian movement came into its own with "gay pride" the important message. Public opinion started to change: now it became less socially acceptable to criticize a person for choosing to love someone of the same sex.

Men's rebellion against the family

The "collapse of the family" is often blamed on women, but men have had their role to play in the changes. Since the late 1950's, men have complained that women "tied them down". Men began to rebel against the family and look to the single male as their role model. Adventure was seen as a male priority, and adventure was "out there", away from the marital home, which "tied men down".

The cult of the single male was reflected in films. After World War II movies changed: the male hero became unmarried rebel: James Dean, Marlon Brando, and later Tom Cruise and Arnold Schwarzenegger, for example. The man most admired by other men was the one who could stay single the longest, keep from getting "caught".

This groovy-male-as-single image continues in rock music culture too. And recent popular research reveals that this role model is influential elsewhere. In an *Esquire* survey in the UK, most men said they only had children because their partners wanted them.

This does not mean that men have stopped falling in love with women; what they are doing is putting "masculinity" before love.

This is not only a Western idea. As Fatima Mernissi has suggested in *Beyond the Veil*, the problem for women in Islam is not that men dislike women, but that men are commanded to put Allah first in their hearts. Love for a woman should always come second: yes, a man should be married and reproduce, but this is part of his duty to Islam: personal love should not be more important in his life than his commitment to men.

Women revolutionizing the family: from the 1970's to . . . ?
With the women's movement of the 1970's came the challenge to the oppression of women within the Western family. Such issues as rape within marriage, abortion rights, equal pay, childcare for working women, financial independence, became important causes. How thin a thread women's rights still hang on is evidenced by such recent events as the anti-abortion campaigns in the US, UK and Germany, and the fact that in all Western countries women are under-represented in parliament and political office.

With many women's current insistence on changing the relationship with men in the family and outside, the family has changed. Most men no longer like the image of themselves as some kind of dictator to their wife and children, but the actual working out of a new emotional contract is difficult indeed, and still to be accomplished—as women describe in *Women and Love*.

The growth in single mother families has been phenomenal in the US and the UK. The divorce rate is soaring—and it is women who initiate most divorces.

One of the biggest changes in the Western nuclear family today is that women are altering their position within it, striving for equality—or often opting out of it altogether.

The fundamentalist backlash
Strong reactionary undercurrents emerging in the 1980's are still with us in the 1990's. The rise of National Socialist parties all over Europe is paralleled by new, correspondingly "fundamentalist" groups in the US and UK. In this mass psychology of "belonging", racism, as always, is combined with sexism.

Matching this reactionary mood, the ideology concerning the family has now reverted in some countries in the West to almost that of the 1950's. Those who do not conform to the stereotype of the "good family" are put on the defensive. It is a time in which, for many, it no longer feels safe *not* to pay lip service to "believing in the family" as a sacred and necessary institution for the continuation of society. In fact, as long as there is reproduction, society will continue: it is not necessary to maintain a "nuclear family" norm to guarantee that.

The Family is a Political Institution

We are told that the family is a religious and sacred institution, but this is not its origin.

We tend to forget that the family was created in its current form in early patriarchy for political and not religious reasons: the new political order, which would allow lineage and inheritance to pass through men, and not women (as it had previously), had to create a special family. Why? Because it had to solve a specific problem, i.e., how could lineage or inheritance flow through men if men do not bear children?

The family, a political institution, was created to solve this dilemma: each man would "own" a woman who would reproduce for him. Thus, laws were set up defining marriage as an institution of male ownership of women and children. Now, each man had to control the sexuality of "his" woman, for how else could he be sure that "his child" was "his"?

Therefore, restrictions were placed on women's lives and bodies by the early fathers;* women's imprisonment in marriage was made a virtue, for example especially through the later archetype of the meek and self-sacrificing Mary, happy to be of service, never standing up for herself or her own rights—because this would be "selfish" and she is above such things—and, of course, always bearing children, especially male children.

Mary, it is important to note, is a later version of a much earlier Creation Mother goddess. In her earlier form, she had many more aspects, more like the Indian goddess Kali than the "mother" whom the Judeo-Christian patriarchal system devised, eventually giving us the obedient and subservient persona of Mary, with her downcast eyes. (Earlier, the most prominent woman in this tradition was Eve, who, because she was sexually alive and curious, caused the "downfall of mankind"!)

Of course, in most pre-Christian religions, there were many goddesses and gods, so that the spectrum of models to follow, or images to draw on, was much more diverse. This diversity doubtless created less rigidity and conformism in human society than we know today.

---

* Patriarchy was "created", to the extent that we know, as far back as the earliest books of the Old Testament; however, patriarchy was *not* the social system of most of the surrounding societies at that time. See the work of Elaine Pagels, Marija Gimbutas and Joseph Campbell.

The Politics of Female Sexuality in the Family

The sexual position of Mary and her daughter

Since there is no daughter icon, are girls supposed to try to be like Mary? And what about their mother?

Women in our socio-religious system are in the strange position of being urged to be like Mary, Mother of God, since she is the most admired woman in the archetypal constellation (also the only woman!).

Can we ever begin to imagine the absurdity of living in a society in which the icon for women is one who has a child without having sex? Of course this is a model no woman can ever (by definition) live up to; therefore all early women are pre-defined as imperfect—are "doomed" to feel inadequate and "not right" somehow. (If you don't have a child, you haven't performed your role; if you do have a child, you have "had sex", and are not "pure" and maidenly.)

In this, we are no more "rational" than ancient societies which we deride for following "crude" myths and symbols. We just as slavishly follow ours: we try to look meek (even the models in fashion magazines have, for the most part, the appropriate and carefully created expressions of acceptance and knowing-their-place, as well as the reproductive, Mary-age).

Women's sexual identity is supposedly nonexistent, at the same time that it is *the* "basic definition" of "who women are" in the politics of the family. (We *are* our sexual organs, we are all called "Mr" or "Ms", this is the basic caste system of a world based on patriarchy.)

And how must men feel, relating to women who are not like the icon, who seem somehow to want sex, to enjoy it? Can a woman "like this" be a "real mother"? Just exactly what kind of a creature *is* this woman he feels drawn to having sex with? She does not exist in icon or myth (except as "Eve"), only in the flesh—a flesh which contradicts the sanctified icon. Thus, are men "doomed" to be always suspicious of the women who "give them" sex—since this, by definition, is not what a "good" or "trustworthy" woman does?

Under patriarchy, men's sexuality too is channelled ideologically, in order to turn it into a driving force for "penetration" of reproductive-aged women—over and above any other sexual activity (anything else is thought "unmanly" and "unmasculine"). Why? Because it has always been a preoccupation of patriarchy to have the highest rate of reproduction possible, since patriarchies are warlike societies, and "need" large populations to control as much territory as possible.

This is not religion, this is politics
The family is a political institution; its purpose is to control women (and especially their bodies), not to give them love.

Are these laws political or religious? The family is often said to be a religious institution, whose real mediator is the Church, not the state. Yet the patriarchal family props up the patriarchal political system.

Must we show respect and reverence for a "religious" tradition which has as its basic principle, at its heart, the political will of men to dominate women? This is not religion, this is politics.

Isn't the Family a "Natural", Biological Institution?

How traditional is the family as we know it? Since it is only about 3,000 years old, the non-patriarchal families that preceded it may in fact have more right to be called "traditional' families.

It is as if we had no historical memory: as we have seen, the two-gender family has not always been the norm—mother–child societies were in existence before patriarchy. And now, an extremely large number of families are mother–child families in the West. (Of course, men too can be single parents.)

Twentieth-century Polynesian families, as documented by Margaret Mead,* were found not to be at all like the nuclear family. There was little concept of "private ownership" of children: children were cared for by the entire society. These island societies are known to be some of the most peaceful and happy in the world.

While both genders are necessary for pregnancy, reproduction is essentially work done by women. And there is a difference between a biological family and an "emotional" family—a family held together by emotional ties. In short, the family is a changeable, political institution. There is a very broad spectrum of families in existence today, although those who believe in the "fundamentalist" family like to deny that any other type of family exists. If the mother–child family was prevalent in pre-history, and indeed is a flourishig form of family in our own societies today, this is something of which we can be proud, not terrified.

* Margaret Mead, *Coming of Age in Samoa* (London, Penguin, 1954).

DEMOCRATIZATION OF THE FAMILY

The Family Creates Human Nature

"It's human nature, you can't change it"

We are told that individual psychology *is* "human nature", even our "animal nature". And unchangeable. Yet, through the family, we shape children's personality, psychology and behaviour: they are formed by humans, not biologically decreed or ordained by heaven.

There is no such thing as fixed "human nature". Rather, it is a psychological structure that is carefully implanted in our minds as we learn the love and power equations of the family—for life. Fortunately the family is a human institution: humans made it and humans can change it.

This research indicates that the extreme aggression we see in society is not so much a characteristic of biological "human nature" (as Freud concluded), nor a result of hormones. Rather it is brought about by the way in which power and love are combined in the family structure: in order to receive love, most children have to humiliate themselves, over and over again, before power.

The Rights of the Child in a Democratized Family

Children Need Choices

In our society, parents have complete legal, economic and social "right" to control children's lives. Parents' exclusive power over children creates obedience. Children are likely to take on authoritarian (or obedient) emotional, psychological and sexual patterns, and see power as one of the central categories of existence.* This has political consequences: an authoritarian family structure's anti-democratic relationships are being translated into the larger political institutions of society. Obedience to authority, especially male authority, becomes a habit, its origin forgotten. People throughout history have deferred to convincing "father figures" even when it was against their interests to do so. Starving Russians at the turn of the century, for example, believed even as they died that the "father" Tsar would come and save them.

Running away from home

Children are often teased about their attempts to run away from home: "Remember the day you tried to run away and you came running back when it got dark?" In this way parents emphasize children's lack of freedom, and the "absurdity" of their challenging the will of their parents. While parents have divorce rights today in most Western countries, children have no means of leaving, or defending themselves, should that become necessary.†

Legal rights for children

Hillary Clinton caused an enormous stir during the 1992 presidential election campaign in the US when she correctly suggested that children should have the right to sue their parents for sexual or physical abuse.

Children should also have the right to work part-time in order to gain some amount of financial independence. Total financial dependence can eat away at a child's integrity and sense of personal honour.

---

* See also R.D. Laing, Florence Rush, Wilhelm Reich, Maria Montessori and Kahlil Gibran.
† However, in September 1993 a landmark case in the US declared that a ten-year-old boy had the right to "divorce" his parents.

Alternative Homes for Children

The key to changing our society's aggressive/defensive emotional make-up is the creation of alternatives for children: homes to which children can choose to go when they are being abused in the parental home. Children could then choose whether to live with their parents or not.

These "group homes" or child houses could be run along the lines of "halfway" houses. Orphanages, or children's homes, need not be, and are not always, terrible experiences, although the names send out chilling messages to many, perhaps because of the implication that the child was left or deserted, never that the child wanted to leave the family, *chose* to go there.

Some parents may read these lines in horror, believing that the real solution is that "good families" should ever be dictatorial, parents should always consult with the children, allow a space for children's opinions too. Unfortunately this is not always what happens. The absolute power of parents can lead to an abuse of that power.

If a child *did* opt for this new form of "home", she or he might of course remain in contact, still love the parents, even at times stay with them. Alternatives for children could in some cases simply give the family breathing space during difficult times.

Alternatives to the family home would make a totally different relationship to the family possible for children, and in turn create a different psychological structure and a less aggressive, more pluralistic and tolerant social system.

Thirty-three Million "Street Children": Where is *Their* Home?

The United Nations estimated in 1993 that there were thirty-three million "homeless" street children in the world, in cities such as Rio de Janeiro, Calcutta and Lagos.

What will our international social and political response be? Should we create traditional nuclear families for them? For how many of these children will we be able to find the "perfect mother-and-father-nuclear-family" homes with heterosexual parents of the "correct age"—and perfect psychological adjustment? (A British court in 1993 ruled that a family with a mother over the age of fifty was ineligible to adopt a child, "since fifty is the age of the natural menopause".)

Children do not need the archetypal family model. What they do need are warm and mature people around them. We should construct positive new families which meet children's needs, not close our eyes because the world is not fitting our icons. We should begin to reach out to one another in new ways, to groups wider than our own nuclear families, and think of the whole society as part of our family too.

The Cult of the "Holy Family" in Twentieth-century Psychoanalysis

Why Psychologizing the Family Doesn't Work

Psychotherapy and its attempted analysis of the family has failed; it may have helped some people but it does not address the underlying problem, that is, the structure of the family itself, as more and more people seek "treatment". It is not so much maladjusted individuals who are "the problem" as the framework into which they are persuaded.

Psychotherapeutic and psychoanalytical theory has a very limited, ahistorical view of individual problems. It asserts that people's problems have their roots in childhood and as long as the individual recognizes this she or he will be able to readjust. Little or nothing is said about the problems inherent in the social structure itself, or the gender roles therein which make adjustment a violation of that individual's human rights. It is assumed that the family is an eternally unchanging biological unit, and that the individual must adapt and change to fit into this unit. Society has benefited enormously from the feminist analyses of gender roles debated in recent years, which have combated the stereotypes this theory endorses.

As Shulamith Firestone* has pointed out, early in the twentieth century the then new Freudianism was used to "answer" the challenge posed to the social system by feminist theory, which called for equal rights for women. Freudianism did this by deflecting "the problem" back onto women, individualizing their pain. In standard therapy, the "talking treatment" continues until the patient learns not to resist the authority of the therapist and to conform to social norms. In the former Soviet Union, for example, governments quickly learned to use these tools for their own benefit, as an effective means of social control.

Taking its cue from Orwell's *1984*, the mass media has also learned

---

* Shulamith Firestone, *The Dialectic of Sex* (London, Cape, 1971) and Naomi Weisstein's pamphlet "Psychology Constructs the Female" (Boston, New England Free Press, 1968).

the refined art of using these psycho-religious symbols of "normality" to control and direct public opinion.

Women in therapy tend to be blamed twice as often as men for their own problems. They are called "hysterical", "irrational", or told they need tranquillizers.* Whereas men, as one woman reports in *Women and Love*, are often seen by therapists as bravely "searching for their existential selves", "on a spiritual quest", when they enter therapy. However, feminist therapies are now using innovative, alternative methods.

* See *Women and Madness* by Phyllis Chessler (London, Allen Lane, 1974) and the American journal *Women and Therapy*, edited by Ellen Cole, for more information on sexism in therapeutic practice.

Definitions of Love and Power

Emotional Categories Created by Patriarchy

Categories of emotion created by a patriarchal social and family system are not the same categories of "basic emotion" that would be created if we lived in a different, gender-equal social system. Dualism, or the mind–body split, is one consequence of the gender division emphasized by our society. Love and power are too often confused. It's as if we can't separate them. Why?

Where is real love? Is the family the place to get it?
Love is at the heart—so to speak—of our belief in the importance of the family. The desire for love is what keeps us returning to the icons. Even when they don't seem to work in our lives, we try, try and try again.

Why is the symbol of the "holy family" so strong in our collective psyche? Because we are told that we will never find love if we don't participate in this family. We hear repeatedly that the *only* place we will ever be able to get "real love" (love that lasts), security, true acceptance and understanding is the family.* That we should distrust other forms of family. That we are only "half a family" or a "pretend family" if we create any other human group. That without being a member of the family we will be forever "left out", lonely, or useless.

No one would want to deny the importance of love, nor of lasting relationships with other people . . . But the definitions of love created by the patriarchal family are distorting, even violent, interlaced with power hierarchies. These make it difficult for love to last, and to be as profound as it could be.

Love and Power Between Parents and Children

How confusing it is for children, the idea of being loved! They are so often told by their parents, "Of course we love you, why do you even

---

* Except, of course, for the thirty-three million street children around the world, as well as many more in "orphanages" in the West, who survive "on their own".

366

ask?" And yet, often they don't *feel* very loved. After all, just because the archetype of a mother or a father is in place, it does not necessarily mean that love is there. Do parents always love their children? Would they admit it if they don't? Why do the feelings so many children describe sound not very satisfying? Is this "just the way things are"—or are there special impediments to real understanding and intimacy in the relationships between parents and children, impediments inherent in the family as we know it?

The biggest problem between children and parents is the power parents have over children.

Should love and power be mixed? What are the effects of mixing these two potent emotions in children's early lives?

Most children here seem to be saying that parents can probably be counted on in some ways—to "be there", let you "stay there"—but the quality of their love is rather vague. One difficulty is that, according to the archetype, parents *must* love their children, parents are not allowed *not* to love the child. Therefore, everything parents do is done in the name of "love". (Punishment too is always "because we love you".)

It is easy for children to believe that the emotion they feel when faced with a powerful person is "love"—or that the inscrutable ways of a person who is sometimes loving and friendly, and other times punitive and angry, are loving.

Must we love others in our families? Why can't we, like the Chinese or Japanese, have a system of respect for our relatives which does not necessarily insist on "love", but only demands "respect" for our elders, as well as responsibility for them? "Love", then, could be free to mean love when this is indeed what we feel.

If not all parents love their children—and maybe many don't know what love is anyway—they shouldn't have to pretend to.

But these may be exceptional cases. Let us consider parents who do love their children, without doubt. The problem then is that, since the parents are still the providers and "trainers" of the children, legally and economically the "owners" of the children, they exercise incredible power over the children. The very power of survival itself. Parents in our society are children's only real access to food, shelter—and "affection".*

Children must feel gratitude ("after all, we brought you into this world, without us, you wouldn't be here") and so, in their minds, this gratitude is mixed with love. How much of the love they feel is really

---

* Yet most people say they get more understanding from their friends.

gratitude and supplication before the power of the parents? If they learn that this behaviour or emotion is "love", or a large part of it, how will they then define love later in life? Won't they be highly confused by passion (either emotional or physical), and what it means? Unable to connect it with other feelings of liking and concern?

As children must, if they stay at home and don't run away, accept and internalize the system of their parents' power over them, they are likely to develop love–hate feelings towards their parents, or have very confused feelings, since both love and punishment come from the same all–powerful source. They learn an emotion that has no name, that we could call powerlove.

Of course, long–term caring for others is something positive that can also be learned in families, but it can be learned in other kinds of families, not just the nuclear model.

Does "Love" Include Sex? The Body?

What definition of love do children learn from the way the parents relate physically?

Isn't it strange to think of your parents having sex?
Finding their parents in any kind of physical embrace comes as a fascinating shock to most children:

"My parents were rarely affectionate, at least in front of us. They just pecked at each other when my father came home from work. But I remember seeing pictures of them with their arms around each other, which fascinated me, since I never saw them that way."

"My folks were only affectionate once that I can remember. We three girls gave them an electric blanket at Christmas, and my dad put his arm around Mum and hugged her when they opened the present. We all commented about this afterwards, that's how unusual it was. They often argued, especially after they'd gone to bed."

"My parents never kissed in front of me. When I was about thirteen they linked arms when we were out shopping. I was amazed. I sometimes wonder whether they've ever slept together!"

"Once I was passing their bedroom door and I saw them in Dad's bed holding each other. I was very surprised and embarrassed (I was about fifteen). It was like, 'Wow! They really do that.'

"They were seldom affectionate in front of me—though I have a lovely memory of seeing them dancing in the front porch and kissing. Once they saw me they stopped."

368

83 per cent of children in this research say their parents seem completely asexual.*

It would be logical if children drew the conclusion that "real love" is never sexual, nor even physically affectionate. But isn't affection a great part of what love is? It feels like that to children when their parents hug and kiss them. However, if the parents don't hug and kiss each other, is the definition of adult "love" different? And if so, what is it?

Is parents' love asexual?†
Why do parents feel that they shouldn't touch each other in front of the children? Because the children would be jealous? Because it would give the children sexual feelings and ideas? Or, do many parents really not want to touch each other?

The questions children have are many: "Is it that our parents really want to be affectionate, but have to hide it in front of us. Should no one see them touch. *Why?* It must be shameful or embarrassing somehow . . ."

Children also wonder, if the parents don't *want* to be affectionate, why exactly are they together (especially if they argue much of the time)? If they are only together "for the sake of the children", this puts an awfully big burden on the children to be "worth it", or to "make their parents happy", and so on, thus confusing the definitions of love even further.

Inequality Between Mothers and Fathers: Is This "Love"?

Another way children learn that power and domination are part of love is through observing the relationship of their parents. Gender tension and especially second-class treatment of the mother by the father is reported by the majority of people from two-parent families in this study. (See Parts II and III.)

Of course, while some of those reporting are children and teenagers, others are now adults looking back; would a majority still be found if

---

* Is this true, in some sense? According to my previous research, probably one-third of parents are not relating to each other physically; another third are having "sex" only irregularly; and most of the final third are probably simply hiding their sexuality from the children. On the other hand, many of these same parents also have active sexual lives of masturbation and/or a relationship outside the family, with a lover.
† Like that of Mary and Joseph? As the Pope stated to a Roman paper in 1993, "There is no sex in Heaven." Why? Because there is no need for reproduction.

I counted only those growing up in the last ten years? Unfortunately yes; one has only to look at the incidence of domestic violence against women to realize that gender inequality is still widespread.

Girls in particular find this gender inequality mixed with "love" confusing, even psychologically violent and terrifying. Why? Because for girls it means also coming to terms with "understanding" what this power relationship will mean for them: will they inherit this gender inequality? Can they avoid being considered lesser beings when they become women? How can they love a father who represents this system? Or a mother who lets herself participate in it?

Is this one reason why girls feel under such enormous pressure to have children of their own, become mothers, as soon as possible? Or alternatively, try to starve themselves, become anorexic so that they cease to exist?

Love Lost and Making the Wrong Decisions

What we have seen in many people's testimonies in this book is the individual's constant quest to come to terms with the unspoken power built into love in the family. People are likely to grow up to believe they don't love someone when they do, that a relationship is "just sex", or they might stay in a relationship out of duty, because they have learned that "real love" is a question of fitting into one of the patriarchal models.

Boys and men especially learn damaging ideas of love from the family, as they are taught to associate love for women with guilt. Or they may discount love that involves sex, since they have learned that sexual attraction is not something to be taken seriously.

To begin to see love clearly, truly to recognize our emotions, we must gain distance from our near-obsession with the "holy family" structure. Perhaps we can begin by looking inside ourselves, for we each hold the key to understanding these feelings.

New Families, Building Bridges

A positive note is that so many people today in the Western world are opting out of the institution as it is rigidly defined and creating their own families. The percentage of those in the UK still in the "traditional family" (father at work, mother at home with the 2.2 children) is, according to *Social Trends* (HMSO), only 7 per cent. And in Germany today, a full half of the population is unmarried, according to a 1993 *Stern* Magazine survey. This trend will continue, despite fundamentalist preaching to the contrary, because people are tired of trying to match the "holy family" model.

Must we feel guilty about revolutionizing our lives?

This profound social transformation is taking place furtively, defensively, even guiltily, as the mythology persists that one is not quite "normal", has not quite "made it", if one doesn't achieve nuclear family status.

Western publics are made to feel that it is important for a political candidate or a head of government to be married and have children, i.e., to be "normal". The subtext seems to be that people should respect, worship and elect the candidate with the family most resembling the "holy family"—the Jesus, Mary and Joseph model.

Why do we feel guilty about the creative ways we have begun to live our lives? Those who would have us conform to just one sort of family are the same people who see nothing wrong with authoritarian forms of government, those who do not believe people are entitled to govern themselves and make choices.

Reclaiming the word "family"

Every family is a "normal" family—no matter whether it has one parent, two or no children at all. A family can be made up of any combination of people, heterosexual or homosexual, who share their lives in an intimate (not necessarily sexual) way. And children can live as happily in an

371

adopted family as with biological parents. A family doesn't have to have children in it. Women are under a great deal of social pressure to have children, but a woman is in no way diminished if she chooses not to have children.

Wherever there is lasting love, there is a family.

Our right to create the family

People make institutions, not vice versa. The fact that individuals are changing the family is a sign of a healthy society. Democracy in politics and education have given society increased vigour, as more and more individuals feel that they have the right to think for themselves.

Single Parent Families

In the UK there are 1.3 million single parent families, over 90 per cent of which are headed by women. There is an unruly debate going on today in most Western countries about women's right to change the family. It is claimed that by doing this women are ruining children and society—never mind that men have opted out even more completely by leaving women *and* children, whereas women are "only" leaving men. Women are taking up the combined work of earning a living and looking after children, and making a valuable contribution to society.

To put the controversy over single parents into some historical perspective: in the UK, for example, marriage was a private matter until legislation in 1753. Rates of cohabitation and "illegitimacy" rose until 1900, when motherhood as synonymous with marriage was firmly established. The turn of the century saw a revival of legal marriage, peaking in the 1950's. Dr Susan McRae states,★ "It may be the single-earner, high-fertility family of the 1950's—against which lone parents and the cohabiting couple are often measured and found wanting—which is at odds with history."

Are single parent families bad for children?

There are very few statistics about the effects of these kinds of households on children, although during World War II, for example, a large number of families were without fathers for several years without this being frowned upon. Today, the assumption of much popular journalism is that the two-parent family is better for children, but there is no real foundation to this belief. The data here shows that there are *beneficial*

★ *Independent*, 23.9.93.

effects for the majority of children living in single parent families. It is more positive for children not to grow up in an atmosphere poisoned by gender inequality.

This conclusion was foreshadowed in *The Hite Report on Men and Male Sexuality*. In that work I was surprised to find that boys who grew up with their mother alone were much more likely to have good relationships with women in their adult lives. 80 per cent of men from such families had formed strong, lasting ties with women (in marriage or long-term relationships) as opposed to only 40 per cent from two-parent families. This does not mean that the two-parent family cannot be reformed so that it provides a peaceful environment for children—indeed this is part of the ongoing revolution in the family in which so many people today are engaged.

The great majority of single mothers, whom fundamentalist groups try to put on the defensive, can indeed be proud of the excellent job they are doing in bringing up their children, often despite financial hardship.

As we have seen, the one-mother family enjoys a long and great tradition in the early mother–child icons of pre-history; and as one mother has astutely pointed out, since most fathers leave childcare to the mother, all mothers are single mothers!

Single fathers

Do girls and boys who grow up with their father only have a different kind of emotional and sexual identity?

Single parent families are mostly single mother families, yet there is an increasing number of single father families too. Is it true that most single fathers don't take much part in childcare, but instead hire female nannies, or ask their own mothers or sisters, or girlfriends, to take care of the children? Men could change the style of families by taking more part domestically, and by opening up emotionally and having closer contact with children. My research here highlights men's traumatizing and enforced split from women at puberty. Healing this is the single most important thing we as a society could do to end the distance men feel from "family".

Single mothers and lesbian mothers

Do girls who grow up with "only" their mother have a better relationship with her? According to this study, 49 per cent of such girls felt that it was a positive experience; 20 per cent did not like it; and the rest had mixed feelings. Mothers in one-parent families are more likely to feel freer to confide in daughters because no "disloyalty" is implied to the spouse. Daughters in such families are less likely to see the mother as a "wimp"—she is an independent person.

Boys who grow up with "only" their mother, as seen in Part III, experience less pressure to demonstrate contempt for things "feminine", and for non-aggressive parts of themselves.

Democracy of the Heart: a New Politics for the Twenty-first Century

Moving to the Future of Family and Society With a More Mature View

We should give up on the outdated notion that the only acceptable families are nuclear families. A more profound historical view of what is happening is needed. We should see the new society that has evolved over the last forty years for what it is, for *itself*, not as a disaster because it is not like the past.

The new diversity of families is part of a positive pluralism, part of a fundamental transition in the organization of society, which calls for open-minded brainstorming by us all: what do we believe "love" and "family" are? Can we accept that the many people fleeing the nuclear family are doing so for valid reasons? If reproduction is no longer the urgent priority that it was when societies were smaller, before industrialization took hold, then the revolt against the family is not surprising. Perhaps it was even historically inevitable. It is not that people don't want to build loving, family-style relationships, it is that they do not want to be forced to build them within one rigid, hierarchical, heterosexist, reproductive framework.

Diversity in family forms can bring joy and enrichment to a society: new kinds of families can be the basis for a renaissance of spiritual dignity and creativity in political life as well.

Private life is in the midst of a welcome process of democratization which will in turn enrich, advance, and transform democracy in the political arena. Continuing this process of bringing private life into an ethical and egalitarian frame of reference—will give us the energy and moral will to maintain democracy in the larger political sphere. We can create a society with a new spirit and will—but politics will have to be transformed by the use of an interactive frame of reference most often found today in friendships between women.*

---

* As documented in *Women and Love* and Carol Gilligan's *In a Different Voice* (NY, Harvard University Press, 1982).

The economic and spiritual difficulties of the West today are often blamed on "the decline of the family", and especially women and "feminism". Single mothers are vilified in a way which the Archbishop of Canterbury argued would be illegal if the same attack were made on a racial minority.* Isn't the problem rather that the West is not living up to its moral promise, that the reality of democracy has fallen well behind its Enlightenment ideal, and that women are in fact in the forefront of the movement for reshaping political and economic institutions, creating a more interactive democracy throughout society?

Diversity in families can form the basic infrastructure for a new and advanced type of political democracy to be created, imagined, developed—a system that suits the massive societies which communications technology today has made into one "global village".

The current fundamentalist reaction to the democratization of private life is trying to return society, both the private and the public social order, to pre-Enlightenment, pre-humanist values. This type of social order has had various names: totalitarianism, feudalism, fascism, authoritarianism and so on.

One cannot exaggerate the importance of the current debate: there has been fascism in societies before; it could emerge again, alongside fascism in the family. They have always gone together historically.

If we believe in the democratic, humanist ideals of the last four hundred years, we have the right, almost the duty, to make our family system a more just one; to follow our democratic ideals and make a new, more inclusive network of private life—a new personal infrastructure for society that will reflect not a preordained patriarchal structure, but our belief in justice and equality for all—women, men and children.

Private life is in the midst of a process of democratization, and this is good. The family has been a repressive, authoritarian institution for too long. Those who would attack women now are trying to reimpose the unequal "holy family" model. Let's continue the transformation, believe in ourselves, and go forward with love, not fear. In our private lives and in our public world, let's hail the future and make history.

* *Independent*, 9.10.93.

Hite Research Questionnaire
on the Family

The purpose of this questionnaire is to better understand how children feel growing up, how they perceive the family and the world around them.

Teenagers, for example, are constantly *told* how to feel, think and behave—on the grounds that adults have "better judgement". But often teenagers completely disagree. What were your thoughts and experiences growing up? Can you remember how you felt, what it was like? Or can you describe what it is like, watching your own child grow up? There are many areas of this subject which are never talked about, especially the physical aspect, and your help in contributing information will be greatly appreciated.

IT IS *NOT* NECESSARY TO ANSWER EVERY SINGLE QUESTION! Answer only those that interest you—but please do answer some of the questions.

The results will be published as an extended discussion of the answers, including many quotes, in the same format as the Hite Reports on female and male sexuality, and *Women and Love*. The replies are anonymous, so *don't sign your answers*.

Looking forward to hearing from you!

Shere Hite invites readers to participate in her future research. Please write to her c/o

Grove Press
841 Broadway
New York, NY 10003

---

1. When you were very little, around three or four, can you remember what it was like being close to your mother? Can you describe her presence, her sounds, her skin, her smell? How she touched you? How she looked?

2. Can you remember your mother breast-feeding your brother or sister? How old were you? What were your thoughts? Were you jealous? Interested? Did you think it was beautiful or repulsive? Did you feel left out? Wish you would be a mother?

3. What things did your parents do that included body contact with you? Held and cuddled you? Bathed you? Washed your hair? Dressed you? Combed your hair? Spanked you? Gave you enemas? Please describe the kind of physical intimacy you had with your parents and how it felt to you.

4. As a child, did you think your mother was beautiful? Wonderful? In what way? Did you like to touch her and be close to her? Did you lie in bed with her? Did she read to you, or did you watch television close together? Describe the feeling you had at these times.

5. Do you remember your mother coming into your room to kiss you goodnight? Was this a pleasant moment? What can you remember feeling?

6. What did your mother and/or father's bedroom look like? Did it have a double bed or single beds? Was it always neat or were the covers usually unmade? Were there lots of pillows? What was the atmosphere there (cold, erotic, friendly, etc.)?

7. What is your earliest memory of this room?

8. Did you spend time in her/his bedroom? Go there often? Or was it slightly mysterious, somewhat off limits? Were you allowed to play there as often as you wanted?

9. At what age did you begin to wonder about your mother's sexuality? Your father's? Or did you assume they didn't have any? Why did you think the bedroom was slightly off limits (if it was)? Or, did you know they did "something" together, but absorb the idea that you shouldn't wonder?

10. Would you have liked to know what your mother's sex life was like? If she masturbated? Your father's? If he masturbated?

11. Did you ever have fantasies of having sex with one of your parents? As a child? Later? What were the fantasies?

12. Did you ever run away from home? Contemplate it? Why?

13. Were you happy at home as a child? Did you have mixed feelings about your parents? Did you sometimes love them (or one or the other), and sometimes hate them? When?

14. Did you ever want to leave home and go and live elsewhere, but you stayed because you had nowhere else to go?

15. When you were a child, did you think it was a problem that you had no money of your own? That you had to ask your parents for money?

16. When was the time in your childhood that you were the angriest with your parents?

17. Who was more controlling of you, your mother or your father? How? Who had more power over you?

18. Did you like other friends' parents more? Other relatives?

19. Did you usually decide, during most conflicts with your parents, that they were right after all?

20. If you did not think they were right, but had to accept their decision anyway, how did you feel about this? Did you sometimes feel that you were living with injustice, but there was nothing you could do about it?

21. If you don't have one parent, how do you feel about it?

22. Do you know how your parents felt about having you?

23. If you are raised by a single parent, does she or he date? If your mother is dating, how do you feel about it if she has a man home with her? A woman? Or if you live with your father, vice versa?

24. Has anyone in your family become HIV positive or contracted Aids? Has anyone you know died? Do you know how to protect yourself against Aids?

25. Do you think your parents read pornography or watch sexy videotapes?

26. Do your parents (or partners) kiss in front of you? Are they sexually affectionate? How? Do you like or dislike it?

27. Do you have a boyfriend or girlfriend? Do you have sex together? Do your parents know?

28. When you fight with your parents, do your parents hit you? Speak a certain way to you? How? Spank you? Punish you? How? Is it usually your father or mother who punishes you?

29. If you were spanked, at what age was this? Were you slapped? Sent to your room? Told you were bad, not lovable, "not fit for human society", etc.? By whom?

30. If you were hit, who did this, and where, on what part of your body? With their hand, or something else? What?

31. Did they pull your dress up/trousers down? What were you wearing? Were you standing up, bending over, or lying down?

Did it really physically hurt? Did you cry? Was it the physical pain that hurt or the humiliation?

32. How often did these things happen? Until what age?
33. How did you feel if a sister or brother was being punished?
34. Were there other forms of violence you experienced as a child? Physical? Emotional? Did you have friends who received physical punishment?
35. Were the girls in your family spanked more than the boys? Were boys "whipped", not spanked? Punished another way? Less or more often than girls?

36. What kind of relationship did you have with your mother by the time you were ten? Fifteen or sixteen? Can you remember conversations or arguments you would have? What did you like least about her? Most?
37. What was your relationship with your father like at that time? What did you spend time together doing? What did he talk to you about?
38. Did you admire him? Why or why not?
39. Did your mother know about any of your sexual activities (masturbation or with a partner)? Did you know anything about hers? Did your father know? Did you know about his? Did you have sex magazines or other "adult" things in your room?
40. What was your parents' relationship? Did you feel comfortable with both of them together, or did you prefer to spend time with one or the other separately? Why?
41. Were you closer to your mother or your father?
42. Were you close to a brother or sister? Were you "pals" or "rivals"? Did you do things together? At what age were you closest? Least close?
43. Who was treated better—you or your sister/brother (if there was a difference)?
44. Did your mother or your father (or someone else) tell you about menstruation? Where/when did you first see a tampon? What were the circumstances?
45. What did your parents tell you about sexuality?
46. Did your father or mother look at pornography? When did you first see it? Where was it? What was your reaction, how did you feel?
47. Did you tell your parents you had seen it? Discuss it with anyone? What did you say?

For Women and Girls

48. Are you like your mother?
49. How do you react when people say you look or act "just like your mother"?
50. If you don't want to be like her, what especially don't you want to be like? Do you look different? How are your looks different?
51. Was there any kind of (buried) competition between you and your mother? Was she ever jealous of you, or were you jealous of her? What for?
52. Did you ever get the message that looking for attention from your father was competing with your mother, that you shouldn't do it? That she could feel angry or left out? Did you try to get his attention anyway? How? Was this only when your mother was not around?
53. Did you sometimes feel you were emotionally in between your mother and father, and had to please both, not take sides? Did different types of behaviour please your mother and father—so that you had to behave differently with each one? Was it easier to relate to them alone than together?
54. Did you have a good relationship with your father? What did you do together? When were you closest?
55. Were you ever called your father's "little girl", or his "special girl"? His "girlfriend" or "best girl"? Did you have "dates" to go shopping, play sports, do errands? Did you enjoy these? What did you enjoy about them?
56. Did your father's behaviour to you change after the age of about twelve, for example, were you told (maybe a year or two later) that you shouldn't wear make-up or lipstick, that it made you look cheap and tarty? Did your mother also tell you things like this? Did either parent warn you about girls with good "reputations" and "the other kind"?
57. Did anyone in your family touch you in ways which made you uncomfortable? How? Were you ever sexually molested by anyone in your family? Who? Please explain. Were you afraid you might be if you didn't watch out?
58. Should daughters sue their fathers in court for incest?
59. Did you have fights with your mother when you were in secondary school? What about? Did she comment on your hair? Your clothes? What did she say?

60. Did your mother or your father supervise your coming and going from the house, with whom, how late you came home, what you wore, etc.? How long you talked on the telephone?
61. What was your first experience of buying a bra? Were you with your mother? Father? Friends? Alone?
62. Did anyone congratulate you at the time of your first menstruation? Or did you get the impression it wasn't too important or interesting? That it was supposed to be kept a secret, hidden, even that menstruation was dirty? What did you think?
63. Did you like your underwear? Did you pick it out, or did someone else? Was it practical? Athletic? Hip? Feminine? How did it make you feel?
64. What was your mother's underwear like? What did it tell you about her "femaleness" and sexuality? Did you like hers better than yours, or vice versa?
65. Did you have a room to yourself, or did you share? Did you ever feel lonely, even frightened, getting into bed by yourself? Or did you like having your own bed and your own room? Did you wish you could get in bed with your parents or your brothers or sisters (if you didn't)?
66. Did your parents expect you to have sex before you left home? Did they know if you did? Did they ask? Did you tell them? If you had a brother, was he allowed more sexual freedom around the house?
67. What was your main source of physical affection between ages seven and fifteen?

For Parents

68. When your children were living with you, were you closer to your son(s) or daughter(s)? Why? (Please answer this section in the present, if applicable.)
69. If you have a son(s), at which age(s) during his childhood was he closest to you? Which was the most satisfying period—infancy? Before kindergarten? During junior school? Secondary school? Why?
70. During which of these ages was your son least close to you? Most hostile and challenging?
71. Your daughter(s)? When were you closest? Most distant?
72. During which ages did your son(s) talk to you most openly and freely about his thoughts and feelings? What did he talk about?
73. Your daughter(s)?

74. Did you like your daughter(s)? What did you like best? Least? What was your biggest complaint?

75. What did/do you most regret about your daughter's childhood/your relationship with your daughter? About your relationship with your son, his childhood?

76. When you punished your children, how did you do it? Physically? Emotionally? Both?

77. If you spanked your children, were these formal occasions, or spur of the moment outbreaks? That is, did you suddenly find yourself reaching out to slap your (screaming?) child, etc.—or, after a certain level of misbehaviour, did you say, "If you don't stop, you're going to get a good spanking." And then later, when it hadn't stopped, proceed to the spanking? Did you do it or ask your spouse to do it?

78. Would spanking or physical punishment be in the living room? Bedroom? Outside? Bathroom? Kitchen?

79. Is it different punishing a girl than a boy? How? If you have both, do you tend to hit one quicker, more often, than the other? In a different place? Which one? Why?

80. What do you think is the most important bond between parents and children?

THANK YOU FOR ANSWERING THIS QUESTIONNAIRE

Please add the following statistical information for research purposes:

age
sex
occupation
in a relationship? married, single, coupled (living together or separately)
sexual preference
religious background
present religious identification
political inclination, if any
nationality, race or ethnic background

Please add anything else you would like to say.

APPENDICES

Quantifying the Emotions:
Methodological Observations on the
Hite Report Trilogy

Gladys Engel Lang, Professor of Communications, Political
Science and Sociology, University of Washington, Seattle

Quantification and analysis of attitudes and emotions is one of the most
difficult tasks faced by social scientists—and one rarely attempted,
almost never on such a large scale as in Hite's work. It has been one
of Hite's contributions to devise an excellent methodology for studying
the attitudes and emotions of a large population, while at the same time
retaining a rich qualitative base: extensive data in people's own words
about their deepest feelings.

When analysing emotions and attitudes in depth, it has been
customary in the social/psychological sciences to use extremely small
samples; indeed, Freud based whole books on a handful of subjects.
Thus for Hite to have used the small samples typical of psychological
studies would have been quite legitimate. However, she also took on the
more difficult goal of trying to develop a larger and more representative
sample, while still retaining the in-depth qualities of smaller studies.
She does the latter by allowing thousands of people to speak freely
instead of forcing them to choose from preselected categories—in
essence, predefining them and prepackaging them, as with so many
studies. It is a method that is hard on the researcher, requiring analysis
of thousands of individual replies to hundreds of open-ended questions,
an analysis that involves many steps.

Hite's work has been erroneously criticized by some members of
the popular press as being "unscientific" because her respondents, though
numerous, are not a "random sample". However, scientists and scholars
in the field of methodology and opinion sampling know that for many
kinds of studies, and Hite's is one of them, a very large non-random

389

sample generating rich data is preferable to a randomly chosen sample. A "random sample" does not guarantee representativeness; frequently, in practice, there is a problem of "who didn't respond". In this kind of sampling, to be perfectly mathematically "representative", all of those chosen must respond. However, in most cases, no such perfection is achieved. Thus, to put it bluntly, there *are* almost no "random samples".* As John L. Sullivan, the noted research theorist, puts it, "Most of the work in the social sciences is not based on random samples; in fact, many if not most of the articles in psychology journals are based on data from college students, and then generalized. . . . Interestingly, these small and non-representative samples have not been criticized in the same way Hite's larger and more representative sample has been." Hite's large and rich sample of over 15,000 is an excellent achievement in itself. Moreover, Hite has matched her sample carefully to the US population at large; the demographic breakdown of the sample population corresponds quite closely to that of the general US population.

Another hallmark of Hite's methodology is the anonymity guaranteed participants. It is this which makes it possible for her respondents to speak so freely about their most private feelings and thoughts, and ensures that they do not feel they must hold back any of the truth about these very personal matters for fear of being ridiculed, judged, or simply "known". It is in fact because the respondents are guaranteed anonymity that one can be confident of the accuracy of Hite's findings. And indeed studies in three other countries testing the findings of the first Hite Report have replicated her basic results.

As Robert L. Emerson of UCLA explains, "Hite's methodology is perfectly suited to her aims . . . the distinctive quality of her data is exactly that it allows men and women to talk about the subjective meaning and experience of a variety of personal matters. The purpose of her research is then to describe and categorize the varieties of such experience . . . so that the whole range of such experiences can be described . . . [and she] has more than fulfilled this goal." Hite is straightforward about her procedures and has done as much and more than other researchers to explain her methods. She makes absolutely clear what she is doing methodologically—in fact, her degree of clarity is not frequently achieved in social science research.

There is a growing literature advocating the use of methods similar

---

* Therefore most survey research today tries to match its samples demographically to the general population in other ways, by, for example, weighting responses to conform to the population profile, as Hite does.

to Hite's in the social sciences. Feminist scholars in particular have developed a sophisticated critique of standard research theory, demonstrating its many built-in biases and distortions (see, for example, the anthology edited by Sandra Harding and Merrill Hintikka, *Discovering Reality*). Hite's work can thus be seen as part of this general rethinking, one of the first studies, in fact, to put new theories into practice.

Nancy Tuana of the University of Texas at Dallas writes: "For centuries, through the guise of science, men have been constructing theories of woman's nature. Although women have been the object of study, our experiences and feelings have not been taken seriously. Shere Hite's work provides a model of a methodology that is based on women's experience. Hite has rejected the silencing of women by recognizing that a theory about women's ways of loving must be rooted in our efforts to give voice to our own experiences. Her work will be valued not only for the insights she provides, but also for her revolutionary approach." And Barbara Ehrenreich, whose background is in the biological sciences, notes that "Tables, graphs, correlation coefficients, etc., do not, in and of themselves make a study 'scientific'. In fact, I would say that any study of human behavior that does not include—and highlight—the element of subjective experience is, in a fundamental sense, unscientific. This was what was wrong with the Kinsey Report and Masters and Johnson's work, and what makes the Hite Reports so ground-breaking: at last we know something about love as women and men experience it and that is the most important thing we can know about it."

In summary, as a scientist and as a human being who obviously cares very much about her subjects, Shere Hite presents in the Hite Reports a deeply penetrating portrait of our culture, based on empirical data, giving us insights into who we are and where we are going. This work is an enormous contribution.

1987

New Trends in the Social Sciences

The Hite Reports are part of an international trend in the social sciences expressing dissatisfaction with the adequacy of simple quantitative methods as a way of defining people's attitudes. More and more the social sciences are turning to various qualitative methods, attempting to find out what people are thinking in a more complex way than projecting into their minds on the basis of preconceived categories. Hite elicits from the populations she studies not only reliable scientific data, but also a wide spectrum of attitudes and beliefs about sex, love and who people are.

JESSE LEMISCH
Professor, Department of History
SUNY, Buffalo

The research methods of the Hite Reports pioneered many current research trends, including the mixing of quantitative and qualitative data. Originally criticized, these techniques are now widely copied by many in the field not only in the US but abroad.

TORE HAAKINSON
Wenner-Gren Centre, Stockholm

There is a growing and highly sophisticated literature critiquing social science methodology and, in fact, Western philosophical concepts of "knowing". Part of this critique is growing out of sociology itself, as predictive models have failed to materialize; and part of it grows out of feminist rethinking of the philosophical assumptions behind various disciplines. Two ground-breaking anthologies of feminist scholarship in this area are: *Discovering Reality: Feminist Perspectives on Epistemology, Metaphysics, Methodology, and Philosophy of Science* (edited by Sandra

APPENDICES

Harding and Merrill B. Hintikka);* and *Theories of Women's Studies* (edited by Gloria Bowles and Renate Duelli Klein).†

The issues are brought out in the following extracts from a fascinating article by Gloria Bowles, University of California, at Berkeley:

"On the Uses of Hermeneutics for Feminist Scholarship"‡

. . . the one discovery of the decade which enables us to understand and to move beyond the tension between discursive inheritance of Western thought and the feminist perspective [is that] what counts as knowledge must be grounded on experience.

SANDRA HARDING AND MERRILL B. HINTIKKA (1983)

Thinking begins only when we come to know that reason, glorified for centuries, is the most stiff-necked adversary of thought.

MARTIN HEIDEGGER (1977)

. . . The scientistic world view, which sits atop the university and defines the social sciences and reaches even into the humanities, has as its goal the so-called "objective knowledge" of mathematics and the physical sciences. Only now are literary criticism, and many other disciplines, wresting themselves from "objective" analysis, whose primary result is a divorce of objective knowledge from evaluation. It is not that the Humanities are merely rebelling against their place on the bottom rung under the Sciences in twentieth-century intellectual history. It is rather that the Humanities are realizing that their subject matter is so thick with personal and interpersonal experience, with moral and evaluative judgements, that the "impersonal" and "value-free" methodological strategies of the Sciences are at best irrelevant and at worst a distortion of the subject matter itself. This critique of scientism/logocentrism in the Humanities, while not inclined to throw all objective analysis out of the window, has been primarily a "negative" critique which has analysed the limits of this borrowed methodology. Feminist scholarship has not only stood critical in a "negative" sense of traditional conceptual

* D. Reidel Publishing Company, London, 1983.
† Routledge & Kegan Paul, London, 1983.
‡ *Women's Studies International Forum*, December 1984.

assumptions, but has made the positive move of putting forth alternative epistemologies which use experience, intuition and evaluation (both of women as individuals and of women as a "class") as modes of knowing. Further, women *qua* women seem to stand in a sort of privileged position in regard to the formulation of such new orientations of thinking. A critique of scientistic thought is not so difficult for women, since we have always used ways of knowing in addition to reason. Throughout male recorded history, men have been the "takers", while women have assumed (or have been forced to assume) the role of "caretakers". Women live in a world where little is impersonal and much is personal, where little is fixed or certain and much is ambiguous and volatile, and where little is value-free and much requires an evaluative response. We have long lived our lives in the intimately personal and non-objective context of the daily needs and concerns of other human beings. We bring all this experience, these skills and perceptions, to our scholarly work and into the academic community. Here we are confronted by the modern form of traditionalism in the scientific mentality and its dictatorial regulations.

In the contemporary academic community, due in part to the recently emerged and broadly based critique of scientism and to the accomplishments of feminist scholarship, this scientistic mentality has become increasingly difficult for traditional scholars to justify. . . . [It is in] the hermeneutic or interpretive tradition where one finds the critique of logocentrism in a powerful form. I am using the most inclusive term, hermeneutics (*Hermeneutik* simply means "interpretation" in German), to designate a constellation of methodologies which stand critical of the objectivism and scientism of the white male tradition. These are the loosely defined movements which have emerged in the post-war years in Continental thinking under the nomenclatures of "phenomenology", "post-structuralism", "hermeneutics" and, most recently, "deconstructionism".

One need not devote one's life to a reading of Heidegger and Foucault and Feyerabend and Derrida (nor do I think Women's Studies scholars should) to see that these writers are saying what we as feminists have been saying all along—that there is something profoundly wrong with the tradition. . . .

For there are common points of interest in the ideas of hermeneuticists and feminists. The "hermeneutical circle", although it has different connotations for different thinkers, means essentially that there is no such thing as a "detached", "neutral" or "objective" place to stand when we know something. We are always speaking from a "prejudiced" (in the sense of pre-judgement) and "interested" and "evaluative" posture. This is the circle, that we are intimately (personally, socially, historically) involved with what we claim to know. This is Heidegger on the nature of hermeneutical thinking:

But if we sense this circle as a vicious one and look out for ways of avoiding it, even if we just "sense" it as an inevitable imperfection, then the act of understanding has been misunderstood from the ground up . . . What is decisive is not to get out of the circle but to come into it in the right way. . . .

Traditional thought claims to be able to leap out of the hermeneutical/interpretive circle and to speak of so-called "value-free", "disinterested", "objective", and "ethically neutral" knowledge. Thus, the hermeneutical/interpretive tradition says all efforts to deny the "circular" and "interested" and "evaluative" nature of thinking are conceptually confused or dishonest. Feminist thought, precisely because it acknowledges and asserts its "prejudices", must, from the hermeneutical perspective, be judged as one of the only available theoretical postures which holds good claim to intellectual integrity and sophistication.

Heidegger contends that the Western tradition does not know how to think; he speaks of openness, receptivity and listening. Both he and Derrida say that truth is to be found in absence or in the spaces between words, a theme common to French literature. Many Women's Studies scholars had our original training in literature; for us, there is both irony and gratification in the "news" that the new model for understanding is the expressive language of the text. Many scholars—not only literary critics but anthropologists and philosophers as well—are talking about the literary text which should replace the machine model as the locus of analysis. For example, feminine biologists have been questioning this model and now some prestigious men in the field are making the same thought. *It is crucial to realize that the literary text, in its paradigmatic form, is an imaginative narrative of those personal interrelations which have long formed the life-world and the existential reality of women.* [Hite's emphasis] Those who have proposed the literary text as the interpretive model have not recognized any special affinity between the literary narrative and the feminist perspective and women's life experience.

However, many white male thinkers are uncomfortable with the hermeneutic circle—and engage in endless discussions of it—because for them it raises the spectre of total relativity, the fear that we will never be able to know anything in an absolutely objective and certain way. Male thought, with its linear habits, would thrust itself out of the circle. It is difficult for men to make the critiques of logocentrism; the few who are trying, from within the tradition, find it hard to embrace intuition and

396

experience as viable ways of knowing. The struggle to affirm what they have been taught to denigrate is enormous. . . . As women, we are not so attached to old ways of thinking since we have been discovering our own. Thus it is that the critique of logocentrism in *Theories of Women's Studies* and other feminist works is more directed and unmediated—feels less cumbersome—than many contemporary male critiques. These feminist essays contrast, for example, with the introduction to a very fine book, *Interpretive Social Science: A Reader*, edited by Paul Rabinow and William M. Sullivan. It painfully and painstakingly elaborates "The Interpretive Turn: Emergence of an Approach", as the only way out of a failed social science: "As long as there has been a social science, the expectation has been that it would turn from its humanistic infancy to the maturity of hard science, thereby leaving behind its dependence on value, judgment, and individual insight" (Rabinow and Sullivan, 1979). The authors mock that polarity, the "hard" and "soft" sciences. Through science, one moves out of the softness and the world of the mother into hardness, which is mature; one leaves a world of dependence, the proper sphere of value and insight. For these writers, it is not easy to say, many pages later: "We propose a return to this human world in all its lack of clarity, its alienation, and its depth, as an alternative to the continuing search for a formal deductive paradigm in the social sciences." . . . Significantly, what they do not say, these male writers, is that they are leaving behind a world of male thought to enter the province of female thought. A growing number of them have been able to make the critique of logocentrism; but so far none of them has been able to analyse their own sexism—and I mean sexism in its many guises, from the denigration of women in prose and in public to a complete ignorance or an appropriation of the enormous advances of feminist scholarship. Moreover, the bulk of male scholarship of the hermeneutic/phenomenological persuasion has been unable to move beyond the preliminary effort of a negative critique of the limitations and irrelevancies of the traditional scientistic methodology. When asked by traditional critics for their alternative ways of knowing, they have little to offer beyond interesting generalities. Some of these thinkers have said explicitly that it is not up to them, it is beyond their capacities, to offer positive alternatives. The problem, and the promise, is that they have not realized that these alternatives will come from us—feminist women scholars who stand removed enough from the tradition to see things differently.

Explication of Scientific Method as Used in Research for the Hite Report Trilogy

Shere Hite

The main concerns of this research were described in the abstract of a paper presented at the American Association for the Advancement of Science annual meeting in May 1985,* entitled "Devising a new methodological framework for analysis and presentation of data in mixed qualitative/quantitative research: the Hite Report Trilogy, 1972–1986":

There were unique challenges to be faced in devising the methodology for the Hite Reports, which comprise a 3-vol. study of over 15,000 women and men in the US, 1972–86. First, although quantification was necessary as part of the final result, a simple multiple-choice questionnaire could not be used, since the theoretical concept for the project stated that "most women have never been asked how they feel about sex" and "most research has been done by men": therefore, it was important not to assume predetermined categories, but to design an essay-type questionnaire which would be open-ended. Also, the data-gathering was designed to protect the anonymity of the respondent. Secondly, compilation of data from essay questions is very difficult, if the data is to be carefully and rigorously treated. . . . Finally, and almost as labour-intensive as compilation and categorization of data, presentation of findings was planned to serve more than an informative function; rather than simply giving readers statistics plus the author's theoretical analysis of data, the aim was to create an inner dialogue within the reader, as s/he mentally conversed with those quoted. Therefore, large parts of text comprise first-person statements from those participating. The format of presentation shows how these fit into intricate categories of social patterns.

The Four Stages of Research

I.

Questionnaire Design

One of the most important elements in the design of *Women and Love* was that the participants be anonymous, because in this way a completely

---

* See published proceedings, statistical abstracts, annual meeting, American Association for the Advancement of Science, May 1985, Washington, DC.

free and uninhibited discussion could be ensured. For this reason, a questionnaire format, rather than face-to-face interviews, was chosen, with respondents specifically asked not to sign their names, although other demographic data were taken. That this anonymity was in fact an aid to communication with participants was verified in statements by respondents in each study, such as the following:

I would find it very hard to say all these things to another person, and I'm sure many women would feel the same as I. I am sick of reading various "advice" columns about what I should be feeling, but I have not found another forum for saying what I think myself, taking my own time, rethinking, not feeling any pressure to be perfect or "in" or anything. I am saving my answers; they have been very important to me.

The second choice to be made regarding format related to how the questions would be asked. In the sensitive realm of personal attitudes, a multiple-choice questionnaire was out of the question, because it would have implied preconceived categories of response, and thus, in a sense, would also have "told" the respondent what the "allowable" or "normal" answers would be. Although a multiple-choice questionnaire is much easier for the researcher to work with, it would have given a subtle signal to the participant that the research categories were equated with "reality", or "allowable reality", whereas the intention here was to permit women's own voices to emerge, for women to say whatever they might feel on the deepest level to be the truth of their situation, with nothing to intervene or make them censor themselves.

Also, the development of the questions in this study has always been an interactive process with the participants. (In a way, this was true of the Kinsey questionnaires as well, since Kinsey developed several questionnaires over his period of research.) In this study, questionnaires were refined and modified at the suggestion of those responding, so that, for *Women and Love*, there were four basic versions of the questionnaire used over several years.

Coming from an academic background with a strong awareness of the ideological elements in the definition of culture, and with a background in the women's movement which gave further emphasis to this idea, it was a constant matter for concern that questions are not simple questions, but always have several layers of meaning. For this reason, the methodology used here was designed to pay special attention to this issue.*

* Points presented at a speech to the National Women's Studies convention, University of Kansas, 1978.

APPENDICES

Many people hold the mistaken belief that multiple-choice questionnaires represent the height of scientific objectivity, in that they can be quantified and need no "interpretation". Nothing could be further from the truth. All researchers, no matter how careful or aware/unaware of their own biases, *do* have a point of view, a way of seeing the world, reflecting the cultural milieu in which they were brought up, and so on—and these assumptions are subtly filtered into categories and questions chosen. (Philosophically speaking, we are all/all life is "biased" and subjective; it is only by combining a mass of subjectivities—all of our "seeing", if you will—that we find, through collective sharing of perception, a "fact"; in other words, for example, we only "know" the sun will come up tomorrow because we have seen it come up every day, and we all agree that the probability is that it will come up again tomorrow.)

Thus, to design the categories of response for a multiple-choice questionnaire is a political act, unavoidably filled with subjective bias, whether consciously or unconsciously so, and whether the researcher considers him/herself to be "neutral" or "apolitical" and so on. * If a study wishes to find out what's "out there", it cannot impose prior categories on that "out there"; it needs to develop its research instrument through an exchange with "them", the participants, before proceeding. This was done in the current study by listening to respondents' suggestions and, indeed, eliciting comment from them as to their feelings about the questionnaire. In other words, there was an ongoing interactive process of sequential refinement in designing the questionnaires for this project. Less meticulous care for research design may mean that a researcher only reifies his or her pre-existing expectations as to the content of the opinions/answers "discovered". †

* As both Elie Wiesel and John F. Kennedy have pointed out, to be "neutral" or "apolitical" is, in fact, to be highly political, because one is endorsing the status quo.
† In the case of *The Hite Report on Female Sexuality*, for example, the point of view was woman-oriented, in that it let women define sex as they saw it, rather than assuming that the male definition of sex which had been predominant for so long was the only possible "correct" definition. For this, the work was described by some as having a "feminist bias". In fact, much of the previous research into female sexuality had been less than "scientific"; rather than taking the information that most women could orgasm more easily during masturbation or direct clitoral/vulval stimulation than during coitus, and concluding that therefore this is "normal", previous studies had started with the assumption that if women did not orgasm during coitus, there must be something wrong with them—that they were somehow defective, "dysfunctional", psychologically or physically abnormal. Research was often geared to finding out what the cause of this "defect" might be. This was a non-scientific approach, not an objective way of looking at female sexuality.
In short, no study is free of bias, or a point of view; the important thing is to recognize this fact, and to clarify, insofar as possible, just what that point of view is.

APPENDICES

The difficulty of studying the emotions

As Judith Long Laws has said, "Most social scientists still avoid the study of feelings and attitudes, because of the difficulty in quantifying such studies, and the belief that this is the 'best' kind of social science. This is not always true; quantification is not always the best way to arrive at understanding. . . . The Hite Report was the first large-scale set of data where women talked about their own experiences in their own voices."

For this reason, essay questionnaires—which are not less "scientific" than multiple-choice, and in fact are recommended for use whenever possible by methodology textbooks—were the research tool of choice. The goal of this study was to hear women's deepest reflections on the nature of love, and to learn how they see love relationships now in relation to the whole spectrum of their lives. The method was important also in that it enabled participants to communicate directly with readers, sharing myriad points of view—in essence debating with each other throughout the text.

II.
Distribution of Questionnaires and Composition of Sample

The questionnaire following this essay and similar versions were distributed to women all over the US beginning in 1980. Their purpose was to discover how women/we view ourselves and our relationships with men and the world now, how we define "reality".

Distribution of the questionnaires was extremely widespread and painstakingly done, in order to reach as many kinds of women with as many varied points of view as possible. In order to ensure anonymity, it was thought best to send questionnaires to organizations rather than to individuals, so that any member who wanted might be able to answer with complete assurance that her name was not on any list or on file anywhere. Clubs and organizations through which questionnaires were distributed included church groups in thirty-four states, women's voting and political groups in nine states, women's rights organizations in thirty-nine states, professional women's groups in twenty-two states, counselling and walk-in centres for women or families in forty-three states, and a wide range of other organizations, such as senior citizens' homes and disabled people's organizations, in various states.

In addition, individual women did write for copies of the questionnaire, using both the address given in my previous works and an address given by interview programmes on television and in the press. However, if an individual woman did write for a questionnaire, whether she returned it or not was her own decision, therefore assuring her complete anonymity, as her reply was unsigned and bore the postmark and demographic information requested, such as age, income and education, but not name or address. All in all, 100,000 questionnaires were distributed, and 4,500 were returned. This is almost twice as high as the standard rate of return for this kind of questionnaire distribution, which is estimated at 2.5 to 3 per cent. A probability method of sampling might have yielded a higher rate of return, but then an essay questionnaire would not have been possible; the purpose here was to elicit in-depth statements of feelings and attitudes, and multiple-choice questions would have closed down dialogue with the participants.

Finally, sufficient effort was put into the various forms of distribution that the final statistical breakdown of those participating according to age, occupation, religion, and other variables known for the US population at large in most cases quite closely mirrors that of the US female population.

Could the study have been done using random sampling methods?
"There are many forms of scientific methodology besides the random sample; those of us in the field know that there is no such thing as a random sample in sex research, but this does not make the work unscientific if, as in the Hite Reports, the study population is carefully matched to the demographics of the population at large."

THEODORE M. MCILVENNA
Institute for Sex Research

Almost no major research using essay questions today is done with the use of random samples. As Dr Gladys Engel Lang has explained at the beginning of this section, most survey research now tries to match its samples demographically to the general population in other ways; for example, by weighting responses to conform to the population profile, somewhat similarly to the methods used here. But an even more important reason for not using random sampling methods for this study is that a random sample cannot be anonymous; the individuals chosen clearly understand that their names and addresses are on file.

Does research that is not based on a probability or random sample give one the right to generalize from the results of the study to the population at large? If a study is large enough and the sample broad enough, and if one generalizes carefully, yes; in fact, the Nielsen television studies, and US political polls generalize on the basis of small, select, non-random samples all the time. However, in a larger sense, no one can generalize from their findings, even if one were to somehow miraculously obtain a completely random sample—the reason being that variables such as psychological state, degree of religious or political fervour and so on are not measured; thus there is no guarantee that those picked in a random sample, although they might represent the population at large in terms of age and income, would also represent the population in terms of psychological make-up.

III.
Analysis of Replies: Measuring and Understanding Attitudes and Emotions

To go from essay statements to mixed quantitative/qualitative data is a long and intricate process.* Of course, some portions of the replies received are already in quantifiable form, i.e., questions answered with a "yes" or "no". But the majority of questions were not so phrased, since the intention, as discussed, was to open dialogue rather than to close it.

There is an ongoing and abstruse discussion in the field of methodology as to how best to study emotions, belief systems, and attitudes—not to mention how to quantify them. For example, not only is the question, "How do you love the person in your current relationship? What kind of love is it?" a difficult one to answer, but also the answer is every bit as difficult to analyse and compare with other answers received, and in some cases build into statistical findings. Nevertheless, it is possible to do this, if such statistics are attached for the reader to numerous examples of definition by the participants, such as is done in this study.

Specifically, the information was analysed in this way: first, a large chart was made for each question asked. Each person's answer to the question being analysed was then transferred onto that chart (usually many pages long), next to its individual identification number. The many months required for this procedure were actually very valuable in that they provided extensive time for reflecting on the answers.

Once the charts had been prepared, the next step was to discover the patterns and "categories" existing in the answers. Usually patterns had begun to stand out during the making of the charts, so that the categories more or less formed themselves. Then statistical figures were prepared by totalling the number of women in each category, following which representative quotes were selected. This procedure was followed for each of the 180 questions.

---

* Thus, in this study, there were over 40,000 woman-hours involved in analysing the answers, plus at least 20,000 put in by the women who answered the questionnaire. This of course does not include the time and effort needed to turn the resulting compilation of data into a book.

In addition, one main chart was kept on which much of the information from other charts was coded for each individual woman, so that composite portraits could be drawn and compared. Any attempt at condensation or computerization at an early stage of the analysis would have defeated the purposes of the study: to find the more subtle meanings lying beneath the more easily quantifiable parts of the replies, and to keep intact each individual's voice so that participants would remain in direct communication with readers, thus reinforcing the integrity of the study. After all the replies had been charted, and the process of identifying categories completed, with representative quotes selected, statistical computation was possible.

Analysing data from essay-type questionnaires, then, is a complex endeavour, but there is no way, if one cares about accuracy and detail or wants to search out and understand the deepest levels of the replies, that lengthy testimonies such as these can be understood quickly—and it is precisely the possibility of reaching these deeper levels that makes the essay questionnaire more valuable for this purpose than multiple-choice. Although multiple-choice questions make the researcher's job easier, only through listening to an individual's complete and free response, speaking in her own way and with her own design, without restriction, can more profound realities be reached.

IV.
Presentation of Findings: a New Interactive Framework

In lectures, Hite's approach is a kind of Socratic dialogue wherein participants are able to question their own prejudices and ignorance, thus learning by thinking through a logical idea for themselves—instead of being simply presented with a "fact". Her method in the Hite Reports is similar. Essentially she carries on an intense dialogue with her readers, making them question assumptions and sharpen their own thinking and critical faculties through identifying with the dialogue she is having with the printed responses. Her readers are thus stimulated to a process of independent thinking and evaluation.

LAWRENCE A. HORNE
American Philosophical Institute, New York

As theorists have pointed out, simple presentation of people's statements is not a rigorous approach to documenting "reality"; people's statements do not "speak for themselves"; there are assumptions and things left unsaid. True analysis requires a complex presentation of subjective data—not just, "people say this, and so that's how it is." For example, in the study of male sexuality, if most men said they have extramarital sex and that it keeps their relationship/marriage working, while it does not bother them—must the researcher conclude simply that since the majority say this, this is "how men are"? It would be simplistic to draw this conclusion. There are many elements in every decision, and it is the researcher's job to search out all the variables.

As it was explained by Janice Green, "In standard social science projects, one researcher's unstated and often unexamined or unconscious point of view is projected onto a research design, and then later also onto the presentation and interpretation of findings, in a rather undigested way. In oral history, at the other extreme (such as that by Studs Terkel), [each bit of] data is allowed to 'speak for itself'—but there is still no clarification of assumptions, biases or other hidden factors."

Dialogue between participant and researcher
Most basic to the methodology of the Hite Reports is the separation of "findings" from analysis and interpretation. This is done by choice of research design, questions, and method of analysis, and, in particular, the style of presentation of the final analysis—that is, separating the interpretation of what people say from what they do say. At times, in the text, participants debate with each other, in their own words; at other times, analysis of what people are saying can bring out several possible sides of a point; researcher and participants can agree or debate at different places in the text. In this way, the metaphysical dilemma of how much of what participants express is ideology can also be addressed. As Janet Wolfe, director of the Institute for Rational Therapy, has explained, "This complex approach has confused some general media reviewers, especially as Hite's work is accessible to a wide audience. But this many-layered structure is another part of Hite's overall methodology, in that she means to involve as many people as possible in the dialogue (not presenting closed "norms")—since it is, after all, a dialogue about social change."

The Issue of Class as Related to Presentation of Data

Much of the important work of the last few years in women's history and sociology has focused on class and economics as the major point for analysis; however, the purpose here is somewhat different.

405

APPENDICES

Although it is important to write about women in terms of class and race, and not to see "all women" as "the same", the focus of this study is not class but gender and gender ideology, that is, the experiences women have in common because of their gender. Also, this book is not built around comparisons of the attitudes of women in the various traditional socio-economic groups for the simple reason that differences in behaviour and attitude are not the major dividing line between women on these issues that some have theorized they might be. But even more importantly, the intention here was not to focus on class differences between women and what should be done about them, but on men's attitudes to women and what should be done to change them, strategies women have devised for developing their own lives while still dealing with the overall society's view of them—and to find the similarities and dissimilarities in women's current definitions and redefinitions of their relationship with men and society.

Nevertheless, women in this study include a vast cross-section of American women from different socio-economic groups and "classes". Great care was taken to ensure that statements by women from all classes are well represented throughout every portion of this book. Women's backgrounds will probably emerge to some extent through their manner of speaking/writing. However, perhaps unfortunately, some grammar and spelling was "corrected" so that answers could be more easily read. While some replies were very appealing when their original spelling reflected a personal style or regional accent, it seemed that in print these misspellings sometimes looked demeaning to the writer, or might be seen as trivializing that respondent. It is hoped, however, that enough of the original syntax in the replies is intact so that readers will get a feeling of the wide diversity among the respondents.

Finally, it does seem that based on this research, there are large areas of commonality among all women. While clearly the experience of a poor woman is different from that of a wealthy woman, and so on, in fact, the emotional expectations placed on "women" as a group by society seem to be much the same. From the statistical charts and from women's statements here, it is clear that, with regard to gender relationships, variables such as "class", income, education, and race are not nearly as influential as the overall experience of being female.

Note on the Use of "Many", "Most", and "Some" in the Text

For ease of reading, not every statement in the text is given with its related statistic; therefore, as a guideline for the reader, it will be useful to know that "most" refers to more than 55 per cent, "many" to any number between 40 per cent and 65 per cent; "some" indicates any number between 11 per cent and 33 per cent; while "a few" will mean a number between 2 per cent and 11 per cent. In addition, tables giving a complete breakdown for all the major findings (of which there are 120) can be found in the statistical appendixes. This is the largest amount of precise data given in any study since Kinsey; certainly Freud never attempted any such large sample. The Schwartz/Blumstein data, while covering relationships, contained less intricate and less numerically coded data relating to the emotions, although this was an excellent study.

Even though, for ease of reading, these general terms are at times used, it is felt that the context makes their meaning clear; in addition the extensive statistical appendixes include the precise data.

The Media and the Hite Reports: Reactions by Scholars in the Field

In the general popular media, there seems to be a widespread misunderstanding of the types and validity of methodologies available in the social sciences—not to mention the subtle debates discussed earlier in these appendixes. For example, even an important medical writer for *The New York Times* in 1976 opened a story on the first Hite Report with, "In a new, non-scientific survey of female sexuality . . ." The press has often made the mistake of equating "scientific" with "representative", and although both criteria are met by these studies, the press has at times insisted on the "non-scientific" nature of the work.★

★ In addition, "hard science" is still considered by many to be truly the province of the "male", as Evelyn Fox Keller points out in her article "Gender and Science": "The historically pervasive association between masculine and objective, more specifically between masculine and scientific, is a topic which academic critics resist taking seriously. Why? . . . How is it that formal criticism in the philosophy and sociology of science has failed to see here a topic requiring analysis? The virtual silence of at least the non-feminist academic community on this subject suggests that the association of masculinity with scientific thought has the status of a myth which either cannot or should not be examined seriously." (From Sandra Harding and Merrill B. Hintikka [eds], *Discovering Reality*, pp. 187–205, Copyright 1978 by Psychoanalysis and Contemporary Science, Inc.)

Many commentators in the scholarly community have tried to inform popular writers of their mistake:

Mary Steichen Calderone, MD, MPH; Founder, Sex Education and Information Council of the US (SEICUS):

The subject of human sexuality is one that closes many minds to any objective approach to it, so much so that panic and anxiety often cause people who have only marginal scientific information to repudiate such an approach to its examination. Hite's has been such an approach. Her studies have given ordinary women and men opportunity to verbalize their long-suffered panics and sexual anxieties, thus making it possible for other researchers and educators in this new field of sexology to understand better what has been going on in human minds, through the centuries, about a part of life that is universal and central to every human being born. We have an enormous store of information about the human reproductive system and its functioning, most of it gained in the past fifty years. . . . Hite's research, as with all research dealing with thoughts and feelings, cannot be expected to be analysed with the same techniques as those that tell us what doses of what drugs give what results in what kinds of patients. . . . We are a scientifically illiterate people, and honest scientists such as Hite are bound to suffer as a result.

Robert M. Emerson, Ph.D., Professor of Sociology, UCLA; Editor, *Urban Life: A Journal of Ethnographic Research*:

Statistical representativeness is only one criterion for assessing the adequacy of empirical data . . . other criteria are particularly pertinent when looking at qualitative data. This is primarily the situation with Hite's research, [in which the] . . . goal can be pursued independently of issues of representativeness, or rather, even demands a logic that is at variance with that of statistical representativeness. The logic is that of maximizing kinds of or variations in sexual experiences, so that the whole range of such experiences can be described; the frequency of any such experiences is another matter, one that is linked to the logic of representativeness.

Much of Hite's work seeks to organize qualitative comments in ways that do not involve an exhaustive set of categories, but again directly convey the more significant themes or patterns, in ways that also identify and explore variations in and from these patterns. Here again, range, breadth, and variation are more important than strict statistical representativeness. . . .

APPENDICES

John L. Sullivan, Ph.D., Professor of Political Science, University of Minnesota; Co-editor, *American Journal of Political Science*, and editor, *Quantitative Applications in the Social Sciences*, Sage University Papers series:

The great value of Hite's work is to show how people are thinking, to let people talk without rigid a priori categories—and to make all this accessible to the reader. Hite has many different purposes than simply stating population generalizations based on a probability sample. Therefore questions of sampling are not necessarily the central questions to discuss about her work. Rather, it is a matter of discovering the diversity of behaviours and points of view. Hite has certainly adequately achieved this kind of analysis. If she had done a perfectly representative random sample, she would not have discovered any less diversity in points of view and behaviours than she has discovered.

Her purpose was clear: to let her respondents speak for themselves, which is very valid. . . . What purpose would it have served to do a random sample, given the aim of Hite's work? None—except for generalizing from percentages. But Hite has not generalized in a non-scholarly way. Many of the natural sciences worry a lot less about random samples, because their work is to test hypotheses. And most of the work in the social sciences is not based on random samples either; in fact, many if not most of the articles in psychology journals are based on data from college students, and then generalized. Interestingly, they are not criticized in the same way Hite has been.

In short, Hite has used a kind of intensive analysis method, but not of individuals—of attitudes and feelings. One might say she is trying to put a whole society on the couch. Hers are works with many different purposes, and scholars and readers can use them in many different ways.

Gerald M. Phillips, Ph.D., Pennsylvania State University; Editor, *Communications Quarterly Journal*:

The Hite studies are important. They represent "good" science, a model for future studies of natural human experience. . . . There have always been serious problems for social scientists involved with studying human emotions . . . they cannot be catalogued and specified . . . the most advanced specialists have difficulty finding and specifying vocabulary suitable for objective discussion of human emotions and their impacts on individuals and societies . . . Hite has acquitted herself of this task remarkably well.

The major share of published studies in the social sciences are done numerically under the assumption that similar methodology produced truth or reliable generalizations for the hard sciences . . . What social scientists obsessed with "objective scientificity" do not seem to understand is that the hardest of scientists, physicists, for example, must engage in argument at the onset of their experiments *and* at the presentation of their data. . . . The problem with numeric measurement in the social sciences is, in the first instance, it works well only when the things being measured behave like numbers. Human data rarely stands still for measurement. . . . A major issue with which social scientists must cope in the future is how to describe and compare ephemeral numbers. . . . It is also the practice of contemporary social scientists to [unnecessarily] obscure their methodologies in complex mathematical formulae . . . [it would be better to give] a statement of what was discovered, presented as simply and succinctly as possible . . . a clear discussion of the theoretical basis for the study . . . and a clear description of the people studied [as in] the Hite model. Hite is a serious, reliable scholar and a first-rate intelligence.

Robert L. Carneiro, Ph.D.; Curator of Anthropology, The American Museum of Natural History, New York:

Hite's work can definitely be seen as anthropological in nature. The hallmark of anthropological field method lies in working intensively with individual informants. And though Hite used questionnaires, they were questionnaires that invited long and detailed replies rather than brief, easily codable ones. . . . And from these responses, presented in rich, raw detail, deep truths emerge—truths which, in many cases, were probably never revealed to anyone else before . . . for every question she presents a broad spectrum of responses. . . . One comes away from Hite's books with a feeling that an important subject has been plumbed to great depths . . . of inestimable value.

1987

Women and Love: Towards a New Feminist Methodology

Nancy Tuana, Columbia University
Presentation of *Women and Love: The Hite Report on Love, Passion and Emotional Violence*

In her first study, *The Hite Report on Female Sexuality*, Shere Hite was an important founder of a methodology now central to the feminist tradition—listening to women's own voices. She was one of the first researchers to develop a model and theory of female sexuality arising out of women's *own* experiences, rather than attempting to force a preconceived model upon our experiences. This methodology of listening to women's voices is the foundation of Carol Gilligan's landmark study of women's moral reasoning in her *In a Different Voice*, and recent studies of women and reason, *Women's Ways of Knowing*, and women's self-image, *The Woman in the Body*. Just as Hite discovered through her first report that the then accepted models of sexuality were lacking, so other theorists, employing the same methodology, have discovered that our philosophical and psychological accounts of reason and morality have been distorted by the omission of women's perspective. Hite's new study, *The Hite Report on Love, Passion and Emotional Violence*, demonstrates that our models of intimacy must be re-examined.

There is much to be learned from Hite's new study. As we listen to women describing what they desire from intimate relationships and what they see as going wrong with them, we hear much discontent. But one who listens closely will also hear the beginnings of change. Women are clearly unhappy with the present state of their intimate relationships with men. Women want more verbal sharing; they want their male partners to express their feelings more often and to take the responsibility for doing so, not always relying on their partners to draw them out; women want men to care about their feelings, truly listening to them when they talk

411

and encouraging such sharing. We also find that when women feel that such intimacy is lacking in a relationship they feel lonely, are upset and angry, and question the relationship. We listen to accounts of failures and successes, pain as well as joy, anxieties and hopes, dreams and fears.

Hite's study is a valuable resource. It provides an exciting confirmation of the results of other psychological studies of intimacy, such as Lillian Rubin's *Intimate Strangers*. In addition, Hite points out directions for future research into intimacy. Her study, for example, reveals patterns of argumentation that exist within many relationships—patterns warranting further examination. Her study also uncovers important relationships between emotional and physical intimacy patterns between women and men—another fruitful area for further research. Furthermore, Hite begins to identify the socio-political structures that ground and reinforce such patterns; a context we must be aware of in order to hear and understand women's voices, as well as to discover ways to transform these patterns.

Hite's study will also be an invaluable resource to scholars. The sustained voices of women provide a text for examining the values and images women associate with intimacy and for uncovering the metaphysic that grounds them.

By listening to the voices of the women in this study we learn that women are looking for a new notion of intimacy—a notion of intimacy that does not dichotomize physical and emotional intimacy; a notion of intimacy that does not set up an either/or choice between women's values and men's values, but rather unites and transforms them. This is a voice well worth listening to.

But, perhaps most importantly, by listening attentively to the voices of these women and the voice of Shere Hite who helps us to weave these voices together, we can learn how to enhance our own intimate relationships.

1987

Index

INDEX

INDEX